"Dennis Snelling's compelling biograph;
tells of the pitcher who, after a sore arm, became
one of baseball's greatest hitters and hitting coaches
before helping to establish the game in Japan."
—DANIEL M. GOLD, *New York Times*

"A well-deserved and rewarding account of a very well-lived life."
—TOM ECKEL, *Spitball: The Literary Baseball Magazine*

"An excellent portrait of a thoughtful and generous man
with a scientific approach to hitting and an unbridled
passion for the game; an athlete, a pioneer, a diplomat,
a teacher—and one of baseball's forgotten greats."
—ANDREW ELIAS, *Ft. Myers Magazine*

"An admirable attempt to elevate O'Doul's place
among baseball's pantheon of greats."
—BENJAMIN HILL, MinorLeagueBaseball.com

"The life of Lefty O'Doul was filled with joy, enthusiasm,
and accomplishment, and no one has told his story
better than Dennis Snelling. This wonderful book fully
describes the many facets of Lefty's personality."
—DICK BEVERAGE, secretary-treasurer for the Association
of Professional Ballplayers of America and president
of the Pacific Coast League Historical Society

"Perhaps the most important twentieth-century figure
not enshrined in Cooperstown, Lefty O'Doul influenced
the game on both sides of the Pacific. . . . Dennis Snelling
brings Lefty to life in this well-written and fascinating
biography. *Lefty O'Doul* should be on the must-read list of
all serious baseball fans. A true Sayonara home run!"
—ROBERT K. FITTS, author of *Banzai Babe
Ruth*, winner of the Seymour Medal

LEFTY
O'DOUL

LEFTY O'DOUL

BASEBALL'S FORGOTTEN AMBASSADOR

DENNIS SNELLING

WITH A NEW EPILOGUE BY THE AUTHOR

UNIVERSITY OF NEBRASKA PRESS | LINCOLN

First Nebraska paperback printing: 2023

Library of Congress Control Number: 2022947683

Set in Scala OT by Rachel Gould.

For my first grandchild, Ellie Noelle Snelling,
and the next generation of readers

CONTENTS

ILLUSTRATIONS

ACKNOWLEDGMENTS

A book like this cannot be written without a tremendous amount of assistance from some great people. Dick Beverage, president of the Pacific Coast League Historical Society and author of two outstanding Pacific Coast League team histories, was an excellent sounding board and kept me on track with his feedback while reading the draft manuscript as I went along. Sacramento baseball historian Alan O'Connor also read through the manuscript and offered helpful suggestions while also lending me one of Lefty's bats as inspiration; Alan also provided an invaluable three-volume, 307-page translation of Japanese newspaper articles from the 1949 tour that had been prepared for San Francisco Seals owner Paul Fagan. My great friend Jim Norby was a source of support and encouragement and always asked thought-provoking questions. He has read each of my manuscripts before publication.

In addition to reading the manuscript, Dick Beverage also introduced me to Rob Fitts, the author of outstanding biographies of Wally Yonamine and Masanori Murakami, as well as the Seymour Medal–winning *Banzai Babe Ruth*. Rob graciously answered questions about Japan and baseball, pointed me to good sources of information, and shared his files on Lefty O'Doul, including important correspondence between O'Doul and Sotaro Suzuki related to the 1934 tour.

Rob in turn introduced me to Japanese baseball historian Yoichi Nagata, a contributor to the landmark *Total Baseball* and author of the definitive history of the 1935 Tokyo Giants tour of the United

States. Yoichi was also incredibly patient in answering questions and pointing me to sources, and he generously provided me with articles and background on early Japanese professional baseball history. Yoichi was invaluable as a resource.

Lefty's second cousin Tom O'Doul was gracious with his time and answered numerous questions about Lefty and his family, as did Tom's son Pat. David Eskenazi opened his vast collection of Lefty O'Doul memorabilia to me—it seemed never ending, as he always pulled out a photo or a letter that I needed. His contributions to this book are especially valuable. Ray Saraceni was generous with his collection as well, including a wonderful tape of a 1956 Vancouver Mounties baseball game, complete with a postgame interview with Lefty. Doug McWilliams, one of the game's all-time best photographers, opened his home and his vast and unique photo collection, and he also provided some files from Dick Dobbins's extensive collection. Dave, Ray, and Doug are three of the best.

Shinichi Hirose of the Japanese Baseball Hall of Fame was always prompt in replying to my questions—and the Hall of Fame graciously provided a photo of Lefty's plaque for the book. Bill Soto-Castellanos, who wrote a wonderful book relating his days as a visiting clubhouse boy for the San Francisco Seals, shared his photos and memories. The research staff at the State Courthouse in San Francisco provided prompt responses to my inquiries about Lefty's will and disposition of assets. I especially want to thank Suzanne Leacy for her research.

Daniel Woodhead shared his mountains of research and correspondence related to his efforts to persuade the Hall of Fame's Veterans Committee to consider O'Doul for induction, including countless letters of support from baseball luminaries and individuals such as General Matthew Ridgway, Warren Buffett, and Bob Costas.

Nonfiction writers almost always build on the research of those who have gone before them. In this case I am indebted to Richard Leutzinger, who produced an entertaining and informative book about Lefty in the 1990s. He sent me the materials he had collected while working on that project. I greatly appreciate his input and generosity. Of course the late Dick Dobbins is owed gratitude for preserving Pacific Coast League history and for leaving his collection for researchers to use. Paula Lichtenberg tracked down and generously shared a number of wonderful stories about Rose Stolz, Lefty's early mentor at Bay View Grammar School—she even found a wonderful photo of Rose Stolz and her first class.

Christina Moretta, Jeff Thomas, and the staff of the San Francisco Library, John Horne and Cassidy Lent of the National Baseball Hall of Fame Library, the staff of the California State Library in Sacramento, and Roberto Delgadillo and the staff of the UC Davis Library were especially helpful in my research queries. Josue Hurtado helped me navigate the collection at Temple University.

Terri Heydari and Cynthia Franco at Southern Methodist University provided copies of material from the Norman Macht Collection that proved especially helpful in understanding the 1934 tour. Mr. Macht himself was generous with his time in answering my questions about the materials, which also included important correspondence involving the 1934 trip to Japan.

Holly Reed at the National Archives helped locate photos taken by the U.S. Army. Joe McCary went above and beyond in making sure a photo from the archives was digitized properly for reproduction. Ciara Crowley and Lorna Kirwan of the Bancroft Library at the University of California, Berkeley, were incredibly helpful in negotiating their photo archives, and flexible with their schedules in allowing me to visit. Debra Kaufman of the California Historical Society was especially helpful in reviewing photographs for me from the Dick Dobbins Collection housed there. Rosemary Hanes, reference librarian at the Library of Congress, provided articles related to the silent film series *Analysis of Motion*. Tricia Gesner of the Associated Press archive was especially helpful in locating a photo of Lou Gehrig and Lefty O'Doul. Maria Louie of the Oregon Health Authority went above and beyond in locating a copy of the wedding certificate for Lefty and his first wife, Abigail, which had been misfiled.

Rob Taylor and Courtney Ochsner of the University of Nebraska Press were as great as everyone had told me they were. My project editor, Sara Springsteen, and copyeditor, Colleen Romick Clark, were incredibly helpful, and patient, in polishing the final manuscript.

Mark Macrae, who oversees an annual reunion of PCL players in Northern California, arranged for me to interview several ballplayers. Becky Biniek and Missy Mikulecky assisted with locating images from the San Francisco Giants' archives. Tom Willman provided a spectacular find from Jimmie Reese's scrapbook—a photo of O'Doul in 1918 with his submarine-base baseball team. Daniel Van DeMortel provided some material that shed light on Lefty's relationship with the San Francisco Giants.

Over the past two decades, I have spoken to numerous players and sportswriters who shared their memories of Lefty for this and other projects, including George Bamberger, Ernie Broglio, Joe Brovia, Ed Cereghino, Cliff Chambers, Bill Conlin, Frank Dasso, Dominic DiMaggio, Bobby Doerr, Ryne Duren, Harry Elliott, Don Ferrarese, Bob Hunter, Larry Jansen, Don Klein, Tommy Munoz, Duane Pillette, Billy Raimondi, Neill Sheridan, and Elmer Singleton. Their insights into Lefty were invaluable.

Others who patiently and promptly answered inquiries and/or shared stories include Marty Appel, Frank Barning, Jim Beaver, Nick Bovis, Matt Dahlgren, Rob Edelman, John Holway, Troy Kinunen, Angus Macfarlane, Bruce Menard, Kerry Yo Nakagawa, Bill Nowlin, Marc Okkonen, John Ring, and Tom Shieber. Dan Harris took author photographs, and Bob Moullete of the Modesto Nuts graciously allowed those photos to be taken at John Thurman Field, the same diamond where Lefty held spring training for the San Francisco Seals in 1951 along with four Japanese stars he invited that year for special instruction. I thank you all.

Most of all I want to thank my wife, Linda, who put up with a lot over the past three years as I made an attempt to bring this fascinating character of Lefty O'Doul into focus. I could not have done this without her help and support.

LEFTY O'DOUL

1

Butchertown

Shortly after celebrating his sixty-first birthday in March 1958, Lefty O'Doul invited a friend of his, sportswriter Harry Brundidge, for a stroll along the streets of San Francisco. O'Doul was, as always, in excellent spirits and chattered incessantly; he was excited that his old team, the New York Giants, had pulled up stakes and was about to open the new baseball season in his hometown. Recently retired after forty years in professional baseball, the two-time National League batting champion, legendary hitting instructor, and successful Minor League manager would soon be opening a restaurant on Geary Street bearing his name, around the corner from a pub he had owned in the 1940s.

As the two men strode through historic Union Square, Brundidge noted O'Doul's always impeccable appearance—this day his sartorial selection featuring an alpine hat with a feather and a herringbone jacket—and marveled at his friend's countenance, which made him appear twenty years younger than he had the right to. O'Doul was on a first-name basis with world-famous athletes, movie stars, and politicians, and the city seemed to belong to him—*San Francisco Examiner* columnist Charles Einstein famously wrote about O'Doul's habit of riding in the front seat of taxis and steering the driver to destinations based on route instructions that were always the most direct, if not always the most legal. In those circumstances, police would invariably halt the vehicle until spotting O'Doul, at which point an officer would smile and wave the driver on his way.[1]

It appeared to Brundidge that the city was devoid of strangers; O'Doul recognized everyone crossing his path—and they him—as he greeted each person by name and spoke softly in rapid, staccato half-sentences, punctuating their delivery with animated facial expressions. Brundidge began to understand why San Francisco Seals owner Charlie Graham had dreaded walking down the street with Lefty O'Doul—it wasn't a walk so much as a never-ending series of interruptions. O'Doul had an easy air about him—a generous spirit that shone through; people were genuinely glad to see him. Brundidge thought to himself that the best word to describe his friend was "dynamic."

During their stroll, O'Doul and Brundidge were suddenly hailed by a group of Japanese businessmen who removed their hats and bowed. "O'Doul-san!" shouted one of the men, clearly delighted at encountering the baseball star. "Konnichiwa!" O'Doul bowed in turn and was introduced to the man's associates.

They shook hands and continued to exchange pleasantries in Japanese. Before parting, the man who had first greeted O'Doul turned to Brundidge and, after apologizing for his rudeness in not addressing him earlier, told the reporter, "In [Japan], O'Doul-san is great national hero. O'Doul [is number one] in Nipponese hearts. Great hero. O'Doul most admired American, including [the] illustrious MacArthur-san."[2]

Lefty O'Doul had visited Japan more than a dozen times as a player and ambassador for the game, including momentous trips in 1931 and 1934—the latter headlined by Babe Ruth—and in 1949, when he was asked to help repair U.S.-Japanese relations with a baseball tour. Brundidge remembered arriving in Tokyo in 1945, shortly after the surrender of Japan, and being peppered with questions from Japanese citizens, including Emperor Hirohito's brother, wanting to know about Lefty O'Doul. Prince Fumimaro Konoe, who twice served as Japanese prime minister, told Brundidge that O'Doul should have been a diplomat rather than a ballplayer.

Pleasantries concluded, the Japanese businessmen continued on their way, as did O'Doul and Brundidge. While they walked, Brundidge remained struck by the adulation accorded O'Doul in

his hometown by men who had traveled several thousand miles
and recognized him during a chance meeting on the street.

• • •

San Francisco was a young city full of ambition in the late 1860s. It
was rough—not only around the edges, but through and through—
and when its aspiration to become a major metropolis collided
with the incompatibility of unsightly industries located within
its city limits, especially butchering and meatpacking (and the
unpleasant by-products), pressure was brought to force the butchers, prosperous though they were, to leave. City fathers acquiesced,
banning the slaughtering of animals within the town proper, compelling the meat merchants to relocate their livelihood to marshy
land purchased from the state of California, at the outlet of Islais
Creek—a former Ohlone fishing spot just southeast of the city on
what was known as Hunter's Point. The area was almost immediately dubbed "Butchertown."

The move proved fortuitous, as San Francisco quickly became
a center for the beef industry, which employed more than three
thousand people; one company, Miller & Lux, emerged as one of
the largest meatpacking operations west of Chicago. The old problems resurfaced, however. Despite the natural barrier of Potrero
Hill, which hid many of the less desirous aspects of Butchertown,
within a few years the muck, the dung, and the stench and pollu-
tion from the slaughterhouses, tanneries, and tallow works spawned
concern on the part of city officials. Instead of cleaning up and properly disposing of the offal produced by their trade, butchers often
extended their slaughterhouses out over the ocean, filling the water
with bloody remains that—sometimes—washed out to sea. Rats
proved a constant problem, and hogs were often stationed under
the wooden floors to devour carcasses dropped into the basement.
This was an embarrassment to officials attempting to convert their
city from a roughshod, ramshackle outpost into the "Paris of the
Western Hemisphere," as San Francisco began vying for the coveted, and lucrative, role of trade center to Asia and the Pacific Rim.
There would be repeated crackdowns.

Butchertown also produced Lefty O'Doul—nearly all of his family members were butchers. Lefty's paternal grandfather, Augustus, was born in Louisiana to parents of French and Italian ancestry and had come to California to make his fortune.[3] For a time, Augustus partnered with his cousin and fellow bayou native Emile Peguillan in a sheep butchering concern.[4] O'Doul's grandmother, Catherine Fitzgerald, was born in Ireland—family lore has Catherine insisting Augustus add a proper Irish apostrophe to his last name of Odoul before she would marry him.

Lefty O'Doul's father, Eugene, was born in 1872, the second of five children, four of whom were boys. In 1895 Eugene O'Doul married Cecelia Suhling, a native Californian born to German parents; two years later, Eugene and Cecelia's only child, Francis, was born on Connecticut Street, the same day as President William McKinley's inauguration, an event that dominated San Francisco newspapers, especially those of a Republican bent. (The family moved repeatedly—some accounts state that O'Doul was born on Galvez Street, while city directories show the family living on P Street. However, according to second cousin Tom O'Doul, Lefty was born on Connecticut.)

Due to its relative isolation from the center of San Francisco, Butchertown developed a separate and, what seems today, surprising identity. Well into the 1930s, cowboys tended livestock on the nearby hills before driving them through the neighborhood streets to their final destination—it was not uncommon for pedestrians to suddenly find themselves flattened against buildings as cattle passed. There were also stereotypical scenes one might imagine in a tight-knit community of that era: O'Doul and his mates, bare feet pounding heavily against the well-worn wooden plank pathway, racing off to the mudflats near the Chinese shrimp camp on Hunter's Point where they would spend hours digging for clams. Then, once the fog cleared in the early afternoon, they would skinny dip in the surf. Milk and ice were delivered to the neighborhood each day, and on sweltering afternoons the boys, likely as not, would launch themselves onto the back of an ice wagon and grab chips from one of the blocks to stick in their mouths, or down each other's backs. The Irish lads of Butchertown would often fight the Italians of North Beach, and O'Doul learned early the fundamentals of fisticuffs—Butchertown spawned more than its share of professional prize fighters. Lefty sided with the Irish even though his bloodlines were tied less to the Emerald Isle than to his French and German roots. He would carry a bit of Butchertown inside him throughout his life.

The family suffered through some hard times. O'Doul's uncle August fled to Seattle following a New Year's Day 1900 bar fight that began with an argument over the price of drinks and escalated into a brawl that allegedly resulted in a death. The police ultimately dropped the charges for lack of evidence.[5] Less than a year later, Lefty's grandmother died suddenly at age fifty-four.[6] Butchertown nearly burned down in 1904, the result of a carelessly tossed cigar under the plank road.[7] Then came the 1906 earthquake, which devastated block after block of buildings in Butchertown; in later years, O'Doul vividly recalled the scene he witnessed as a nine-year-old: "A lot of packing houses . . . were on the bay shore and they just shook down. Couple of days later . . . I walked into town. There were beds hanging out of the houses, where the walls had fallen away."[8] O'Doul's family was fortunate in that they were able to move back into the home they had been renting on Sixth Avenue since 1904, remaining until around 1911.[9]

Lefty enrolled at Bay View Grammar School, where it was said he excelled at geography—other subjects, not so much. His reputation was that of an extremely likable and unfailingly polite young man with a quick sense of humor and a gift for leadership.[10] O'Doul's education ended somewhere in the vicinity of the eighth grade because his father felt it vital that he learn a trade—specifically the family tradition of butchering. Eugene O'Doul, who was often subjected to good-natured shouts of "Froggy" because of his French blood and bayou lineage, had labored in the slaughterhouses but by 1908 was a salesman. That position eventually enabled him to secure a spot in the Don Biggs Company for his teenage son, whom Eugene's friends playfully dubbed "Young Froggy."[11] Lefty, who became a card-carrying member of Amalgamated Meat Cut-

ters Union Local 508, regretted the premature end to his school-
ing, but his quick mind, insatiable curiosity, and love of people
ultimately fostered within him a talent for self-education.

O'Doul always claimed that, prior to abandoning his formal education, he was instructed in the fundamentals of baseball by his
teacher, a woman in her midthirties named Rose Stolz, who recognized and encouraged the development of his athletic talent. Under
her mentorship, fifteen-year-old Lefty led Bay View to the finals of
the San Francisco grammar school championship.[12]

"Sure I had always played some ball ever since I learned to walk,"
explained O'Doul. "[But] she taught me the essential fundamentals
of the game. She taught me to pitch, field and hit. . . . Miss Stolz,
alone, is responsible for my success in baseball."[13] Lefty always took
great pride in pointing out that a woman had taught him to play ball.

It was an exaggeration that made for a good story—Rose Stolz
was the first to admit she was far from a baseball expert. Her interests tended more toward drama and literature—she had obtained
autographs from nearly every prominent actor who had appeared
in San Francisco, dating back before the turn of the century.[14] She
coached sports at the school despite her lack of knowledge because
she saw a need and no one else was willing. As a result, she became
a lifelong fan of O'Doul, and he credited her with his success.[15]

Rose Stolz did teach Lefty and his teammates to be gentlemen.
All of the members of the grammar school team wore carnations
in their lapels as they marched to the ballpark for the championship game. "She insisted flowers were not sissy," remembered
O'Doul, "and that washing your ears, combing your hair and wearing your Sunday-Go-to-Meeting clothes made you a man. I learned
a lot from her."[16]

While possessing the same piercing blue eyes and fair complex-
ion as his father, Lefty would outgrow him by a good three inches,
rounding out at an even six feet tall.[17] And Rose Stolz was correct.
He was indeed a gifted athlete—both fast and strong. Lefty O'Doul
would always consider himself lucky, and accordingly made it a priority throughout his life to assist those less fortunate; the discovery
of his athletic prowess proved one of his luckiest breaks.

However, after taking the job at the Don Biggs Company, it appeared that O'Doul had abandoned sports in favor of females—or at least one member of the fairer sex—while settling into a life of grueling six-day work weeks, herding sheep through the streets of Butchertown and cutting meat at the slaughterhouse; he relished being on horseback and would always admire the cowboys of his youth. O'Doul's future seemed set. Other than a brief stint pitching for what he called a "bush league" team in the Visitacion Valley Athletic Association in 1914, he largely forgot about baseball.[18]

That changed in 1916 when O'Doul's father convinced the nineteen-year-old to join the South San Francisco Parlor of the Native Sons of the Golden West, a social organization open exclusively to native-born Californians and dedicated to preserving California history.

The Native Sons also sponsored a baseball league.

Games were scheduled on Sundays and involved some eighteen teams, representing various parlors in and around San Francisco. Admission was free but the competition intense; some teams hired former professional players. Contests were generally staged at Ewing Field, Golden Gate Park, or on a ball field located at Fourth and Bluxome, only a few blocks from the present-day home of the San Francisco Giants.

Lefty did not immediately join the baseball team—as enamored as he had been with the game, he was more enamored with his girlfriend and continued passing his Sundays with her. Then, as so often would be the case for Lefty O'Doul, fate stepped in.

According to a 1932 interview conducted by Ed Hughes of the *Brooklyn Daily Eagle*, O'Doul insisted, "I wasn't what you call crazy about the game. I also had liked the girls some too, and one in particular at that time. But it seems that this particular charmer liked another fellow, also. I had an engagement to take her to a picnic one Sunday, but the other kid got there first. That left me with an afternoon on my hands."[19]

So, instead of squiring an attractive female that summer day in 1916, Lefty accompanied his father to a Native Sons baseball game being played by the Butchertown-based South San Francisco Parlor. One of the team's scheduled pitchers was ill (according to

another account, he was missing following an unlucky night shooting craps.) South San Francisco's manager, Jack Regan, who had
been attempting without success to persuade O'Doul to play for
his team, finally convinced him to take the mound.[20]

"I won that game," recalled O'Doul, "and made quite a hit all
around. Guess it gave me the yen to be a big league star."[21] O'Doul
gave up the slaughterhouse—and the girl—and grabbed what he
recognized was an opportunity. He went undefeated for South San
Francisco and was also their best hitter. At least that's the way the
story is always told—and it is technically true.

Four weeks into the season, O'Doul threw a one-hit shutout, and
followed up the next Sunday with a four-hit, 3–2, victory, pushing
his team's record to five wins without a defeat.[22] On the first of October he tossed another shutout, allowing only three hits, and it was
announced that the San Francisco Seals of the Pacific Coast League
(PCL) had signed him for the 1917 season.[23] O'Doul's instant success was unusual, as was the reaction of his family. At a time when
parents almost never encouraged ball playing by their sons, Lefty's
had no qualms. "My dad didn't think a thing about it," remembered
O'Doul. "He was elated, if anything."[24]

By the end of the month, South San Francisco was 13-0, and only
the Stanford Parlor, at 13-1, remained within striking distance. It
was announced that those two teams would meet for the league
title on November 12 in a game played at Recreation Park, home
field of the Seals, with a special admission charged to raise funds
for homeless children.[25]

More than three thousand were on hand for the championship
contest—O'Doul had never before played in front of a crowd that
size. There was considerable interest in the game throughout the
city. Ping Bodie, a Seals outfielder bound for the Philadelphia Athletics, offered ten dollars to the first player hitting a home run. A
local judge matched Bodie's offer for a triple. The A. G. Spalding
Company supplied gold watch charms intended for each member of the winning team. As a measure of O'Doul's popularity, the
game was halted when he came to bat in the second inning so fans
could present him a floral horseshoe for good luck.[26]

Stanford, which featured two former PCL players in its lineup, took the lead in the third inning on a walk, two stolen bases, and a bad throw by the South San Francisco catcher. But O'Doul, batting sixth in the order, tied the score in the fifth with a single—one of his three hits that day—stole a base, and then scored on a daring play that brought fans out of their seats. On a grounder to deep short, O'Doul, emboldened by his first opportunity to perform on a grand stage, displayed the reckless daring of a young man unfamiliar with failure; instead of stopping at third, Lefty kept on going, startling the shortstop to such a degree that he scored when the infielder's throw to the plate went awry. South San Francisco added three more runs in the sixth, and the game seemed well in hand.

But O'Doul, presaging a career-long tendency for his arm to tire after seven innings, faltered in the eighth. He hit a batter, walked two others, and allowed a pair of hits. In all, he surrendered seven bases on balls as South San Francisco lost, 5–4.[27] Jack Regan reacted by filing a protest that Stanford had used an ineligible player, second baseman Jack Kennedy. The protest was upheld, and the teams were ordered to replay the game on Thanksgiving Day.[28]

On the day of the rematch the grounds were clumpy with mud, the result of recent rainstorms. The atmosphere was nonetheless festive, with bands playing and local dignitaries jockeying for attention. O'Doul relished getting a second chance. He once again batted sixth and pitched, and once again collected three hits. But he surrendered two runs in the first inning and was knocked out of the box by the fifth, at which point he was shifted to centerfield. Stanford won, 6–3, yet for some reason had again used Jack Kennedy.[29] Eagle-eyed Jack Regan again protested, and once again he was successful. Wisely resisting any thought of yet a third "championship" contest, those in power declared South San Francisco the winner, and both of their defeats—and thus O'Doul's—were wiped away.[30]

Having obtained his first extended look at Lefty O'Doul, an impressed Al C. Joy of the *San Francisco Examiner* looked forward to the coming season and speculated, "Frank O'Doul may be considered by San Francisco next spring for a position other than that of pitcher. This boy takes a healthy clout at the ball and is a streak on the bases."[31]

The San Francisco Seals were an important baseball franchise, a member of one of the highest rungs of baseball outside of the Major Leagues, within a circuit that served as a direct conduit to the big time—in reality, to those in the west, they *were* the big time. Baseball had become immensely popular there during the last two decades of the 1800s—people from all over the country had settled in the Bay Area, bringing the game with them. A remote outpost at the edge of a vast continent, California retained much of its wealth of baseball talent, providing a home for several fast teams that could give the "Major Leaguers," who often barnstormed the state each winter, a run for their money.

The Seals became part of the Pacific Coast League when that circuit was formed in 1903 by expanding the independent California State League from four teams to six through the theft of Seattle and Portland, the two largest cities in the Pacific Northwest League. (Ironically, the PCL's golden era would end in 1958, when the Major Leagues utilized the same tactic, picking off San Francisco and Los Angeles and making the PCL decidedly minor once again.)

The circuit managed to survive the 1906 earthquake, which not only destroyed the Seals' home field, Recreation Park, but league headquarters as well. By that time the San Francisco franchise was under the control of Cal Ewing, who constructed a new Recreation Park farther west from the old one, spanning the entirety of Valencia Street between Fourteenth and Fifteenth Streets, in time for the 1907 season.

The Minor Leagues of that era were far more independent of the Eastern "Majors," since the "farm system" had not yet been invented. Relationships between Major and Minor League teams were more of the handshake variety, based on personal connections and favors—although Major League teams were allowed to draft a limited number of Minor League players at the end of each season, a source of irritation for local owners desirous of building a strong franchise rather than losing their talent at far below market value.

The PCL possessed a greater independent streak than most, and the league's franchises unrepentantly hoarded the top-notch athletes residing in their backyards. They also paid well throughout their history; it is not difficult to find instances of players taking pay cuts when they reached the Major Leagues.

The Seals had featured a number of exciting and interesting players over the years. Future "Black Sox" third baseman Buck Weaver had played infield for them. Ping Bodie, a likeable but incurable braggart, slugged a record thirty home runs in 1910—an incredible number for the Deadball Era. Jimmy Johnston stole 124 bases in one season. Pitcher Spider Baum would win more than 260 games during a long PCL career.

Following a dispute with a partner, Cal Ewing chose to relocate the Seals elsewhere in the city in 1914, erecting an impressive edifice that he modestly christened Ewing Field. While aesthetically pleasing, it was unfortunately constructed in an area of San Francisco plagued by a relentless, Arctic-like fog that rolled in every afternoon from the Pacific Ocean. Patronage declined precipitously. Other owners, alarmed by their plummeting share of gate receipts, pressured Ewing to abandon the stadium after one season, and the debacle led him to divest himself of the franchise at year's end.

The team traipsed back to Recreation Park and, aided by connections to the Detroit Tigers through new manager Harry Wolverton, won the PCL pennant in 1915, the Seals' first in six years; one of the key young players supplied by the Tigers was San Francisco native and future Hall of Famer Harry Heilmann.[32]

But the Seals slipped to fourth place in 1916 as their pitching faltered. Harry Wolverton was determined to bring in new talent—including a young left-hander from the baseball league fielded by the Native Sons of the Golden West.

San Francisco sportswriter Harry B. Smith was immediately impressed with O'Doul, telling readers that he "carries himself with a lot of confidence."[33] But in embarking on his first year as a professional, O'Doul was actually unsure of himself for one of the few times in his life. "As a kid from Butchertown," he remembered, "I was kind of timid, you know, just out of the sticks and all." Eager to stand at the plate and show what he could do, O'Doul encountered resistance, with one veteran ordering him to drop his bat and move along. "So I went to the outfield and shagged balls and never got up to the cage again until I got some kind of reputation. That's the way it was in those days."[34] He was, however, able to demonstrate his athleticism—and competitiveness. During an interview given in 1955, O'Doul claimed that Harry Wolverton placed a ten-dollar gold piece on home plate and had the entire team line up in the outfield and race for it. The twenty-year-old rookie beat everyone, sliding into home plate to grab the gleaming prize.[35] As would prove true throughout his career, he attracted attention. Up to now, he had always been known simply as Frank; before the end of training camp, Harry B. Smith was calling him "Lefty" O'Doul.[36]

The still raw pitcher began 1917 in a San Francisco Seals uniform, granted a look-see consisting of three appearances encompassing a grand total of eight innings.[37] In early May, he was loaned to Des Moines in the lower-level Western League for more seasoning against less experienced competition.[38] The Midwest proved a quite different experience for the twenty-year-old—especially the travel; road trips could stretch as far as Denver, seven hundred miles west of Des Moines.

"What a life!" O'Doul exclaimed during an interview for Lawrence Ritter's classic book *The Glory of Their Times*. He reminisced about rickety trains featuring equally rickety seats, and locomotives belching thick black smoke everywhere while rattling along all night and the next day to reach Wichita, or some such destination. O'Doul recalled, "If you opened the window you'd be eating soot and cinders all night long. If you closed the window you'd roast to death."[39]

The local baseball team, nicknamed the Boosters, had played in the Western League since 1908, and was two years removed from its last pennant. The team's player-manager, Jack Coffey, had suited up for Boston in the National League nearly a decade earlier, and coincidentally with San Francisco the prior year (thus explaining the pipeline from the Seals to the cornfields of Iowa). Coffey also moonlighted as head baseball coach for his alma mater, Fordham University, where he had played shortstop; his college double-play partner had been Francis Cardinal Spellman, future archbishop of New York.[40]

The Boosters' home field, Holcomb Park, was a typical sports facility of the time, consisting of a wooden grandstand and bleachers extending down each foul line. (It would later achieve notoriety for hosting the first night game under permanent lights in organized baseball history.) The franchise was owned by Tom Fairweather, a Des Moines city councilman and close friend of Chicago White Sox owner Charles Comiskey; Fairweather later served as president of several Minor Leagues into the 1940s.

O'Doul won his debut for Des Moines at Sioux City on May 19, despite struggling through seven innings in the midst of a heat wave that saw the temperature top out at eighty-eight degrees around game time. Exhausted, he was lifted in the eighth after walking the first batter of the inning and hitting the second.[41] He allowed two runs in the same number of innings in relief four days later, one day after unsuccessfully pinch-hitting for pitcher Rudy Kallio.[42] His next start was an uneven, complete game loss to Sioux City, in which he dug himself a hole by allowing a triple and four singles in the second inning.[43]

But O'Doul found his rhythm, pitching a three-hitter against the Lincoln Links on June 1 to move Des Moines into first place while toiling in weather similar to that he was accustomed to in San Francisco—temperature in the low sixties with skies threatening rain.[44] After failing to make it out of the first inning in his next start, he tossed back-to-back five-hitters against Omaha and St. Joseph.[45] O'Doul also displayed his raw ability as a batsman; on June 18 he smacked three hits in six at bats while tossing a fourteen-inning complete game victory against Wichita, improving his record to 5-2.[46]

Then, when it appeared he had arrived as a professional ballplayer, O'Doul suffered a badly broken middle finger on his glove hand thanks to a line drive smashed back through the box. An infection set in, resulting in several days' hospitalization and knocking him out of action for nearly two months.[47] The finger never healed properly, remaining permanently crooked—O'Doul would call it his "funny finger."[48]

Lefty finally made his return on August 30, matched against

veteran Harry Gaspar, a former big leaguer who was pitching for the St. Joseph Drummers. Neither man was particularly effective, but O'Doul got the better of the duel, winning 7–4.[49] Clearly not as sharp as he had been before the injury, he lasted only one inning in his next start, and then surrendered eleven hits and six runs the day after that. Although he won a seven-inning contest against Omaha in early September, Jack Coffey began utilizing O'Doul as a reserve outfielder—his picture-perfect left-handed hitting stroke and impressive foot speed proving hard to ignore.[50] He remained a reserve through the playoffs, pitching only intermittently.[51]

The Pacific Coast League season was longer than that of the Western League, so the Seals recalled O'Doul from Des Moines to serve as a potential reinforcement, although he would not see any action.[52] Despite his uneven performance—typical for a youngster—he had demonstrated his potential and raw athletic ability. What Lefty O'Doul could not have foreseen was that he would spend the remainder of his four-plus decades in baseball exclusively in either the Major Leagues or the Pacific Coast League.

2

He Can Be Just as Great a Ballplayer as He Cares

Japan's baseball genesis resulted from a pair of unrelated events. The first was its initial introduction around 1872 by American educator Horace Wilson, a Civil War veteran who had relocated from San Francisco after being hired to serve as an English teacher at what would later become Tokyo Imperial University. Legend has it that Wilson, recognizing that his pupils lacked a proper exercise regimen, introduced them to the game and it was instantly embraced.[1]

The second event began five years later when Hiroshi Hiraoka returned from his engineering studies in the United States, where he had become a rabid baseball fan. He established the first baseball club in Japan, the Shimbashi Athletic Club, constructing a baseball diamond on rented land and defeating all comers for several years.[2] Prep schools followed suit, establishing teams on a competitive level, most notably one at Daiichi Koto Gakko, which in 1896 famously challenged and several times defeated a group of Americans from the Yokohama Cricket and Athletic Club. By the turn of the twentieth century, universities in the Tokyo area were attracting large crowds for their games—and continue to do so today.

Reciprocal visits between American and Japanese baseball teams began. In 1905 Waseda University became the first Japanese collegiate team to visit the United States, and several months later the University of Washington returned the favor—the first of a number of exchanges over the next twenty-five years.

In a trip organized by San Francisco entrepreneur Mike Fisher, the first American professional players traveled to Japan in November 1908 under the sponsorship of the Reach Sporting Goods Company. The team was originally to be headlined by Ty Cobb, Hal Chase, Orval Overall, Frank Chance, and other big league stars. However, at that time Japan was an isolated and mysterious locale, and travel across the ocean was an endeavor not lightly taken. One by one the stars backed out. The roster ultimately consisted of marginal Major Leaguers and Pacific Coast League players.[3]

Despite the defections, that 1908 tour was so successful that Japan was added as a stop on the 1913–14 World Tour staged by the Chicago White Sox and New York Giants. This was followed by visits in 1920 and 1922 by Minor and Major League All-Star teams, but those efforts at baseball diplomacy were marred by less than exemplary behavior on the part of the Americans. A team of women, the Philadelphia Bobbies, toured in 1925, with a male battery consisting of Washington Senators Earl Hamilton and Eddie Ainsmith.[4] A group of Negro League All-Stars headlined by Biz Mackey staged a very successful tour in 1927. Ty Cobb visited a year later, playing nine games during a tour arranged by Herb Hunter and also including Bob Shawkey. Cobb's close friend, Seals part-owner George Putnam, also made the trip.[5]

In 1920 thirty-year-old Sotaro Suzuki left Japan for New York, thanks to his employment with a silk trading firm, and, like Hiroshi Hiraoka, became a rabid fan of the American game, haunting the Polo Grounds at every opportunity. It was there that he met John McGraw and the two became friends. When Lefty O'Doul joined the New York Giants in 1928, Suzuki struck up a friendship with him as well. Suzuki returned to Japan in 1930 to work for newspaper publisher Matsutaro Shoriki, who successfully underwrote a team of Major League stars that toured Japan in the fall of 1931, a squad that included O'Doul, who was also a good friend of Babe Ruth.[6]

That tour was wildly successful and led to further exchanges, including one in 1934 that finally brought Babe Ruth to the Far East, thanks in large part to the efforts of Lefty O'Doul. That event helped usher in the formation of Japanese professional baseball, also due in no small measure to O'Doul's influence and efforts.[7] O'Doul returned several times during the 1930s, providing instruction and support, and facilitated tours of the United States by Japanese professionals in 1935 and 1936. He made another visit in 1937 and was planning more when hostilities made trips too dangerous to undertake.

Then came December 7, 1941.

• • •

The San Francisco Seals were acquired by a new ownership group in 1918, headed by ex-PCL and Boston Red Sox catcher Charlie Graham, who partnered with Sacramento newspaperman George Putnam. Requiring additional operating capital, they enlisted a San Francisco dentist and former college teammate of Graham's, Charles "Doc" Strub, to join them. Together the triumvirate would field some of the greatest Minor League teams in baseball history, and along the way threaten the Major Leagues' monopoly on acquiring and developing talent.

The Seals were coming off a tumultuous season that had seen manager Harry Wolverton dismissed in June during a power struggle with the previous ownership, even though the team was in first place at the time. The Seals won the 1917 pennant anyway, but owner Henry Berry declared bankruptcy at the end of the season and also exited.

By that time the team's ballpark, Recreation Park, was a dilapidated relic consisting of splintered wooden planks and chicken wire—a home by default following the debacle of Ewing Field. "Old Rec" (or more appropriately "Old Wreck," as it was known even when comparatively new) featured an upper deck literally nailed on top of a lower one, creating an enclosed space at ground level protected by wire mesh that enveloped eight rows of seating, all within whispering distance of the baselines. The area became universally known as the "Booze Cage," where drinking and gambling were perpetually within earshot of the players. It was a rough-and-tumble atmosphere, the catcalls of the wise guys echoing around the wooden structure—it was not a place for the thin-skinned or the easily tempted.

Recreation Park shared with all PCL stadiums of that era the tendency of being what one today would term a hitter's venue; it was arguably the best for batsmen outside of the high altitude and short fences found in Salt Lake City. Its right-field fence material-ized rather abruptly at only 235 feet from home plate, a fifty-foot-high screen tacked atop the wall as if an afterthought intended to render the playing field at least somewhat fair to pitchers, which it most decidedly was not. The park's idiosyncrasies also meant that lackadaisical base runners were easy targets when trotting to first base—it was not uncommon for the right fielder to throw out a clueless batter after fielding a line drive snagged on the rebound off the fence.

It was here that Lefty O'Doul encountered Charlie Graham, one of the greatest influences in his life. Graham was sympathetic to players, often sharing a portion of his profit from their sale to other teams when he was under no obligation to do so. He knew what it took to get to the big leagues, and he recognized O'Doul as quite possibly the best all-round athlete he had ever seen.

O'Doul demonstrated his impressive speed that spring, outrac-ing an Olympic Club sprinter who was visiting the team's training camp in Fresno.[8] The twenty-one-year-old also attracted attention for his speed with the ladies, noted in particular for his flirtation with a young girl who worked the counter of the cigar store in the Seals' hotel.[9]

Graham and his partners had hoped to sign veteran outfielder (and future Hall of Famer) Sam Crawford, recently released by the Detroit Tigers, but were beaten to the punch by the Los Angeles Angels. Then they attempted to acquire ex–Santa Clara College star Harry Wolter—and thought they had a deal finalized with the Chicago Cubs—but Cubs owner Charlie Weeghman received a better offer from Sacramento, and Wolter instead landed with a Seals rival. As a result, O'Doul was in center field on Opening Day; and although he doubled and scored a run in his first game, his lack of experience was exposed before another nine innings had passed.

The *San Francisco Chronicle* described O'Doul's attempts to catch fly balls as resembling "a small boy trying to sprinkle salt on the tail of a sparrow." He broke in when he should have stayed back, and stayed back when he should have broken in. Seals manager Red Downs showed mercy and took him out.[10]

O'Doul finally made a start as a pitcher against Oakland and lost. Then he shut out Sacramento on four hits, and a week later relieved Tom Seaton with one out in the first inning and allowed only three hits the rest of the way.[11] When another outfielder suffered a knee injury in late April, Downs returned O'Doul to center field, starting him five straight times.[12] During the season's first month, O'Doul bounced back and forth between pitching and the outfield or pinch-hitting. By the beginning of May he had been in the starting lineup thirteen times—three times as a starting pitcher and the remainder in either left or center field.

Then on May 3, O'Doul endeared himself to Charlie Graham by pitching a thirteen-inning complete game to defeat Sacramento while striking out Harry Wolter four times—O'Doul's confidence was such that he retired Wolter the fourth time after intentionally walking a batter with two out in the twelfth inning so he could pitch to him, despite the fact that doing so loaded the bases.[13]

When Red Downs suspended pitcher Chief Johnson for breaking training—a euphemism for hitting the bottle (which of course is another euphemism)—he sent O'Doul to the mound again on only one day of rest. The twenty-one-year-old impressed everyone by keeping the game close before tiring in the ninth.[14] After that, excepting for pinch-hit or emergency situations, O'Doul was a pitcher in 1918. Once Lefty settled into the role, he developed rapidly, as did his reputation. He stood out. O'Doul threw hard and possessed a deceptive curve ball; despite his inexperience, general opinion held that the young left-hander was clearly big league caliber—only the threat of his being drafted into military service was keeping him off a big league roster.

O'Doul enjoyed pitching full-time—and did not miss the criticism of his outfield play. While prone to fits of wildness at times, O'Doul won six of his final seven decisions, three by shutout, and closed the season—which ended in mid-July that year because of the country's increased entanglement in the war in Europe—on a winning note, capturing his twelfth victory against eight defeats. Five of his victories were shutouts.

Even with the shortened season and shifting of positions, O'Doul's raw talent was obvious, and he was drafted from the Seals by the New York Yankees. O'Doul was living with his parents on Twentieth Street near Van Ness at the time, having enlisted in the navy rather than return to the slaughterhouses following the government's orders to "work or fight." Not that O'Doul fought—he first was assigned to a submarine base in San Pedro, California, where he was trained as a torpedoman and played for the installation's baseball team along with Harry Heilmann, Bob Meusel, Howard Ehmke, Herb Hunter, and Jimmie Reese.[15]

Later that year, O'Doul returned to San Francisco and toiled in the shipyards during the week while pitching weekends for the company team in the Shipbuilders League; in mid-November he defeated a team representing Alameda that included several Major Leaguers, throwing a two-hit shutout and striking out eight while walking only two. O'Doul's catcher was Yankees starter Al "Roxy" Walters, and the San Francisco Chronicle predicted that "when Walters tells [Yankees manager] Miller Huggins how good O'Doul is, that shrewd little manager will want a good look at the kid, and will give him a thorough tryout."[16]

But the winter season had its harsh side for O'Doul. "Sad thing is, my dad died in 1918 while I was in the Navy," he recalled while reminiscing nearly fifty years later.[17] O'Doul's forty-six-year-old father had lost his battle with tuberculosis, taking a turn for the worse in September at about the same time the Spanish flu was sweeping through San Francisco. Eugene O'Doul succumbed on December 9, 1918.[18]

Lefty O'Doul continued pitching into the spring, representing the Mare Island Naval Station under the watchful eye of soon-to-be Yankees teammate Duffy Lewis. O'Doul made his final appearance in San Francisco on St. Patrick's Day 1919.[19] That same day, his contract arrived in the Yankees offices and he prepared to leave for Jacksonville, Florida, where his new teammates were training.

Yogi Berra once famously said, "When you come to a fork in the road, take it." That odd saying more than aptly described the next several years of Lefty O'Doul's baseball career.

Before departing San Francisco, O'Doul was filmed by a new type of motion picture camera for the first in a series of shorts entitled *Analysis of Motion*.[20] Utilizing a new technique dubbed "slow motion," the film captured O'Doul throwing a baseball, the images projected at one-tenth of normal speed so audiences could catch every nuance of his arm actions during the delivery of curves, fastballs, and other pitches. Originally screened at baseball's winter meeting for sports-writers and other "experts," who lauded the achievement equally for its entertainment value and potential use in training, the film was shot and distributed by the Novagraph Film Corporation and exhibited in New York City at the Strand Theatre in January 1919.[21] The silent motion picture garnered considerable attention in New York—and afforded Yankees fans the opportunity to glimpse the San Francisco phenomenon well before his arrival.[22] It also influenced O'Doul, who later utilized film to study his own hitting. But cinematic appearances did not necessarily translate into fame—at the beginning of training camp, everyone rhymed his last name with "towel" rather than "tool."[23]

The Yankees that O'Doul joined in 1919 were not the Yankees we think of today. They had yet to win a pennant, with three second-place finishes their best showing to that point. The arrival of Babe Ruth remained a year away and, despite owner Jacob Ruppert's willingness to open his wallet, the team had little to show for his four years in charge—not even a home field. Instead, the Yankees shared the Polo Grounds with John McGraw and his New York Giants. The team's manager, the diminutive but spunky Miller Huggins, was in his second year in charge, having replaced Bill Donovan in 1918 after spending five seasons as player-manager of the St. Louis Cardinals. A scrappy former second baseman who led the National League four times in drawing bases on balls, Huggins was nervous and contemplative, but also competitive and tenacious. And he was a master at studying people.

Mispronunciations of his name aside, O'Doul quickly estab-

lished himself as one of the Yankees' best athletes. It was thought
that his success as a pitcher despite the cramped confines of Recreation Park would translate well into coping with similar dimensions at the Polo Grounds, but he surprised the Yankees with
his athleticism. Having played all winter, O'Doul was in the best
shape of his life, and as a result enjoyed a head start on most of
his new teammates. He was timed in a seventy-five-yard run, in
full uniform, in eight and three-fifths seconds.[24] O'Doul's hitting
also drew attention, and Miller Huggins began assigning him outfield drills with an eye to getting his bat in the lineup more regularly. Huggins also worked with him in the sliding pit, as his
lack of experience in that area became painfully evident in early
workouts.[25]

O'Doul was ramrod straight, clear of eye, and fleet of foot. He
consistently demonstrated his powerful throwing arm and a beautiful swing. He was charismatic. Quick to laugh and smile, and slow
to take offense, O'Doul had an ingratiating personality that served
him well, even as a rookie, although his penchant for pursuing a
good time—as well as his lack of fear when it came to authority—
would later negatively influence Huggins's opinion of him.

Another rookie making a strong impression was ex–University
of Illinois multi-sport star George Halas; he and O'Doul made for
the dominant story out of Yankees training camp that spring. An
outfielder, Halas displayed great speed, a solid bat, and an impressive throwing arm; whispers began circulating that he would be
the Yankees lead-off hitter and right fielder when the team opened
the season. Like O'Doul, Halas was in top physical shape, having
played football and basketball over the winter with the Great Lakes
Naval Training team after starring for its baseball squad during
the summer. Two years older than O'Doul, Halas had two months
earlier been named Most Valuable Player of the Rose Bowl, catching a touchdown pass and intercepting another in a game played
between two teams of military personnel.[26] It was open to debate
whether O'Doul or Halas was the fastest player on the Yankees.

Both young men were overenthusiastic and prone to showing
off; Huggins found it difficult convincing either of them to hold

back. O'Doul soon injured his arm throwing too many curveballs, relegating him to pinch-hitting and the outfield for much of the exhibition season.[27]

Halas hustled constantly, like an early day Pete Rose, and threw the ball so hard during practice that other players were complaining. More than once, Huggins was heard to scream at Halas, "Watch that arm!"[28] Huggins continually counseled Halas to slow down, especially after the rookie pulled a hip muscle. Heeding that advice proved difficult for a player that New York Tribune sportswriter W. O. McGeehan labeled "one of those youngsters who have to play for all that is in them all the time."[29]

Huggins was unabashedly enthusiastic about the two young players. And as spring training rolled on, the Yankees manager clearly became enamored of O'Doul more as a hitter and less as a pitcher. Huggins announced during the first week of April, "It may be that I hold on to as many as six outfielders, counting O'Doul among them. Of course, O'Doul also is a left-handed pitcher, and as he fortifies us in two departments the chances favor him greatly."[30]

As spring training drew to a close, O'Doul remained on the team, despite his sore arm, and Huggins continued expressing confidence in him, telling the press, "That boy O'Doul is here to stay."[31]

Lefty O'Doul made his Major League debut on April 29, 1919, as a pinch hitter in the third game of the season, at the Polo Grounds against the Philadelphia Athletics. He batted for Yankees starting pitcher George Mogridge in the bottom of the seventh with New York trailing, 7–0; Athletics spitballer Russell "Jing" Johnson, making his first start after spending all of 1918 in the navy, made short work of the rookie, striking him out.[32] O'Doul did not appear in another game for two weeks.

The other spring training phenomenon, George Halas, was likewise seeing little action. His pulled hip muscle kept him out of the lineup until the ninth game of the season. Halas then started four straight games but was benched after collecting only two hits in seventeen at bats. O'Doul's second game appearance consisted of an unsuccessful pinch-hitting attempt for Halas, who had already struck out three times that day—there was grumbling that Halas's name should be changed to "Alas."[33]

Six weeks into the season, Lefty O'Doul collected his first Major League hit, off the great Walter Johnson. The Yankees were trailing in the eighth inning, 5–1, when O'Doul was asked to pinch-hit for pitcher Luke Nelson. Johnson was easing up with the big lead and O'Doul took advantage, lining a solid single into right field.[34]

But other than earning him a few more pinch-hit opportunities, O'Doul's success against Walter Johnson did not earn him any playing time. He spent most of the season practicing in the outfield, with Huggins occasionally having him throw batting practice.[35] O'Doul finally pitched for the first time on July 5, in the ninth inning of a lopsided loss against Washington at the Polo Grounds; he surrendered a hit, walked two batters, and allowed a run.[36]

O'Doul pitched twice more that season—with little success— pinch-hit a few times, and on September 26 played a couple of innings at the end of a game in right field, replacing Sammy Vick. O'Doul not only played sporadically for the Yankees—he was used almost exclusively when the cause was hopeless. The Yankees finished third in the American League with a record of 80-59, but lost fifteen of the nineteen contests in which O'Doul appeared. He earned neither a win nor a loss as a pitcher, and collected four hits in sixteen at bats.

But he went home with $500 in his pocket—each Yankee player's share for finishing third.[37] Miller Huggins continued lavishing praise on the youngster at the end of the season, insisting to reporters that his confidence in O'Doul was unshaken and that he viewed him as a natural ballplayer who only needed time to develop.[38] Huggins made no mention of George Halas, who, after being released midseason, had since retired from baseball to pursue what would become a Hall of Fame career in professional football as founder and owner of the Chicago Bears.[39]

The day after Christmas 1919, the Boston Red Sox sold Babe Ruth to the New York Yankees for $100,000, contingent on Ruth and the Yankees reaching agreement on terms.[40] Ruth would soon be twenty-five years old and was already one of the game's biggest stars. As a pitcher he had twice won twenty games in a season. As a hitter he had broken the season record for home runs, blasting twenty-nine in 1919. Ruth had played for three World Series champions in Boston, pitched twenty-nine and two-thirds consecutive shut-out innings in the Series, and now had the opportunity to become the biggest drawing card in America's biggest city.

Ruth might have acted foolishly at times, but he was no fool. He reached an agreement and the deal was formally announced to the public on January 5, 1920.[41] Ruth was handed the position of starting right fielder for New York—he had played more often in left for the Red Sox—and fans began excitedly recalling his prodigious feats, including his hitting a ball completely out of the Polo Grounds the previous September, and a grand slam some two years earlier that he had launched five hundred feet into a pen filled with alligators during an exhibition game at Little Rock.[42]

A triumphant Jacob Ruppert declared, "[Ruth] is entirely satisfied and New York fandom may rest assured the big fellow is determined to set such a home run record in 1920 as has never before been imagined."[43] A week after the deal was finalized, the *New York Times* opined, "The coming season will see the game's greatest drawing card, his power in this respect enhanced through that record deal, performing in the largest city of the major leagues. It will not be surprising if the Yankees of 1920 set new records for home attendance in a season."[44]

When Lefty O'Doul arrived in Jacksonville for his second spring training with the Yankees, many sensed a greater intensity on his part—at least at the beginning of camp. Huggins continued praising the youngster, pointing to O'Doul's California winter league encounter with Ruth, during which he allowed a home run to the slugger but also struck him out twice.[45]

There appeared to be little opportunity for O'Doul in the Yankees outfield. In addition to Ruth, returnees included Ping Bodie, Duffy Lewis, and Sammy Vick. Huggins had also acquired Lefty's former submarine base teammate Bob Meusel. O'Doul once again

worked out both on the mound and in the outfield, and was careful not to overwork his throwing arm.[46] But Huggins showed little inclination to play him, even as his raw talent continued to
impress observers.

Detroit Tigers scout Bobby Lowe labeled O'Doul one of the fastest players he had ever seen, more than the equal of Ty Cobb when
it came to sprinting from home plate to first base. W. J. Macbeth of
the *New York Tribune* also raved about O'Doul and, with a nod to
Lowe's assessment, insisted, "He can be just as great a ball player as
he cares. Whether or not he possesses the Cobb temperament and
ambition remains to be seen."[47] For his part, Cobb—who within a
year would become player-manager of the Tigers—declared, "The
Detroit club will claim the Coaster [O'Doul] in a minute if Huggins wants to waive him out of the league."[48]

Huggins still failed to play O'Doul, whose winning personality
made him a favorite of reporters, who nicknamed him "O'Doodle"
(since he was a *Yankee*). "Hug" was no different from other managers throughout history, who have never taken kindly to the press
telling them how to fill out the lineup card. Yet Huggins seemed
particularly stubborn when it came to O'Doul. *New York Evening
Post* sportswriter David Walsh posted a lengthy argumentative piece,
pointedly questioning Huggins about sitting O'Doul "while other
and less deserving individuals are given enough rope to hang by
the neck until dead." Walsh went on to write, "All we are capable
of is a reasonably accurate resume of O'Doul's activities to date,
which include a potpourri of timely base hits in the practice games
and a graceful posture on the bench."

But Walsh also criticized O'Doul for his tendency to hurt his
own cause with "a personality that refuses to take anything seriously beyond the matter of getting his meals promptly." Walsh
added, "He is inclined to be something of a buffoon on the ball
field, and by his negligent attitude toward affairs in general gives
one the impression that the whole thing is quite a merry jest, with
the laugh distinctly on the other fellow."[49]

O'Doul did have an influential champion within the Yankees
hierarchy—team business manager Harry Sparrow—and it is

entirely possible that Huggins was forced to keep O'Doul when he did not really want to. Sparrow's position would today be considered akin to general manager, although he was definitely more administrator than talent scout; he had joined the Yankees upon their sale to Jacob Ruppert five years earlier at the recommendation of Sparrow's close friend John McGraw. Like Bobby Lowe, Sparrow saw in O'Doul a potential Ty Cobb. Responding to rumors that O'Doul would be traded or sold, Sparrow declared, "If this club ever trades O'Doul or lets him get away, it will be over my dead body."[50]

When O'Doul did play during the exhibition season, it was usually in the outfield. Near the end of training camp he finally took the mound, pitching five innings against the Brooklyn Dodgers and earning the win. He surrendered only two runs, both in the first inning, while also collecting two hits in two at bats.[51] But Huggins could not seem to make up his mind about O'Doul, and O'Doul was not helping matters with his desire to pitch rather than play every day. The consensus among scouts was that O'Doul showed great promise as a hitter, but that his throwing motion put too much strain on his arm and he would likely find it difficult to last long as a pitcher at the Major League level.[52]

When pressed by Huggins about playing the outfield, O'Doul would make an excuse that his "funny finger" kept him from properly closing his mitt.[53] A decade later, after winning his first batting title, O'Doul would relate that Huggins had told him, "You should be an outfielder. The way you hit that apple, you ought to forget pitching." But O'Doul did not heed that advice: "I still believed I could be a great pitcher, and would not listen."[54]

Lefty O'Doul played even less in 1920 than he had in 1919. He sat on the bench all season, batting only twelve times. He pinch-hit twice in April, six times in May, and once in June. In frustration, he reportedly took to tossing peanut shells at Miller Huggins when the manager was not looking.[55] Over the years, O'Doul repeatedly insisted that Huggins was so oblivious to his presence that he once sneaked off to the horse races with another teammate who rarely played, Chick Fewster, when they thought that day's doubleheader was going to be rained out. Upon discovering the games had been played after all, both were certain heavy fines awaited them, and maybe even suspensions. But Huggins had not even noticed they were gone.[56]

While the story seems typically self-deprecating on O'Doul's part, it is more than likely pure fiction. But it is also more than likely an accurate reflection of frustration with his role, or lack of same, with Huggins and the Yankees. He impatiently sat and watched the Yankees ride the talent of Babe Ruth, with the team either tied for first or a close second for much of June and July, as the slugger easily raced past his old mark of twenty-nine home runs.

Ruth and O'Doul became fast friends, the San Franciscan accompanying the slugger and his wife to Coney Island on several occasions. It was the beginning of the "Jazz Age" in New York, and there was no better companion during that era than Babe Ruth. O'Doul learned about the high life, the speakeasies, dressing well, and mingling with the rich and famous. He and Ruth played golf on a regular basis. Ruth quickly became popular among his teammates, thanks to his personality and the fact that he was one of the few team members who owned an automobile—a luxury that remained well beyond reach of the average American.[57]

O'Doul finally took the mound for the first time on July 26, the second of three pitchers used in the fourth inning against the Boston Red Sox. He faced six batters, allowing two hits, a walk, and a hit batsman.[58] He appeared again five days later, in a mop-up role against St. Louis, although he was in the game long enough to bat twice. On a day when Ruth smashed his thirty-seventh home run of the season over the right-field bleachers and into an adjacent street, O'Doul entered the game with New York trailing, 13–4, and pitched three innings. He acquitted himself well, allowing only two hits and no runs. In the ninth inning he slammed a double to tally a run, and then scored ahead of Wally Pipp's home run.[59]

O'Doul would appear in only one more game that season—the game in which Cleveland shortstop Ray Chapman was killed by a Carl Mays fastball.[60] Huggins had O'Doul pinch-hit with two out in the ninth—his thirteenth and final appearance in a game that year, and only his thirty-second in his two years with the Yankees.

With the tying run on first, he hit a sharp grounder to Harry Lunte, Chapman's replacement at shortstop, and Lunte threw to second base for a force out to end the game.[61]

The Yankees came up short in their quest for the American League pennant in 1920, finishing third, three games behind Cleveland, despite the prodigious feats of Babe Ruth who, as predicted, set a previously unimaginable Major League home run record with fifty-four—more than the number hit by any other Major League *team*, save for the Philadelphia Phillies, which bested him by ten.

After the season there were rumors of division among the Yankees players, with several reportedly acting in a mutinous fashion toward Miller Huggins. An incident that supposedly brought matters to a head involved O'Doul. Huggins had tapped Sammy Vick to pinch-hit one day, and several of the Yankees objected. Blocking Vick's path, they told O'Doul to grab a bat. When O'Doul attempted to do so, Huggins stopped him and a shouting match ensued.[62] According to press reports, Huggins insisted on total control over the roster if he was to continue as manager in 1921; Harry Sparrow, who had been an obstacle to that request, had succumbed to a heart attack in May 1920—roughly three weeks after the dugout incident involving O'Doul and Vick.[63] Yankees ownership acquiesced to Huggins's wishes, and the manager jettisoned several players over the winter.[64]

Two Major League seasons of no note behind him, Lefty O'Doul barnstormed his way to the West Coast with a team of "all-stars" assembled by Philadelphia Phillies outfielder Casey Stengel, and then found himself back home in San Francisco, but this time playing for Charlie Graham and the Seals—he was indeed being sent away by the Yankees over Harry Sparrow's dead body. Despite his differences with O'Doul, Miller Huggins publicly predicted he would be back with the Yankees within a year or two.[65] But it was notable that the Yankees could only send O'Doul to the PCL if he went unclaimed on waivers by every other team in the league, which is exactly what happened despite Ty Cobb's proclamation several months earlier.

Charlie Graham was not only running the Seals' front office, he had taken over as manager late in the 1918 season, holding that position while Lefty O'Doul sat on a Major League bench for two years. The 1920 season had been a rough one for Graham—the PCL had been hit hard by gambling scandals that had resulted in the banishment of several players, including two of San Francisco's star pitchers. Graham saw O'Doul as both a drawing card and a piece he needed to reboot his pitching staff.[66]

Graham was not lacking for talent on his roster; he had a comer, Willie Kamm, at third base and another, Jimmy O'Connell, at first. The Seals began 1921 successfully, winning their first ten games, but O'Doul was hardly the reason for the fast start—Lefty retained his deceptive curve ball, but ever since suffering his arm injury during training camp with the Yankees in 1919, his fastball had lost its zip.

O'Doul lasted only three batters in his first appearance, against a Portland Beavers squad that would turn out to be one of the worst in PCL history with a final record of 51-134.[67] One sportswriter derisively sneered that O'Doul's throwing arm was "no nearer right than raisins in real beer." But Charlie Graham remained hopeful that San Francisco's legendary trainer, Denny Carroll, could revitalize the left-hander's career.[68] O'Doul did not win his second game until the first of May, when he outdueled Los Angeles Angels spitballer Doc Crandall for a 1–0 victory.[69]

O'Doul then established a rhythm, reeling off nine straight victories. After he defeated Oakland with his second straight shutout while collecting three hits in three at bats, teammate and ex–White Sox star Jim Scott effusively proclaimed, "Lefty is not only a great pitcher, but he can play the outfield better than most gardeners. He is a .300 hitter, and can just about outrun any man in the league. Why the New York Yankees let him go and why the other major league clubs granted waivers on him is one of the mysteries of baseball."[70]

O'Doul was fooling hitters with his curve ball, but each appearance took something out of him. He had to be used carefully at times—he was at his best on five to six days' rest. That weakness could be hidden in the PCL, but Charlie Graham knew it would be a different story in the Major Leagues.

Graham was not at all shy about using O'Doul as a pinch hitter, calling on him twenty-one times in that role in 1921. He even utilized O'Doul as a pinch runner on several occasions.[71] Thanks to lessons gleaned from his former teacher, Rose Stolz, O'Doul also developed a reputation as a sharp dresser always in perfect tailored style, something for which he would be known the rest of his life. When he defeated Doc Crandall for a second time in June, *San Francisco Chronicle* sportswriter Ed Hughes referred to him as "the Beau Brummel southpaw."[72]

O'Doul fashioned another nine-game winning streak between August 20 and September 22, topped off by his twenty-fifth win of the season—a complete-game four-hitter against Portland. Not only that, as a batter he matched the entire Beavers lineup with four hits all by himself, plus a walk, in five times at the plate.[73]

But his efforts were for naught. The Seals led the PCL every day, save one, between Opening Day and Labor Day, but were overtaken in September by the Los Angeles Angels, which had been purchased in late August by the owner of the Chicago Cubs, chewing gum magnate William Wrigley. Charlie Graham blamed himself for the Seals' late-season collapse and would return exclusively to front office duties over the winter, acquiring infielder Dots Miller from the Phillies to succeed him on the bench.

Thanks in no small measure to the PCL's atypically elongated 188-game season, O'Doul ended 1921 with an impressive record of 25-9 while pitching more than three hundred innings—a total that would nearly match his output in all of his other seasons combined. In addition, he hit .338 with five home runs in 136 at bats. But the strength of O'Doul's arm remained in question—he tired easily when his workload increased.

Seals co-owner George Putnam traveled to the East Coast in September 1921, searching for prominent Major Leaguers willing to venture out to Northern California and captain local all-star teams for a two-month winter schedule. Putnam returned bearing agreements signed by four of baseball's biggest stars—St. Louis Browns first baseman George Sisler, St. Louis Cardinals second baseman Rogers Hornsby, Detroit Tigers star Harry Heilmann, and Putnam's close friend Ty Cobb. O'Doul was selected to play for Heilmann's team and played right field in the early going, save for two starts on the mound, including a five-hit shutout. When Earl Sheely was signed to play first base after the season began, Heilmann shifted to the outfield and O'Doul went back to pitching and pinch hitting.

Near the end of the impromptu winter league season, O'Doul received word that the Yankees were exercising their option. True to Miller Huggins's prediction, he was going back to New York.[74]

The Yankees team that Lefty O'Doul rejoined in 1922 was more accomplished than the one he had left a year earlier; these Yankees were the defending American League champions, having captured the 1921 pennant. Unfortunately, they lost the World Series to the New York Giants in eight games—the Series was then a best-of-nine affair—despite not only taking the first two contests but also shutting out the Giants both times.

The San Francisco Seals had wanted to keep O'Doul, reportedly offering prize prospect Jimmy O'Connell to the Yankees in exchange.[75] The Chicago White Sox were also interested, dangling veteran outfielder Amos Strunk.[76] The White Sox offer was especially tempting to New York—Babe Ruth and Bob Meusel were serving six-week suspensions, the result of ignoring Commissioner Landis's edict against winter barnstorming by players who had appeared in that year's World Series.[77] But the Yankees also had only one left-handed pitcher on the roster, Harry Harper—and he was threatening to retire. O'Doul served as double insurance in Miller Huggins's mind. Ed Barrow, who had succeeded Harry Sparrow as Yankees business manager, put the final damper on any trade speculation, declaring, "We have decided to keep O'Doul."[78]

Lefty arrived at training camp in New Orleans the day before his twenty-fifth birthday—the first time he had journeyed to the land of his grandfather's birth.[79] Of course, his surroundings at the opulent Hotel Grunewald, with its Italian marble staircase and famous Cave dining room featuring big-budget music revues on a nightly basis, was somewhat more upscale than the surroundings to which his family members would have been accustomed.

O'Doul was a pitcher during spring training, and he was hit hard in his first appearance, this time by the St. Louis Cardinals. But he also hit well that game, slamming two triples and a single.[80] His primary shortcoming on the mound was an inability to control his curve ball—he seemed to either hang his breaking pitches out over the plate or surrender bases on balls because they strayed too far from the strike zone. And his lack of arm strength prevented him from throwing the kind of fastball that kept hitters honest.

O'Doul remained on the roster when the season began, but as in his first stint with the Yankees, he did not play. Despite Ruth and Meusel serving out their suspensions, which lasted until May 20, O'Doul appeared in only two of the team's first thirty games—once as a pinch hitter against Boston, and the other when he pitched a one-two-three inning in relief against the Detroit Tigers.

On May 23, O'Doul relieved Carl Mays in the eighth inning of a game against St. Louis in which the Yankees trailed 6–3. In an effort to improve Lefty's control, Miller Huggins instructed him to focus his eyes on the plate as he pitched. He did—bouncing pitch after pitch off of it—and walked the first two batters he faced. After he settled down, Frank "Home Run" Baker committed an error at third with two out and the bases loaded. By the end of the inning, the Browns had scored five unearned runs.[81] O'Doul did not pitch again for three weeks.

He continued drawing his paycheck, $397.96 a month, but O'Doul's behavior toward Huggins proved little better than during his first stint.[82] Waite Hoyt remembered watching the Yankees manager as he nervously eyed the action on the field, his body literally shaking while he stood with one foot at the top dugout step, refusing to peek at the scoreboard and constantly inquiring as to the count on the batter. O'Doul would then spit on Hoyt's shoes when the pitcher wasn't looking, resulting in an argument that would finally cause an exasperated Huggins to call out, "Come on down here alongside of me O'Doul, and cut out the foolin'." While Huggins kept his eyes fixed on the diamond, O'Doul would skip down the bench, hand on hip, while singing out, "All right teacher. I'll take the front seat."[83]

Lefty tossed three good innings against St. Louis on June 13, and then came back three days later and surrendered eleven hits in five innings against Detroit. He hit a two-run pinch-hit single against the White Sox on July 17, pitched two innings against the Browns a week later, and that was it—save for a pair of exhibition game appearances against International League teams. The first was against Syracuse on August 10, in which he pitched a 3–2 complete-game victory.[84] The second appearance probably ended any possibility of O'Doul pitching in the World Series—a 12–12 tie on September 26 against the Buffalo Bisons. O'Doul started and pitched the first five innings, allowing six runs, including a home run to Bill Kelly that landed on the roof of a building across Masten Street, outside of the Buffalo Baseball Park.[85]

With playing time scarce, O'Doul spent the year renewing his friendships with Babe Ruth and Bob Meusel. He discovered that the Yankees had a private detective tailing them when they, along with teammate Whitey Witt, dined one evening at an illegal brewery—Prohibition having been in effect for going on three years. The detective, who posed as a fan, turned them in and they were fined by the ball club.[86]

The Yankees repeated as American League champions in 1922, and repeated as losers of the World Series to the Giants, this time in five games (four losses and one tie). During the Series, O'Doul was limited to throwing batting practice and sitting on the bench. In mid-July the Yankees had traded Chick Fewster, Elmer Miller, Johnny Mitchell, and cash to the Boston Red Sox for Joe Dugan and Elmer Smith. The Yankees were also to include a player to be named later. After the Series, it was officially announced that O'Doul was that player.[87] His days as a Yankee were over.

New York Times sportswriter John Kieran wrote the epitaph to Lefty O'Doul's Yankees career, saying that he was "the owner and operator of a magnificent curveball. It fooled every batter—once. But it never fooled any batter twice."[88]

O'Doul returned to San Francisco for the winter, heading back to his old neighborhood, where he visited Rose Stolz and the children of Bay View School and served as an honorary floor manager for the popular Butcher's Orchestra.[89] At the end of January he met the *Korea Maru*, the ship returning the first Major League All-Star team to tour Japan, when it docked in San Francisco. Headed by his old Seals teammate Herb Hunter, the team won fifteen of sixteen games with a squad led by Casey Stengel, Waite Hoyt, Herb Pennock, and Joe Bush. O'Doul was captivated by the treasures they brought with them—camel's hair coats by the armful, ladies' furs, and cages of exotic birds.[90] He chatted with the players as they excitedly talked of their adventure. He'd seen a lot in his twenty-five years, having lived in San Francisco and New York, but nothing like that.

Lefty O'Doul remained incredibly popular in his hometown despite three nondescript Major League seasons, and the fact that he had spent three of the past four years on the East Coast. One measure of that popularity was revealed in the recognition he received on Thanksgiving Day in 1922, during a visit to San Quentin Prison for the prisoner's Annual Field Day, an event always featured prominently in the San Francisco newspapers. O'Doul joined other local Major Leaguers and members of the prestigious Olympic Club to officiate the proceedings, as inmates competed in events ranging from running various distances to a tug of war. Every inmate, save for the seven on death row, was allowed to compete in a series of contests judged by the professional athletes.

The seven condemned men were marched to a special area where they remained under the watchful eye of armed guards; the civilian judges and members of the press were instructed not to converse with any of them. One of the death row seven, who would soon be hanged for the murder of a Los Angeles policeman, recognized O'Doul and pleaded for the chance to play catch with him. Guards relayed the request to the warden, who granted it. So it came to be that as the fifty-yard dash was being contested in the center of the prison yard amid a chorus of shouts and whistles, in a far corner Lefty O'Doul quietly played catch with a man condemned to the gallows.[91]

It would be unquestionably trite to employ an obvious and tired literary cliché by suggesting that somehow San Quentin was symbolic of O'Doul's "imprisonment" by the New York Yankees. But he must have felt a freedom of sorts in no longer being chained to the bench by Miller Huggins, and receiving a new start in a new city under a legendary baseball manager.

And Frank Chance was indeed such a legend, although by the time he assumed command of the Boston Red Sox in 1923 he was in poor health and had been out of baseball for six years—ever since resigning midseason in 1917 as manager of the PCL's Los Angeles Angels. More than a decade had passed since Chance's days as player-manager for one of the most successful teams in Major League history, the 1906–10 Chicago Cubs, who averaged a record 106 wins per season. Chance was attempting a comeback—against his wife's wishes—and success was indeed a long shot. The Red Sox, after being raided for several years by the Yankees, were terrible.

Chance was under no illusion, but he was anxious for any opportunity, his wife's misgivings aside, to get back into the harness. He said all the right things during spring training, telling the press, "We have got a lot of good youngsters and we are going to start building up from the bottom." He even displayed a bit of friskiness, donning a mitt and catching O'Doul and teammate Dan Fowlkes.[92] Boston's roster included a number of ex–Coast Leaguers—living in Los Angeles, Chance had seen nearly everyone who played out there, including O'Doul during his stellar 1921 season with the Seals. He voiced praise for the left-hander, faint as it was, announcing, "I am satisfied his work there was good enough to make the grade in the big league."[93]

In the early going, perhaps because of his catching him during practice, Chance asked O'Doul to drill in the outfield, and in the early intersquad contests he hit four balls over the fence.[94] O'Doul also displayed his impressive speed, winning races staged against other Red Sox that cost Chance twenty dollars for betting against him.[95] Chance did ask pitching legend Mordecai "Three Finger" Brown to coach O'Doul, with limited success. It was clear that O'Doul's arm still bothered him—he simply could not cut loose with his fastball—and he was not ready to be a Major League outfielder.[96] Once again, Lefty O'Doul was to be a benchwarmer.

On April 18, 1923, the Red Sox helped the Yankees open their new state-of-the-art facility, Yankee Stadium, by losing. And they kept on losing. O'Doul came in to pitch late in the second game of the series and received a rousing ovation from the twelve thousand on hand. He faced Ruth, who tapped harmlessly back to the mound for an easy out, and went on to pitch a scoreless inning, allowing only one single.[97] O'Doul started the final game of the series, but was chased in the fourth inning and charged with the defeat.[98] It would mark the only starting pitching assignment of his Major League career.

It was depressing sitting on the bench for a terrible team. O'Doul did play more than he had with New York, but the results were similar. He was again employed almost exclusively in mop-up roles; the Red Sox lost twenty-five of the first twenty-six games in which O'Doul took part.

The one victory resulted in Lefty O'Doul's first and only Major League win as a pitcher, at the Red Sox home opener at Fenway Park against the Yankees on April 26. O'Doul entered the game in the top of the ninth with one out in relief of Howard Ehmke. The score was 4–3 in Boston's favor, with Yankees runners on first and third and Babe Ruth the next hitter. Ruth hit a sacrifice fly to tie the game. O'Doul then struck out Wally Pipp to end the inning and earned the victory when the Red Sox scored the winning run in the bottom of the ninth.[99]

Lefty O'Doul did set a Major League pitching record while with the Red Sox—one that has unfortunately stood for nearly a century. On July 7 the Red Sox lost to the Cleveland Indians by a score of 27–3. O'Doul surrendered sixteen of those runs—only three of which were earned—including a record thirteen in one inning. In three innings of relief, O'Doul allowed nineteen base runners. During the barrage he continually looked to the dugout, killing time by walking around the mound between pitches, but no help was forthcoming.[100] In later years, O'Doul would claim Chance left him on the mound as punishment for missing curfew while spending a night on the town with his former Yankees teammates.[101]

O'Doul pitched three more times that July, his final appearance representing his longest Major League stint, seven and two-thirds innings of relief against Washington, during which he allowed three runs. But he pitched only ten more innings over the final two months of the season.

The Red Sox finished last again in 1923, in both standings and attendance. The team was sold, Frank Chance was out (and would be dead within a year), and Lefty O'Doul would soon be headed back for his fourth stint in the PCL.[102] It would prove to be one of the best things that ever happened to him.

3

This Fellow Frank O'Doul Is a Sure Frank Merriwell

The former empire of Japan was an occupied nation in the immediate aftermath of World War II, administered by the United States through its assigned agent, General Douglas MacArthur, whose mission was to transition the nation to democracy. The country's economy was in shambles and its citizens were attempting to reconcile themselves to the final outcome of a war that had terminated at their doorstep—a humiliating turn of events for a people who had thought themselves invincible, who believed that the "Land of the Rising Sun" could never be defeated and that their leader, Emperor Hirohito, was divine. MacArthur recognized the delicate tightrope he must navigate—the emperor could no longer be considered infallible, but a nation adrift is a nation with its future up for grabs. Communists were beginning to make headway, manufacturing grand promises pitched to an increasingly desperate populace.

The general was deeply concerned; he suggested a revival of competitive athletics as a possible remedy. One of MacArthur's first lieutenants, a Japanese American named Tsuneo "Cappy" Harada, was aide-de-camp to General William Marquat, whom MacArthur tasked with overseeing the proposed rebirth of sports in Japan. Within a year of the war's end, Marquat and Harada had restored stadiums around the country, facilitating the reestablishment of professional, college, and high school teams in several sports.

But three years on, MacArthur detected little improvement in the morale of the Japanese. Alarmed by what he recognized as a growing danger, he convened a staff meeting in the spring of 1949 to vet possible solutions to the problem. While sumo remained the national sport, baseball retained its immense popularity—a monument had recently been unveiled in Kobe honoring Babe Ruth, who had succumbed to cancer the previous August.[1]

Harada recognized the positive and lasting impact of earlier visits by Americans, especially the 1934 junket headlined by Ruth. He decided to speak up, suggesting a new baseball tour as the best opportunity to improve morale. When asked who could organize such an endeavor, Harada replied that the obvious choice was Lefty O'Doul, the most revered of living American stars—the man who had convinced Ruth to come to Japan fifteen years earlier. MacArthur, responding with a question that carried the unmistakable ring of an order, looked at Harada and said, "What are you waiting for?"[2]

• • •

Lefty O'Doul was headed back to the Pacific Coast League for the fourth time in the spring of 1924, purchased by the Salt Lake City Bees. Boston Red Sox general manager Bob Quinn had leaned toward keeping O'Doul, but his new manager, Lee Fohl, felt otherwise. "Lee and I did differ regarding O'Doul," Quinn admitted. "The outcome of the matter is that Lee done as he saw fit, for I have no intention of overruling him on such matters. I hired him as a manager and that comes under his duties."[3]

The sale was made "outright," meaning that the Bees were free to sell or trade him to another team if they so wished.[4] The Bees' interest in O'Doul was due in no small part to Duffy Lewis, O'Doul's former Yankees teammate, who had become Salt Lake City's player-manager.

While with the Yankees, Lewis had openly lobbied Miller Huggins to make O'Doul a full-time outfielder, but O'Doul remained stubborn, telling San Francisco reporters he had no intention of giving up the mound, "despite the opinion of some of his well-wishers that he would make an excellent outfielder."[5]

Not yet ready to press his old teammate, Lewis insisted publicly, "O'Doul will make us a dependable southpaw pitcher, a crackerjack hitter, a good base runner and the sort of a fellow whose presence on a club strengthens the morale."[6] Lewis was prepared to bide his time, certain in the knowledge that, sooner or later, the thin air of Salt Lake City would convince the left-hander to shift his focus away from the mound.

Lewis also hoped matrimony would result in a newfound maturity for his pitcher—in late April, the twenty-seven-year-old O'Doul married Abigail Lacey in a small civil ceremony during an off day in Portland, with teammate Clarke "Pinky" Pittenger as his witness.[7]

Upon reporting to training camp in Fresno, California, O'Doul had immediately set about expanding his pitching repertoire. New weapons included a screwball and a changeup developed under the tutelage of Detroit Tigers star Dutch Leonard—a Fresno native who had been recently pitching for an outlaw team because of a feud he was engaged in with his manager, Ty Cobb.[8]

O'Doul made his debut in Salt Lake City, as a pitcher, in the second game of the season, and did so in remarkable fashion, taking a 16–2 lead into the ninth inning against Oakland before coasting and allowing four runs. Duffy Lewis and Roy Leslie both hit home runs over the Rotisserie Inn sign posted on the outfield fence, earning them their choice of two chicken or trout dinners. O'Doul homered as well, but not in a spot where he could win a meal; while he may have good-naturedly whined about the injustice, he was quite satisfied that he had proven his larger point—he could be an effective pitcher in one of baseball's most challenging venues.[9]

Duffy Lewis was aware of O'Doul's physical limitations—he did not use him again for nine days following his first appearance. But Lewis stuck to his plan; other than some pinch-hitting assignments and late-inning outfield appearances, O'Doul was a pitcher for the first three months of the season, although with far less success than had been the case early on.

When July rolled around, Lefty had lost as many as he had won, with an earned run average of nearly six runs per game—certainly not numbers that would get him back to the big leagues. And as Duffy Lewis had calculated, Bonneville Park began humbling the left-hander. Later in his life, O'Doul reflected on the unforgettable experience of playing baseball in Salt Lake City, exclaiming, "What a city for pitchers! With that near mile-high altitude, somebody hits a ball and it sails out of the park on wings, mountain-bound!"[10]

O'Doul pinch-hit between pitching assignments, and after three consecutive successful appearances raised his batting average for the season to an even .400, Lewis used a rash of injuries to convince Lefty to become an everyday outfielder. And O'Doul was finally ready to listen. Sometimes he played in left field, and sometimes in right, but he was in the lineup every day. And, as Duffy Lewis had hoped, he was an instant success.

O'Doul collected four hits on August 6, including a three-run, ninth-inning home run that defeated Portland.[11] He smashed three home runs and drove in eight against San Francisco eleven days later.[12] A week after victimizing the Seals, O'Doul stroked eight straight hits in a doubleheader versus Los Angeles, going six for six in the first game.[13] During a twenty-nine-game stretch spanning September 9 to October 9, O'Doul collected fifty-seven hits in 116 at bats—one hit shy of a .500 batting average. Outside of his winning streaks on the mound during the 1921 season, he had never experienced such success on the diamond. His days as a pitcher were over, and furthermore he was fine with that.

O'Doul made one more emergency pitching appearance for Salt Lake City, in relief at home against Portland on September 20. It was an experience that served to reinforce the notion that his move to the outfield was indeed the right one. In four and two-thirds innings, O'Doul was battered for ten runs and nineteen hits; years later, he claimed that during the barrage, he threw a high curve that Portland's Jim Poole slammed out of the park while swinging the bat one-handed, a feat that O'Doul claimed had convinced him to give up pitching once and for all.[14]

O'Doul maintained his torrid hitting pace all summer, finishing in a virtual tie with Duffy Lewis for the PCL batting crown with a .392 batting average, while driving in 101 runs in only 416 official at bats. Salt Lake City ended its 1924 season with 101 wins—which seems impressive until one realizes that the team played 201 games. Dissension was a problem for the Bees—it had always seemed to be so for some reason—and the latest fissure came to light when

Duffy Lewis emerged from the clubhouse one day with a black eye, courtesy of pitcher Harry O'Neill, with whom he had been feuding for most of the season.[15] Lewis was relieved of his managerial duties at year's end and replaced by third baseman Oscar Vitt.

Before taking his leave, Lewis reminded reporters of O'Doul's successful conversion from pitcher to everyday player and, shaking his head over the struggle it had been to get the ballplayer to see the light, declared, "O'Doul would be a major leaguer today if he had followed not only my advice, but the advice of others."[16]

Salt Lake City had been a controversial candidate to replace Sacramento as a PCL city, after the California capital's franchise had foundered following a last-ditch transfer to San Francisco at the end of the 1914 season. But the Salt Lake City contingent gradually won over the other PCL owners and the city was awarded a slot for the grand sum of $15,000.[17]

Utah's capital was a good sports town—bicycle racing had been wildly popular for years, and citizens had consistently supported lower-level professional baseball teams. The city at first proved a boon to the fortunes of the PCL. Attendance exceeded expectations and crowds were enthusiastic. But by 1925 the bloom was off the rose.

Enterprising young boys were selling rocks to patrons for the purpose of chucking them at umpires. Travel to and from other PCL cities was expensive, and owner Bill Lane was repeatedly rumored to be moving the team to California—Fresno, Long Beach, and San Diego the most commonly mentioned destinations. The uncertainty surrounding the franchise depressed attendance and made Lane extremely unpopular.

The Bees' home field, Bonneville Park, had gained a reputation as a sort of joke, its short fences combined with the high altitude of Salt Lake City conspiring to bring about ridiculous offensive numbers once the "lively ball" was adopted. Outfielder Paul Strand, who won back-to-back batting titles and the Triple Crown in 1923 for Salt Lake City, was acquired by the Philadelphia Athletics and promptly flamed out within two months—the numbers he had posted in the PCL, including a still-standing organized baseball record of 325 hits in one season, proving a mirage in the desert. In May 1923, Vernon outfielder Pete Schneider—a converted pitcher like Strand and O'Doul—hit five home runs at Bonneville Park. *In one game.* During the 1924 season, the Bees and Seals had combined for 170 runs and 264 hits during a seven-game series; San Francisco's Bert Ellison crashed out twenty-five hits in thirty-seven at bats that week. *The Sporting News* scoffed, "Is that baseball? You are right, it is not. It is cricket."[18]

Lefty O'Doul's enjoyment of life and carefree attitude had branded him as someone who was less than serious about his profession. That perception had hampered his Major League career—Miller Huggins had been loath to turn over a regular position to a man even his supporters admitted could be a bit of a buffoon.

O'Doul fit in well in the PCL, which had a long tradition of tolerating—even promoting—the entertaining and the unorthodox. Baseball *was* entertainment. Lefty O'Doul understood that. Furthermore, he enjoyed the attention. He was a showman—and a talented one. Although appearing lackadaisical at times, he could be surprisingly combative on the diamond, especially when he felt slighted. Many whose lives intersected with O'Doul's did not understand that; their resulting misperceptions—combined with his stubbornness in continuing to pitch for so long—served to obscure the talent of a man who at his core was very analytical, and competitive.

That analytical nature was revealed in his working with Dutch Leonard in an attempt to develop additional pitches, and in his golf game, which by this time he had mastered. Although he would later claim that a golf swing was in no way comparable to swinging a baseball bat, golf did prove key to understanding Lefty O'Doul's hitting philosophy.[19] He did not copy Babe Ruth, whose stance began with his feet together before striding into his swing, almost launching his body at the ball in order to maximize the force generated by the bat head through the strike zone. Ruth thought place hitting a fiction. Not so O'Doul. Although he considered the swing completely different, O'Doul utilized many of the same skills necessary for success on the links—keeping one's head still, keeping one's eye on the ball to the point of contact, and shifting one's weight through the hips rather than striding. O'Doul's remained, to be sure, an evolving philosophy. But before long he would be providing batting instruction to teammates. And they would listen.

In order to return to the Major Leagues, O'Doul would not only have to convince skeptics that he was through with pitching once and for all, he also had to overcome the prejudice against Salt Lake City hitters, of whom it was thought effectiveness more a measure of where they played than their ability. O'Doul began 1925 as he had ended 1924. A dozen games into the season—all played at Bonneville Park—he was batting an even .500; his fast start included three-hit games thrice against Portland, and eight hits in eleven at bats in the final three games of a series against Vernon.

During another series against Vernon in July, with New York Yankees scout Ed Holly sitting in the stands, O'Doul collected six hits in six at bats—and then repeated the feat two days later.[20] At one point, he slammed out nine consecutive base hits, the last a home run that sent a game into extra innings. After making an out, he had ten more hits in a row, raising his batting average to .422.[21] Between June 21 and August 2, O'Doul hit safely in forty-four of forty-five games, batting .475 over that span with nine home runs and sixty-three runs batted in. It was no secret that Ed Holly's main target was Bees shortstop Tony Lazzeri, who was on his way to hitting an incredible sixty home runs (and setting a still-standing organized baseball record of 222 runs batted in), but it was also thought that with the Yankees in a freefall to seventh place in the American League, they would give serious consideration to O'Doul—surely a batting average greater than .400 in late July would convince Miller Huggins that Lefty was finally ready to be a full-time Major League outfielder.[22] The Yankees were said to be combing the PCL, willing to spend a quarter million dollars securing talent. Yet even Ed Holly's confirmation that marriage had curtailed O'Doul's heretofore prodigious taste for nightlife—he spent four weeks tailing Lefty and reported the ballplayer was home every night by six o'clock—was not enough to put him on the Yankees shopping list.[23]

Cincinnati was rumored to be interested—their scout was

O'Doul's old Des Moines manager Jack Coffey—as were the Chicago Cubs. Then, Lefty was hurt in a game against Seattle, sustaining an injury initially thought to be season-ending. During his second at bat in the first game of a doubleheader, O'Doul took a fastball on his right (non-throwing) elbow, fracturing the bone. He finished that game and started the nightcap, but was unable to continue after his first at bat.[24] He then missed three games. The Reds and Cubs backed off. Sensing his future hanging in the balance, O'Doul returned to the lineup, grimacing with every swing.

The injury undeniably hampered O'Doul's hitting; after spending nearly the entire season with a batting average above .400, Lefty hit less than .300 following his injury, dropping him well behind both Paul Waner and Frank Brazill in the batting race. Although he compiled a still impressive .375 average for the 1925 season, plus 63 doubles, 17 triples, and 191 runs batted in during 198 games played, O'Doul would finish a distant third in the race. Waner became the league's first-ever .400 hitter, while Brazill followed closely at .395. Tony Lazzeri was purchased by the New York Yankees, while Waner, who had hit 75 doubles to go along with his .401 batting average, was headed to the Pittsburgh Pirates. (Brazill, a notorious hothead who had already flunked a trial with the Philadelphia Athletics, remained in the PCL.)

But there was good news for O'Doul: despite his injury-influenced batting slump down the stretch, he had been purchased by a Major League team.

The undoubtedly romanticized story of the time—which to be fair may contain an element of truth to it since it sounded like something Cubs owner William Wrigley would do—had Wrigley, who also owned the PCL's Los Angeles Angels, conversing with Salt Lake City owner Bill Lane when the Bees visited Los Angeles late in the 1925 season. Wrigley's attention was captured when O'Doul stepped to the plate. Nudging Lane, he asked, "Who is that fellow?"

Lane allegedly replied, "That is the guy one of your scouts wanted to buy some time back. He's the best hitter in the league, a swell fielder and a valuable man."

"What did you say his name was again?" asked Wrigley.

"O'Doul," said Lane. "O-D-O-U-L."

Wrigley snapped, "All right. Wrap him up—I'll take him."[25]

One can be excused for expressing a degree of skepticism as to the veracity of this version of events—certainly there is fiction in Lane characterizing O'Doul as a "swell fielder." Even O'Doul would have admitted that. But several years later Wrigley would tell much the same story, without the dramatic flourishes. And to the end of his days, William Wrigley maintained Lefty O'Doul was the only player he ever personally acquired for the Chicago Cubs.[26]

The Chicago Cubs had last won the National League pennant seven years earlier, at the same time leading the Major Leagues in attendance. The team had accomplished neither feat since, finishing in the National League cellar in 1925—the first time that had happened in the fifty-season history of the franchise. (It would not happen again until 1948, after which last place became more routine—a habit even.)

The Cubs had some talent in 1926—Gabby Hartnett was a good young catcher, and first baseman Charlie Grimm was a star, one year after being acquired from the Pittsburgh Pirates. But the Cubs' best pitchers, Wilbur Cooper and the great Grover Cleveland Alexander, were most definitely nearing the end of the line—Alexander was thirty-nine years old.

William Wrigley possessed many qualities, but being patient while losing was not among them. He had hired a new manager, Joe McCarthy, fresh from capturing his second American Association pennant. McCarthy, a career Minor Leaguer in his first big league job, was in charge of thirty-five players at the team's training base on Wrigley-owned Catalina Island.[27] The Cubs had used twelve men in the outfield in 1925, with Cliff Heathcote playing in the most games, ninety-nine; McCarthy correctly concluded this as one of the squad's weak areas.

Tasked with rebuilding the franchise and dealing with the team's many prima donnas, McCarthy set out an ambitious schedule, including two-a-day workouts topped off by a mountain hike. And he meant for the team to be serious in going about its business, banning poker among other pastimes. Of course, on his second day in camp, the fun-loving O'Doul ignored the hint, making a resplendent appearance in rainbow-colored golf garb, joined by Charlie Grimm, Howard Freigau, and Sheriff Blake.[28]

The weather was warm and the players' conditioning was such that McCarthy soon shortened the workout sessions, recognizing that wearing everybody out before the season began was an unwise strategy.[29] The first intrasquad game saw O'Doul in the outfield with the first team, along with fellow newcomers and Minor League sluggers Joe Kelly and Hack Wilson.[30] But McCarthy had his reservations about O'Doul—and the rest of that outfield alignment.

After Wrigley arrived on the island, O'Doul played left field during intrasquad games, rather than in center as originally planned.[31] McCarthy felt much less enthusiasm for his new acquisition than did his boss—especially when it came to O'Doul's defense—and McCarthy seemed to be feeding his doubts to Irving Vaughan, who was covering training camp for the *Chicago Tribune*. It was Vaughan who first sounded an ominous note for O'Doul's chances. "Knowing how McCarthy feels about matters," wrote Vaughan, "it wouldn't surprise us to see [Pete] Scott in left, Wilson in center and Kelly in right when the season opens."[32]

Next, Vaughan wrote a piece for *The Sporting News*, declaring that one of the outfielders originally projected to start (probably Kelly) was slow and another (almost certainly O'Doul) had "a weak arm and is not sure fire on fly balls."[33] Later, Vaughan wrote, "[O'Doul] has shown some glaring defects as a fielder and hasn't lived up to his hitting reputation."[34] Whether O'Doul's injured elbow was hampering his hitting is a matter of speculation, but his lack of instinct in the outfield was definitely hurting his chances with McCarthy.

O'Doul started in the first exhibition game, against William Wrigley's other baseball team, the Los Angeles Angels, and was the only Cub batter to collect more than one hit in a 5–2 loss.[35] He collected two hits the next day as well. But before long, McCarthy was playing Heathcote in left and Wilson in center, having decided that O'Doul was not worth the money the Cubs would have to pay to keep him, reportedly $50,000.[36] He was quietly returned to Bill

Lane, who had since moved his Bees to Hollywood. O'Doul did not have far to go; the Cubs were playing an exhibition series against Hollywood at the time.[37] A week later O'Doul played against the Cubs and had a stellar day—playing right field, he threw out a runner at third and hit a home run.[38] It was satisfying, but O'Doul would not forget how McCarthy had shown such little regard for his talent. Not by a long shot.

Bill Lane had finally abandoned Utah for Los Angeles in the off-season. William Wrigley had wanted Lane as a tenant of the new stadium he had finally completed for the Angels—Los Angeles' Wrigley Field opened in September 1925—and to accomplish that had brokered a deal to move the other Los Angeles–area franchise, the Vernon Tigers, to San Francisco, where it would become the Missions and play second fiddle to the Seals.

To differentiate his team from the Angels, Lane arranged to have it represent Hollywood—although the team would never play there, and would eventually be moved again by Lane to San Diego after ten seasons. A second Hollywood team, the Stars, would emerge in 1938 (ironically, the very same team that had moved to San Francisco a dozen years before) to become one of the most glamorous franchises in baseball—owned by Bob Cobb of Brown Derby restaurant fame, with shares sprinkled among scores of Hollywood celebrities, who flocked to the ballpark. These were not those Stars.

Undoubtedly disappointed in his treatment by the Cubs, and in losing out on yet another shot at the Major Leagues at age twenty-nine, O'Doul got off to a slow start in 1926 and chafed under the authoritarian, and sarcastic, Oscar Vitt. Despite O'Doul's clearly being the team's best hitter, Vitt began the year platooning him, generally benching him against left-handers. Vitt also accused O'Doul of being a clubhouse lawyer of sorts, plotting along with second baseman Johnny Kerr to undermine him.

During a game in mid-May, Hollywood was down one run in the ninth, with a runner at first and no one out. Vitt flashed a bunt sign to O'Doul, who ignored it and swung away, hitting into a double play. That was the last straw for Vitt; he demanded that Lane place both O'Doul and Kerr on waivers.[39] After two days, Lane and Vitt reversed themselves; later that week O'Doul hit a grand slam off Joe Oeschger to win a game at Wrigley Field.[40] But Vitt continued to irritate O'Doul, and vice versa. For three weeks in June and July, Vitt batted O'Doul fourth against right-handers and eighth against lefties.

O'Doul was unhappy, and his offensive production dropped. Whether that was a result of his unhappiness, the shift from the thin air of Bonneville Park, or his still painful elbow remains unclear; he *was* sidelined with "water on the elbow" during September, missing a week of action.[41] O'Doul's batting average dropped nearly forty points from a year earlier, even after concluding the season with eighteen hits in his final thirty-one at bats. He had been the team's leading hitter by far, with twenty home runs and a .338 average, seventh-best in the PCL. But Hollywood had finished sixth.

Bill Lane was still grumpy about O'Doul's carefree attitude and, after unsuccessfully attempting to peddle him to San Francisco's second PCL team, the Missions, sent Lefty a contract that included a cut in pay.[42] Then Lane found a taker.

As an early thirtieth birthday present of sorts, O'Doul learned he was returning for a fourth stint with his hometown Seals, who paid $7,500 for his services. Save for word of a return to the Major Leagues, O'Doul could not have been happier.[43] San Franciscans were happy as well; Abe Kemp of the *San Francisco Examiner* wrote that Lefty's acquisition brought to the Seals "speed, power, personality and charm."[44] O'Doul had come full circle—a decade earlier he had signed with the Seals before being farmed out to the cornfields of Iowa. The 1926 season had been a disappointment—in a span of three months going from the Chicago Cubs to being placed on waivers by a Minor League team. But 1927 would serve as the springboard to the next phase of O'Doul's baseball career.

Lefty O'Doul remained extremely popular in his hometown and relished the prospect of taking aim at the short right-field fence at Recreation Park for an entire year.[45] He also wanted to cause regret on the part of Bill Lane and Oscar Vitt for letting him go.

The San Francisco Seals had become a powerhouse since O'Doul had last played for them six years earlier. During a time when the PCL strictly limited the ability of the Majors to draft its talent, Charlie Graham, George Putnam, and Doc Strub had gained a reputation for signing players and selling them, most often to big league teams, at great profit. Third baseman Willie Kamm had been sold to the Chicago White Sox for six figures. Jimmy O'Connell had gone to the Giants for $75,000. The Seals had won pennants in 1922, 1923, and 1925—teams arguably among the greatest in Minor League history. In addition to Kamm and O'Connell, during the 1920s the Seals signed and sold Earl Averill, Paul and Lloyd Waner, Lefty Gomez, Gus Suhr, Lew Fonseca, Dolph Camilli, Curt Davis, Alvin "General" Crowder, Babe Pinelli, Roy Johnson, Frank Crosetti . . . and Lefty O'Doul.

O'Doul began the 1927 season with a nineteen-game hitting streak, including thirteen multi-hit games out of fourteen between the third and the sixteenth of April. He was blanked by spitballer Frank Shellenback in his first appearance against Hollywood, but then collected hits in each of the remaining six games, including three—two of them home runs—in the series finale. When Hollywood visited San Francisco in mid-May, O'Doul stroked six hits in fourteen at bats, including two home runs, during the first four games of the series. During a nine-game stretch in late July and early August, O'Doul cranked out twenty-four hits in forty-two at bats. He was making it clear to Lane and Vitt how he felt, and the Seals were reaping the benefits, finishing in second place after a last-place finish in 1926.

As the season wore on, kids began flocking to the left-field bleachers, many of them O'Doul's guests, and many of them from his old neighborhood. They screamed out his name as he stood on the field in front of them, and screamed even louder when he sneaked away baseballs between innings and tossed them into the stands. What O'Doul had, they wanted. And he was going to give it to them. The kids organized a rooting section and wore buttons bearing his image.[46]

Lefty regularly visited his old school, calling on Rose Stolz, who had since become the school's principal, and lectured the students about baseball and life.[47] He also made sure to always have a treat for the school's canine mascot, Bay View Bill.[48] As a result of his loyalty, each morning after the flag salute in the schoolyard, Rose Stolz had the children of Bay View School turn and face the direction of Recreation Park and shout "Hip Hip Hooray!" in Lefty's honor.[49]

Though O'Doul was an only child and had no children of his own, he knew how to relate to them. He never forgot that he had once been one of them. And they could not get enough of their hero.

Preparations began for a "Lefty O'Doul Day." But O'Doul was not interested in a day for himself—he wanted it to be about the kids who were his biggest fans. As a result, the *San Francisco Chronicle* agreed to supply miniature bats and baseballs to the boys and girls attending the game, all of whom would be admitted free of charge. After the game, kids would be grouped together in center field and O'Doul would stand at the plate hitting five hundred baseballs to them—gently, it was said.[50]

The *Chronicle* took up a collection, printing the names of those contributing to what was hoped to be a large check handed to O'Doul on his day. Rose Stolz made a donation. So did Emma Rulan of San Jose, who enclosed a note indicating it was a "thank-you" to O'Doul for hitting a home run for her bedridden son, who listened to Seals games on his radio. The Seals kicked in $250. Colorful San Francisco character Gus Oliva, often portrayed as a local gangster—it was said that he went together with hot water like soap—gave $225.

After $1,000 was collected, the *Chronicle* limited further donations to no more than a dollar, so that everyone could feel they had contributed. Ballplayers Eddie Mulligan, Bob Geary, and Harry Krause pitched in. Former lightweight boxing star Jimmy Britt did too. A San Quentin inmate who listed himself only as "A Friend" sent a dollar. Boys from Lefty's old neighborhood collected nickels to make up a combined donation. Nearly $2,000 in all was mailed to the *Chronicle*.

It was announced that 5,000 bags of peanuts and some 1,500 miniature bats autographed by O'Doul would be distributed to youngsters in attendance. After the game, children would be allowed to come onto the field while O'Doul and his teammates swatted the five hundred autographed baseballs into the crowd. Not only that, O'Doul announced he would pitch the afternoon game of the September 11 doubleheader—his first mound appearance in three years.[51]

The Seals easily won the morning contest, 15–1, with O'Doul collecting three hits in three at bats. After the stadium was emptied, the next crowd began lining up for the two-thirty afternoon start. The "Standing Room Only" sign quickly went up as children, amped with anticipation, filled the bleachers, first swelling against the enormous Christensen Lumber Company sign on the back wall before spilling onto the grass in left field.

There were preliminaries, including a roping demonstration by one of the Butchertown Cowboys. O'Doul rode with the horsemen as they galloped around the diamond and tossed miniature bats to children who had taken over the infield, talking to players, swarming the benches, and swinging players' bats. O'Doul and his teammates waded into the stands and tossed bags of peanuts. It was a kid's dream—and Lefty's, too.

The Butchertown Cowboys, assisted by the police, finally shooed the crowd back into the bleachers and grandstands so the game could begin. During a ceremony broadcast on local radio, Lefty was presented his check as well as other gifts, including a loving cup, a floral arrangement, and a wristwatch.

Pregame festivities completed, O'Doul took the mound to face the Missions, who must have been licking their chops at the idea of facing him—even though it was expected he would pitch only three or four innings at best. At first it appeared that prediction would prove optimistic. O'Doul surrendered a lead-off double, followed by an infield error to give the Missions two runners on base with no one out. But he settled down, getting a strikeout and a double play to escape the inning unscathed.

O'Doul then brought the crowd to its feet in the bottom of the inning when he smacked a double. Even though he was stranded at second, he already seemed larger than life to those who had come to honor him.

The Seals scored in both the second and third innings, while O'Doul retired the Missions in order. Bill Rodda lined a single off

O'Doul to lead off the fourth, but was doubled off first base on a fly ball; it was the last hit O'Doul surrendered. Other than a walk to opposing pitcher Ed Bryan, O'Doul did not permit another man to reach base. Meanwhile, the Seals scored in the fifth to stretch the lead to 3–0.

In the eighth, Earl Averill made a spectacular catch to save extra bases, and O'Doul responded by saluting the outfielder with a wave of his cap. O'Doul did not have a lot of velocity on this day, but he had command of his curve ball and repeatedly used it as his out pitch. As the game continued he gained confidence, and when Bill Rodda lofted a lazy fly ball to Smead Jolley in right field to end the game, the crowd erupted, and not because the notoriously poor-fielding Jolley had actually caught the ball. It was because O'Doul had thrown a two-hit shutout, striking out four batters while walking only one; once again he had proven himself a master showman. With the pressure on, he had more than delivered—and it was a moment O'Doul would always rank among the most satisfying of his career. The *Chronicle* crowed, "This fellow Frank O'Doul is a sure Frank Merriwell."[52]

His adrenaline pumping, O'Doul clambered onto the roof of the grandstand and, rather than hitting autographed baseballs into the crowd, tossed them to the kids excitedly chattering below. One father, clearly as thrilled by O'Doul's performance as the sea of children surrounding him, turned to his son and asked, "Well, what do you think of Lefty now?" The son shouted back, "Gee dad, he's keen!" The *Chronicle* put it simply, declaring, "Say brother, it was a wow!"[53] Concessionaire Tom Stephens was so enthused he exclaimed, "Let's have another kid's day next year and I will give away 10,000 sacks of peanuts!"[54]

There was no doubting it had been a great season for Lefty O'Doul. As usual he concluded the year with a flourish, collecting 13 hits in his final 23 at bats to finish with a .378 average, second-best in the league. O'Doul hit 33 home runs and drove in 158, while leading the league with 278 base hits, 40 stolen bases, and 164 runs scored. He was named the PCL's Most Valuable Player.[55]

That October, Babe Ruth and Lou Gehrig embarked on a nation-wide barnstorming exhibition engineered by Ruth's manager, Christy Walsh. The two stars captained teams of local players at each stop of a tour that left New York on the eleventh, visiting eighteen states before arriving in Northern California.

O'Doul, along with George Putnam and Gus Oliva, met Ruth and Gehrig on the Oakland side of the Bay to welcome the two stars and accompany them by ferry to San Francisco. Once there, the Knights of Columbus, of which Ruth was a member, made a special presentation and arranged for the two great players to distribute baseballs and handkerchiefs to local children.[56]

Ruth's "Bustin' Babes" took on Gehrig's "Larrupin' Lou's" that afternoon at Recreation Park. O'Doul batted second and played left field for the "Babes," whose lineup also included Smead Jolley, Eddie Mulligan, and Gus Suhr. Willie Kamm, Lew Fonseca, and Jimmie Reese were among those on Gehrig's team. The "Lou's" won, 10–7, although O'Doul did hit a home run over the left-field fence, and Jolley added two more. Gehrig also homered, but Ruth did not—although the Babe pleased the crowd by pitching two innings.

The teams played two games the next day, one in the morning in Oakland and the other at Recreation Park in the afternoon. In a ceremony prior to the latter contest, Lou Gehrig presented O'Doul a check for $1,000, his reward for being named Most Valuable Player of the PCL.[57] O'Doul later reciprocated by purposely missing a foul fly ball hit by Gehrig so the Yankees star would have another chance to swing the bat.[58] Constantly shadowed in the outfield by young fans screaming to get his attention, O'Doul also "lost" a couple of other fly balls so the kids crowding the field would have an opportunity to grab a souvenir.[59]

O'Doul skipped games in Marysville, Sacramento, and Stockton before rejoining Ruth and Gehrig in San Jose. He again played for Ruth's team, but this time as the right fielder. And O'Doul seemed to have developed a new fan club—every time he went out to take his position, a horde of screaming females would race onto the field trying to touch him. When he later posed for photographers, the young women were literally hanging off him. A local reporter dubbed O'Doul "The Sheik." Inspired, he robbed Gehrig of a home run with a leaping catch.[60]

Ruth insisted that O'Doul play in the tour finale in Los Angeles on October 30. To make room for Lefty, Ruth announced he would play first base and O'Doul would take left field. It was announced that Cubs pitcher Charlie Root would play for the Larrupin' Lou's—Ruth had claimed Root would be easy to hit, which had raised Root's ire; at least that's the way the publicity went.[61]

Twenty-five thousand crammed into Wrigley Field to see baseball's two biggest stars. Ruth batted third for his team, with O'Doul right behind him in the batting order. Ruth would only collect one hit in four tries off Root, same as O'Doul, while Gehrig homered twice and led his team to victory, 5–2. After the game, Ruth and Gehrig autographed dozens of baseballs and then threw them to a crowd of children, who made a mad scramble to secure a souvenir.[62]

O'Doul was in great spirits—and he had reason to be. A couple of weeks earlier, at the baseball winter meetings in Pittsburgh, he had been drafted by the New York Giants.[63] The Seals had made a tactical error in leaving him unprotected; reasoning that with his thirtieth birthday having come and gone he was unlikely to be drafted, they rolled the dice and lost. If Charlie Graham and his partners had recognized the certainty of losing him, they could have set up a bidding war and collected far more than the draft price for their best—and most popular—player. Instead they were left with a poor deal that represented what the PCL resented about the Major Leagues: O'Doul had been purchased a year earlier for $7,500, half what the Cubs had paid for him on option; now the Giants were getting him for the draft price of $5,000, far below market value. That being said, Charlie Graham would never have stood in O'Doul's way, even if he could have.[64] Lefty O'Doul was headed back to the big leagues—and to the Big Apple. And this time he was going to stick.

He Always Could Play Ball,
Now He Gets It Earnestly

General MacArthur endorsing Cappy Harada's pursuit of Lefty O'Doul as a panacea for Japan's problems seemed foolhardy to many insiders—not that anyone planned to take that up directly with the general. There had been other recently proposed junkets; Minor League president Frank Shaughnessy had suggested one for the 1949 postseason involving champions of the American Association, International League, and Pacific Coast League.[1] But the shaky Japanese economy, racked by inflation, and the considerable financial risk of such an undertaking—including the issue that yen could not legally be exchanged for dollars—made it nearly impossible to compensate players. (Yen could be used for operational expenses in Japan, but American dollars could not legally be used to pay athletes, who fell under the category of entertainers.)

Harada was undeterred—he believed that sports, particularly baseball, were a big key to reengaging the Japanese people. When Harada had learned that Shigeru Mizuhara, star third baseman of the Tokyo Giants team that had toured the States in 1935 and 1936, was a Soviet prisoner of war, he undertook a massive effort to effect his release and repatriation. One of Mizuhara's first appearances was at a Tokyo Giants game where, in a moment best rivaled in American baseball history by Lou Gehrig's "luckiest man" speech, the baseball star addressed the crowd, emotionally declaring, "I, Mizuhara, have finally come home."[2]

Harada was also ready to come home—although certainly not under circumstances nearly as dramatic as Mizuhara's. But chasing down a baseball legend in his home state represented a big moment in Harada's life. He was not someone easily discouraged; like O'Doul, he'd survived a hard-knock early life, although his "hard knocks" lasted longer into adulthood than O'Doul's. Harada was born in the United States in 1921 and his mother died soon after. As a result, when little more than a child, he worked as a field laborer alongside his father, harvesting grapes, celery, strawberries, and other crops grown in the fertile soil of California's Santa Maria Valley, 120 miles northwest of Los Angeles.

Harada knew that Lefty O'Doul had become enamored with Japan and its people during his first trip there as a player in 1931. Over the course of several subsequent visits, O'Doul had eagerly sampled the food, familiarized himself with the language, and immersed himself in the culture—in the process becoming, with the exception of Babe Ruth, the most popular of America's baseball players in the eyes of the Japanese.

Making another visit had also been on O'Doul's mind. He had been shocked by the bombing of Pearl Harbor, almost taking it as a personal affront. But only a few months after the war's end, he had traveled to Japan on his own, eager to reestablish ties. "I knew if we brought a baseball team over there," he reasoned, "it would cement friendship between their people and us."[3] No trip had materialized from that first visit. Nor had one developed from requests he submitted to Occupation forces in 1947 and 1948. But O'Doul had remained certain the day would arrive.

Lefty eagerly welcomed Harada in San Francisco and listened intently to his proposal. O'Doul never hesitated, although he had one condition: rather than a Major League All-Star team, he insisted on bringing his San Francisco Seals to Japan following the 1949 season. Harada returned to Japan with the message—now it was up to General MacArthur and the Occupation forces to determine whether the plan was feasible.

• • •

There was no middle ground with John McGraw. He was that kind of guy—the proverbial "love him or hate him" character. He was brilliant and bombastic. He was generous. He was rude. He was kind, even empathetic. He was loyal. He never forgot a slight. He had friends you would not want to cross.

McGraw was one of the first celebrity managers, a nonplayer recognized as the face of his franchise. Charisma and force of personality, coupled of course with success, served him well in that role over the entirety of his career. During his reign—a not wholly inaccurate characterization of his tenure—only Christy Mathewson came close to matching McGraw as the symbol of the New York Giants.

At fifty-five years old, John McGraw was commencing his twenty-seventh season at the helm of the Giants when Lefty O'Doul arrived in 1928. He had captured ten National League pennants and three World Series and had endured only two losing seasons with New York—the first in 1915, when Christy Mathewson's talent diminished at age thirty-four. Following that stumble, McGraw rebuilt, winning his sixth pennant in 1917, followed by four in a row beginning in 1921.

McGraw's only other losing season as a manager came in 1926, when the Giants finished in fifth place and one of his favorite players, star outfielder Ross Youngs, was sidelined permanently by kidney disease that would claim his life a year later at age thirty. McGraw paid tribute with a framed memorial photo of Youngs, prominently displayed on his office wall at the Polo Grounds alongside one of Mathewson, who had succumbed to tuberculosis in 1925.

Three seasons removed from his last pennant, John McGraw had acquired Lefty O'Doul to add hitting and speed to the Giants' lineup. McGraw was of course quite familiar with O'Doul, not only because the Giants and Yankees had shared the same city, and ballpark, during O'Doul's first big league stint, but also because of McGraw's late friend Harry Sparrow—the man who had, with unintentional prescience, declared that the Yankees would trade O'Doul only over his dead body.

McGraw addressed the widespread skepticism that O'Doul would suddenly become a successful Major Leaguer at age thirty-one, or further that he even deserved another opportunity following his failed trials with the Yankees and Red Sox. Ignoring the naysayers,

McGraw staunchly defended the acquisition, insisting, "The New York club's scouts on the Coast, who watch O'Doul in many games, are sure he will make good as a big leaguer this time."[4]

When it became clear that O'Doul was going to make the team—and likely become popular in doing so—McGraw began taking more credit for bringing him to the Giants, granting an interview with Al Lamb in the *Binghamton Press* that contradicted his earlier statements. He now insisted that his scouts had completely over-looked O'Doul.

According to McGraw's revised version of events, he handed a slip of paper to Giants team secretary Jim Tierney immediately before Tierney entered the draft room. The slip read, "First choice, Frank O'Doul, of San Francisco." McGraw went on to explain that his scouts had been recommending Smead Jolley and a couple of other Pacific Coast League prospects, but that the asking price was far too high. "I had not a single report boosting O'Doul," McGraw told Lamb. "In the meantime I kept watching the weekly averages and noticed that O'Doul was up there all the time. And I got a warning that Jolley could not run. I made up my mind that O'Doul was my man."[5]

Reporting to Augusta, Georgia, on March 1, O'Doul enjoyed an impressive spring with the Giants.[6] In the intrasquad games he was "hitting the ball on the nose."[7] He even played well on defense, showing off his speed and making several diving catches; near the end of training camp, Frank Graham of the *New York Sun* declared O'Doul "the best the Giants have had in left field since Irish Meusel hit the chutes."[8]

Fred Lieb interviewed O'Doul early in spring training and the outfielder admitted, "In a way I was sorry to leave the Coast. They thought pretty well of me. . . . An O'Doul Day out there netted me $2,500. Then I got $1,000 for the most valuable player prize. Then they named a candy bar after me. However, on the other hand, it is mighty pleasant to get another crack at the game in New York." O'Doul admitted he wished the Yankees had given him more of an opportunity, but he also declared his respect for Miller Huggins and admitted to having been stubborn about changing positions.

He confessed to Lieb, "Perhaps I made a mistake in devoting the early part of my career to pitching. I always was fast and could run. Then I injured my arm pitching, which held back my career. Had I gone right into outfield work I would have gone ahead faster."[9]

Lefty O'Doul definitely went about his business in 1928 with a different mind-set—one might even dare say a maturity. He had been labeled his first time around as one of the playboys of the diamond. Now at an advanced age in baseball terms, and receiving what he knew could be his last chance in the Major Leagues, O'Doul was determined to give it his best. *New York Sun* sportswriter Will Wedge declared that O'Doul had become "a pillar of intense effort."[10]

Also reporting to spring training that year was forty-one-year-old Ty Cobb, about to begin his twenty-fourth Major League season. He'd received Connie Mack's permission to work out with the Giants during the early stages of spring training and join the Philadelphia Athletics when they arrived in Augusta for an exhibition game after training in Florida. At that time veterans, especially from opposing teams, did not offer advice to other players. But Cobb was ready and willing to provide tips and O'Doul took full advantage, asking "The Georgia Peach" to tutor him in hitting to left field, something John McGraw had been nagging Lefty to master.[11] Cobb also corrected O'Doul's habit of gripping his bat too tightly.[12] Cobb's generosity in sharing his wisdom and experience led O'Doul to do the same for the rest of his life.

Like O'Doul, the Giants looked sharp that spring. Near the end of training camp they won thirteen consecutive exhibition games, the last six against the Washington Senators, two seasons removed from back-to-back World Series appearances. Senators manager Bucky Harris, impressed with O'Doul's performance, responded to reporters' questions by saying, "He should be a big favorite at the Polo Grounds. He always could play ball, now he gets it earnestly." Harris admitted he enjoyed seeing O'Doul run the bases, although he wished that he had done so against a team other than his.[13]

O'Doul led the Giants in batting during the preseason with a .436 average, and collected at least one hit in every exhibition game he started.[14] McGraw announced that he would utilize a platoon outfield in 1928—O'Doul, George Harper, and Edd Roush against right-handed pitchers, and Roush, Art Jahn, and Les Mann against left-handers.[15]

The headline for New York's 1928 opener was the debut of second baseman Andy Cohen, whom John McGraw hoped would be his long-sought Jewish star—the savior who would bring fans flocking to the Polo Grounds instead of crossing the Harlem River to Yankee Stadium to see Babe Ruth, whose presence had enabled the team in the Bronx to eclipse the Giants as favorites among New York baseball fans.

At five minutes to two, McGraw led the march of Giants players from their center-field clubhouse. Joe McGinnity, making his first appearance at the Polo Grounds in years, waved from the press box. Fans shouted greetings to New York's manager, that bulbous physique of his instantly recognizable, encased by the team's new home uniform—a gleaming cream white jersey with red and black trim, sans pinstripes, plus a red-billed white cap adorned with a black "NY" monogram.

It was the kind of day that, as James Harrison of the *New York Times* put it, "wintry breezes . . . went straight to the marrow of the bones."[16] The cold did not matter to Lefty O'Doul. He had been waiting his entire career for this moment: a spot in the Opening Day lineup of the New York Giants, playing left field and batting second. When O'Doul stepped from the clubhouse and onto the grass of the Polo Grounds that day, he basked in the familiarity of the place, the upper deck ringing the top—excepting the bleachers—evoking the image of a bathtub, grandstand tucked hard against Coogan's Bluff. The Yankees had since built their own stadium across the river, but the Giants had remained, as they would for three more decades.

O'Doul spied men in hats, coats, and ties, leaning against the railing and clutching cigars and scorecards while whistling and cheering their heroes in anticipation of a big game. He had come to know every inch of the place, having spent three years there rooted to a seat on the bench. Its sights and smells revived within

him a feeling most likened to comfort. It was definitely more pre-
cious to him—he had lost it once. He did not want to lose it again.

A clearly enthusiastic McGraw, on the field in uniform on Opening Day for the first time in seven years, stood at home plate direct-
ing practice as if a general. He even hit grounders to Cohen and
the other infielders. Once warm-ups were complete, Mayor Jimmy
Walker threw out the first ball in front of thirty thousand cheering
fans, the first of whom, Irving Stallman of Long Island, had arrived
at eight-thirty, four and a half hours before the gates opened, and
seven hours prior to the first pitch.[17]

If O'Doul was nervous, it did not show. In his initial at bat—
his first in the Majors in nearly five years—he lined a single to left
field, just as Cobb had preached. In the fifth inning, he was robbed
of extra bases by an excellent running catch. He made a nice running catch himself in the sixth. Andy Cohen played the hero that
day as if it had been scripted, winning the game with a two-run
double; after the final out, fans streamed from the stands and carried him around the Polo Grounds on their shoulders.[18] But Cohen
was not the only Giants player to receive a positive review that day.

Joe Vila of the *New York Sun* was clearly impressed with O'Doul's
performance and recognized its importance to the Giants. "There
is no reason to doubt Lefty O'Doul's quality," wrote Vila. "He is a
big leaguer through and through. A natural hitter, O'Doul is made
to order for the Giants."[19]

Lefty's breakout game came in the season's third contest, against
the Philadelphia Phillies in front of nearly forty thousand people, who braved a bitter cold wind that whistled virtually unim-
peded through their clothing. Andy Cohen would again steal the
headlines, collecting three hits to give him seven in the first three
games of the season, along with seven runs batted in. But it was
O'Doul who drew first blood, leading off the fourth inning of a scoreless game against veteran Phillies right-hander Jimmy Ring with a
line shot over the right-field fence and into the promenade. It was
O'Doul's first Major League home run, and the first of the season
for the Giants. The feeling could not have been more exhilarating
for O'Doul, especially after sitting on Major League benches for

four years, from the hellos of Opening Day to the goodbyes of each
fall, almost never seeing action—and never seeing action that was
meaningful. Fans applauded O'Doul as he rounded the bases, his
easy gallop reminding *New York Sun* sportswriter Will Wedge of a
thoroughbred—the man simply looked like an athlete.[20]

O'Doul added a pair of doubles for good measure, impressing
everyone with his speed as he churned the ground digging for second base, arms alongside his torso with hands splayed and palms
downward as if he were an umpire signaling a safe call, easily
devouring distance with effortless strides among the longest in
baseball. The Giants romped to an 8–1 victory, and at long last
the thirty-one-year-old O'Doul had tasted true success in a Major
League uniform.[21]

Three days later, the Giants won despite the Phillies holding
them to five hits, largely because two of those were home runs by
O'Doul. His first blast off Augie Walsh, a twenty-three-year-old
right-hander making his third Major League appearance, was a
"herculean shot" that ricocheted off the railing of the upper right-
field pavilion of the Polo Grounds. The second was hit as hard,
or harder, but on a lower arc and landed deep in the lower deck.
The third time around, Walsh wised up and walked O'Doul, even
though it resulted in loading the bases.[22]

Lefty seemed to be making up for lost time—the *Philadelphia
Inquirer* was labeling him "the latest bid as rival for Babe Ruth."[23]
Kids began congregating outside the players' entrance at the Polo
Grounds, knowing Lefty would sign their autograph books and talk
to them too. But O'Doul's headlong rush for stardom was interrupted when he twisted his ankle so badly tripping over first base
that he had to be carried from the field by his teammates. The ankle
sidelined him completely for more than two weeks, and he would
not appear in the outfield for a month.[24]

O'Doul's ankle injury would linger throughout the season, imped-
ing his ability to shift his weight and drive the ball with authority,
but he remained productive with a bat in his hands. He collected
nine hits in seventeen at bats during a series against Brooklyn as
May became June. No one struck him out for nearly two months,

a span of 107 at bats that covered nearly the entirety of June and July. Nevertheless, John McGraw continued platooning Lefty even as his batting average remained above .300; O'Doul would make only four starts against left-handers during the 1928 season.

The Giants were in contention, but John McGraw recognized that in order to compete he needed more pitching beyond Freddie Fitzsimmons and Larry Benton. A year earlier, McGraw had acquired Benton from the Boston Braves at the June 15 trade deadline (correcting a mistake made several years earlier when an impatient McGraw had sent Benton to the Braves before he ever pitched for the Giants). The right-hander had responded with thirteen wins in eighteen decisions during the remainder of the 1927 season; and Benton was on his way to a league-leading twenty-five wins in 1928.

McGraw once again pulled the trigger at the deadline, this time sending little-used rookie catcher Al Spohrer and three pitchers, including veteran Virgil Barnes, to the Braves for Joe Genewich, a talented right-hander with a mediocre 57-76 career record and a reputation for being less than completely motivated.[25] It was a deal that would pay off handsomely, as Genewich would capture eleven of fifteen decisions, complete ten games, and save three more out of the bullpen.

A month later came an acquisition that, along with the emergence of nineteen-year-old Mel Ott as an everyday player during the 1928 season, would boost the Giants' fortunes for the next decade. For a reported $25,000, McGraw purchased a left-hander from the Beaumont Exporters of the Texas League, a pitcher who had washed out two years earlier in a tryout with the Detroit Tigers. Within a month, Carl Hubbell would become a mainstay of New York's pitching rotation.[26]

The Giants began August by winning thirteen of sixteen to move within a half game of the first-place St. Louis Cardinals. But they ended the month with an eight-game losing streak to fall into third place, six and a half games out of the lead.

The Giants manufactured another push, highlighted by winning streaks of five and nine games, putting them right back into the race. O'Doul heated up in tandem with his team; during a seven-game series against Boston in mid-September, he collected fourteen hits in twenty-five at bats. On September 24, a day after going hit-less in six at bats against Cincinnati, he slammed two home runs to help defeat the Reds.[27]

But in the end the Giants fell short, losing their chance at the pennant in part because of a controversial play in the first game of a doubleheader against the Chicago Cubs on September 27, when Andy Reese was caught off third base in a rundown and tagged out, after making contact with Cubs catcher Gabby Hartnett in the base-line and falling to his hands and knees a foot shy of home plate.

The moment umpire Bill Klem bellowed "*Out!*" John McGraw exploded from the bench, screaming that Reese should have been declared safe because Hartnett had interfered by standing in the baseline without the ball. Klem screamed back that Hartnett was in the baseline expecting to make a play, so it was not interference.[28]

The Cubs won the game, 3–2. A New York victory would have put the team in a flat-footed tie for first with the Cardinals; instead, the Giants were a game back with only three remaining, including the nightcap of that day's doubleheader. Between games, the Giants and Cubs joined in an emotional ceremony, dedicating memorial plaques to Christy Mathewson and Ross Youngs—three-foot square bronze markers affixed to either side of the center-field entrance. Despite the solemnity of the occasion, McGraw was fuming.

The Giants won that afternoon, but they lost the next day and were eliminated. According to McGraw's biographer Charles C. Alexander, the Giants manager always blamed Bill Klem for cost-ing him the 1928 pennant; as a reminder of the wrong that he per-ceived had been inflicted upon him, McGraw had a photograph of the play framed and hung on his office wall alongside the portraits of Mathewson and Youngs.[29]

O'Doul hit an impressive .319 during the 1928 season, with eight home runs and forty-six runs batted in, while striking out only eight times in 354 official at bats. But John McGraw decided he needed to make additional changes in order to get back to the World Series,

and one of those changes involved trading Lefty to the Philadelphia Phillies for Fred Leach, a proven everyday player who had hit
.300 four straight seasons for Philadelphia.[30] Like O'Doul, Leach
was a left-handed-hitting outfielder and, while representing himself as being twenty-eight years of age, he was in reality only eight
months younger than the soon-to-be thirty-two-year-old O'Doul.
McGraw told reporters that he liked Lefty, but ultimately decided to
trade him because he wound up like a pitcher when making throws
from the outfield.[31] Years later, San Francisco sportswriter Bob Stevens would famously say that O'Doul "ran like a deer but, unfortunately, he threw like one too."[32] Leach, who had long wanted out
of a losing situation in Philadelphia, was a more combative ballplayer than O'Doul; many were of the opinion that Leach would play
even better with a team fighting for a championship in September.

The opinion of the deal in Philadelphia was decidedly mixed. S.
O. Grauley of the *Philadelphia Inquirer* saw O'Doul as a "stiff-hitting
outfielder," but added he was "not so sure in his fielding."[33] James
Isaminger, of the same publication, praised Leach and suggested
that the cash acquired in the deal was as valuable to the Phillies as
O'Doul, or perhaps even more so.[34]

Despite his frustration at being labeled a platoon player, O'Doul
likewise had mixed feelings about the move, leaving New York for
a third time in his career for one of the worst teams in baseball.
The Phillies were more than a decade removed from their glory
days—if three consecutive winning seasons highlighted by a solitary
World Series appearance, in 1915, can be considered a run of glory.

When O'Doul joined the Phillies in 1929, they were coming
off the worst season suffered by any National League team since
the end of syndicate baseball and the circuit's contraction to eight
teams in 1900.[35] Over the previous decade the Phillies had finished
in last place seven times. But they had uncovered promising rook-
ies during the 1928 season in outfielder Chuck Klein and infielders Don Hurst and Pinky Whitney.

Phillies manager Burt Shotton had been a fair center fielder in
his day, a speedy ballplayer, and a close friend of Branch Rickey,
serving as manager of the St. Louis Cardinals on Sundays when

the devout Rickey observed the Sabbath. Like his crosstown coun-
terpart Connie Mack, Shotton would later be noted for managing
in his street clothes, but at this early juncture in his managerial
career he manned the coaching lines and wore a standard uniform. Shotton was a calm, patient manager who believed in getting
to know his players and using psychology to help him help them
improve. He was the antithesis of John McGraw; O'Doul, who had
characterized the Giants legend as nice enough off the field, but
a tough man on it, appreciated that.[36] Furthermore, Shotton signaled that O'Doul would play every day. He appreciated that even
more. Lefty O'Doul was about to become an overnight sensation
at the age of thirty-two.

5

I Feel as Though I Am Going
to Have a Great Year

General MacArthur quickly gave his approval for O'Doul and the San Francisco Seals to visit Japan. Seals general manager Charles J. Graham, whose late father had been the longtime, greatly revered owner of the team, proposed a twenty-two-game tour for October and November 1949. An enthusiastic O'Doul declared, "I think we can contribute something to postwar Japan."[1]

Graham assured reporters that money was not the motivation for undertaking the trip, underlining his pledge by announcing, "Any profit will be turned over to General MacArthur for whatever purpose he sees fit."[2]

When Graham visited Japan in July 1949 to meet with the legendary general, he stepped off the plane and was handed a cardboard replica of a seal balancing crossed baseball bats on its nose. An amused Graham assured newsmen, "I am quite confident that financial arrangements can be made. I would not have made this trip if I was not optimistic."

Graham was driven to the American Embassy and ushered into General MacArthur's residence. At one point during their conversation, MacArthur stressed the importance he placed on the event, both in its timing and its potential to boost the morale of the Japanese. "The arrival of the Seals in Japan would be one of the biggest things that has happened to the country since the war," he explained. "It takes athletic competition to put away the hatred of war and it would be a great event for Japan politically, economically and every other way."[3]

Although for financial reasons the length of the schedule had to be trimmed substantially, from twenty-two games to ten, arrangements were completed to Graham's satisfaction; his task complete, the Seals' executive returned home to collaborate with O'Doul on forming a roster for the trip—some of the Seals were unwilling or unable to go, so other players accepted invitations to fill out a roster expected to include at least twenty players.[4]

O'Doul was doing his part to show the Japanese he cared. Back in April, a Japanese teenager had written to an American friend about his love for baseball, and especially the Yomiuri Giants, but lamented the fact he could not afford to see them play. A San Francisco sportswriter learned of the letter and wrote about it, which caught the attention of *Yomiuri Shimbun*, Japan's largest newspaper and the financial underwriter of the famous 1931 and 1934 tours. The Japanese publication provided a season pass to the seventeen-year-old. O'Doul noticed the story as well, and during a ceremony that summer at Korakuen Stadium, the boy not only received his season ticket, he also received a San Francisco Seals baseball cap and a baseball autographed by O'Doul.[5]

Sotaro Suzuki began promoting the upcoming tour, highlighting it in various Japanese baseball magazines. He informed fans that he had received a special letter from O'Doul in which the American had extolled the virtues of baseball to Japan's youth. Suzuki made sure to mention, "Mr. O'Doul even signed his name in Japanese."[6]

The Japanese were very interested in O'Doul's return—players relished the opportunity for competition. Forty-one-year-old Hanshin Tigers player-manager Tadashi Wakabayashi—a Hawaiian-born pitcher who had visited Japan with his high school team two decades earlier and stayed—had become one of the country's legendary hurlers, the winner of 233 games in the Japanese major league to that point.

Wakabayashi had toured the United States with Hosei University in 1931, and had waited a long time to once again play against Americans. He told Japanese reporters, "I won't go so far as saying we will make the San Francisco Seals bark, but I'm sure we'll give them a stiff rub."[7]

A week before O'Doul and his squad were to depart for Tokyo, the New York Yankees and Brooklyn Dodgers met in the 1949 World Series. Among those covering the event was Shogi Uno, a reporter for *Yomiuri Shimbun*.

Uno was granted an audience with Baseball Commissioner A. B. "Happy" Chandler, and the two discussed the changes in Japan and in its professional baseball league. Impressed by the skill of the Yankees and Dodgers, Uno lamented that Japan did not have players of that caliber. Chandler assured Uno, "But you will if you stick to it."

After Uno noted that Japan had only eight professional franchises, and at least six more potential owners, Chandler suggested it would be wise to form a second league in order to make room for those with the means and desire to field professional teams. The alternative, he warned, might be open warfare, as had occurred several times in American baseball. Borrowing from Benjamin Franklin's famous Revolutionary War quote, Chandler told Uno, "If you don't hang together, you will all hang separately."

Chandler also recommended that Japan promote the game aggressively to its youth, insisting, "Baseball is one of the greatest and surest means of inculcating the spirit of competition, fair play and democracy in any people. People who love and play baseball don't start wars."

Uno responded that an event like Pearl Harbor would never happen again. He assured Chandler, "Now we stick to baseball."[8]

• • •

Lefty O'Doul eagerly awaited the New York Giants in Philadelphia on Opening Day in 1929—enduring two days of bad weather and resulting cancellations to do so, which only added to his determination. John McGraw, back in an overcoat and tie, started left-hander Carl Hubbell against the Phillies, partly to demonstrate he had been correct in platooning O'Doul, who was playing left field and batting second. O'Doul was determined to show McGraw there was a price to pay for slighting him. Fred Lieb spotted O'Doul before the game and asked the former Giant how he felt. His response was firm and unequivocal. "I feel as though I am going to have a great year," he told Lieb.[9]

Hubbell struck out O'Doul his first time up, bringing an "I told you so" smirk to McGraw's lips. There was a catcall or two as O'Doul trudged back to the bench. But in his next at bat, O'Doul crushed a pitch over the right-field fence and onto Broad Street to tie the game. Phillies fans rose to their feet and gave their new hero a rousing ovation as he circled the bases. Encouraged, O'Doul responded later in the game with a second home run onto Broad Street, this one off Larry Benton, giving him four runs batted in on the day. The Phillies fell to the Giants, 11–9, but O'Doul had more than made his point with what was already the third two–home run game of his big league career.[10]

A week later the Phillies faced Hubbell again, this time at the Polo Grounds. After collecting two hits in his first three attempts, O'Doul was standing in the on-deck circle, waiting for his next turn at the plate. During a lull in the proceedings he screamed sarcastically, "I can't hit left-handers!"—making sure that everyone, especially John McGraw, could hear. He then stepped to the plate and promptly lined out another single to center, his third hit of the day.[11]

O'Doul later explained his obvious frustration with John McGraw. "I had to learn," he said. "I made mistakes. Then when I finally did come up to the Giants[,] . . . McGraw wouldn't let me hit against lefthanders. Of course, I couldn't hit lefthanders because I didn't get the practice. Shotton kept me in there every day, regardless of who was working against the Phillies." He closed his discourse with a nod, assuring everyone within earshot, "I hit lefthanders."[12]

Fred Leach would miss much of the season's first month with an ear infection, while Lefty O'Doul smashed nine hits—three of them home runs—in twenty at bats against the Giants. While taking obvious pleasure in showing up McGraw, O'Doul was circumspect about his early success. When asked about his leading the league in hitting through the first week of the season, O'Doul laughed and said, "It's something like holding a cake of ice on a sunny street. You can't eat it, you can't drink it, and you know it's going to melt soon."[13]

The Phillies' offense was greatly improved in 1929, thanks to O'Doul, Chuck Klein, Don Hurst, and Pinky Whitney. O'Doul roomed with Klein; he not only dispensed advice to the young slugger when it came to swinging a bat, he also tutored him in the finer points of men's fashion. The first thing that had to go was Klein's garish, country bumpkin yellow shoes.[14]

The home diamond of the Phillies, the Baker Bowl, was two years older than O'Doul and made of steel, concrete, brick, and grime. The stadium had been constructed in 1895 to replace a seven-year-old wooden structure destroyed by fire. Its right-field fence, only 280 feet from home plate, had to feel familiar to O'Doul, recalling Recreation Park. The forty-foot-high wall, encased in tin and displaying a newly painted ad hawking Lifebuoy Soap, had a twenty-foot-high screen tacked atop it. O'Doul quickly gained confidence, certain he could bang line drives off that wall anytime he wanted. It was a ballpark made for Lefty O'Doul.

Philadelphia's roster was most definitely improved in 1929, and younger—O'Doul was the only front-line player in his thirties. However, the team's pitching remained a constant weakness. During their first extended home stand in May, the Phillies were defeated by scores of 14–12, 16–0, 13–9, 14–13, and 20–16. Yet somehow, at the end of a doubleheader in Boston on May 22, Philadelphia sat in fourth place with a record of 13-13. By that point O'Doul was playing against both right-handers and left-handers, inflicting damage on all comers with an impressive .410 batting average in twenty-six games. He had driven in twenty-seven runs while striking out only three times.

O'Doul hit two home runs off Brooklyn's Dazzy Vance on May 16, and then went four for four and scored four runs the next day.[15] He continued fattening up on the Giants, drilling five hits in six at bats during the first game of a doubleheader on June 19, and adding a single in the nightcap.[16] By this point McGraw was being heckled in Gotham's newspapers for letting the colorful outfielder go; and O'Doul was not above playing up to the typewriter brigade, which loved his act, and him.

Lefty cooled off a bit in June, his batting average dropping into the .360s. After collecting only one hit in his previous sixteen at bats, O'Doul and the Phillies met New York in a doubleheader on June 30 at the Polo Grounds. In the first game, against who else but Carl Hubbell, O'Doul hit a screamer in the first inning destined for extra bases, but Bill Terry made a leaping grab of the line shot behind first base.

His second time up, O'Doul sent another screamer, this time at Terry's feet and to his right, but once again the Giants' first baseman was up to the task and smothered the ball. O'Doul, who according to the *Brooklyn Daily Eagle* had "knocked everything loose from Carl Hubbell but the pinstripe on his uniform," displayed an exasperated grin as he trotted back to the bench. Between innings, O'Doul eased his frustration by good-naturedly conversing with Giants fans seated near the Phillies dugout.

O'Doul launched yet another rocket in the sixth inning, this time toward Giants second baseman Andy Cohen. But it was not hit high enough, and Cohen gloved the line shot above his head.

It seemed O'Doul could not buy a break. Meanwhile, the Giants were slaughtering the Phillies. In the bottom of the sixth, Fred Lindstrom slammed a home run off the left-field grandstand roof and the ball rebounded to O'Doul, who in mock anger picked it up and fired it over the roof from whence it had come, and out of the stadium. The crowd loved it. So did O'Doul—so much so that when Travis Jackson duplicated Lindstrom's feat later that inning, he favored the fans with a repeat performance, this time throwing the ball toward the right-field bleachers.

In the eighth inning O'Doul again faced Hubbell, who was nursing a three-hit shutout with a runner on first. With his slump now standing at one hit in his last nineteen at bats, O'Doul gave up trying to hit one through the infield and opted to drive the ball. He connected solidly, launching Hubbell's delivery into the right-field grandstand. Always the showman, and relieved at finally getting a ball past the Giants infielders, O'Doul tipped his cap to each base as if to reintroduce himself as he completed the circuit to home plate.[17] The Giants won the game, 14–2, but O'Doul had again won over the Polo Grounds faithful.

The slump, such as it had been, was over; during a twenty-game stretch beginning on the Fourth of July, he hit .512 and raised his batting average back to the .400 range. In the six weeks between June 20 and August 3, he struck out only once; along the way he collected five hits in five at bats against St. Louis, had an eleven-for-eighteen series against the Cubs, a four-hit day against Pittsburgh, and finally a four-for-four day, again victimizing the Cardinals. (O'Doul would hit .462 against St. Louis in 1929, including a .500 average at Sportsman Park.) His offensive output was staggering; O'Doul was treating pitchers as if they were no more than his old Pacific Coast League competition, accomplishing this despite the disadvantage of not being able to hit against the Phillies' pitching staff, which would compile a ridiculous 6.13 earned run average for the season.

As Lefty O'Doul battled Brooklyn's Babe Herman for the National League batting title, their approaches were contrasted by Brooklyn sportswriter Tommy Holmes. According to Holmes, Herman simply went up to the plate to swing his bat at whatever he saw, while Lefty had evolved into what Holmes called "a scientific hitter."

O'Doul would generally use a thirty-six-ounce bat during spring training, and then switch to a model one and a half ounces heavier once the season began. He would also add a rubber sponge to the handle to absorb shock.[18] He jotted down notes on every pitcher he faced, and continually adapted his approach depending on whom he was facing. He sprayed the ball to all fields and would either choke up or hold the bat at the end of the handle, depending on the situation, nervously twitching the bat as the pitcher delivered the ball. He also developed an uncanny ability to almost always hit the ball in the direction he wanted.[19] Whenever he could, O'Doul reviewed films of his hitting, and he constantly studied pitchers and situations. He also constantly altered his stance—on one pitch he might crouch, on another he might point his right foot toward the pitcher.[20] And he almost never swung at anything outside of the strike zone. O'Doul's adage was "get a good ball to hit."[21]

O'Doul told Harold Burr of the *Brooklyn Daily Eagle*, "It's all in the stance and the timing." To demonstrate, he jumped to his feet and rolled up the newspaper he had been reading. "The bat should be brought around this way. It starts from the hips," he said, nearly decapitating a nearby hotel lobby lampshade. "I could knock a golf ball out of the park if I'm timing a pitch right," he explained. "If my timing is faulty I couldn't hit a medicine ball. It's all in the timing."[22]

When in one of his rare slumps, O'Doul would convince a pitcher who had the same delivery as his next opponent to throw batting practice, or he might forgo practice entirely and play golf instead, entering the game cold.[23] Whatever put him in the proper frame of mind—according to O'Doul, that was the real key to successful hitting.

O'Doul studied ballparks as well—he had trouble with left field at Wrigley, as did most left-handed hitters. On warm days, the white-shirtsleeve crowd filled the bleachers, making it difficult to see the baseball as it left the pitcher's hand. Experimenting with different stances, O'Doul finally discovered a crouch that afforded him a better view, out of some green woodwork on the outfield wall. He hit .333 lifetime at Wrigley against some great pitchers, and struck out fewer times there per at bat than at any other ballpark, excepting Cincinnati.[24]

If "scientific" and "studious" served as accurate adjectives for Lefty O'Doul, so did the word "superstitious." And he became, if anything, more so as his success grew—after all, there was more to lose. He sought out "lucky" lockers, not only at his home park in Philadelphia but also around the league—although he admitted to difficulty locating one that brought satisfactory results at Wrigley Field. Once, another player grabbed a bat, intending to dispatch a spider that had made its home in front of O'Doul's locker. "Hey, don't touch that [spider], you dumbbell!" O'Doul screamed. "That's the best talisman of good luck a man can have!"[25]

If O'Doul had a big day at the plate after consuming a particular dish, he would eat that meal every day as long as he continued hitting. Abbie O'Doul complained about having to sit at the same seat in the same restaurant every day when her husband was on a hitting streak.

He was also particular in the manner he discarded items at home.

Abbie told a reporter, "Often he leaves a shirt or a tie hanging on a doorknob in our apartment, and I would like to move it but I don't, for I know he has put it there for some reason."[26]

"I don't mind your laughing at the [superstitions]," O'Doul confided to reporters. "I do them and I have a reason for them. They may handicap some players, but my little superstitions seem to help me. They give me confidence when they work out right. And confidence is everything to a hitter."[27]

It was in Philadelphia that O'Doul bought his first green suit. After a successful day with the bat, the suit was soon followed in short order by a green shirt, a green tie, green socks, and a green handkerchief. It was a wardrobe he would continue to wear even after it became threadbare. Playing up his slice of Irish ancestry beyond its relevancy, O'Doul became known as "The Man in the Green Suit."[28]

On September 1 Lefty O'Doul smacked a single in the sixth inning of a game against Brooklyn. It was his third hit that day and, more important, it made him the first batter in 1929 to reach two hundred hits.[29] The question now was whether he would eclipse Rogers Hornsby's National League record of two hundred fifty hits in a season. After going hitless in the nightcap, during which he drove in his one hundredth run of the year, his batting average stood at .389—a full eleven points behind Babe Herman, whose three hits in seven at bats that day brought his average to an even .400.

O'Doul then caught fire. He slammed three home runs during a four-game series at St. Louis, including his thirtieth of the season, and collected ten hits in fifteen at bats. When O'Doul left St. Louis on September 9, his batting average stood at .398, allowing him to surge past Herman, who had dropped to .392. Herman would be unable to regain his advantage.

O'Doul's average remained in the .390s during September, but he could not quite reach the .400 mark. Going into the final three games of the season, with a shot at .400 on the line and four hits shy of Hornsby's mark, the Phillies were going to play, who else, the New York Giants. It was the theme of Lefty O'Doul's year.

In the first game at the Polo Grounds on September 29, McGraw
started a left-hander, Bill Walker. O'Doul did not mind. He engaged
in good-humored banter with Giants fans while collecting a pair
of singles to move within two of Hornsby and put his batting average at .394.[30] Due to a quirk in the schedule, neither the Phillies
nor the Giants played again until they met on October 5 for a doubleheader at the Baker Bowl, the final games of the season for the
Phillies. John McGraw, wanting to make O'Doul earn the hit record
and/or a .400 batting average, started Hubbell and Walker.

With roughly ten thousand people looking on, O'Doul was a perfect four for four against Hubbell. His third time up he slammed
his thirty-second home run of the season, emphatically breaking
Hornsby's National League hit mark. In the nightcap he collected
two hits in five at bats in a rematch against Walker.[31] That gave
him a new National League record of 254 hits (George Sisler held
the American League and Major League marks with 257). Fifteen
years later, O'Doul would look back on 1929 and shake his head.
"What a season that was!" he told Gene Karst. "The ball looked
like a balloon to me that summer. It seemed I could hit anybody
and everybody."[32]

Reports had O'Doul ending the season with a batting average
of .400, but after the official figures were released in December,
it was discovered that two unsuccessful at bats had been missed
and O'Doul had in fact hit .398. One more base hit would have
put him at .400—no Major League batter has ever come closer to
.400 without reaching that figure, and only two men, Bill Terry and
Ted Williams, have since posted a higher batting average in a big
league season. O'Doul's .398 mark still ranks as the fifth-highest
batting average by a National Leaguer since 1900—and the highest by an outfielder—while his 254 hits remain a National League
record, shared with Terry.

Batting second in the lineup most of the year, Lefty scored 152
runs and ended the season with 32 home runs and 122 runs batted
in; despite suffering a broken toe and two strained hamstrings, he
did not miss a game. He finished a close second to Rogers Hornsby
in the National League Most Valuable Player balloting.[33]

O'Doul hit .400 or better every month except June, when he batted .298. He hit for an incredible .453 batting average at the Baker
Bowl and struck out only nineteen times all year—he remains the
only man in Major League history to hit more than thirty home
runs in a season and strike out fewer than twenty times.[34] After the
season, Babe Ruth apologized for leaving Lefty off his celebrated
All–Major League team, explaining that he had selected its members before it was certain O'Doul would win the batting title; he
admitted to being concerned that if Babe Herman bested O'Doul,
people would say he had chosen Lefty because of their friendship
and shared love of golf, which they had famously played from San
Francisco to New York.

For the Phillies it had been a season of improvement, a fifth-
place finish—their best showing since 1917—and seventy-one victories, a gain of twenty-eight over the prior year. Meanwhile, the
Giants were never closer than four games out of first from July on
and finished a distant third to the pennant-winning Chicago Cubs.
Fred Leach hit .290—108 points less than O'Doul.[35]

For the first time, Lefty O'Doul was an established Major League
star. He was featured in a Louisville Slugger advertisement in *The
Sporting News*.[36] As had been the case in New York, he became the
idol of kids, and of their parents. "I like kids," he said. "They wait
around the entrance of the Baker Bowl until I'm dressed, and I
always answer their greetings, sign their autograph books, give 'em
an old ball. No matter where I happen to be playing, I always like
to leave people happy. Smiles are what count in life."[37]

Like many who had bought stocks on margin, O'Doul was wiped
out in the stock market crash, and he hoped his newfound success
and popularity would result in Phillies owner William Baker offering him a substantial raise; he asked for a one-year deal at $17,000,
or a two-year contract for $30,000. Baker countered with $11,000
for one year—with one thousand of that provided when O'Doul
reported to spring training. Baker offered an additional thousand
should the Phillies finish 1930 in the first division.[38]

O'Doul was not hard and fast in his demands; when Burt Shot-

ton wired Lefty in San Francisco on his thirty-third birthday, warning him that no better offer was forthcoming, O'Doul wired back,
"Have mailed contract. Am leaving for camp immediately."[39] He
arrived in Tampa on March 16 and sat on the bench watching his
teammates lose to the Detroit Tigers.[40] O'Doul boasted to reporters that he felt great and would finish in the top five in hitting.[41]

During spring training, Burt Shotton predicted that the Phillies'
pitching staff would be 30 percent stronger. "And if I am a good
prophet," he declared, "you know what that will mean. The Phillies
will be right up with the leaders when the season ends."[42] But the
pitching staff was not 30 percent better. In fact, Shotton had been
so desperate to improve it, he traded for forty-three-year-old Grover
Cleveland Alexander.[43] An overenthusiastic Shotton seemed to forget himself, predicting that the ancient Alexander, winner of nine
games in 1929, would be a twenty-game winner in 1930 "if he is
not hampered by his friends."[44] It was a not-so-veiled reference to
Alexander's well-known struggle with alcohol.

Alexander made his return in a Phillies uniform by losing the
third game of the season against the New York Giants, 2–1, allow-
ing seven hits and four walks in six innings. Beat writer Stan
Baumgartner observed, "Alexander was patently not at his best."[45]
Unfortunately, that *was* his best. Over eight additional appearances,
Alexander allowed twenty runs in slightly more than fifteen innings.
By the end of May he had pitched his last Major League game, hav-
ing dropped his only three decisions.

Meanwhile, despite battling tonsillitis and claiming that "this
spring, somehow, I haven't felt right against any kind of pitching,"
O'Doul started as strong in 1930 as he had in 1929.[46] During his first
trip to Wrigley Field, he banged out ten hits in fifteen at bats. The
defending National League batting champion went five for five the next
day against the Cardinals at Sportsman Park, including three doubles;
sixteen games into the season, O'Doul's batting average stood at .500.

He also built on his reputation as a showman, instructing Phillies
bat boys in the proper protocol for greeting him following a home run.
Forty years later one of them, Fred Hunter, general manager of a Minor
League franchise in Charleston, West Virginia, remembered, "We were

to stand on either side and Lefty would reach out and grab each of us by the hand as he crossed home plate." Hunter laughed, "It made a great picture, and Lefty never missed a bet for publicity."[47] As O'Doul later told Lawrence Ritter, "Maybe I was a ham, I don't know. . . . But what's the use of doing something when no one's looking?"[48]

Despite O'Doul's heroics, by the middle of their first long road trip at the beginning of May, the Phillies had fallen to last place. There they remained virtually the entire season—save for a brief spurt to seventh during June. Their longest winning streak of the year was three games. They finished last in attendance, drawing fewer than four thousand fans per home date. As a team the Phillies hit .315, yet their opponents outscored them by more than a run and a half per game. The pitching staff compiled a horrendous 6.71 earned run average—and it could not all be blamed on the Baker Bowl. While the staff mark was 7.04 at home, it was only marginally better—6.36—on the road.

O'Doul enjoyed another outstanding year in 1930; on September 1 his batting average stood at .380. Then he was sidelined by a badly bruised shin and a flare-up of his infected tonsils that reduced him almost entirely to pinch-hitting duties for the final month of the season, costing him a chance to battle Bill Terry and Babe Herman for the batting title—Terry would win with a .401 mark, while Herman ended the year at .393.

Nevertheless, O'Doul would long remember, and be long remembered for, the pinch-hitting show he put on that September. It was a performance many thought cost Joe McCarthy his job as manager of the Chicago Cubs.

A hobbled Lefty O'Doul pinch-hit against Cincinnati on September 9, smacking a two-ball, two-strike pitch over the right-field wall for a three-run home run to tie a game that Philadelphia eventually won.[49] When the Chicago Cubs arrived in Philadelphia three days later, he remained on the bench.

The Cubs, who were defending National League champions, had fashioned a five-game lead at the end of August over their nearest competitors. But the team was a bit wobbly. Veteran pitcher

Hal Carlson had died suddenly in May, the result of a ruptured ulcer.[50] Rogers Hornsby, the reigning National League Most Valuable Player, was, like O'Doul, reduced to pinch-hitting duty as he recovered from a broken ankle. Star pitchers Guy Bush and Charlie Root were nursing sore arms—Root would pitch fewer than five innings total after Labor Day. Chicago had lost ten of fifteen, its lead slipping to a mere half game over both St. Louis and Brooklyn.

The Cubs won the first game of the series, but the second game on Saturday, September 13, would prove a turning point for them—and not for the better. The Phillies twice rallied from behind and battled Chicago to a 5–5 tie as the game moved to the bottom of the eighth. With two out and a runner on first, Burt Shotton called for O'Doul. Picking up one of his red-labeled bats, O'Doul limped to the plate. Skies threatened rain that would ultimately wash out the nightcap of what was supposed to be a doubleheader; the storm clouds were an apt metaphor for the Cubs' situation. With a pitcher in the on-deck circle, it seemed possible, even likely, that the Cubs would walk O'Doul, even though it would result in moving the winning run to second base. Shotton hoped McCarthy would call his bluff, wagering that with O'Doul swinging a bat for the first time in four days and unable to run, the Cubs would decide he was more or less harmless, despite his reputation. And the Cubs did not walk him. Pat Malone fired the first pitch wide for ball one. A second was just off the plate. O'Doul now realized that Malone was not pitching around him. Malone's next delivery was fatter and O'Doul got his bat on it, but fouled it off.

With the count at two and one, Malone fired his fourth pitch and it caught too much of the plate. O'Doul did not miss. The ball soared over the right-field wall. The crowd erupted.

O'Doul limped around the bases and as he reached home plate, the batboys were in their proper place, allowing for a triumphant photo in the *Philadelphia Inquirer* of Lefty crossing home plate while Cubs catcher Gabby Hartnett stood hands on hips, a helpless witness to the spectacle that was Lefty O'Doul.[51] Hal Elliott retired the Cubs in order in the top of the ninth and it was all over.

Joe McCarthy shadowed Pat Malone to the clubhouse, chewing

him out the entire distance for pitching to O'Doul instead of walking him.[52] With one swing of the bat, Lefty O'Doul, the player who
had gotten away from the Cubs in 1926, had dropped Chicago from
first place to third; William Wrigley, a native of Philadelphia, was
on hand and caught an earful from ecstatic Phillies fans.

Guy Bush attempted to defend his teammate and fellow pitcher.
"Pat was throwing low to Lefty, just as any of us would have done,"
said Bush. "Some fans will say O'Doul should have been walked,
but that would have put the winning run on second[;] . . . in my
judgment there was only one thing to do and that was to try to get
O'Doul for the third out."[53] Bush predicted that the Cubs would
win the pennant anyway; Chicago's front office seemed to agree,
announcing that the team was taking applications for World Series
tickets.[54] But Lefty O'Doul would have something to say about that.

After a day off, because Sunday baseball remained illegal in Philadelphia, the teams met for a doubleheader on Monday, September
15. The first game was a slugfest, with the Phillies jumping out to
a 5–0 lead; at one point, Joe McCarthy and Rogers Hornsby were
seen arguing, with McCarthy wagging a finger in Hornsby's face.[55]
The Cubs were feeling the pressure.

Chicago rallied to score seven runs in the fifth, and then added
single runs in the sixth inning, on Hack Wilson's fiftieth home run
of the season, as well as in the seventh and eighth innings, stretching their lead to 10–5.

In the bottom of the eighth, Shotton sent O'Doul to pinch-hit
for pitcher Hap Collard. He singled and later scored as the Phillies thrilled the home crowd by scoring six times to take an 11–10
lead. Despite Lefty's infirmities, Shotton put him in left field, and
after the Cubs scored again in the top of the ninth to tie the game,
O'Doul came to the plate in the bottom of the ninth with no one
out and pitcher Hal Elliott on first.

Shotton flashed the bunt sign to O'Doul, but Elliott broke too
early on the sacrifice attempt and was picked off, eliciting an audi-
ble groan from the crowd. However, one unidentified visitor in the
press box immediately proclaimed, "That is the play that is going
to beat the Cubs, for O'Doul is going to hit a home run."[56]

After dusting himself off, ex-baserunner Elliott glumly skulked back to the Phillies' dugout, walking near O'Doul on his way. As he passed by, Lefty nodded and assured him, in a voice raised sufficiently for those in the box seats to hear, "Never mind, kid."[57]

With the bases now empty and one out, O'Doul was given the green light. Cubs left-handed relief pitcher Bud Teachout, a twenty-six-year-old rookie who had pitched a complete-game victory earlier in the series, looked in for the sign and nodded. O'Doul then made a prophet of the press box with a lightning strike.

O'Doul's bat was described as performing "like a slingshot," launching the ball over the right-field wall and onto Broad Street for a walk-off home run—his second crushing blow in as many games. The Phillies had won, 12–11. While rounding the bases, O'Doul—still miffed at McCarthy for cutting him in 1926—shouted at the Cubs' manager, "There goes your bag of gold!"[58]

It was Lefty's third home run in his last four at bats, and his fourth hit in a row.[59] Although the Cubs won the nightcap, despite O'Doul once again pinch-hitting successfully, drilling a ninth-inning run-scoring single—his fifth straight hit and two hundredth of the season—Chicago had dropped behind St. Louis for good. The Cardinals finished two games ahead of the Cubs.

Confined to a pinch-hitting role for nearly all of September, O'Doul completed the season just shy of one hundred runs batted in—he had ninety-seven—while batting .383. His former teammate Bill Terry tied O'Doul's one-year-old National League record with 254 hits. Despite the disappointment of being unable to pad his statistics down the stretch, nearly a year later O'Doul was still crowing about sending the Cubs to a bitter defeat. "I'll let Wrigley figure out how much I cost him," he told Tommy Holmes in July 1931. "Personally, I figure . . . I cost the Chicago players four or five thousand dollars apiece." O'Doul added that he always relished playing against the Cubs and exacting revenge for the slight of 1926. "I don't know any other series of the year in which I'd rather come up with plenty of base hits."[60]

After O'Doul had almost single-handedly knocked the Cubs out of the 1930 pennant race, with William Wrigley on hand to witness the debacle, the Cubs' owner was forced to endure hazing from Phillies fans about the player that got away. "Do you know," said Wrigley, "those fans forgot about the game and started to kid me about my team. It was all good-natured, of course, and I took it that way. They wanted to know how much I would give to get O'Doul back. They said it would spare me watching my Cubs take another [World Series] trimming from the Athletics. I now know how an umpire feels. They made me think I was friendless. And Philadelphia is my home town."

Wrigley went on to admit, "When they yelled to me about buying O'Doul they touched a tender spot."[61]

A year earlier, shortly after O'Doul had won the batting title with the Phillies, Wrigley told *The Sporting News*, "As long as I have been in baseball I've only bought one player myself. That one was Lefty O'Doul. I still call him, 'My O'Doul.' O'Doul reported to our training camp in 1926, the first year McCarthy was in charge. But Joe didn't think O'Doul was so good, so we released him to Hollywood. But he seems to be back in the majors again. Since then I've never butted in on my baseball men. I have a fine club president and a grand manager, and I rely implicitly on their judgment."[62]

That may have been the case, but less than two weeks after O'Doul's pinch-hitting pyrotechnics, William Wrigley fired Joe McCarthy and replaced him with Rogers Hornsby.[63]

"I realize that Joe McCarthy is one of baseball's greatest managers," conceded Wrigley, who had entered the season upset about the Cubs 1929 World Series loss. "But I must have a winner."[64]

McCarthy quickly signed to take over as manager of the New York Yankees and declared, "I'd jump off the Brooklyn Bridge to nip the Cubs in the World Series."[65]

Like O'Doul, McCarthy would eventually gain revenge on the Cubs—in the 1932 World Series when Ruth "called his shot" and the Yankees swept Chicago in four games. Meanwhile O'Doul, despite his heroics and hitting .391 while driving in 219 runs over two seasons, was about to discover that the Phillies considered him expendable.

6

The Fellow Has Plenty on the Personality Ball

Lefty O'Doul was ecstatic about bringing a baseball team to Japan for the first time in fifteen years. He sent a message through the press to Japanese baseball fans, proclaiming, "I am happy with the prospect of going to Japan with the Seals for the purpose of goodwill. It will be a pleasure to meet old pals—Japanese, GIs, and American businessmen in the Orient. I am anxious to play the college teams, which are the backbone of Japanese baseball."[1]

When the Seals touched down in Tokyo on October 12, 1949, to begin their nearly three-week sojourn, O'Doul led his players off the plane and was greeted by thousands of people eager to glimpse the Americans. The official delegation was led by prominent Japanese film actress Kinuyo Tanaka.[2]

News of the tour had dominated the press, and placards bearing each player's likeness were posted all over the city. Demand for tickets to the first game, to be played three days later between the Seals and the Yomiuri Giants at Korakuen Stadium, was unprecedented. Buyers were allowed to purchase only one ticket; additional ticket booths were hastily constructed to handle the crush, and the game sold out in ninety minutes. Thousands of fans stood in a line stretching two miles, a large percentage of whom had camped out all night for the privilege—many of them carrying straw mats or folding chairs for their sleeping arrangements.[3]

Fans were also snapping up several sets of baseball cards depicting the visiting players and some of the Japanese stars, created especially to commemorate the occasion. A 122-page program was produced for the series, thirty pages of which were printed in Japanese. A seal balancing a baseball on its nose graced the cover, along with images of a Japanese shrine and Mount Fuji.

Seals players were astounded by their reception. "It got the boys off on the right foot," said Seals owner Paul Fagan. Charles J. Graham added, "I couldn't believe it. Never have we seen such a demonstration anywhere."[4]

As the automobile caravan carrying the Americans wound through the streets of downtown Tokyo, the players were showered with confetti in five colors and greeted with shouts from the thousands lining the sidewalk—by some estimates, one million people witnessed O'Doul and the Seals players pass, the largest crowd to gather in Japan since the end of the war.[5] The fans crowded the street to the point they could reach out and shake hands with the players. Many shouted Lefty's name; O'Doul remarked to no one particular, "This is the greatest ever."[6]

At the same time, something gave O'Doul pause. When he triumphantly shouted "banzai" to people along the route, he did not receive the greeting in return. The Japanese were more reserved than had been the case fifteen years earlier—they seemed almost somber in comparison.

"I noticed how sad the Japanese people were," recalled O'Doul in an interview twenty years later. "When we were there in '31 and '34, people were waving Japanese and American flags and shouting 'banzai, banzai.' This time, no banzais. I was yelling 'banzai' at them, but the Japanese just looked at me."[7]

O'Doul turned to Cappy Harada and asked, "How come they don't yell banzai?" Harada replied, "That's the reason you're here, Lefty. To build up the morale so that they will yell 'banzai' again."[8]

The caravan completed its five-mile route at Hibiya Park and the players checked into their hotel. The next day, the Seals were hosted by General MacArthur at a luncheon in his home within the grounds of the American Embassy. MacArthur addressed the players, thanking them for making the journey, and reminding them of the great importance he placed on the tour. He closed his remarks by telling O'Doul and his men, "There is no substitute for victory."[9]

The general, who in his youth was an outfielder for the West Point baseball team, spent the remainder of the affair talking baseball with O'Doul and the other players; at one point he noted the amazing and, more important, spontaneous reception Lefty had received and told him, "You've finally come home."[10] One of MacArthur's officers remarked, "That was one luncheon the Old Man really enjoyed."[11]

That evening, a rally was held at the Tokyo Sports Center. Fifteen thousand people, some having lined up nine hours early, filled the building. The arena shook when O'Doul was introduced. He assured the crowd that the Seals were not taking their opponents for granted, and added that he expected "many surprises" from the Japanese. He also said that he hoped to do some pinch hitting. Then he flashed a smile and waved to the fans, who once again exploded in an incredible display of affection.[12]

Meanwhile, another two thousand people, who were stranded outside when the doors were locked, grew increasingly frustrated at their inability to gain entrance to the event. As the crowd began venting its anger, the Tokyo Metropolitan Police dispatched an additional 150 officers to help quell a potential riot. O'Doul became aware of the situation and came outside, where he apologized for not being able to admit the unlucky fans and added, "I think speaking to you personally will no doubt serve to promote goodwill and friendship." Satisfied, the crowd dispersed.[13]

• • •

With the Philadelphia Athletics capturing their second straight world championship and outdrawing the Phillies by a margin of more than two-to-one in 1930, Burt Shotton had to find more pitching in order to compete—or find another job. He would have to sacrifice offense in order to do so.

Lefty O'Doul, who would be thirty-four years old on Opening Day, had value both as a hitter and as a drawing card. So he was on the move again, this time to Brooklyn. On the same day that Joe McCarthy signed a two-year deal to manage the New York Yankees, O'Doul was shipped, along with second baseman Fresco Thompson, to the Dodgers (at the time informally nicknamed the Robins, in honor of their longtime manager, Wilbert Robinson) in exchange for three players and cash.[14] Shotton gave his rationale for the deal: "If you have stars and they cannot win for you, get rid of them and try someone else. I thought I had a winner last spring and when the team failed I was one of the most disappointed men in baseball. I hated to part with O'Doul because he was one of the finest men I ever handled, and one of the greatest hitters in the game, but he was the pawn for hurlers I wanted from [Brooklyn]."[15]

Of course, Dodgers president Frank York took an opposite view of the transaction. He assured his team's fans, "O'Doul and Thompson will strengthen our club in the only two positions in which it was really weak in 1930, and so I think that the deal is one that guarantees to put Brooklyn in the thick of the fight next season."[16]

Thrilled to be playing for a contender, an exuberant O'Doul vowed that he had but a single goal. "I won a batting title two years ago," he declared. "This year my great ambition is to play in a World Series. I was a member of the Yankees in the days of their early pennants, but my being a bullpen pitcher my chief mission then was to sleep out in the sun."[17]

As an outfielder, O'Doul lacked a knack for getting a jump on fly balls—he would never master that. His arm, ruined during his days as a pitcher, was mediocre—Dodgers shortstop Glenn Wright had to venture far into left field to take his relay throws.[18] Ground balls—forget about it. But the man kept the clubhouse loose, and he could hit and he could run. And he was now partnered with one of his rivals for the past two seasons, Babe Herman, equipping Brooklyn with a heavy-hitting lineup second to none. Brooklyn fans began dreaming about the team winning its first pennant since 1920, ecstatic that the Dodgers had surrendered little of value while acquiring two starting players.[19]

Lefty O'Doul arrived in Florida for spring training, pulling on his Brooklyn togs for the first time. Like a kid at Christmas, he sat in front of his locker and eagerly unpacked his shipment of new bats, carefully personalizing them with red tape and adding skulls and crossbones to those he felt particularly worthy.[20] During his first practice session in Clearwater, O'Doul slashed line drives all over the park—and more than a dozen out of it—lining pitches equally hard down either baseline and drawing the attention of his new teammates, almost all of whom stopped to watch. According to Tommy Holmes, when O'Doul connected solidly, the sound of the ball hitting the outfield wall boomed as if an echo emitting from the crack of the bat that had sent it on its way. Few hit the ball as hard as O'Doul—it was one thing to handcuff infielders with line drives, but O'Doul handcuffed outfielders.[21] Holmes concluded, "O'Doul is just a great hitter."[22]

In late March 1931, the Dodgers concluded spring training with a trip to Havana. After landing at the pier, the players were paraded by automobile while local girls showered them with roses. The Cuban capital would prove popular with the players, especially after discovering the bar in the back of the grandstand that sold nickel beer—even better, the Cuban promoter provided a free keg to the team after each game.

During player introductions, O'Doul, Babe Herman, catcher Al Lopez, and Havana native Dolph Luque received the loudest ovations from the Cuban baseball fans, who quickly bestowed Spanish nicknames on many of the visitors. One day, Herman proudly paraded a newspaper blaring headlines featuring what he thought was his Cuban moniker. Teammate Gordon Slade, who taught Spanish in the off-season, broke the news to Herman that the headline instead reported that he had struck out twice. Pausing to process this new information, Herman suddenly brightened and declared, "Well, I must be pretty good when they put it in big type when I fan."[23]

Near the end of training camp, O'Doul badly bruised the heel of his left hand, and it contributed to a poor start. After singling in his first at bat as a Dodger, he was retired twelve times in a row. Fans remained patient—they saw Lefty as one of them; in Brooklyn, as elsewhere, he was incredibly popular among spectators, teammates, and the press. Glenn Wright noted the more obvious aspects of O'Doul's personality: "He was a born politician. . . . Before we were in some new town half an hour, Lefty knew everybody in the place."[24]

O'Doul, who took up residence in Brooklyn, had been acquired in part for his potential to become the face of the franchise, another Ruth or McGraw, creating an identity for a team that, manager Robinson aside, had always struggled to find one.[25] But there were obstacles. In addition to his hand injury, O'Doul found the hitting background at Ebbets Field far from ideal. There was also the matter of the new baseball, which had been introduced in response to the unprecedented offensive barrage of the previous two years.[26] The new spheres featured raised seams, enabling pitchers to produce more movement on the ball during its journey to home plate. In addition, umpires no longer automatically discarded baseballs when they became scuffed or discolored. O'Doul told reporters that .350 would be an excellent average for any National League hitter in 1931—and quickly added that he planned to be the one to do it.

But he continued to struggle, squandering an opportunity to win a game against Pittsburgh with two out in the ninth by uncharacteristically swinging for the fences—and even more uncharacteristically swinging at a bad pitch; Pirates lefthander Larry French retired him on a chin-high fastball to end the game.[27]

Eighteen games into the season, the Dodgers sat in seventh place; with the pitchers acquired by the Phillies winning games, and O'Doul suffering the first protracted slump of his career, some members of the press began whispering that perhaps Philadelphia *had* gotten the better of the deal.

O'Doul gamely worked to right himself, adding an hour and a half to his practice regimen. He studied the copious notes he had made on every pitcher he had ever faced. And he retained what he considered that most valuable of tools necessary for a hitter— confidence. In early May, despite his batting average registering a paltry .197, he insisted, "My slump isn't going to last all season. It is taking me a long time to shake it off, but when I do, all of the pitchers will know it."[28]

O'Doul finally began breaking out of his doldrums in early June when the Dodgers visited St. Louis. Altering his strategy from swinging for the fences to an approach more aligned with place hitting, Lefty went seven for thirteen, plus four walks, in a four-game series, raising his batting average past the .250 mark. By the time the Dodgers returned from the road trip, O'Doul was hitting .274.

But frustration simmered just below the surface. He would be ejected four times that season—the worst incident occurring at the end of June when he received five days' suspension for uncharacteristically charging an umpire after he was called out at first base on a close play.[29]

O'Doul admitted afterward, "Of course I was wrong in charging the umpire as I did. I know I was safe on that play at first and what looked at that time to be the winning run was crossing the plate just then. I'm not one for arguing with umpires without some provocation, but I guess I'm too Irish to stand for one that's wrong without a squawk."[30]

It was about this time that Wilbert Robinson decided to let O'Doul make his own decisions at the plate, rather than giving him signals from the bench.[31] Lefty responded with a hitting barrage impressive even by his standards; wherever pitchers threw the ball, he hit it. He moved his feet, constantly repositioning himself to best advantage in the batter's box, using all of his allotted space and more. This maneuvering served the purpose of closing the few holes in his strike zone as he attempted everything he could to gain the upper hand. O'Doul was in a zone.

Lefty went four for four against Boston on July 9, and then repeated the feat twice more in three days against St. Louis. He cracked out ten hits in thirteen at bats against the Cubs at Wrigley Field, even while complaining about the poor hitting background there.[32] That was followed by eleven hits in twenty-four at bats during a six-game series at Pittsburgh, including five hits in five at bats on July 24.[33] By the end of July, after a long western road trip during which he collected forty-two hits in eighty at bats, O'Doul's batting average had risen to .340.

Wilbert Robinson was dumbfounded. "In all my fifty years of baseball," he declared, "I have never seen anything to compare with the scientific hitting that Lefty has done on this trip. That goes for all the hitters I have seen in my half century in the game, including Willie Keeler, my old Baltimore Oriole teammate. Keeler is generally rated as the most scientific hitter of all-time, but without taking anything away from his reputation, I want to say that O'Doul's exhibition since on the road beats everything I ever knew Keeler, or any other smart batter, to show in any one period."[34]

Relieved by the return of his batting eye, O'Doul told Murray Robinson of the *Brooklyn Standard Union*, "If there's nothing else I can accomplish, it's to show Robbie that he didn't make a mistake when he took me from the Phillies."[35]

Despite O'Doul's prodigious offensive output, Brooklyn was not making much headway. After briefly reaching second place, the Dodgers became mired in the middle of the pack. And that is where they remained. O'Doul had another excellent season, although not quite up to his recent standards—a .336 batting average, good for fifth-best in the National League, thirteen points behind fellow Bay Area native Chick Hafey of St. Louis; O'Doul's prediction of .350 being the upper limit of batting average that season proved quite accurate. As intended, the new baseball dampened offense—the league-wide batting average dropped from .303 in 1930 to .277 in 1931. Switching to a strategy of place hitting had resulted in a drop in home runs for O'Doul from twenty-two to seven, reflecting a similar change seen throughout the National League—892 home runs were hit in 1930, versus only 492 a year later. Pitchers breathed a little easier as earned run averages decreased by more than a run per game.

O'Doul participated along with his teammates in a postseason round-robin City Series against the Yankees and Giants, an event that raised more than $100,000 for charity. Babe Ruth and the Yankees took the title, but O'Doul surprised everyone during the field events, setting a new record by sprinting down the first base line in 3.3 seconds—at age thirty-four he had broken the record set by the great Jim Thorpe.[36]

And O'Doul was not done playing in 1931. He had been selected to join a team of Major League stars bound for Japan to engage in a series of exhibition games.

The All-Star coterie of Major League players arriving in Japan following the 1931 season was by far the best collection of talent ever to visit that country. Ostensibly fronted by Lefty O'Doul's ex–San Francisco Seals teammate Herb Hunter—who had spent much of the 1920s establishing a relationship with the Japanese—the trip was blessed by Commissioner Landis only after respected newspaperman Fred Lieb agreed to coordinate the venture; Hunter had reportedly angered players on previous trips with his lack of organization and inability to handle money—at least in a way other than it seeming to end up in his own pocket.

The trip across the Pacific Ocean aboard the Japanese luxury liner *Tatsuta Maru* took two weeks; to pass the time, players amused themselves with various contests. O'Doul won them all—everything from dice and cards to more physical feats of running and long jumping.[37]

When the All-Stars docked at Yokohama in November 1931, they were uncertain of the reception they would face; Japan had invaded Manchuria only a month before, and as a result relations between the United States and Japan were strained.

They need not have worried. Despite a measure of disappointment in Babe Ruth's absence—he had declined an invitation—thousands of enthusiastic Japanese baseball fans were on hand for the arrival of the Americans. The mayors of Yokohama and Tokyo made brief presentations before the party boarded a special train bound for the capital. There, the players were met by limousines waiting to convey them through the streets of downtown Tokyo. They rode in open cars as thousands lined the boulevard, waving special flags created for the occasion and cheering for Lou Gehrig, Lefty Grove, Al Simmons, Frankie Frisch, Lefty O'Doul, Mickey Cochrane, and Rabbit Maranville. The celebratory outburst was said to be greater than that accorded Charles Lindbergh several months earlier.

"I will remember this reception to my dying day," remarked an obviously moved Gehrig. "I do not know that anything has touched me as much as this welcome." A flabbergasted Frankie Frisch sputtered, "It made me feel like a great military hero or a man who had flown across the Pacific."[38]

Unaware that Japanese newspapers carried detailed accounts of

American baseball, the players were taken aback by the fans' familiarity with them. Japanese baseball enthusiasts knew that Lefty
Grove had won thirty-one games, and that Lou Gehrig had lost a
home run that ultimately cost him the title in that category when a
teammate trotted to the dugout instead of running the bases when
he mistakenly thought Gehrig's fly ball had been caught.

Although the local teams were no competition for the All-Stars,
who rarely fell behind in any of the games, the contests in Tokyo
were played before crowds as large as forty thousand. At one point,
the American contingent traveled to Sendai, a city of two hundred
thousand in the north of Japan nicknamed "The City of Trees."[39]
The players were greeted at the train station at seven in the morning by ten thousand people, virtually all of them frantically waving American flags.

The Americans were provided lodging at a traditional Japanese
hotel, many of them forced to stretch out in one common room
in the fashion of the natives. While some deemed the experience
uncomfortable, others, such as O'Doul and Maranville, relished
the adventure. It was the same with the food—Boston Red Sox
outfielder Tom Oliver, born and raised in Alabama, could not cot-
ton to the methods the Japanese employed in preparing chicken.
But, nine years after being fascinated by the goods—and stories—
brought back to San Francisco by big league players returning from
Japan, O'Doul was finally able to see it himself, and he loved it all.

The game in Sendai drew fifteen thousand; according to Fred
Lieb, it was said to be the largest crowd to ever gather in the city
for any purpose. Most of the city's automobiles had been commandeered for use by the players, so roughly half the crowd was forced
to slog their way on foot to the top of a hill some five miles from
town in order to reach the ballpark. Others took the streetcar line,
which terminated some two miles from the field. The remainder
arrived in buses. Regardless of the mode of transportation, everyone was on hand three hours before game time, so as not to miss
any of the batting or fielding practice.[40]

Between games, the players were treated as celebrities at official
receptions and during a seemingly endless string of parties. Rabbit

Maranville celebrated his fortieth birthday on Armistice Day at the home of a Japanese aristocrat; he received several presents, including a cake with a chocolate rabbit perched atop it, and a brand new baseball glove signed by O'Doul and the rest of the team.

Maranville, whose physical dimensions were similar to most of the Japanese he played against, became one of the favorites on the trip, especially when he caught pop flies in his vest pocket, or in his lap while sitting on the infield. Japanese players attempted to imitate him, and fans roared with laughter as baseballs bounced off the players' heads.[41]

At one point the Americans were hosted by Japanese prime minister Reijiro Wakatsuki, who apologized for not throwing out the first pitch at a recent game in Tokyo. He explained that having never played baseball, he did not think he could complete the task without embarrassing himself, so he reasoned that it would be better to invite the team over for tea instead. The American ballplayers and their wives happily posed for a group photo; Abbie O'Doul, wearing a flashy new dress, managed to slip to the front as the photo was taken, explaining afterward, "I wanted to show some of the Shanty Irish in San Francisco what company I was now traveling in." Unfortunately, as Fred Lieb put it, several of the party acted as "Ugly Americans" during the visit to Wakatsuki's residence. When the prime minister was called from the room by an urgent message, several players began taking various items—filling their pockets with cigars, pens, and figurines. Even Lieb's wife succumbed to the temptation.[42]

While all seemed relaxed and festive on the surface, danger—real and present—lurked. Wakatsuki's government resigned only a few weeks after the reception, in large part due to its inability to control the Japanese military. That task fell to his successor, Tsuyoshi Inukai. In January 1932, a Korean activist made an attempt on the life of Emperor Hirohito.[43] Four months later, Inukai was shot to death by eleven junior officers inside the prime minister's residence.[44]

The Americans remained blissfully unaware of the danger churning just below the surface of the world they were visiting. When they weren't cavorting on the diamond or being feted at banquets, they cavorted elsewhere, usually on a golf course. Mickey Cochrane, Muddy Ruel, and Bruce Cunningham were considered, outside of O'Doul, the best golfers among the pro ballplayers—Lefty won a tournament arranged by a Japanese sports enthusiast and was awarded a jewel case.[45]

Lou Gehrig was knocked out of action five games into the tour when he was hit by a pitch that broke several of his fingers.[46] As a spectator, Gehrig became most taken with the Japanese fans. "The enthusiasm of the Japanese for baseball borders on the fanatical," he said. "Never had I seen anything like it even in our biggest championship years at [Yankee] Stadium. The games didn't start until 2:30 in the afternoon, but each day the gates had to be locked at 10:30 in the morning."[47]

Like Gehrig, O'Doul was sidelined in the midst of the tour— during a game in which the Americans took to verbally berating their Japanese counterparts. Most of the opponents took the abuse stoically, thinking it an odd American custom, but one hot-tempered player, Osamu Mihara, who had been nicknamed "Nosey" by the Americans, began firing back in broken English. This irritated the Americans, and O'Doul declared that he would take care of the matter by bunting down the baseline and forcing "Nosey" to field the ball, at which point Mihara would receive his comeuppance.

O'Doul executed his plan and tore down the line. Mihara streaked over to cover first base but recognized Lefty's intention. The two collided, but Mihara was ready for the impact and angled his body in such a way that O'Doul took the brunt of the violent collision. O'Doul struggled to his feet, clutching his ribs. He was out for the series—even worse, he was unable to play golf for the duration of the tour. O'Doul spent the rest of his time on the bench next to the "Iron Horse."

Despite his injury, Lefty was easily the best hitter on the tour, batting a robust .615—Frankie Frisch was second-best at .404—winning O'Doul another jewel case, this one awarded by *Yomiuri Shimbun* to the player with the best batting average.[48] After being sidelined with his battered rib cage, O'Doul spent his days instructing Japanese players and visiting with old friend Sotaro Suzuki, who especially enjoyed sitting in the hotel lobby in Yokohama with its spectacular views of the harbor, talking baseball with O'Doul and the other American stars.[49]

Despite winning every game, the Americans insisted they were impressed with the play of their Japanese counterparts. Although doubting the Japanese would ever produce Major League–caliber batsmen, Frankie Frisch commented, "Outside of hitting, the Japanese are just as good as American players. They field like cats."[50] Unfortunately, the Americans behaved condescendingly at times, showboating during games in ways that insulted their hosts. Outfielders—including O'Doul—would lie down at times when Lefty Grove pitched, certain the Japanese batters could not hit successfully against him.[51]

But the Japanese were impressed with O'Doul, and his performance. And having the time to get to know the country and its people after his injury, he became impressed with them. Lefty began corresponding regularly with Sotaro Suzuki, and made arrangements to return the next winter with Herb Hunter, Ted Lyons, and Moe Berg.

O'Doul was in fine spirits after returning from Japan in December, even after receiving his contract and seeing that it included a pay cut. With the Depression in full swing, few options existed beyond taking what was offered, so O'Doul wired back his acceptance: "Have received 1932 contract and, while not exactly pleased with the slight reduction in salary, have signed and returned it to the club only in view of the wonderful treatment accorded me last season. Feeling fine and enjoyed Japan immensely. Am in the pink of condition and looking forward to a highly successful season."[52]

Later he confided, "It seems to me that they could have got along without cutting my salary. But maybe they were a little disappointed in me. As a matter of fact I was disappointed in myself. But I'll lead the league [in hitting] this season and get it back."[53]

Brooklyn had a new manager in 1932. Max Carey was chosen to replace sixty-eight-year-old Wilbert Robinson, fired after eighteen seasons at the helm of Brooklyn.[54] There were other changes;

for the first time in its forty-plus years of existence, the franchise would officially be known as the Dodgers (they had been variously and informally dubbed Bridegrooms, Superbas, Robins, Dodgers, and Trolley Dodgers over the years).[55] Carey indicated he was ready and willing to make trades, although he denied a rumor that O'Doul would be dealt to the Cubs for Hack Wilson.[56] O'Doul was not traded, but holdout Babe Herman was, to Cincinnati. Following consecutive second-place finishes in the batting race with averages of .381 and .393, Herman had slipped to .313 in 1931 and, combined with his holdout, was deemed expendable by Carey. Ernie Lombardi and another player were also sent in a package deal for three Reds, including young second baseman Tony Cuccinello.[57]

And the Dodgers acquired Hack Wilson after all—obtaining him from St. Louis, one month after the Cubs had traded him to the Cardinals.[58] Wilson was a nearly unequaled drinker among Major Leaguers and, after hitting fifty-six home runs and driving in 191 in 1930—the climax of a sensational five-season run—had become expendable after his offensive production plunged to a mere thirteen home runs and a .261 batting average in 1931.

Thirty-five years old when the season began, and determined to avoid a slow start in 1932, Lefty O'Doul took even more batting practice than usual; despite freezing weather that kept most of his teammates indoors, he wore out several pitchers, including forty-eight-year-old Jack Quinn, because he was dissatisfied with his stroke.[59] But his plan for a fast start was derailed by Minor League pitcher Les Barnhart, who struck him on the wrist during an exhibition game, costing Lefty three weeks, including the first week of the regular season.[60]

O'Doul finally made his season debut against the Braves in Boston; despite a heavily bandaged hand, he collected two hits, one an infield roller he beat out for a single, and the other "a rousing double to left center."[61] He began using a glove to protect his injury while he batted—making him the first to use a batting glove in a Major League game.[62] In spite of the pain, O'Doul confided to teammate Fresco Thompson that he was confident in his chances to win his second batting title.[63]

Although O'Doul did not get off to the start he had hoped for, he was hitting better at Ebbets Field in 1932. Responding to his complaints of the previous year, the Dodgers had affixed strips of green canvas to the lower center-field stands.[64] It had an impact—after batting only .300 at home in 1931, versus .366 on the road, O'Doul hit for a .356 average at Ebbets Field in 1932, only twenty-three points below his mark away from the Dodgers' home park. As the weather began to warm, so did O'Doul. A three-for-four day at Pittsburgh on May 18 bumped his average across the .300 threshold. A seventeen-for-thirty-five surge at the beginning of June moved him past the .340 mark. At the end of June, a month during which he batted .404, he was pushing .350 and his slugging average topped .500. The ball may not have been as lively as it had been two years earlier, but O'Doul's bat certainly was.

Even as he enjoyed one of his typical batting surges, O'Doul constantly analyzed his hitting stroke. Brooklyn teammate Joe Stripp remarked, "If I'm on second base and O'Doul is put out, he'll come to me with all sorts of questions, 'How was I standing? Just where was the ball? Did I come through with my swing?' If Lefty doesn't get a hit, he wants to know why."[65] Stripp later added, "He carries more in his head up to the plate than any other batter I know."[66]

O'Doul loved talking about hitting—probably even more than hitting itself. As time went on, one could see him refining his philosophy. More and more he talked about looking for the fastball and limiting one's stride as being keys to success—rules that would become the bedrock of the hitting approach he would espouse over the next three decades.

He told *Brooklyn Daily Eagle* columnist Ed Hughes that he had abandoned crouching for the most part, saying that he felt a straight-up stance was the only way to consistently hit anything, whether a baseball, a golf ball, or a fighter's chin.

O'Doul confided that he often lay awake at nights trying to figure out how to get the best of pitchers. "I experimented a lot before landing the correct method . . . I believe in crowding the plate," he told Hughes. "You can sock the balls that are straight over the plate, and you're in line to nail 'em when the pitcher sneaks one over the corner. I hit the way they pitch to me. I'm a wrist hitter. That's where a lot of my walloping comes from, and I swing the bat well from my hips . . . but most of all I should say I hit with my feet." (Hall of Fame umpire Bill Klem attested to O'Doul's ability to shift his feet during a pitch in order to hit the ball where he wanted, and called Lefty the greatest hitter he had ever seen.)[67]

O'Doul continued, "The feet have an awful lot to do with good hitting, as much as the eyes, wrists, or anything else. When I get into a batting slump, it's almost always because of poor footwork. My stride is a little off, either a few inches too long or too short."[68]

He also spoke to Hughes about the challenges in shaking a slump: "You've got to use some psychology on yourself. You can't worry about it too much because then you start pressing. That's bad. I try, almost subconsciously, to get the proper stride again. When success begins to come . . . I don't rush it. I'm content almost to tap the ball, as long as I know it's going right. Then when I feel sure of myself I gradually apply the pressure and try for the extra base clouts." He insisted that playing golf helped his batting stroke.[69]

O'Doul added to his ever-expanding roster of superstitions. He decided that if he tossed his glove to the ground at the end of an inning and the fingers pointed toward right field, he would get a hit his next time up. He continued affixing skulls and crossbones to his best bats. Hughes noted that after a swing and a miss, O'Doul would spit on the end of his bat, scrape it, and then grind it in the dirt like he was chalking a pool cue. "That gives him the idea that he won't strike out," explained Hughes.

Hughes concluded the profile with the traditional canard portraying star athletes as role models, dutifully reporting that O'Doul and his wife lived in a Brooklyn Heights apartment and asserting with a straight face—or pen as it were—that the Dodgers outfielder abstained from alcohol, watched what he ate, and was "a home-loving young man."[70] In truth, the marriage was a bit rocky—Lefty lived life on his terms.

As Lefty's hitting improved, so did the Dodgers. On July 23 they sat in seventh place with a record of 42-50. Over the next month Brooklyn won twenty-four of thirty to move into second place, a game and a half behind the Cubs. During that stretch, O'Doul hit .432 with eight home runs. He scored thirty-four runs in thirty games.

On August 4 he slammed three home runs in a doubleheader against the first-place Pittsburgh Pirates, all three either tying or winning a game. After his home run in the first contest provided the winning margin, O'Doul sat in front of his locker, shoveling his way through a pint of ice cream, and boasted to reporters that he was going to win the batting title. "I feel great," he told them. "The ball looks like a balloon. I've got more confidence than at any time since I came to the Dodgers. I wish we were playing three games today."[71]

No truer words were ever uttered. O'Doul slugged two home runs in the nightcap; the first in the eighth inning cleared the scoreboard in right to tie the game, minutes after he made an outstanding running catch of a fly ball while colliding with the outfield fence. Two innings later, he hit a ball so hard that right fielder Paul Waner never bothered turning around to see where it landed. Pitcher Bill Swift started for the dugout as soon as he saw O'Doul meet the pitch—he knew instantly it was a walk-off home run.[72] Less than a week later, O'Doul slammed two home runs off Cincinnati's Red Lucas.[73]

Despite O'Doul's prodigious hitting feats, Brooklyn managed no more than a break-even record following their surge and finished a distant third, while the Chicago Cubs returned to the World Series for the first time since 1929.

Although the Dodgers failed to win the pennant in 1932, O'Doul did capture his second National League batting title, as he had predicted to Fresco Thompson in April. Topping his nearest challenger by eighteen points, O'Doul became Brooklyn's first batting champion since Zack Wheat in 1918. Two days before season's end, when O'Doul had all but clinched the title, Thompson sneaked up to the press box. Waiting until Lefty stepped to the plate, Thompson suddenly yelled into the microphone, "Winnah—and new champeen!" A startled O'Doul looked up at the press box and, after spotting his teammate, grinned. Then he smashed a line drive that nearly knocked over Mel Ott in right field; Ott held onto the ball for an out, but as the Giants outfielder struggled to retain his balance, the runner from third tagged up to score the game's first run.[74]

A night earlier, O'Doul had been honored at a father-son dinner sponsored by the Brooklyn YMCA. He promised to form a "Y" club baseball team and outfit it from his own pocket—and even coach whenever he could. The lettering and piping on the uniforms would, of course, be green. When asked to dispense some advice to young hitters, O'Doul offered, "Always look for a fastball and the pitcher can't cross you. If you're set at the plate to meet speed, you can shift in time to meet a curve or change of pace. But, if you try to guess with the pitcher and prime yourself for a curve or slow ball, there's not a chance in the world of hitting him if he throws a fast one."

"Sounds like simple advice," wrote the sportswriter who had posed the question, "but maybe you've got to be an O'Doul to follow it."[75]

O'Doul's final record for the 1932 season included his league-leading batting average of .368, plus 219 hits, 120 runs scored, and 90 runs batted in. Once again he had more home runs, 21—good for sixth in the league—than strikeouts, 20. It was the third time he had accomplished the feat in the past four years. O'Doul finished third in the voting for Most Valuable Player, behind former teammate Chuck Klein and Cubs pitcher Lon Warneke.[76] Before leaving for Japan, he signed his Dodgers contract for 1933—having won the batting title, his pay cut was restored.[77]

As O'Doul bid his goodbye to Brooklyn for the season, Tommy Holmes remarked on Lefty's popularity, both at home and abroad. While crediting part of it to his athletic prowess, Holmes also noted, "The fellow has plenty on the personality ball. He is one of the dapper and debonair men of sport, with a sartorial perfection and a manner worthy of a diplomat. He knows his stuff."[78]

O'Doul arrived by ferry in San Francisco four days after the season ended, stepping onto San Francisco soil as a two-time batting champion. A delegation was on hand to greet him and he was applauded by a large crowd, anxious to glimpse their hero. Dressed impeccably as always, in a coat and tie complete with a carnation in his lapel, he clambered onto a truck and was paraded down Market Street to City Hall, waving his hat in greeting to those gathered on the sidewalk. There was no doubting San Francisco loved Lefty O'Doul; the *San Francisco Chronicle* crowed, "He is one of the most popular players who ever played here and he is popular because he wears the same size hat he did when he was a kid."[79]

A week after arriving in San Francisco, O'Doul and Herb Hunter, joined by their wives, headed off for Japan, with a stop in Honolulu to pick up Ted Lyons and Moe Berg. During the five weeks he spent working with collegiate players in Japan that October and November, O'Doul noted how impressed he had been with their play in 1931: "A year ago we had a team that could have won a pennant in either [Major] league by ten games. We were afraid that the games would be too one-sided, and [Herb] Hunter, who knew what the Japanese could do, was willing to bet us that we couldn't score twenty runs in any one game. And by George, we never did. Not against the defense they have. Their outfielders go for miles for fly balls and never miss what they reach. I saw at least four plays out there which surpassed any outfielding stunts I've ever seen in this country."[80]

But he also noted that the Japanese tended to play "mechanically—everything by rote. No competitive spark." He added, "They are quick to master the technical moves, but as soon as they got that far, they fell into habitual systems that you couldn't shake them out of."

There were definite idiosyncrasies that had developed during the evolution of baseball in Japan. O'Doul recalled that Ted Lyons could not break the habit of Japanese pitchers throwing a ball high and inside every time the count reached two balls and one strike. "There was nothing Ted could do about it," said O'Doul. "That was their system—maybe it got results once—and they stuck to it."[81]

He also noted that hitting backgrounds were not given consideration in Japan, and were in fact detrimental to batters. "They have no green background," he remarked. "The result is these boys have been pushing the ball rather than swinging. They haven't been able to see the ball."[82]

O'Doul was impressed by the extent to which the Japanese were anxious to learn. During sessions that lasted upwards of four hours, they peppered the Americans with questions: How long should the bat be? How should I hold the bat? What is the best way to catch the ball? When should we use the bunt?

Lefty managed to get into a little hot water while on that trip when he, Ted Lyons, and close friend Joe Cohen were strolling along a fish market on the Tokyo Bay waterfront, taking photographs—an illegal practice. A Japanese policeman spotted them and made an arrest on the spot. O'Doul finally met another officer who recognized him, and he was able to talk himself out of that jam. According to Lefty, "They hissed at us all over the joint and generally raised hell until they found out who we were."[83]

O'Doul later explained, "I knew it was against the law to use a camera, but I had previously asked a couple of other cops if it would be all right. They nodded, but while I was setting up my shots a couple of others rode up on bikes and told me I was under arrest. They don't want 'enemies' running around taking pictures."[84]

The mysterious Moe Berg, who was surreptitiously taking photographs that may or may not have later been used by the United States during the Second World War, afterward joined O'Doul and Lyons for a beer at a Tokyo restaurant. Berg scribbled some nonsensical syllables in Japanese on a scrap of paper and handed it to the young waitress without either Lyons or O'Doul noticing. Berg then asked her to read the note aloud.

"Frank O'Doul," she began, "has the ugliest mug I have ever seen. His face would stop a clock. He is also a lousy baseball player. Someday he will get hit by a baseball and killed." As a flustered O'Doul tried to make sense of what the waitress had said, and Lyons began convulsing in laughter, the waitress confessed softly in what was likely the limit of her English, "Me no understand."[85]

During the trip, O'Doul did uncover a talented player. Like O'Doul, twenty-three-year-old Waseda University reserve outfielder Haruyasu Nakajima had been converted from the pitching mound. Seeing something in him, O'Doul took Nakajima aside and provided some tutoring, as well as encouragement. Nakajima eventually became Japan's first Triple Crown winner, and the third player ever inducted into the Japanese Baseball Hall of Fame.[86]

Always gracious to his Japanese hosts, O'Doul, after returning home from the trip, autographed his favorite bat and sent it to the chief steward of the *Chichibu Maru* as a thank-you for his treatment during the trip home; Lefty also appeared in court on behalf of a stowaway he and Joe Cohen had discovered on the final leg of the return trip to San Francisco. O'Doul persuaded the judge to dismiss the charges.[87] Between his stint in Japan and spring training, Lefty spent much of his time as a volunteer coach for several youth baseball teams at Funston Park in San Francisco and attending various functions around the city. Near the end of February, he arrived at San Quentin with Willie Kamm and Lew Fonseca to play in the annual baseball game against the prisoners there. That night, he held a public screening at City Hall of his nearly confiscated photos from his trip to Japan.[88] The day before leaving for spring training, he paid a special visit to Rose Stolz and the kids at Bay View School and fascinated them with tales of his Japanese adventures.[89]

The 1932 season had marked a comeback of sorts, and proof that O'Doul's first batting title had been no fluke. The year was topped off by his being named left fielder on the *Sporting News* Major League All-Star team, as chosen by the Baseball Writers Association; he easily beat out Babe Ruth and Al Simmons for the honor.[90] Going into the 1933 season, O'Doul's lifetime batting average stood at a gaudy .359.

And he was becoming a national celebrity. There were endorsements for bats, shoes, and gloves. He was on the cover of *Baseball Magazine*. His image was depicted on baseball cards. In early 1933, every Major League ballplayer, coach, and manager was asked to sit for a formal portrait that would accompany each man's full-page profile in an ambitious new book, *Who's Who in Major League Baseball*. O'Doul's write-up noted, "He is one of baseball's greatest and most popular players."[91]

7

Banzai O'Doul

Eager to get his players acclimated, Lefty O'Doul put them through a two-hour workout on Korakuen Stadium's skin diamond on the eve of the 1949 tour's first game; the Seals were taken aback when twelve thousand Japanese baseball enthusiasts materialized for the practice session. Seats behind home plate were filled with Japan's professional, amateur, and university players, closely watching every move made by the Americans.[1] Temporarily forgetting he was fifty-two years old and had not swung a bat in anger in four years, or with any regularity in more than a decade, O'Doul spied the short fences down each line—less than 260 feet—and attempted to entertain the crowd by taking batting practice. He hoped to thrill his fans by depositing at least one ball over the fence; although he failed to do so, the crowd was nonetheless pleased with his attempt.[2]

Three days after their arrival in Tokyo, the Seals made their debut in Japan, against the Yomiuri Giants. For those players having never before visited the country, the previous seventy-two hours had to seem like stepping into another world. The culture, the food, the language—everything was disorienting. Even at the ballpark, the one place that should have felt familiar, the atmosphere was almost similar to a World Series. Fifty-five thousand fans jammed the stadium for that first contest, the largest crowd ever to attend a game there. The stands were packed three hours before the first pitch, despite a steady drizzle that had threatened cancellation of the contest—something General Marquat was determined to prevent.

Yomiuri Shimbun reported, "The opening game seemed to be the only topic of conversation throughout the city."[3] Radios blared onto the streets from seemingly every shop, while newspapers wheeled out mobile electronic scoreboards throughout the city, fans huddled around them for pitch-by-pitch updates.

O'Doul was asked to address the fans before the game began, his first opportunity to do so in that setting in more than a decade. The crowd roared its approval when O'Doul began his speech with a single word—a word that reflected his sincere feelings. A word he knew they would appreciate. The word was "tadaima," translated in English as "I am home."[4]

O'Doul added to the ceremony by presenting a dozen coveted American bats to the manager of each of the Japanese professional teams, and then Cappy Harada introduced the Seals players to the crowd, followed by Mrs. Douglas MacArthur throwing out the ceremonial first ball.[5]

The day was not without controversy. The Japanese were surprised and thrilled when the national anthems of both nations were played and their flags flew together, the first time that had happened since the war. It was an incredibly emotional moment—and one that raised eyebrows among the American military contingent.

Cappy Harada then added to the symbolism, going beyond what had already seemed unthinkable a few moments earlier by saluting both the American and Japanese flags, a gesture that did not go unnoticed by the crowd, or by Harada's military compatriots. That salute, coming from a Japanese American no less, infuriated Harada's fellow American officers, who wanted him punished immediately. A group of officers bitterly complained to General MacArthur, but to their surprise he betrayed no reaction to the news. Instead, he matter-of-factly told the officers that he not only had no problem with Harada's salute, he had expressly advised him to do it.[6]

O'Doul agreed that raising the flags of both countries was entirely appropriate. "I looked at the Japanese players and fans," he remembered, reliving the emotion of that day nearly two decades later. "Tears. [Their eyes] were wet with tears. Later, somebody told me my eyes weren't too dry either."[7] That the Seals won the game hand-

ily was of secondary importance to the event itself. It was an important moment that sent a strong message to the people of Japan.[8]

• • •

The baseball world was changing in 1933, and Lefty O'Doul was at
the age where he began to recognize the passage of time—in what
seemed little more than a blink, he was beginning his seventeenth
season in professional baseball. John McGraw had retired. Miller
Huggins was dead. William Wrigley had succumbed to a heart
attack a year earlier. Wilbert Robinson was fired, and retired. Babe
Ruth was pushing forty—O'Doul was thirty-six. There was a new
president in the White House, and Prohibition was about to end.

Although O'Doul began the 1933 season solidly enough, he felt
his timing was off. Soon it became evident to everyone, as he became
mired in the worst of the few slumps he'd experienced in his career.
After going two for five against the Giants on April 16, O'Doul failed
to hit safely for nearly two weeks. He habitually wore his lucky green
suits—and added new green socks, hats, ties, and shirts. Nothing
worked.[9] It was a slump that ate at him like no other in his career.

"I was out there for an hour before the game Saturday," he moaned
to a reporter. "Hit them until the blisters came. I was getting desperate. I had people watch me, old-timers who can usually tell
you what's wrong. I had movies of myself. I looked at them, but I
couldn't tell. And that slump went on and on."[10]

O'Doul thought he had finally traced his problems to gripping
the bat handle too tightly, which was altering the arc of his swing.
When he finally collected a base hit on April 29, after twenty-nine
consecutive hitless at bats, O'Doul—as only he could—literally
dropped to the ground and kissed first base.[11] But he could never
quite get on track.

There were moments when it appeared he might be on his way
to a hot streak. On May 11 he had five hits against Cincinnati's Paul
Derringer.[12] Ten days later he homered twice off Chicago's Charlie
Root, but dropped a line drive while avoiding a collision with the
left-field fence, allowing the winning run to score for the Cubs.[13]

Criticism of O'Doul began to appear in the Brooklyn press, particularly from the pen of young sportswriter Harold Parrott, who complained, "No outfielder in the league is weaker on ground balls now than O'Doul, but he refuses to hustle in practice. He is the slowest to get the scent of a fly ball, yet he lags in shagging. The outfield has given away as many runs as it has batted in, and O'Doul has been the worst offender."[14]

Lefty did not take the criticism well, and he let Parrott know of his unhappiness the next time he saw him. The situation did not improve—after going hitless in eight at bats in a doubleheader against Boston, O'Doul's average fell to .245. He was found at his locker after the second game, fishing a broken bat out of the bottom of his cubicle.

As reporters gathered close, he confessed, "It never rains but it pours. You make one mistake and you make ten. First, I get off to a slow start. I don't hit and I worry about it, and it affects my fielding. So my fielding gets terrible. Then, because I am playing bad ball, I am benched and I get worse. And then, to top it all off, I have an argument with a newspaperman, which is another mistake."[15]

O'Doul's stock was plummeting—in the 1930s, a player of his age was on a short leash. A simple slump that would be diagnosed as nothing more than that for a player in his twenties was quickly interpreted as meaning the end was near for a player enduring the same struggle in his mid-thirties—never mind that he was coming off his second batting title in four years. Everybody looked for signs of the death knell. Rumors circulated in early June that Max Carey was shopping O'Doul to the Giants; Dan Daniel reported that the 1932 batting champion had passed through waivers, unclaimed by every National League team.[16]

The rumors of O'Doul being available were true. He was eating breakfast at a hotel with Hollis Thurston when he learned of his being traded to the New York Giants with pitcher Watty Clark for first baseman Sam Leslie. Lefty immediately declared himself "tickled to death to play for the Giants."[17] Clark learned the news upon his return to the hotel and thought it was a joke. O'Doul wandered past in one of his green suits and told the pitcher, "Don't be afraid to tell the boys you're glad to go to the Giants, Watson." Clark said, "I'm not afraid, but I still think they're kidding me."

"No, they're not," replied O'Doul. "The trade has been made."[18]

The transaction was front-page news in Brooklyn, and Dodgers fans found it difficult to understand the trading of the defending National League batting champion and a pitcher coming off a twenty-win season in exchange for Bill Terry's understudy, no matter how poorly the team was playing. They did not realize the Dodgers were hemorrhaging cash; the deal was part of what today would be termed a salary dump. For Lefty O'Doul, the transaction represented another complete cycle. The first phase of his career had begun in San Francisco and ended with a return to his hometown ten years later. The second phase of his baseball career had begun with the New York Giants in 1928 and would now end with the same franchise.

O'Doul's new Giants teammates dubbed him "The Mayor" because it seemed he had friends at every stop; he possessed an incredible capacity for people—they energized him. He had once confided to Harold Burr of the *Brooklyn Daily Eagle*, "I like people. People and cities. Some of the fellows get bored when it rains on the road, but I'm never at a loss for amusement. I go places—museums, theaters, zoos. I like to hang around the waterfronts watching the boats go out to sea. Every city's different. I like to study people."[19] O'Doul also revealed that he was a Revolutionary War buff and that a favorite pastime was visiting Paul Revere's house in Boston. He also favored New York's Museum of Natural History, the Metropolitan Museum of Art, and the Bronx Zoo.

Frank Graham noted Lefty was a native of San Francisco, but called him "a citizen of the world at large."[20]

O'Doul's superstitions continued—led of course by his never-ending parade of green suits. It was said that if he ate bean soup and hit well that day, he'd eat bean soup "until they stop him from getting a hit."[21] He also brought along his good-luck charm "Miss Murphy," an on-deck practice bat he had pieced together from one of his favorite war clubs after it had split in half. Named in honor of a particularly hefty female Dodgers fan, O'Doul had refashioned the cudgel by tacking it together with two dozen nails and filling the remaining holes with lead and tape. It was used by the Giants as a warm-up bat for years, even after O'Doul had moved on.[22]

Lefty seemed energized by his reunion with the Giants. On his first day at batting practice, he sent eleven straight pitches into the right-field stands.[23] His habit of long practices continued; he was soon recruiting Mel Ott to work with him hour after hour, the two of them pulling balls down the right-field line of the Polo Grounds. The work paid off as O'Doul began hitting—.350 in his first thirteen games for the Giants—further souring the mood of Brooklyn fans.[24]

Lefty did seem a bit maniacal at times—and he always knew his batting average. But his teammates also recognized he was a clutch player. So did National League fans—they voted him into the first Major League All-Star Game.[25] The brainchild of *Chicago Tribune* sports editor Arch Ward, the game was originally conceived as a one-off event connected to the World's Fair. It was an immediate sensation—Chicago fans lined up for tickets three days beforehand.

John McGraw came out of retirement to manage the National League side, and his original starting lineup honored the fans' vote by including O'Doul. But detractors argued that Lefty was too slow for spacious Comiskey Park.[26] And his batting average was a mediocre .270—an improvement on the .185 mark he had carried at the end of April, but a long way from the type of performance National Leaguers expected in order to beat their hated counterparts. The National and American Leagues were strong rivals, and players rarely changed leagues during their careers—generally only if released or returned to the Minors and subsequently sold to a team in the other league did they switch. A player was usually either a National Leaguer or an American Leaguer for life. As a result, the game was considered an important measurement of superiority.

McGraw acquiesced and benched O'Doul in favor of Chick Hafey, although the shift was made so late that Lefty's name remained in the preprinted scorecard, listing him as batting sixth and playing left field. The American League won the game, 4–2, with Babe Ruth hitting a two-run homer and Lefty Grove closing out the game with three shutout innings before a crowd of more than forty-seven thousand fans.[27]

O'Doul did make an appearance, leading off the sixth inning as a pinch hitter for Jimmie Wilson. The National League trailed, 3–0, and O'Doul grounded out to Charlie Gehringer against Washington Senators right-hander Alvin "General" Crowder. A few weeks later, members of the Brooklyn Central YMCA traveled to the Polo Grounds to honor O'Doul for his work in establishing youth baseball teams in their borough. O'Doul was presented a gold statuette from a committee of twenty representing hundreds of youngsters from the "Y" who were in attendance, wearing uniforms that bore his name.[28] He did not play, but that failed to dampen the spirits of the kids who had come to honor him—the baseball fans of Brooklyn still saw Lefty O'Doul as one of their own.

To the chagrin of those fans, O'Doul did help the Giants win the pennant. When Lefty arrived, New York was in a virtual tie for first place with the St. Louis Cardinals. O'Doul was put into left field and the second spot in the batting order, and by the Fourth of July, New York led by five games. They were never headed.

Along the way O'Doul compiled several of his usual impressive hitting streaks. In early August he was moved to right field when right-handers faced the Giants, with Mel Ott displacing Kiddo Davis in center. O'Doul fashioned back-to-back four-hit games against Philadelphia. During that five-game series against his old team, he drove in eleven runs and slapped out thirteen hits in twenty-two at bats. He also hit two home runs in one game versus the Phillies, including the one hundredth of his career, off the submarine delivery of Ad Liska. At the end of August, O'Doul slugged three-run home runs in consecutive games during a key series against St. Louis. But in early September, Bill Terry returned Kiddo Davis to center and Ott to right. O'Doul became for the most part a pinch hitter; in Terry's estimation, Lefty's offense no longer outweighed his defensive shortcomings.

O'Doul hit nine home runs for the Giants—third-most on the team, behind only Mel Ott and Johnny Vergez—despite playing only a half season for New York. That brought his total to fourteen on the season, placing him eighth in the National League. He batted .306 for New York, bringing his season average to .284—by far his lowest since becoming an everyday player. O'Doul had to admit to some disappointment in how the year had turned out, but there was a bright side. The Giants were going to play in the World Series against the Washington Senators.

In profiling the players participating in the 1933 World Series, *The Sporting News* said of O'Doul, "The Man in the Green Suit . . . Colorful. Not afraid to talk up. Man in love with life. Favorite among newspapermen as he is one of the boys, a smiler. Seems to be consigned to nothing more than pinch-hitting role in big series. Too bad."[29]

The Giants took the first game behind Carl Hubbell while O'Doul sat, undoubtedly stirring within him memories of his frustrating World Series experience with the Yankees eleven years earlier. The morning of the second game, Abbie O'Doul suggested to Lefty that he drag his threadbare emerald green suit out of the closet and wear it to the ballpark.

At first he scoffed at the suggestion, protesting that he was unlikely to play, and that the suit had not brought him any luck all year, anyway. Abbie gently prodded her husband: "Just take it for old-time's sake." So he did.[30]

Washington was leading, 1–0, in the sixth inning, when the Giants loaded the bases. Bill Terry, standing as a baserunner on second, called time and signaled for O'Doul to bat for Kiddo Davis, who had collected three hits in his first six at bats in the Series to that point.

O'Doul approached the batter's box and prepared to face Alvin Crowder, the pitcher who had retired him in the All-Star Game three months earlier. Carefully placing his right foot on the outside chalk line, he held his bat in his left hand and used it to knock the dirt off his left cleat, then did the same to the right. Satisfied, he stepped out of the box and planted a good luck kiss on the end of his bat. Ritual complete, O'Doul stepped in and readied himself for the biggest moment of his career.[31]

Crowder's first pitch was a ball, outside. O'Doul, looking for something he could drive so the runner could score from third, then fouled off two pitches. The next delivery was off target and O'Doul let it go by.

With the infield drawn in and the count at two balls and two strikes, O'Doul abandoned trying for the fences and decided to level his swing, aiming to hit a line drive through the infield. He measured Crowder's next pitch but mistimed it, the top of his bat barely tickling the ball as it went by. Fortunately, catcher Luke Sewell was unable to hang onto it and it became a harmless foul tip. O'Doul was surprised at missing the ball and called time. Worried, he walked over to Travis Jackson in the on-deck circle. "Ain't I leveling right at the ball?" he asked Jackson. The Giants shortstop assured him, "Keep on leveling, you're doing all right and you'll get hold of it."[32]

O'Doul returned to the batter's box and focused on Crowder—the Senators pitcher was now threatening to blank him in both the All-Star Game and the World Series. To prevent O'Doul from pulling the ball, Crowder chose to go with a curve on the outside of the plate. O'Doul was ready and, following Jackson's advice, leveled his swing, meeting the ball near the end of his bat; the crowd reacted, thousands of people springing to their feet with a roar while Lefty ran to first as if "running on clouds."[33] O'Doul later told reporters, "I met it squarely and sent it right where I wanted to."[34] Crowder could only turn his head and watch O'Doul's line drive land in center field, while Hughie Critz and Bill Terry crossed the plate. The Giants had taken a 2–1 lead.

Years later, during an interview with Bob Stevens, O'Doul still reveled in the moment. "I wasn't going to let Crowder throw a ball past me . . . so with each pitch I moved a little closer. Finally I was darn near standing on the [plate]." When Crowder threw the fateful pitch, O'Doul said he "chased it as though it was the pot of gold at the end of the rainbow." He also admitted that he probably stepped across the plate. "However, [the umpire] didn't see it, nor did anybody else, and I certainly wasn't going to call his attention to it."[35]

Travis Jackson followed with another single to score Mel Ott, while O'Doul sprinted safely to third. Bill Terry signaled for the next batter, slow-footed Gus Mancuso, to lay down a squeeze bunt. Not expecting the tactic, the Senators were caught off guard and O'Doul scampered across the plate for the Giants' fourth run. The Giants plated two more runs before the inning was over, chasing Crowder and taking a 6–1 lead, which would prove to be the final score.[36]

The inning over, O'Doul headed to the clubhouse while Homer Peel took over in left field. As O'Doul reached the steps leading to the clubhouse, several fans broke free of the police cordon and patted him on the back. He went directly to his locker, where the clubhouse boy witnessed the veteran outfielder bury his face in that old, threadbare green jacket and dab tears from his eyes.[37]

Fred Lieb, writing for the *New York Evening Post*, declared O'Doul's hit the turning point of the World Series, which the Giants ultimately captured in five games, their first Series triumph in eleven years.[38] Bill Terry told reporters, "O'Doul came through as I expected he would. . . . His hit was just what we needed, when it could do the most good."[39] A beaming O'Doul told Will Wedge of the *New York Sun*, "That was the best big money wallop I ever got." He added that he was dedicating the hit to fellow Bay Area native Johnny Vergez, the Giants third baseman who was recovering from a ruptured appendix and unable to play in the Series.[40]

Fourteen years after his Major League debut, O'Doul finally had his shot in the limelight, with something at stake. The pinch-hit single was his only appearance in the Series, but it did not matter. It remained forever the proudest moment in O'Doul's life, the only moment that topped the original "Lefty O'Doul Day" in 1927. It was a splendid way for O'Doul's season to end, especially considering that it began with a tortuous batting slump and a trade from Brooklyn. He had delivered on the biggest stage in team sports.

The day after the 1933 World Series ended, Lefty O'Doul prepared to leave for his home in San Francisco. Before departing, he was asked to pose for a simulated "farewell" scene along with teammates Hughie Critz, Mel Ott, and Bill Terry. The premise of the photograph involved the three World Series stars saying goodbye to Terry before leaving New York for the winter. The resulting image reflects a lot about Lefty O'Doul; while the other three men seem stiffly posed and all too aware of the camera, Lefty is leaning in, grinning widely, and appearing as natural as if the photographer had happened onto the scene. Lefty not only looked natural in that pose, he seemed natural in every situation life threw at him.[41]

A week later, O'Doul and Washington Senators star Joe Cronin boarded a ferry in Oakland for the trip across the bay to San Francisco and a celebration in their honor. Upon arriving at the Ferry Building on the Bay side of their home city, they were greeted with hearty handshakes from San Francisco mayor Angelo Rossi and police chief Bill Quinn. The two Major League stars were introduced to a throng of fans who had been waiting expectantly for several hours; the crowd was determined to greet what they saw as *their* World Series heroes—especially Lefty O'Doul, whose clutch pinch-hit single had turned the tide against Cronin's Senators.

The two ballplayers maneuvered through the crowd shortly after arriving at eight-thirty, jostled repeatedly by the multitude surging around them, as seemingly detached hands thrust out from the mass of humanity, eagerly attempting to pat one or both of their favorite sons on the back. While the city's municipal band blared "California, Here I Come," O'Doul, clearly savoring the moment, remarked to no one in particular, "This sure is sweet!"

The crowd surrounded the Ferry Building and strung itself all along Market Street as the band switched to "Take Me Out to the Ballgame." Handed a microphone, O'Doul invited everyone to the charity baseball game to be played the next day at Seals Stadium, promising, "Tomorrow [you will] see some baseball that is baseball." Rose Stolz and her kids from Bay View Grammar School were out in force, hoisting an enormous yellow banner as testimony of allegiance to their hero. O'Doul posed for a photo among that sea of young boys from his old neighborhood, boys he would have been among thirty years earlier. It was one of the proudest moments of his life.

Lefty then caught a glimpse of a familiar and welcome sight, and a wide grin stretched across his face. It was the Butchertown Cowboys, wearing their handsome chaps and ten-gallon hats, led by district attorney Matt Brady, astride the horses that had so impressed O'Doul as a boy—a reminder of his roots. The Native Sons were

also out in force—the organization that had sponsored the baseball league in which O'Doul received his start.

Cronin and O'Doul stepped into an open automobile and were
driven up Market Street, greeted by vigorous shouts and applause
along the route, and from what seemed to be every office window
above them. The ballplayers called out to friends they recognized,
and rode past the St. Francis Theater, where highlights of the 1933
World Series, including Lefty's big hit in the second game, were
being screened. "All the guys that won a bet on that hit of Lefty's are
on Market Street today," claimed one observer. It was also observed
that he was probably right.

The celebration proceeded to City Hall, where local politicians
spoke of the noble way the two men had played and the great credit
they were to the city. The temporary grandstand groaned under the
weight of the dignitaries, as the multitude of ordinary folks surged
closer to hear from their heroes, who were presented loving cups
to commemorate the occasion, as well as passes to the prestigious
Olympic Club. When O'Doul took the microphone, young children
screamed out his name and he could not suppress his delight. "This
homecoming," he finally began, "is the happiest day of my baseball
career." He insisted that the Senators could just have easily won—
provided they had Carl Hubbell—and closed his remarks by saying, "And I want to thank those Butchertown Cowboys out there,"
which ignited yet another round of pandemonium.[42]

Lefty O'Doul had returned to San Francisco as a World Series
hero, and his off-season was packed with testimonial dinners and
benefit baseball games. One of those games, staged at Seals Stadium under the sponsorship of the Elks Club, drew fifteen thousand fans eager to see their hometown favorite play alongside and
against the likes of Ty Cobb, Joe Cronin, Chick Hafey, Tony Lazzeri,
Willie Kamm, and other stars boasting local connections. The bat
O'Doul had used in the World Series was placed on display as if
a holy relic.[43] O'Doul was presented a chest of silver dinnerware
before the game and was said to be besieged by autograph seek-
ers both during and after the contest. The event raised more than
$6,000 for local charities.[44]

A couple of weeks later Babe Ruth breezed into town, his wife and daughter literally in tow following a trip to the Hawaiian Islands, where Ruth had played several exhibition games. The Babe, who was stopping over on his way to Los Angeles for the Stanford-USC football game, was met by O'Doul at the dock, and the two almost immediately set off for Lake Merced Country Club, where they played thirty-six holes of golf, newsmen and photographers joyfully tagging along.[45]

The winter's whirlwind of activity culminated in yet another trip to Japan for O'Doul, this one to complete negotiations for a tour to top all previous tours—one that, should O'Doul be successful, would include Ruth, who, after turning down several previous invitations, would finally make his first appearance in the Orient.

The seeds for finally bringing Babe Ruth to Japan had been sown some six months earlier by Lefty O'Doul. Soon after returning to America following the 1931 tour, O'Doul wrote Sotaro Suzuki about how much he had enjoyed playing in Japan, and of his desire to return.[46] Suzuki in turn wrote to O'Doul about his interest in starting professional baseball in his country. Over the next year, the two worked on potential business deals involving sporting goods in both America and Japan, principally involving Hillerich & Bradsby.[47] After O'Doul made his visit in the fall of 1932 with Herb Hunter, Ted Lyons, and Moe Berg, he expressed to Suzuki his dream of starting a baseball school in Japan—hopefully with financial assistance from *Yomiuri Shimbun*.[48]

O'Doul desperately wanted to bring another All-Star team to Japan—and he wanted to do it without Herb Hunter's involvement. His old friend Suzuki was the person who could help him do so. "Let me know if your paper wants to take a team to Japan," O'Doul wrote in April 1933. "If they want a big league team, let me know in plenty of time so to bring a first class club over there to your country." Then O'Doul wrote something he knew would grab Suzuki's attention.

"I think it would be a wonderful thing . . . if we could get Babe Ruth to come to Japan. If you let me know in plenty [of] time I will talk to him and his manager and try and arrange to get him to make the trip."[49]

Suzuki had to have felt a jolt of adrenaline upon reading that sentence. He wrote back that he would take O'Doul's proposal to the publisher of *Yomiuri Shimbun*, Matsutaro Shoriki, who had long sought to bring Ruth to his country.[50]

Matsutaro Shoriki seemed an unlikely person to underwrite baseball tours. A graduate of Tokyo Imperial University, he was not a baseball fan in particular. His sport was judo, at which he was a master. After graduating from law school, Shoriki was with Tokyo's Metropolitan Police for more than a decade—his courage during a major riot, which he stopped single-handedly without the use of a weapon or physical force, made him a legend. He was also a rabid anticommunist and repeatedly used the police to infiltrate universities, earning him the permanent enmity of many leftists in Japan.

He lost his position in 1924 in the aftermath of an attempted assassination of prince regent and future emperor Hirohito—unfortunately on his watch—but retained influential friends in the government. Unemployed, he purchased a small newspaper, *Yomiuri Shimbun*, which had a circulation of a little more than fifty thousand. A determined and relentless worker and aggressive risk-taker, Shoriki decided to emphasize sports and sensationalistic news and within a decade had the publication on its way to boasting a readership approaching 1.5 million.[51]

During the summer of 1933, O'Doul and Suzuki discussed not only arrangements for the proposed exhibition series, but also the prospect of O'Doul adding his expertise to existing efforts in establishing professional baseball in Japan. Suzuki had convinced Shoriki to underwrite the tour at great financial—and, as it turned out, great personal—risk, and Shoriki in turn made an effort to provide stiffer competition than had been produced by the college players in 1931.

Shoriki was also quite willing to leave Herb Hunter out in the cold—his newspaper had lost money on the 1931 tour, while Hunter had collected a tidy sum. Hunter had also spread rumors that it was Shoriki who had made a financial killing. Through Suzuki, Shoriki again insisted Ruth had to be a part of any deal and, mindful of the poor behavior of the players during the previous visit—as well as the lack of a novelty factor in their return—told O'Doul he did not want any of those players back, with the exception of deferring to Lefty on whether to include Lou Gehrig. Shoriki also preferred that the tour occur after the 1934 World Series, reasoning it would take a full year to generate the kind of publicity necessary for success.[52] That would also provide Shoriki time to develop stronger opposition for the Americans, which he felt important to generate maximum fan interest.

Shoriki's support secured, the next step was to implement the plan while keeping it secret from Herb Hunter; O'Doul worried that if Hunter, who was actively attempting to negotiate a deal with the Tokyo Six University League for a tour in either 1933 or 1934, discovered what he was up to, he would cut out O'Doul entirely.[53] At the same time, Suzuki expressed concern that Ruth might retire, which would dampen interest in his appearance.[54]

Shoriki held firm that there would be no underwriting the tour without Ruth. The Japanese had seen top American players, but they had not seen the home run king. "Japanese fans are very anxious to see Babe before he quits," Suzuki explained. "These are the views given by Mr. Shoriki and the circumstances now prevailing in Japan, and we must have Babe Ruth in the next major league team at any rate. You may consider that if Babe is not coming, Mr. Shoriki might turn down the proposition."[55]

Although O'Doul had been unsuccessful to that point in persuading Ruth to participate, he *had* made a deal with Earle Mack, son of Connie, who had been granted exclusive rights by Commissioner Landis to bring a Major League Baseball team to the Orient. "Mr. Mack is a very fine man," O'Doul wrote, "and he wants the baseball players to get the money, not one man [Hunter] like 1931."[56] Mack wrote to Shoriki, referencing the efforts of Suzuki and O'Doul, and suggested O'Doul as the best intermediary to secure an agreement.[57] Shoriki agreed that O'Doul would make a satisfactory representative to finalize the deal.[58]

The Japanese Department of Education had forbidden university players appearing in games against professionals, and O'Doul was assured that Hunter, who would soon arrive in Japan, would have no success in changing the decision. O'Doul was also told that if Shoriki was likewise unsuccessful in his efforts to persuade the Department, he would form a professional team—really an All-Star squad—to play against the Americans.[59]

Unaware of the deck being stacked against him, Hunter arrived in Japan and encountered a distinct lack of enthusiasm for his proposal. Then he received a telegram from his wife, warning him that Suzuki and O'Doul were working with Earle Mack against him. Hunter scrambled back to the United States, hoping there remained a chance he could somehow cut a deal.[60] Among his efforts was contacting Babe Ruth as he vacationed in Hawaii following the 1933 season, shortly before the Bambino visited San Francisco and played golf with O'Doul.[61] But there was not much Hunter could do—O'Doul held the upper hand.

Following the 1933 World Series, and the subsequent celebration in San Francisco, O'Doul visited Japan to complete tour arrangements and was invited to provide instruction to a high school team in a small community some twenty miles outside of Tokyo. As he neared the town, he was welcomed by a motorcade, each car with a sign affixed to it that said, "Welcome, Frank."[62] He did feel welcome—one of Lefty O'Doul's strongest personality traits was his ability to feel at home wherever he went.

He granted an interview to the English language *Japan Times and Mail*, in which he began helping to lay the groundwork for Japanese professional baseball. "It is remarkable to see the progress that has been made by baseball players in Japan both in hitting and teamwork," he observed. "I feel[,] however, that baseball will never really reach its height in Japan until a professional league is organized. . . . It would give the baseball players of Japan a chance to continue the game after they leave school.

"In America, the average baseball player does not reach his prime until he is at least twenty-six. In Japan, the average player quits the game at twenty-four and in most cases is finished with the game for life."[63]

Upon returning to the United States, O'Doul repeated his claim that the birth of professional baseball in Japan was imminent, mentioning that such a team might soon tour the States.[64] He would spend the 1934 season recruiting players for the grand tour, including the biggest name of them all; his promise to bring Babe Ruth to Japan had set the plan in motion. Now he had to deliver.

There had been rumors of O'Doul clearing waivers after the 1933 season, paving the way for his release by the Giants so he could sign up for a fifth stint with his hometown San Francisco Seals. But when spring training rolled around in March 1934, O'Doul was again wearing a New York uniform.[65] Although happy enough to be returning for another big league go-round, O'Doul recognized that he would play a lesser role during the upcoming season; it was no secret that he and player-manager Bill Terry did not get along. Like John McGraw, Terry rarely employed O'Doul against left-handed pitchers. And when it came to playing every day, at age thirty-seven and with the Giants seeking to repeat as National League champions, O'Doul's body was no longer up to the task.

But Terry was also mindful of O'Doul's talent, and employed him accordingly in key situations. When utilized judiciously, the San Franciscan remained a potent offensive weapon, and O'Doul provided some outstanding moments for the Giants during the 1934 season, the first of which came on the second of May when he "emerged from the depths of the New York dugout," as John Drebinger put it, and reminded the Brooklyn Dodgers why it was dangerous to trade Lefty O'Doul.

Brooklyn had taken a 4–3 lead in the top of the eighth. New Dodgers manager Casey Stengel counted on left-hander Charlie Perkins to close out the game and earn his first Major League victory, but after retiring the first batter in the bottom of the eighth, Perkins allowed a single to Bill Terry and walked Mel Ott, who had homered earlier. With the dangerous right-handed-hitting Travis Jackson due up next, Stengel called time and brought in his ace, hard-throwing right-hander Van Lingle Mungo.

Terry, standing out at second base, anticipated the move and signaled for O'Doul to pinch-hit for Jackson. The switch caught Stengel off guard—O'Doul had batted only four times to that point and was still seeking his first base hit of the season; Travis Jackson was the team's best run producer outside of Mel Ott.

But, as he had in the 1933 World Series, O'Doul made Terry appear a genius. Mungo, unaccustomed to pitching in relief, and anything but a control pitcher under normal conditions, fell behind the patient O'Doul by a count of three balls and one strike. O'Doul knew a fastball would be coming—Mungo would not want to load the bases. Guessing correctly, O'Doul swung and sent an arcing line shot, the baseball's flight stopped only by its crashing against the right-field balcony.[66] His three-run home run sank the Dodgers—and by the end of the month, Charlie Perkins was back in the Minors, never to win a game in the big leagues.

After playing right field for a week and a half in mid-May, O'Doul returned to his role coming off the bench, with considerable success. He jumped on the first pitch he saw for a three-run pinch-hit home run against Pittsburgh on May 27 at the Polo Grounds, and for good measure smashed a pinch-hit grand slam three weeks later into the upper right-field tier at Forbes Field—the first and only grand slam of his Major League career.[67] O'Doul added back-to-back two-run pinch-hit singles against the Phillies in early August.[68]

Given an extended run in the Giants' lineup during the middle of the 1934 season, O'Doul provided a reminder of his past prodigious offensive streaks. Subbing for injured outfielder Jo-Jo Moore during the first week of July, he smashed sixteen hits in thirty-four at bats, including two triples and four home runs, to raise his batting average to .393; in one of those games he again homered to defeat the Dodgers, but O'Doul also provided fodder for those pointing to his reputation as a defensive liability when he nearly squandered the game by dropping a fly ball after initially losing track of it in the sun.[69]

O'Doul's hot streak with the bat did earn him more time as a starter, and later that month he drove in runs in five consecutive games. However, despite registering ten extra-base hits while driving in twenty runs during a twenty-six-game streak, his appearance in the outfield during a July 29 doubleheader at the Polo Grounds against Philadelphia would prove his last. Terry's confidence in him as an outfielder had run out. From the end of July, O'Doul was employed exclusively as a pinch hitter.

That summer, a man wearing a green suit and claiming to be Lefty O'Doul began frequenting drinking establishments in Greenwich Village. The imposter paid his tab with bad checks, an incident nearly identical to one that had occurred previously in San Francisco.[70] Over the years, the story of the imposter gave rise to one of O'Doul's classic, exaggerated, self-deprecating tales, in which he claimed to have visited a victimized bar owner—while at the same time explaining why he was no longer in the Giants' lineup.

According to O'Doul's repeated tellings over the years, after the bar owner admitted he had never before laid eyes on him, O'Doul slapped a twenty-dollar bill on the bar, more than covering the amount of the phony checks, and told the barkeep to forget about it. The punchline comes when he offers the man some advice: "If a guy comes in here again claiming to be me, take him out back and hit baseballs to him. If he catches them, you know he's a phony."[71]

The day after Labor Day 1934, the New York Giants were leading the rest of the National League by seven games and seemed a near lock to capture their second straight pennant. But then the Giants dropped eleven of nineteen games, and their lead completely evaporated. Suddenly, the surging St. Louis Cardinals and their electrifying young right-handed pitcher, Dizzy Dean, were within a single game of the lead with two left to play.

Back in January, a cocky Bill Terry had predicted the Giants would repeat as National League champions, with Pittsburgh, St. Louis, and Chicago posing the most serious threats. When asked if he feared the Dodgers, Terry paused and then explained to the assembled reporters, "I was just wondering whether they were still in the league."[72]

The remark had, predictably, come back to haunt him. The Giants were desperate for a victory—any victory—and their final two games of the season were, of course, against Brooklyn. And neither the

Dodgers nor the New York press had forgotten Terry's flippant dis-
missal of his inter-borough rival. During Saturday's penultimate
contest, an inspired Dodgers lineup tallied single runs in the fifth,
sixth, and seventh innings, two of which were directly attributable to
singles launched from the bat of pitcher Van Lingle Mungo. Brooklyn added a pair of runs in the top of the ninth to take a 5–1 lead.

Eager to close out the game, a fired-up Mungo struck out the
first two batters in the bottom of the ninth. Terry, no doubt remembering O'Doul's success earlier in the year against the Brooklyn
right-hander, called on him to pinch-hit for catcher Gus Mancuso.
But Mungo was up to the task; O'Doul uncharacteristically took
three called strikes, never lifting the bat from his shoulder. The
game was over.[73]

The next day, Terry again called on O'Doul to pinch-hit for Gus
Mancuso, this time in the eighth with one out and one on. Dodgers manager Casey Stengel countered Terry's move by replacing
his right-hander with veteran lefty Tom Zachary.

Terry in turn reacted to Stengel's move by recalling O'Doul and
substituting Harry Danning, who promptly grounded into a double play to end the inning. The Dodgers ultimately won the game
in extra innings.[74] Meanwhile St. Louis, behind Dizzy Dean and
his brother Paul, swept the Cincinnati Reds to steal the pennant
from New York. Just like that, it was all over for the Giants. Tommy
Holmes penned the epitaph to the Giants' season: "Whatever doubt
there may have been in Manager Terry's mind regarding the existence of the Dodgers," he wrote, "the truth was brought home to
him with vengeful, not to say tragic, suddenness."[75]

It also was all over for O'Doul as a Major Leaguer—instead of
ending his big league career in a World Series, his final appearance
in a Major League box score resulted in a cameo appearance that
culminated with his being called back to the dugout without seeing
a single pitch. Lefty O'Doul's Major League career had ended as it
had begun fifteen years earlier—with a whimper rather than a bang.

Despite the disappointing ending, O'Doul had been extremely productive in 1934. Pinch-hitting as often as he played the outfield, for

the fourth time in his big league career he garnered more home runs than strikeouts (9 to 7), adding to his reputation as one of baseball's all-time great contact hitters. O'Doul, whose final batting average was .316, drove in an impressive 46 runs on 56 hits in only 177 at bats—a ratio greater than that of teammate Mel Ott, who led the league in RBIS with 135.[76] O'Doul's lifetime batting average in the Major Leagues stood at .349, fourth-best in history. Interestingly, O'Doul's career at bats as a professional are almost equally divided between the Majors and the Minors, with uncannily equal results. He had 3,264 at bats and 1,140 hits in the Majors versus 3,255 at bats and 1,146 hits in the Minors. His lifetime Minor League batting average—with all but a handful of his at bats coming in the Pacific Coast League—was .352. Interestingly, his home-road splits were also very similar: researcher Bill Deane cataloged that O'Doul hit .352 in his Major League career at home and .347 on the road.[77] His record as a Minor League pitcher was a more than respectable 53-32.

Despite rampant speculation that the rumors of the previous spring regarding his release would finally come true, leading to his becoming manager of his hometown San Francisco Seals, O'Doul did not necessarily close the door completely on his big league career. He spoke of wanting to play two more years, and shortly after season's end was photographed with Mel Ott at the Louisville Slugger factory in Kentucky as the two stars placed their bat orders for 1935.[78]

Meanwhile there was the matter of the 1934 tour to Japan. O'Doul had successfully conspired to freeze Herb Hunter out of the picture, but the path to securing Babe Ruth proved challenging. It took months to sway him; O'Doul ultimately utilized his wife to convince Ruth's wife, and she in turn finally convinced Ruth during the summer. The official announcement was made in early July 1934 and generated headlines in both countries.[79] "I expect to have a lot of fun," volunteered Ruth, "and maybe it will be my last showing in baseball."[80]

But shortly before it was time to depart, Ruth again changed his mind, his mood soured toward any undertaking after learning the Yankees had no intention of allowing him to ever manage the team. The situation had come to a head after Ruth, who had already declared he would no longer be an everyday player in 1935, chose to force the issue with Yankees owner Jacob Ruppert about becoming manager. Ruppert told Ruth that Joe McCarthy, winner of only one pennant in four years in New York, was returning as manager.

Ruth responded by informing Ruppert that he would not sign a new contract as a player. He was quitting the Yankees. One of the most successful and lucrative partnerships in the history of team sports was at an end.[81]

O'Doul faced other obstacles. The National League reversed its decision to allow its players to participate, which meant O'Doul could serve as a coach and tour guide on the trip, but could not play in games since he remained under contract to the Giants. Pittsburgh Pirates president William Benswanger had earlier framed his reluctance to allow his players to participate due to "the boat hazard; the danger of Oriental disease, etc., and the possibility of playing too much baseball, thereby unfitting the player for his summer's work."[82] Senators owner Clark Griffith and Red Sox owner Tom Yawkey also withdrew their support for the junket, costing the team Joe Cronin, Heine Manush, and Lefty Grove.

It seemed as if the entire trip was jinxed. Injuries began to creep up: Bill Dickey broke his finger and could not play. When Griffith relented and allowed pitcher Earl Whitehill to go, there was hope he could be convinced to allow Manush and Cronin to participate after all, but each suffered injuries that ended their seasons.[83] And now, enraged by his divorce from the Yankees, Ruth was in no mood to go to Japan. The other issues were simply that—issues. They could be dealt with. But without Ruth there would be no tour.

Unaware of the drama unfolding thousands of miles away, Sotaro Suzuki traveled to the United States to cover the World Series for *Yomiuri Shimbun*, planning to return to Japan afterward with the American baseball stars. Following a meeting with Ruth's manager, Christy Walsh, Suzuki rendezvoused with Ruth in a New York barbershop. O'Doul was to join him there.

According to Robert Fitts in *Banzai Babe Ruth*, his definitive book about the 1934 tour, Suzuki arrived first and the Bambino was in a decidedly negative frame of mind; he was having none of what Suzuki was offering. O'Doul and Walsh arrived and they fared no better. Ruth was adamant. He was not going. In a last-ditch effort, a shaken Suzuki reached into his case and pulled out a coat bearing Ruth's image, pleading with Ruth that the men delivering the *Yomiuri* newspaper would wear it. That got Ruth's attention.[84]

In 1956, in an interview Suzuki gave to Carl Lundquist of United Press International, he said he told Ruth, "Babe, there are thousands of boys over there waiting to see you play ball, kids who never saw the great Babe."[85] Suzuki then showed Ruth the poster created for the tour, featuring the ballplayer's portrait, his eyes altered to look Asian.

Ruth looked at the poster and let out a big laugh. "Aw, if that's the way it is," he told Suzuki, "sure, I'll go."[86] Air once again filled the room. The tour was on.

After playing their way across the United States and Canada in October 1934, the All-Stars made an appearance in Vancouver, British Columbia, before heading across the Pacific for Japan. Both Connie Mack and Babe Ruth were in a jovial mood, posing for numerous photos on the deck of the luxury liner *Empress of Japan*. At one point, the two men swapped hats to comic effect, Ruth perching Mack's bowler atop his cranium—it was at least two sizes too small—and Mack, smiling broadly, wearing Ruth's beret, which flopped loosely about the legendary manager's head.

Before taking off, Mack sat the players down and read them a letter from Commissioner Landis, stressing the importance of the trip and the need for the players to behave as true ambassadors for the game.

The next leg of the trip, to Honolulu, was marred by heavy seas, resulting from a severe storm that had made playing conditions miserable in Vancouver and caused widespread destruction across the Pacific Northwest. Moe Berg wrote to nationally syndicated sports columnist Harry Grayson from aboard ship, "How they turned out for Ruth at every stop, grownups and school kids. Ruth put on a great show as usual for the newsreel cameramen, just before we sailed." Berg indicated that after a rough couple of days at sea, the ocean had calmed, allowing the players to emerge from below deck for some light pitching and catching.[87] Although Connie Mack was in charge, Ruth was assigned the role of manager and supervised the impromptu workouts; speculation arose that Mack was auditioning Ruth as his eventual successor as manager of the Athletics.

Meanwhile, Japanese baseball fans waited anxiously for the arrival of the contingent from America, including the greatest player of them all. Fred Lieb, who had been part of the 1931 tour, knew those making their first trip were unaware of the riotous welcome that awaited them. He wrote that Gehrig and O'Doul, as repeat visitors, were quite popular and could expect a special level of adulation. But Lieb also recognized what was likely to be different about this venture.

"Within the next fortnight," wrote Lieb, "the cry 'Banzai' will be shouted from thousands of lusty Japanese throats as another crew of distinguished American ballplayers are driven through the Ginza, the Broadway of Tokyo. Again it will be 'Banzai Lou Gehrig' and 'Banzai O'Doul,' but this year, instead of shouts of 'Banzai Grove' and 'Banzai Simmons,' it will be 'Banzai Babe Ruth.' . . . Yes, I believe the 'Banzais' for the honorable Babe will be the loudest and most vociferous ever extended to a foreigner in the land of Cherry Blossoms."[88]

Lieb was absolutely correct in his assumption, not that the prediction was a particularly difficult one to make. The players docked in Yokohama and were greeted by two dozen Japanese girls, who presented each player a hapi jacket—a special linen coat traditionally worn at festivals—with his name embroidered in Japanese characters. Then everyone boarded a special train for the twenty-mile trip to Tokyo.[89]

Once in the capital, the motorcade was mobbed all through the city by fans reaching out in the hope of touching the great Babe Ruth—as if the adoration they felt for him would be returned in some way. Ruth was photographed with a group of blind children; he allowed them to touch his face in order to "see" him.[90] Lefty

O'Doul remarked, "I think a million people saw Ruth, or tried to see him. Talk about your hero worship. There was never anything like it."[91] The party was amazed by the red and green electric signs along the Ginza—making the city seem as if it were ablaze. There were bicyclists everywhere, along with men pushing handcarts loaded with every imaginable item.[92]

Ruth had to be provided a special cordon of police protection every time he ventured from his hotel. He was continually accosted by fans seeking his autograph, especially children, and did his best to oblige—in truth he was thriving on the attention. One would be hard-pressed to find someone who understood and was as comfortable with the mantle of celebrity as Babe Ruth. And it was a wonderful salve for the wounds suffered from a subpar season—only twenty-two home runs and a sub-.300 batting average, not to mention the ego-puncturing end of his Yankees career.

But as in 1931, there was an undercurrent of danger lurking just beneath the surface. The same day the players arrived in Japan, three weeks of talks broke down in London, talks designed to address Japan's demands for naval equality by altering a decade-old treaty that had been enacted to prevent an arms race in the wake of World War I.[93] The treaty, often called the Five-Power Treaty, limited the Japanese naval presence to 60 percent the size of Britain and the United States. As a result of Japan's refusal to bargain further, relations between the countries were further strained, and there was talk that war was inevitable. And those in Japan wishing to move that country to a war footing were all too active behind the scenes.

Ruth's mood only improved as the tour continued. He was mobbed by fans everywhere he went, baseballs constantly thrust into his hands to sign. The first game was played in front of sixty-five thousand fans at Meiji Jingu Stadium in Tokyo—the opening ceremonies included the president of the Japan Baseball League, Marquis Nobutsune Okuma, throwing the first pitch to seventy-one-year-old Connie Mack, who crouched behind home plate. Ruth failed to hit a home run, but the Americans won anyway, 17–1.[94] The team took the field in uniforms designed especially for the tour, white togs patriotically trimmed in red and blue, with a shield representing the United States on the shirt front, over the heart, and the words "All-Americans" surrounding the emblem. "U.S." was emblazoned on the cap and each sleeve.[95]

When the stars later played in Osaka, site of the country's largest stadium, seating eighty thousand, the atmosphere was like that of a World Series.[96] But Ruth seemed rusty the first few games—indeed, the weather was cold and the pitchers seemed to be ahead of the hitters early on. Lefty Gomez threw spectacularly in the third game, winning despite a light snowfall, 5–2, before a crowd of thirty thousand. Earl Averill's first-inning grand slam proved the telling blow. Two days later Gomez pitched a 10–0, two-hit shutout, striking out nineteen batters, including four in one inning when Jimmie Foxx, playing catcher despite nearly missing the tour after a serious beaning before coming to Japan, let a pitch get away on a swinging third strike and the Japanese batter reached first safely.

Ruth finally warmed up in the fourth game of the tour, hitting two home runs at Sendai on November 9.[97] The next day, Ruth and Connie Mack headlined a radio broadcast back to the States via NBC. O'Doul spoke briefly, along with several other players. Ruth reported that a team of Japanese ballplayers would be visiting the United States in the spring.[98]

Ruth had homered in Gomez's nineteen-strikeout effort, and two days later he added a pair of circuit clouts.[99] In all, he homered in six consecutive games, four times hitting two home runs, demonstrating to the amazement of teammates and Japanese fans alike that, even as he neared forty years of age, he could still rise to the occasion.

The Babe even found time to play some golf, joining Lefty O'Doul and the American ambassador to Japan, Joseph Grew, for a round at the Tokyo Golf Club, or at least fourteen holes or so before the newsreel cameraman became too much.[100]

On November 14 the players attended an America-Japan Society luncheon held in their honor at the Tokyo Imperial Hotel. Prince Iyesato Tokugawa, president of the Japanese House of Lords and also president of the committee organizing the 1940 Olympics, scheduled to be held in Japan, spoke of the great passion the Japanese had for baseball and declared that it was no longer only an American sport. He also gave a nod to the impact of the American tour, saying, "There are no national differences which cannot be solved through sportsmanship."[101]

Three days later, the All-Americans played their final game in Tokyo before moving on to other parts of the country. Jimmie Foxx played all nine positions and Ruth seven, including shortstop and third base. The Babe clouted two more home runs, one a grand slam, in a 15–6 victory. The players were presented an incredible array of gifts, and representatives from *Yomiuri Shimbun* awarded Ruth a valuable vase in recognition of a 440-foot home run he had hit.

The game in which Ruth's home run streak ended remains largely responsible for the tour's enduring legacy—and a historic moment for Japanese baseball. It was on November 20 in Shizuoka that high school student Eiji Sawamura, who had surrendered his amateur status and the opportunity to play for one of Japan's prestigious Big Six universities in order to pitch against Babe Ruth and the Americans, battled Earl Whitehill to a scoreless tie for six innings. At one point, Sawamura struck out Charlie Gehringer, Ruth, Lou Gehrig, and Jimmie Foxx in succession. A frustrated Ruth, worried that as manager he might lose a game to the Japanese, fumed about the sun being in the batters' eyes. He exhorted the team to watch for Sawamura twisting his mouth—a sign that he was going to throw a curve; it was a habit Ruth knew well, since he had also been plagued by it early in his pitching career.[102] Gehrig, heeding Ruth's advice, waited for the curve and drove a home run in the seventh to give the Americans a 1–0 lead that proved to be the final score.[103] Despite losing, Sawamura had become a hero; Connie Mack inquired about Sawamura's interest in playing for the Athletics, but the teenager indicated he had no desire to leave Japan.

Inspired by the near victory, the Japanese battled hard in the next game at Nagoya, leading 5–3 in the eighth inning, before finally losing, 6–5; they never again came close to victory. The final game in Japan was played on December 1, and as thanks for his work on the tour, Ruth asked Sotaro Suzuki to manage the All-Americans, who easily defeated Eiji Sawamura, 14–5, after spotting the opposition three runs in the first.[104]

Ruth homered thirteen times during the tour as the Americans won all sixteen games they played against Japanese competition, plus two more against mixed teams. The contests drew more than three-quarters of a million fans. Despite the one-sided nature of the contests, the junket seemed an unqualified success—the players left enraptured with Japan, which had proven much more modern than they had supposed; to a man they felt the likelihood of war between the United States and Japan had been greatly diminished thanks to the tour. But they were unaware that on the same day Eiji Sawamura pitched his 1–0 game against the Americans, arrests were made that disrupted a coup attempt fomented by junior military officers who were part of a secret society dedicated to overthrowing the government in favor of a totalitarian regime.[105]

Shoriki and his newspaper once again lost money, same as in 1931.[106] But Shoriki also recognized that his gamble had again raised the profile of his newspaper, and its circulation.

One interesting side note to the trip appeared at the end of an article in *The Sporting News* on December 6. Moe Berg had sent a letter to a friend in Newark, New Jersey, telling him he had "met many of his old friends and has taken a variety of pictures with his camera." Berg would later become a spy for the forerunner to the Central Intelligence Agency, and it has often been speculated that some of his shots of Tokyo Harbor, taken when he stole away to the top of the highest building in the city, may have been used by American intelligence during the war.[107]

Although his inability to play, and the presence of Babe Ruth, had shunted O'Doul to the background during the tour, he was far from disappointed. He was thrilled at the success of the event, and sure of its impact on the people he felt he had come to know, and that he felt had come to know him.

O'Doul joined Ruth and the remainder of the party for games in Shanghai and Manila before returning to Japan. The tour complete, some of the players headed home while others, including Ruth and Gehrig, set off for around-the-world excursions. O'Doul remained behind for several weeks, working with Sotaro Suzuki to form the genesis of Japanese professional baseball.

Eiji Sawamura, Osamu "Nosey" Mihara, and Shigeru Mizuhara signed on to the new endeavor. The team was originally christened the Dai Nippon Tokyo Yakyu Club, and O'Doul was named as an official advisor; during that first meeting on December 26, 1934, he was given two hundred shares of stock in the new team. He suggested to Suzuki that the name be shortened a bit to the "Tokyo Kyojin"—in English, the Tokyo Giants. Uniforms were designed that mimicked those worn by O'Doul's famous New York team, and plans were made for the Japanese professionals to visit the United States in February 1935 for a barnstorming tour. In mid-January, Lefty and Abbie O'Doul returned to the States.

But there were reminders of the dangerous conditions in Japan, and it became clear that the risks taken by those sponsoring Ruth and the American tour were not only financial. As the Japanese players were heading off to tour America, a man brandishing a samurai sword approached Matsutaro Shoriki on the street, at the entrance to the offices of *Yomiuri Shimbun*. He slashed Shoriki's head, leaving a six-inch gash that nearly resulted in the newspaper publisher's bleeding to death.

Shoriki's assailant claimed to have attacked him because the newspaper publisher had defiled Japan by bringing Ruth and the other professionals to the country. The truth was that Shoriki had been attacked by a thug from the ultra-nationalist War Gods Society who was an employee of *Tokyo Nichi Nichi*, a rival of *Yomiuri Shimbun* that had seen its circulation drop due to the increased popularity of Shoriki's paper. Concerned that Ruth's trip would further bolster *Yomiuri*'s success at the expense of *Nichi Nichi*, and convinced that Shoriki was the key to the paper's success, an assassin was sent to dispatch him.[108] The violence, and the publicly stated reasons for it, dashed the hopes of many Westerners that the 1934 tour had made a lasting impact on improving relations between Japan and the United States.

Ignorant of the political machinations in Japan, O'Doul remained enthusiastic about his efforts, and certain that baseball could serve as a bridge to better relations between America and Japan. He was equally certain that, with proper coaching, there would eventually be Japanese baseball players in the Major Leagues. The question for O'Doul was not if, but when. The answer would be three decades— and another three after that before Japanese players would begin making a serious and lasting impact on American soil.

Prior to leaving for Japan, there had been rumors that O'Doul would spend the 1935 season in San Francisco as manager of his hometown Seals. Those rumors only grew in intensity, even as Charlie Graham feigned ignorance about the prospect, swearing, "I have not been informed, nor do I know whatsoever anything about it."[109] When the Seals finally went public with their interest, Graham was quoted, "I wouldn't want to get O'Doul here unless he would be satisfied." Giants secretary James Tierney responded that O'Doul had been sent a contract to play for New York in 1935. When informed of Bill Terry's remark that the Giants were willing to let O'Doul go if the price was right, Tierney insisted he did not know what Terry meant by that.[110]

When O'Doul returned from Japan in January 1935, he told reporters, "I take it for granted I will be with the New York Giants, as had there been plans to the contrary, I am satisfied Terry would have made an announcement."[111] He added, "I don't think my major league playing days are over, and I'd like to get back under Bill Terry and help the Giants win that pennant. There's no getting around the fact New York is the team to beat in the National League."[112]

Under the rules of the time, no Major Leaguer with ten years or more of service time could be sold directly to the Minor Leagues—he had to be released. Since O'Doul had played eleven years in the big leagues, he fell into that category.[113]

In early February, the Giants sent O'Doul a contract for one dollar, to meet a deadline that otherwise would have made him a free agent. A furious O'Doul took that as a sure sign the Giants had intended to release him all along, only to pull back when they thought there was some money to be made. O'Doul wanted to return to San Francisco, but he also wanted the $4,000 demanded by the Giants for his contract. As requested, Commissioner Landis took up the matter, but he ruled in favor of the Giants.[114] Lefty did not receive a penny.

On the bright side, O'Doul was coming home one more time; he agreed to a three-year contract as player-manager for a San Francisco Seals team coming off back-to-back losing seasons for the first time in twenty years. When asked about the roster, O'Doul begged off, declaring, "I can't go into detail . . . as I don't know anything about it except what I have been told."

He went on to add, "It is the ballplayers that make the manager and not the manager that makes the ballplayers. Under McGraw, Huggins and Chance, I found out that their great success was in getting the work out of their players and in keeping them keyed to a high pitch. Toward that end I intend to bend all my energies. This is the big opportunity of my baseball life and I'm going to make the most of it."[115]

At the same time, he insisted on continuing as an active player. "I'm going to play as much as I can," he said. "But I'm not going to keep a better man on the bench in order to be in the lineup myself."[116]

Charlie Graham could not have made a more popular choice for manager. O'Doul was charismatic, a hometown hero, and a box office draw. And he still could hit. Lefty O'Doul was about to begin his fifth, and longest, stint with the San Francisco Seals. Graham also had an incredible young prospect recovering from a knee injury that he wanted to have tutored by baseball's foremost "scientific hitter."

8

Baseball's Greatest Hitting Instructor

During the 1949 trip, O'Doul met the young man to whom he had sent a baseball cap and an autographed baseball during the summer. Shigenobu Sadoya was ushered into O'Doul's room in the Gajoen Hotel as Lefty was greeting a stream of guests welcoming him back to Japan. Sadoya pulled out a letter O'Doul had written to him expressing his interest in meeting Sadoya when he came to Tokyo. They visited for a few minutes and had their photo taken together. As the teenager started to say goodbye, O'Doul said, "Wait a minute. I want to say a few words to Japanese boys. . . . They should get used to playing ball rather than trying to learn to play ball. If I should have a chance I should like to coach you Japanese boys." In fact, O'Doul was already coaching them by showing them how Americans played baseball—seriously and with teamwork.

The Seals easily won the tour's first game, shocking the Yomiuri Giants by scoring five runs in the first inning and pulling away to a 13–4 win—the Japanese players, having watched the Seals practice at half-speed during their first workout, had underestimated them. Afterward, the Japanese press criticized Giants manager Osamu Mihara, the same man who had knocked O'Doul out of the lineup during the 1931 tour.

While O'Doul used his ace pitcher, Con Dempsey, for the first game, Mihara decided against doing the same, instead using his third-best pitcher, Tokuji Kawasaki, because he thought his delivery would be more effective against San Francisco. However, the Japanese press argued O'Doul had shown respect toward Yomiuri by using his best, and by not doing so, Mihara had been less than honorable. Former Japanese pitching star Kyoichi Nitta, acting as a baseball critic for *Yomiuri Shimbun,* said that after he learned Kawasaki was to start, "I felt a certain amount of anxiety."[1] After the tour, Mihara was replaced as Yomiuri's manager by his coach, the revered Shigeru Mizuhara.

Yomiuri Shimbun convened a roundtable of Seals and Giants players, as well as members of the Japanese press, and O'Doul was asked, in light of his efforts to start the professional game in Japan, his impression of the host players. O'Doul responded, "Since my arrival I have been able to see with my own eyes that Japanese baseball has developed along sound lines, and I have been very pleased at this."[2]

O'Doul also noticed that the Japanese retained their insatiable desire to learn. During the tour there were repeated references in newspapers about players wanting O'Doul's opinions and advice in the light of Japanese baseball being cut off from the world over the previous decade. The language echoed that of the mid-1800s, when Japan had been forced into the modern world by Commodore Perry and, when recognizing their deficits, responded by hiring teachers and other professionals, including Horace Wilson, to help them progress.

Every game—indeed every movement—by the players was dissected and analyzed. *Yomiuri Shimbun* arranged on several occasions to have Japanese and American counterparts talk to each other, with the Japanese querying Americans about their technique, and for advice that would lead to improvement in their play.

Near the end of the tour, the newspaper had Japan's best at catcher, second base, and the outfield interview their opposite numbers on the Seals, with the discussion transcribed for the edification of Japanese baseball fans and titled *The Essence of American Baseball.* In it, the editors at *Yomiuri Shimbun* stressed, "It is our firm belief that the visit of the San Francisco Seals will contribute greatly to the improvement of baseball in the future in Japan."[3]

The Japanese asked about American training regimen, techniques for catching and throwing, and proper strategy in various situations. They also went over batting stances and asked about their weaknesses as players. The result was surprisingly candid and very informative.

Joe Sprinz, coaching for the Seals, was impressed by the level of play on the part of the Japanese and their willingness to accept criticism. Sprinz noted they fielded well, but he felt they were lacking in other areas. "What they need is instruction in hitting," he said. "Somebody to work with them for about a year. It doesn't take them long to catch on."[4]

• • •

When Lefty O'Doul rejoined the San Francisco Seals in 1935, he was already considered one of the great teachers of hitting. Although he would serve as a manager for the next two decades plus, his greatest impact would be as an instructor—a combined hitting theorist and amateur psychologist of sorts who helped develop and inspire a number of great baseball players along the way.

Charlie Graham had O'Doul's first prize pupil ready; the young man's name was Joe DiMaggio, and he hailed from San Francisco's North Beach. A generation earlier he would have been one of the neighborhood kids O'Doul and his mates considered mortal enemies—the Irish versus the Italians.

Joe DiMaggio was quite a baseball player. A natural. He had actually abandoned baseball in his teens, favoring tennis, basketball, and touch football, but had resumed using a bat and ball after his older brother, Vince, signed as an outfielder with the San Francisco Seals.[5] He first joined the Seals during the final weekend of the 1932 season, a seventeen-year-old shortstop dragged to Seals Stadium by Vince when the Seals' regular at the position—future National League All-Star Augie Galan—received permission to go home a few days early. However, by the spring of 1933, it was clear that Joe DiMaggio was no shortstop.

Seals manager Jake Caveney moved Joe to the outfield, costing his brother Vince a job; Vince subsequently signed with the Pacific Coast League (PCL) team in Hollywood. Eighteen-year-old Joe then spent the summer of 1933 compiling an amazing record, highlighted by a sixty-one-game hitting streak that instantly made him the most sought after prospect in baseball. DiMaggio was stoic, rarely speaking, and just as rarely betraying emotion; during his epic streak, he had earned the moniker "Deadpan Joe." But his quiet nature did not reflect a lack of confidence.

With Charlie Graham financially dependent on the fortunes of his baseball team—and on a strong seller's market for players he signed and developed—the temptation was great to auction DiMaggio immediately to reap the benefits. At the same time, Graham knew that another season in the PCL would likely increase the young star's value, so he decided to gamble and hold onto the teenage sensation. It appeared the gamble was lost when DiMaggio injured his knee during the 1934 season, missing two months. Amid concerns that he had not fully recovered, interest from Major League teams waned.

However, New York Yankees scout Bill Essick kept tabs on DiMaggio through his West Coast bird dog, Joe Devine, who assured Essick that DiMaggio's knee had healed. Essick in turn convinced the Yankees to acquire the young outfielder, on the condition that DiMaggio remain with San Francisco in 1935. New York sent two players to the Seals immediately and promised three more if DiMaggio proved as healthy as Essick said he was.[6]

Lefty O'Doul and Joe DiMaggio could not have been more different in terms of personality, but Joe was similar to Lefty in one important way—his approach at the plate involved remaining nearly motionless in the batter's box, and taking a very short, quick stride when he swung. DiMaggio also exhibited superior defensive skills, impressing O'Doul by throwing out two runners at home plate from deep right field in a game against Portland in May.[7]

Because he was a new manager recently arrived from the Major Leagues, local sportswriters were soon seeking O'Doul's opinion of the Seals' best player. They asked him to compare DiMaggio to former Seals outfielder Paul Waner, who had become a star with the Pittsburgh Pirates, capturing two National League batting titles and carrying a lifetime average of .348 through his first nine seasons. "DiMaggio I believe," declared O'Doul, "is faster than Waner, a more polished outfielder, certainly a greater thrower and without question a better flyhawk. He may not hit any harder, or any oftener than Waner, but it's my guess he'll go just as far, if not farther."[8]

Lefty took DiMaggio under his wing, dispensing hitting advice the future Hall of Famer would consider the best he ever received—whenever he struggled, he would recall O'Doul's instruction. "Keep your left toe pointed toward the pitcher," O'Doul lectured, "and lay off the bad balls."[9] That oversimplifies what O'Doul was telling DiMaggio—in baseball shorthand he was explaining how Joe could best utilize his impressive power while hitting to all fields. O'Doul knew that was the right amount of advice to impart—with his talent DiMaggio would do the rest; O'Doul's number one job was to get the most out of the now twenty-year-old, and prepare him for big league life. In August, at the request of the Yankees, the Seals switched DiMaggio to center field, the position New York expected him to play for them. He, of course, excelled.

DiMaggio powered the Seals to the 1935 pennant with an incredible season that included thirty-four home runs among his one hundred extra-base hits, and a .398 batting average; the numbers were especially impressive considering that he played more than half of his games in pitcher-friendly Seals Stadium, which had replaced rickety bandbox Recreation Park in 1931. There was little question about Joe DiMaggio's inevitable march to stardom—he joined the Yankees in 1936 and became one of the greatest outfielders in baseball history, as well as an American icon.

O'Doul was eager to let New York baseball fans know the treat they were in for, insisting that DiMaggio was as good as any player ever to come out of the PCL. "Barring injuries," said Lefty, "he will be voted the Most Valuable Player in the American League in three years."[10]

Ted Williams was a junior at San Diego's Herbert Hoover High School in the spring of 1936. It was an exciting time—the city was booming, welcoming the world to Balboa Park for the California-Pacific International Exposition. Numerous attractions were added to the famous venue in the city's center, including the Starlight

Bowl—where outdoor events are still held today—and the Old Globe Theatre, an homage to William Shakespeare's original theatrical facility several thousand miles to the east; it too remains an important San Diego landmark, even after having to be rebuilt following its destruction by an arsonist in 1978.

San Diego had also become home to a new baseball team, the Padres, which were members of the PCL. The franchise had moved so quickly from Hollywood over the winter that owner Bill Lane almost literally threw together a ballpark on the site of a motorcycle race track at Broadway and Harbor Boulevard; a shortage of new uniforms resulted in the team's first official photograph including a smattering of Hollywood jerseys.

The city of San Diego, which had long coveted membership in the PCL, was thrilled to have the Padres there. Among those most excited was Williams, who made his way to the team's new home, Lane Field, a few days before Easter Sunday in 1936, not to attend the game between the Padres and the San Francisco Seals—he had no money for a ticket—but rather for a chance to soak up the atmosphere and maybe peek through the fence for a glimpse of some honest-to-goodness professional ballplayers.

There was indeed an empty knothole, and Williams wasted no time. The first player he glimpsed was a left-handed hitter, same as he was, taking batting practice. "I was looking through the knothole," he remembered, "and I said, 'Geez, does that guy look good!' And it was Lefty O'Doul, one of the greatest hitters ever. The swing was fluid, compact. The man's head never moved and his stride was almost non-existent. The whack of his bat was true and indicated a cleanly hit ball, every time. A kid copies what he sees is good. And if he's never seen it, he'll never know."[11]

Within two months, Ted Williams would be playing in the PCL himself, a prodigy soon to be ranked among the greatest hitters of all time. Not long after joining the Padres, the not quite eighteen-year-old Williams was struggling a bit. When the Seals visited San Diego, he approached O'Doul for some advice. After watching his swing and assuring the youngster that he had nothing to worry about, O'Doul looked Williams in the eye and said, "No matter what manager or coach tries to change your stance, don't listen to them."[12] Williams would always think highly of O'Doul; in 1941 he would use a Lefty O'Doul model bat, manufactured by Hillerich & Bradsby, as he became the last Major Leaguer to hit .400 in a season.[13]

O'Doul lobbied Charlie Graham to acquire the youngster, but San Diego owner Bill Lane knew what he had and was not interested.[14] "Williams has drawn more praise from O'Doul than any other manager in the Pacific Coast League," wrote San Diego sports columnist Earl Keller, who said O'Doul told him, "That kid is the best prospect this circuit has seen since Joe DiMaggio. He has the makings of a great player and, if he is handled right, he will go places. I would like to be his teacher."[15]

Following his first Major League season in 1939, Williams was asked about the source of his picture-perfect swing. "I've always had it," replied Williams. "Lefty O'Doul told me to never change it. That is good enough for me. No one will ever change it and if anything ever goes wrong with it, I'll go back to Lefty and get it straightened out."[16]

Before Lefty O'Doul came along, it was widely assumed that hitting was instinctive—although one might improve with experience, batters had to hit their own way; they could not be taught. Peter Morris, in his excellent book *A Game of Inches*, pointed to Charles Ebbets as hiring the original scientific hitter, Willie Keeler, to spend spring training with Brooklyn in 1913, making him the first documented case of an individual hired to teach hitting at the big league level.[17] Certainly others taught informally on occasion— Rogers Hornsby regularly dispensed hitting advice, and Ty Cobb of course had helped Lefty O'Doul back in 1928.

Although professionals were hired as hitting coaches for colleges in the 1800s, it would not be until the 1950s that full-time hitting instructors began appearing regularly at the Major League level.

Cobb, for one, thought such coaching valuable. In 1917 he told *Baseball Magazine*, "I believe that it would pay every major league club to have a man do nothing but coach batters. A fellow gets into a slump for no reason that he can see. But a trained man who knows batting could see the reason, and coach a batter out of his slump."[18]

O'Doul became the next "scientific hitter," and he began to produce results with his instruction. It was revolutionary. In 1948 the Hillerich & Bradsby Company, maker of Louisville Slugger baseball bats, asked O'Doul to write a feature on hitting for their *Famous Slugger Yearbook*. Titled "How to Bat," O'Doul's article began with an illustration.

"The best way I can describe hitting," wrote O'Doul, "is to say that it is like swinging an ax at a tree. A man who takes an ax and swings at a tree does so naturally because he has no worries about the tree doing anything to him. He is certain he is going to hit the tree, and whether he knows it or not, he could replace the ax with a bat and have a sound baseball swing.

"Most hitting faults come from uncertainty, lack of knowledge, and fear. Lack of knowledge can be removed as an obstacle to good hitting by simple teaching. Fear can only be conquered by a batter gaining confidence in himself."

O'Doul continued for six more pages, discussing the importance of holding the bat at the proper angle and keeping the head still. He cited Babe Ruth as someone who held his bat vertically before going into his swing, making him an outstanding low ball hitter. He used Tris Speaker as an example of a batter whose strength was hitting the high pitch—he held his bat horizontally, almost parallel to the ground, peeking over his elbow at the pitcher. "Joe DiMaggio," wrote O'Doul, "carries his bat in a position I call the happy medium between the vertical and the horizontal. The angle of the bat in his hands is such that he can swing as easily and swiftly at a low pitch as at a high one."

But O'Doul's overriding mantra was keeping the head still. O'Doul wrote that in observing the hitters he deemed the greatest—Ruth, Speaker, DiMaggio, Ty Cobb, Harry Heilmann, and Ted Williams—they had in common keeping their head still through their swing.

"A man who knows the secret of keeping his head in one position will not stride too far. He will keep his back foot anchored securely to the ground. His hips will move out of the way so that the bat can come around. He will not dip his hips or his body[;] . . . he will hit the ball out in front and he will hit it hard and full."

O'Doul cautioned against what he called a common fault—dipping the body while swinging, brought about by bending the knees. This, he said, causes batters to pull back their hips and "wave at the ball as it goes by." O'Doul also noted that some batters slide forward, dragging the bat behind them on their swing. This, he said, results in locking the hips, which in turn locks the arms. Thinking a long stride generates power, these hitters are instead dissipating it.

"At the point of contact of bat and ball, the wrists will un-cock as the ball is hit," he wrote. "This is the last action and gives the bat its final speed. Both arms will be straight and reaching as far as they comfortably can to provide a wide arc which increases power. This is where Ted Williams, I think, gets his power—from the wide spread of his arc."

O'Doul also reflected on the mental aspect of hitting, and the importance of picking out a good bat—thirty-four inches long and thirty-five to thirty-six ounces was his recommendation. He concluded the piece by dispensing another bedrock of his hitting theory.

"Good hitters don't swing at bad pitches, balls over their heads, or too wide or low. They make the pitcher come into the strike zone and that's the way you want to stand, so that your bat covers the vital strike zone.

"The good hitter will always look for the fast ball. If he's ready to hit the fast ball, he can adjust his timing for the slower curve and change of pace. But if he's looking for the curve, the fast ball will be thrown by him."[19]

After the sale of Joe DiMaggio, the San Francisco Seals struggled to develop talent due to the financial limitations of Charlie Graham and his partners. The Seals did possess one holdover of value, Joe Marty, who was moved back to center field in 1936. The twenty-two-year-old Marty was quiet, like DiMaggio, but not as shy. He surprised people with his poise in front of a microphone, and impressed many as being a potential emcee or radio broadcaster. He had initially joined the Seals in 1934, taking up some of the slack when DiMaggio was injured that year. In 1935 he had a solid season, stroking twenty-nine doubles and sixteen triples while batting .287.

But there was always the impression that he was capable of more. Marty had a reputation for laziness. Lilio Marcucci, who served as a Seals clubhouse boy in the mid-1930s and later played for the rival Sacramento Solons, did not think Joe Marty really wanted to play baseball. "When he was on the American Legion team and semi-pro clubs in Sacramento," said Marcucci, "they'd have to go pick him up at his house each morning just to make sure he'd come out and play."[20] Sacramento owner Lew Moreing had decided against signing the youngster after he saw him plop down under a shade tree between innings rather than come in all the way to the bench.[21]

Marty showed a greater interest in playing football, and he had enrolled at St. Mary's College in Moraga with the intention of doing so. But Charlie Graham's partner, George Putnam, recognized that Marty possessed the tools to become a successful Major Leaguer—speed, power generated from strong wrists, and a good throwing arm. Putnam convinced Marty that baseball was his ticket.

O'Doul made a special project of Joe Marty in 1936, recognizing that the young center fielder was not one to be prodded—he did not respond well to direct criticism, tending to mope when he was not hitting well. He had to be encouraged, constantly.[22] O'Doul assured Marty that he had talent, and that he needed to have confidence in that talent and be patient at the plate, waiting for the pitcher to put the ball in his spot. Then, swing hard without hesitation.

O'Doul showed Marty film he had taken of himself in the Major Leagues to assist the young outfielder in correcting the flaws in his swing.[23] He tutored him in bunting, pointing out that with his speed, he could take advantage when the third baseman played deep. O'Doul explained that following a few successful bunts, the infield would creep in, creating the perfect opportunity for Marty to swing away. Marty's timing at the plate was impeccable—despite being a right-handed hitter, he could smash line shots down the first base line. Sam Crawford, the former Detroit Tigers star umpiring in the PCL at the time, was impressed by what he saw.[24] So was

the PCL's top umpire, Jack Powell, who insisted Marty was as good
as DiMaggio was in his third year.[25]

Marty took to O'Doul's lessons—after the first thirty-five games
of the 1936 season, he was hitting .442. O'Doul continued gently
pushing the young outfielder, insisting he was "utilizing only seventy percent of his ability" while at the same time declaring, "Marty
is potentially as great, or greater, than Joe DiMaggio."[26]

Marty's misfortune was following Joe DiMaggio to the Major
Leagues—comparisons, however unfair, were inevitable. But those
comparisons worked to the advantage of the Seals; Charlie Graham needed a big sale to boost Seals finances after DiMaggio's
knee injury had substantially lessened the amount that the Seals
would have otherwise realized from the Yankees. Certainly DiMaggio's incredible rookie season in New York—88 extra-base hits,
125 runs batted in, and a .323 batting average—did not hurt Marty's market value.

Marty won the PCL batting title in 1936 with a .359 average and
was sold to the Chicago Cubs after the season.[27] Graham would
often credit the sale of Joe Marty—and O'Doul's coaching of him
that increased his value—as saving the Seals franchise from bankruptcy. For his part, Marty would hit .290 as a rookie for the Chicago Cubs and bat .500 with five runs batted in during the 1938
World Series, including a home run off the Yankees' Monte Pear-
son. But alcohol and an inability to rein in his temper would ham-
per Marty's big league career, and he was back in the PCL to stay
after the war. He was, like so many of his generation, a ballplayer
whose career was unalterably impacted by extended military service. But raised expectations have also proven the ruin of many a
player, and that might have been the case for Joe Marty. He was
not—and never would have been—another Joe DiMaggio. Unfortunately, that was how he was measured.

As Ty Cobb had, O'Doul eagerly provided baseball counsel to both
his own players and opponents who came to him for help. Bobby
Doerr, who had joined the Hollywood Sheiks as a sixteen-year-
old second baseman in 1934, before they moved to San Diego to

become the Padres, always remembered O'Doul's generosity in dispensing advice.

"We used to go to Lefty and ask him things," remembered Doerr. "They didn't have hitting coaches or anything. You just had to go around and ask questions. You worked out all your own problems.

"I was having a little trouble with dipping [my bat] under balls. I wasn't pivoting my hips. I remember [O'Doul] telling me, 'Just think of your head, your shoulders, and your hips being these three spools and that they are turning rather than dipping.' That made a big impression on me. I worked at that to get a more level swing."[28]

Other managers sent players to work with O'Doul—during spring training in 1942, Connie Mack had a young, gangly, six-foot-four-inch shortstop named Jack Wallaesa he wanted to convert into a switch hitter. Babe Ruth had been impressed with the twenty-two-year-old, briefly taking him aside to dispense some batting tips, as had O'Doul.[29] After observing Wallaesa, the wheels started turning in O'Doul's head. He begged Mack to let him have the infielder for a year, telling the venerable manager he would turn him into another Ted Williams.[30]

Mack refused the offer, but he did allow the shortstop to work with O'Doul for a few hours. O'Doul tied a rope to Wallaesa's chest and anchored his feet. He had him hold his elbows high, learn the strike zone, and swing through the ball while keeping his bat on an even plane.

When Wallaesa returned to Philadelphia, he began getting results. Each night he would look in the mirror and practice his swing, chanting over and over, "O'Doul . . . O'Doul."

"At first I thought he was a little screwy," remarked Dee Miles, Wallaesa's unfortunate Philadelphia Athletics roommate. "Then I recalled he was concentrating on his hitting and using the name O'Doul to keep him doing the right thing."[31]

Six weeks into the 1942 season, Wallaesa was hitting .300 and appeared to be Mack's shortstop of the future. However, a couple of weeks later he received a call from his draft board and chose to enlist in the army.[32] Wallaesa was out of baseball for nearly four years—and unlike many other professional ballplayers, he did not

play at all during his final three years in the service. By the time
he returned in 1946, he had lost whatever edge he had. Wallaesa
enjoyed several solid Minor League seasons, but never again topped
.200 in the Majors.

After Joe Marty was sold to the Cubs, he was replaced in center field
by a brand-new face with an old, familiar name. Dominic DiMaggio was a slight, frail-looking twenty-year-old who wore glasses and
weighed less than 160 pounds. This DiMaggio's physique was nothing like that of his brothers.

The legendary Spike Hennessy, who had coached baseball on
the San Francisco sandlots for decades and touched the careers of
almost every player to come out of the city during that time, repeatedly urged O'Doul to take a good look at Dominic.[33]

DiMaggio was finally given a chance during an open tryout at
Seals Stadium, held jointly by the San Francisco Seals and the Cincinnati Reds. He may have been small, but O'Doul immediately
recognized the possibilities in Dominic. Hennessy had been correct, and O'Doul made sure the Seals signed him right away. There
was one stipulation—the youngest of the DiMaggio brothers could
not be farmed out. "They worried that if I was sent to a Seals farm
club in a hot climate, they might have to sop me up with a sponge,"
DiMaggio remembered.[34] A special ceremony was held for Dominic's signing, which included his being carted into Seals Stadium
in a wheelbarrow pushed by his brother Joe.[35]

O'Doul set to work on eliminating a bad habit DiMaggio had
developed on the San Francisco sandlots. "I used to lunge," Dominic recalled more than fifty years later. "My body would go forward
into the ball. I thought I would get more power that way. It was
wrong. I had to keep my body back."[36] O'Doul decided to convert
Dominic into a pull hitter, which would make him more attractive
to big league scouts; DiMaggio later changed that approach when
he went to Boston and realized that his line drive stroke was not a
good match for the Green Monster.

There was skepticism about this youngster going straight from
the sandlots to the fastest Minor League in the country. Some of

those skeptics whispered none too quietly that Charlie Graham was merely cashing in on a popular San Francisco name.

O'Doul broke Dominic in slowly, but the kid began making a case for himself a couple of weeks into his career when he threw out two Seattle runners attempting to stretch singles into doubles.[37] Barely out of his teens, DiMaggio played 140 games in 1937 and batted .306. He improved his batting average by one point the next year while playing in twenty-three more contests. Despite his success, there were many continuing to doubt that the small, bespectacled outfielder was Major League caliber. But O'Doul knew.

DiMaggio added nine pounds to his frame for the 1939 season and began pounding the ball with authority. He increased his slugging average 130 points and his batting average by more than 50. In May, the Yankees were said to be interested in having Dominic join his brother in their outfield.[38] A month later the Chicago Cubs sent their chief scout to look him over.[39] In July, the New York Giants made a serious pitch, but only on the condition that he join them immediately. Charlie Graham, with his team in contention for the PCL pennant, turned them down.[40]

O'Doul would often say that Dominic DiMaggio's 1939 season ranked among the finest years any ballplayer ever had at any level. He was named the PCL's Most Valuable Player, and the Boston Red Sox acquired him.[41] O'Doul was effusive in his praise, telling Jack Malaney of the Boston Post, "The fans of Boston will love that kid by the Fourth of July. He may not have Joe's power, but he can do everything he can do . . . except hit for high average and distance. Yes sir, they'll love that kid up there in Boston."[42]

Asked about his brother during spring training in 1940, Joe DiMaggio volunteered, "I haven't seen much of him myself, but I'll take Lefty O'Doul's word for it. Lefty said to me, 'Joe, I don't like to say it to your face, but he is a better fielder than you are.'" Grinning as he finished buttoning his shirt, DiMaggio added, "I'll wait and see for myself. He'll have to prove it to me."[43]

Dominic DiMaggio would fashion a long and successful career, appearing in seven All-Star games for the American League. And he would always credit Lefty O'Doul for helping make him successful. "He was, very definitely, the one person who helped me to be the hitter that I was," recalled DiMaggio. "[He was] an outstanding teacher, especially as a batting instructor. He was the best, as far as I was concerned, in the history of the game."[44]

In November 1939 Lefty O'Doul attended one of the events of the season in San Francisco—surpassed perhaps only by the World's Fair, held that year at Treasure Island. It was the wedding of Joe DiMaggio and Dorothy Arnold, an actress two days shy of her twenty-second birthday. The pair had met two years earlier in New York on the set of a film, *Manhattan Merry Go Round*, in which both had minor roles.

The ceremony took place at Saints Peter and Paul Catholic Church on Filbert Street, in North Beach across from Washington Square, into which the overflow crowd, well, overflowed. It was said that the wedding marked the first time the church had motion picture cameras trained on it since being utilized as a location for a scene in the silent film *The Ten Commandments* while under construction nearly twenty years earlier. The crush was such that it took the wedding party nearly fifteen minutes to navigate the crowd and enter the building; Joe's brother Vince was accidentally locked out, eventually gaining entry only by squeezing through a side entrance. Plainclothes policemen served as ushers—and to maintain order, as much as they could.

Afterward, Lefty O'Doul joined hundreds of others at the reception, held at DiMaggio's Grotto on Fisherman's Wharf. There was a three-foot-tall wedding cake and a three-piece band playing swing music, mostly Italian, including the ever-popular "Funiculi Funicula."[45]

During the reception, O'Doul was approached by another guest, New York Yankees first baseman Babe Dahlgren, a San Francisco native who had taken over for Lou Gehrig when the famous star was diagnosed with his ultimately fatal disease. Dahlgren had played well under the circumstances, drawing raves for his defense while driving in eighty-nine runs. He also hit a home run off Cincinnati's Bucky Walters in the second game of the World Series. But Dahlgren had batted a disappointing .235 and asked O'Doul for assistance, especially in eliminating his habit of committing to pitches a tick too early, which caused him to swing at too many bad offerings. O'Doul assured Dahlgren he'd be only too happy to help.[46]

Thus unfolded what remains to this day one of the more controversial incidents of O'Doul's career. He and Dahlgren were originally to work together over a week's time, but circumstances reduced that to a single day in mid-February, at Boyes Hot Springs, where San Francisco Seals pitchers and catchers had reported to spring training.[47]

Although O'Doul enjoyed helping other players, according to Dahlgren this would be one time that O'Doul's help backfired— the Yankees' manager was Joe McCarthy, and Dahlgren claimed that he unwittingly reignited the old feud between the two men that dated back to the spring of 1926, and O'Doul's revenge against the Cubs in September 1930.

While the Yankees had publicly declared they were fine with Dahlgren being tutored by O'Doul, years later Dahlgren insisted that he and O'Doul had barely worked together, and that he had not received any useful advice from the former big league star. "I went up to Boyes Springs," said Dahlgren, "and he looked at me swing a few times. [He said] he couldn't find anything wrong."[48]

But during spring training in March 1940—a week after meeting with O'Doul—Dahlgren told James Kahn of the *New York Sun* that while he had only worked with O'Doul for one day, he had come away with a "head full of ideas" he planned to try. "Of course, I know what my main fault is," Dahlgren told Kahn. "Joe McCarthy has told me dozens of times, and so have many of the other fellows. I hit at too many bad balls. I'm too eager, that's what. If I can lay back and wait, with my bat high, as O'Doul taught me, and not step into the ball, I think I ought to hit better."[49]

Dahlgren reported to spring training with the Yankees and was stinging the ball to all fields.[50] "McCarthy called me over," remembered Dahlgren, "I thought to pat me on the back. Instead he asked if I was doing anything different at the plate. I said, 'No.'"

Dahlgren's grandson, Matt, wrote a book about the incident, *Rumor in Town*, that in part draws on a unpublished manuscript penned by his grandfather. In it, Babe Dahlgren says that he learned

O'Doul had been chiding McCarthy in baseball circles for having to send his players, such as Dahlgren, to him in order to learn how to hit.[51]

In reviewing spring training coverage, it appears Dahlgren was doing *something* different at the plate—whether that was due to O'Doul's influence was never clear. Not that O'Doul was failing to take credit—in a *New York Times* article on February 27, 1940, it was reported that Dahlgren was working with O'Doul, who was helping him spray the ball around more by eliminating a lunge.[52] It is not a big leap in judgment to infer the source of that information regarding Dahlgren's improvement being O'Doul himself. When Dahlgren reported to spring training with the Yankees and worked out for the first time, it was noted by reporter James P. Dawson that he had "changed his stance at the plate."[53]

At the same time, McCarthy was having Tommy Henrich work out at second base despite his being a left-handed thrower; the strange explanation had it related to Henrich's being insurance at first base in case Dahlgren didn't hit.[54] It would not be a stretch to believe that McCarthy may have resented the article published ten days earlier about O'Doul working with Dahlgren.

Dahlgren ultimately appeared in every game for the Yankees in 1940 and improved his batting average by nearly thirty points. When Dahlgren made an error in a key game late in the 1940 season that McCarthy felt had cost New York a pennant, McCarthy told reporters that Dahlgren's arms were too short to effectively play first base. Dahlgren asserted that McCarthy also told reporters that the first baseman was a marijuana smoker—a shocking charge that in those days ruined careers; Dahlgren vehemently denied the accusation about marijuana use for the rest of his life, insisting that he had asked for and passed a drug test in 1943 in an attempt to clear his name.[55] He would spend the remainder of his days convinced he had landed on a blacklist of sorts.

Dahlgren was traded away by the Yankees after the 1940 season and bounced around the Majors for a few years before Branch Rickey learned of McCarthy's accusation and made it common knowledge within baseball circles.

"Unfortunately," wrote Dahlgren in a letter some fifty years later, "I was hurt by Lefty when he 'used' me to get at Joe McCarthy."[56]

Whatever happened, it is undeniable that McCarthy spewed venom toward Dahlgren following his departure from the Yankees. In June, after trading him to the Boston Braves, McCarthy suddenly delivered an unsolicited soliloquy about his former first baseman, telling reporters who had questioned McCarthy's personnel decision, "I don't see any more headlines about Dahlgren breaking up a ball game. What's the matter? Isn't he playing? I looked in the box score the other day and he wasn't there. What's he hitting, around .220, eh?"[57]

Had O'Doul disparaged McCarthy, and the news got back to the Yankees manager? Was McCarthy upset by Dahlgren's admitting to the press that McCarthy had given him the same advice as O'Doul, but that he had not heeded that advice until it came from Lefty?

This much is certain. Old rivalries die hard. Sometimes they never die. And sometimes they create collateral damage.

In 1942 Lefty O'Doul was assigned another high-profile batting pupil—Academy Award–winning actor Gary Cooper, who was to play the role of Lou Gehrig in the biopic *Pride of the Yankees*. Sam Goldwyn had hired O'Doul for $6,000 to serve as the film's technical advisor, specifically to work with the actor.[58] Cooper had previously played the role of a pitcher in the film *Meet John Doe*, and the consensus was that he would need to be a lot more convincing in order to impersonate Lou Gehrig. So O'Doul was brought in. The task was monumental—not only had Cooper never played baseball, but he was also right-handed.

The actor swung a bat until he ached all over. "[O'Doul] even made me go down to the Venice amusement pier last night," moaned Cooper, "and spend the whole evening in one of those automatic ball pitching booths."[59]

That March, Yankees great Bill Dickey, who appeared in a few of the film's scenes, remarked that Cooper reminded him of Gehrig, especially in his mannerisms. "Lefty O'Doul spent two weeks before the shooting started showing Cooper how to hit and throw," said Dickey. "They must've worked like dogs, because Cooper really swings the bat as if he knows what he's doing."[60]

Dickey did allow that there were not a lot of baseball scenes, which helped disguise Cooper's lack of athletic ability. While Cooper performed in the close-ups, Babe Herman handled the long shots of Gehrig. (Over the years there were rumors that Cooper never learned to hit left-handed, so the images were reversed, with Cooper wearing mirror-image letters on his uniform—even Cooper lent his name to the speculation at one point. But research by film and photograph analyst Tom Shieber has convincingly laid that theory to rest. Other than in a few frames, it is almost certain that the scenes involving Cooper were shot with him performing as a lefty.)[61]

As a thank-you to O'Doul for his work with Cooper, a character in the film—a policeman—was named in his honor. After filming was completed, Cooper presented O'Doul with a photograph. It was inscribed, "To a great guy who put up with a lot trying to teach me to hit."[62]

O'Doul did not limit himself to instructing only men. One of his more interesting projects was Alice Tognotti, who was attempting to sign with the All-American Girls Professional Baseball League. Tognotti had gained O'Doul's attention as a teenager while managing a youth team called the Baby Seals, which featured children of San Francisco Seals players Gus Suhr, Tony Lazzeri, and Del Young.[63]

She worked out with O'Doul and the Seals during the spring of 1946 before being selected as an outfielder by the Fort Wayne Daisies, where she played under manager Bill Wambsganss, the only man to turn an unassisted triple play in a World Series game (for the Cleveland Indians in 1920).[64]

Unfortunately, Tognotti batted only .067 in twenty-one games for Fort Wayne, and her professional career ended at age nineteen. Three years later, she was named manager of the first souvenir shop at Seals Stadium, an innovation introduced by Seals owner Paul Fagan.[65]

O'Doul did seem to have a growing obsession with teaching players to become pull hitters—and one player who claimed to be less than enamored with that approach, at least later in his life, was Ferris Fain. O'Doul worked during the 1940 season to teach Fain to be a pull hitter, but the nineteen-year-old had a tough time of it, hitting only .238. In 2001 Fain told author Brent Kelley, "O'Doul had a theory that the scouts loved to see pull hitters and just worked on me all the time . . . and that just was not my type of hitting."[66]

Fain felt that O'Doul was attempting to enhance player values to assist Charlie Graham and the Seals, who were struggling to remain in business, relying on the sale of young talent to keep going. Fain told Kelley that in 1941, when O'Doul was sidelined for several weeks, coaches Larry Woodall and Tony Lazzeri told him to forget about what O'Doul was saying and just hit to all fields; Fain responded with a .310 batting average that season. But Fain was urged by O'Doul to return to pulling the ball the next year, and the results were awful—his batting average plummeting more than ninety points.

O'Doul used his old rope trick on Fain to keep him from lunging, yanking him off his feet as he sputtered, "Stop it! Stop it! Ye gods, what swinging! The only thing wrong with your stance is your heart is in the right place, but your keister is three blocks away."[67] Fain told Brent Kelley, "I can remember him standing back of the batting cage with a rope tied to my belt, and when I started to go forward with my body I ended up in the back of that batting cage."[68]

Fain entered the military after the 1942 season and did not return until the conclusion of the war. At that point, O'Doul—perhaps no longer pressured by Seals management since the franchise was setting Minor League attendance records and infused with money thanks to new partner Paul Fagan—welcomed back Fain and stopped insisting that he constantly pull the ball. Fain responded with his greatest season for the Seals in 1946, driving in 112 runs and batting .301. Drafted after the season by the Philadelphia Athletics, Fain went on to win two American League batting titles, play in five All-Star games, and retire as one of the greatest-fielding first basemen in Major League history.[69]

Despite his later stated disagreements with O'Doul, at the time Fain was quoted as saying that he lunged at everything until O'Doul pulled out the rope trick.[70] And in 2001 he told Brent Kelley that he idolized Lefty and considered him the best manager he ever played for. "You couldn't help but love him," he told Kelley.[71]

Once in a while, an unorthodox hitter would come along and O'Doul would leave him alone. One such player was Joe Brovia, who had first arrived in Seals training camp in 1940 as a pitcher. Once O'Doul saw Brovia swing a bat, he told him to toss aside the toe plate and get into the outfield. Farmed out to the Arizona-Texas League that April, Brovia hit .383 for El Paso, and followed that up with a .318 average the next year as a nineteen-year-old reserve outfielder for the Seals. The war then cost him the better part of four years.

Anyone who ever saw Joe Brovia play never forgot it. He wore his cap low over his forehead and peered menacingly at the pitcher. Standing in the left-hand batter's box, he held his hands at his belt and the bat straight up, grinding the handle in his hands—Brovia looked like he would never be able to get around on a fastball, but he feasted on them. And he could feast on other pitches as well. In 1948 he sent a curve ball thrown by Bob Feller during an exhibition game back through the box and narrowly missed hitting the pitching great in the head; afterward Brovia reenacted the plate appearance for reporters and boasted, "Did ya see that line drive I strung back at Feller, the bum? Ooof what a poke."[72]

Brovia played with a rage—he claimed to hate pitchers, especially left-handers—and was a fanatic about hitting. Not so much about fielding. Teammate Larry Jansen recalled that Brovia would frequently sneak into the batter's box for extra practice; when O'Doul would spy him from Charlie Graham's office, he would open the window and yell out, "Brovia! We all know you can hit—get out into the outfield!"[73]

Although O'Doul did not tinker with Brovia's technique, he did impart advice the left-handed slugger took to heart—keep the head still, keep your stride short, and look for the fastball. "I took his advice and had good success hitting," said Brovia.[74]

After returning from the war, it took Brovia a year to regain his batting eye before making it back to the Seals to stay in 1947. He was patient at the plate, also heeding O'Doul's advice to wait for a good pitch to hit. His oddball stance made him susceptible to fouling balls off his instep, but he was surprisingly tough to strike out. Brovia batted .309 in 1947, following that the next year with a .322 average. With his distinctive style and aggressiveness at the plate, Joe Brovia became, with the exception of O'Doul, the most popular member of the Seals in the eyes of their fans.

O'Doul also assisted several other excellent career Minor League hitters, such as Brooks Holder, Ted Jennings, Neill Sheridan, and Ray Perry. He rejuvenated the career of George "Catfish" Metkovich, after he had bounced around the Minors for four seasons.[75] Froilan "Nanny" Fernandez, a hard-hitting shortstop who fell into the Seals' lap in 1941 after injuries had opened up a slot, said of O'Doul, "Lefty's a great psychologist. He never said a word to any of the boys when they were going well, but always volunteered helpful advice when they were in a slump. All of us profited from his common sense suggestions."[76]

Dino Restelli, who had grown up across the street from the DiMaggio family, had a pretty swing that O'Doul had filmed as an example to other hitters.[77] Restelli, who briefly took the National League by storm during the summer of 1949 as a member of the Pittsburgh Pirates, told reporters that O'Doul had taught him two things—concentration and determination.[78]

One of O'Doul's greatest successes came in 1948 when Gene Woodling joined the Seals. The twenty-five-year-old had been found wanting by the Cleveland Indians and Pittsburgh Pirates, for whom, as Woodling put it, he consistently hit "the prettiest 400-foot outs in baseball."[79]

Woodling had already won three Minor League batting titles, but that was not translating into success at the Major League level. After watching Woodling for a few days, O'Doul approached him. "I take it you do not want to spend the rest of your career in the Pacific Coast League. You want to get back to the majors. Well, they don't want singles hitters up there. An outfielder, especially a left-handed batter, has got to be able to pull the ball in the major leagues or they don't like him."[80]

O'Doul instructed the five-foot-nine outfielder to crouch, reducing the size of his strike zone, and close his stance by putting his feet close together. That, explained O'Doul, would force pitchers to give him better pitches to hit. Woodling's new stance reminded some observers of Stan Musial.

"O'Doul had never hit that way himself," said Woodling. "But he had devised a system for me and it worked wonders."[81]

That it did. After hitting eight home runs and driving in fifty-four while batting .289 for Newark in 1947, Woodling slammed twenty-two home runs for the Seals in 1948 while leading the league with a batting average of .385. Despite missing six weeks after tearing several ligaments in his ankle on a slide into second base, Woodling drove in 107 runs. His home run total nearly matched his career sum to that point, which had encompassed more than two thousand Minor and Major League at bats. His slugging percentage increased nearly two hundred points compared to a year earlier at Newark.

"Thanks to Lefty O'Doul," wrote Woodling in 1992, "I regained my batting eye and career as a major league ballplayer."[82]

After the 1948 season, the Seals sold Woodling to the New York Yankees, for whom he was seen as insurance for Joe DiMaggio, who was battling a serious heel injury. Woodling won five World Series rings, hit .318 in World Series play, and batted .300 or better five times while playing in the Major Leagues until age thirty-nine.

Woodling had a simple reply when asked about the success he enjoyed in his career. "Lefty made it possible," he said.[83]

1. O'Doul in his navy uniform as part of the
San Pedro Submarine Base baseball team.
He is second from the right in the middle
row. Also on the team were Harry Heilmann
(back row, far left), Howard Ehmke (next to
Heilmann), Bob Meusel (next to Ehmke),
and Jimmie Reese (front row, second from
left). Courtesy of Tom Willman.

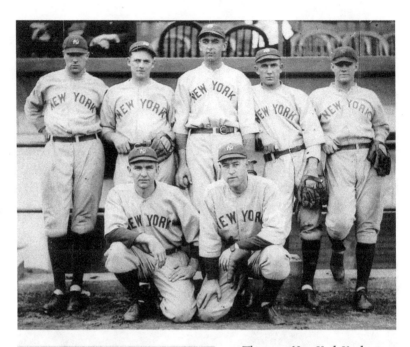

2. The 1922 New York Yankees pitching staff. Back row (left to right): O'Doul, Waite Hoyt, Clem Llewellyn, Sam Jones, George Murray. From row: Bob Shawkey, Bullet Joe Rogan. Carl Mays is not pictured. From the Doug McWilliams Collection.

3. O'Doul during spring training in 1927 with the San Francisco Seals. He would become the second "30-30" man in Pacific Coast League history and would make his return to the Major Leagues at age thirty-one. San Francisco History Center, San Francisco Public Library.

4. Lou Gehrig and Lefty O'Doul look at the $1,000 check O'Doul received for winning the 1927 MVP Award of the Pacific Coast League. The uniforms, the Larrupin' Lou's and the Bustin' Babes, represent barnstorming teams captained by Gehrig and Babe Ruth during their famous cross-country tour following the 1927 season. AP Photo.

5. In 1929 and 1930 for the Philadelphia Phillies, O'Doul became a star, hitting .398 and .383 in back-to-back seasons and setting a still-shared National League record for hits. National Baseball Hall of Fame Library, Cooperstown NY.

6. O'Doul on his first trip to Japan in 1931, wearing the All-Star Team uniform. David Eskenazi Collection.

7. O'Doul with Brooklyn in 1932. He would win his second National League batting title that season with a .368 average. National Baseball Hall of Fame Library, Cooperstown NY.

8. Joe Cronin and Mayor Angelo Rossi pose with O'Doul during a celebration in San Francisco following his game-winning pinch hit in the 1933 World Series. San Francisco History Center, San Francisco Public Library.

9. In November 1933 Babe Ruth arrived in San Francisco from Honolulu and played a couple of rounds of golf with O'Doul, who was beginning his effort to convince Ruth to go to Japan after the 1934 season. Courtesy of PristineAuction.com.

10. O'Doul with the New York Giants in 1934. *National Baseball Hall of Fame Library, Cooperstown NY.*

11. Connie Mack, Sotaro Suzuki, Jimmie Foxx, and O'Doul aboard the *Empress of Japan* before departing from Vancouver, British Columbia, on October 20, 1934. *Stuart Thomson Collection, City of Vancouver Archives.*

12. Lefty poses in 1935 with Tokyo Giants second baseman Takeo Tabe, measuring him with an oversized bat given to him as a gift by the visiting Japanese ballplayers. San Francisco History Center, San Francisco Public Library.

13. O'Doul Day in San Francisco was always an event. Here Lefty poses with a giant scrapbook presented to him in 1940. Dick Dobbins Collection on the Pacific Coast League, courtesy of California Historical Society, MSP 4031.022.

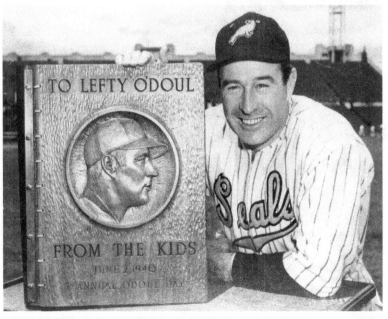

14. O'Doul was asked to prepare actor Gary Cooper for his role as Lou Gehrig in *Pride of the Yankees*. The two take a timeout in Sun Valley, Idaho. David Eskenazi Collection.

15. The Seals trained in Hawaii in 1946 and 1947, thanks to the largesse of Paul Fagan. While Charlie Graham (pictured on the left in the photo on the program cover) was almost a second father to O'Doul, Paul Fagan (center) would prove a thorn in Lefty's side. Ray Saraceni Collection.

16. (*Opposite top*) During the San Francisco Seals' tour to Japan in 1949, the flags of the United States and Japan flew together for the first time since before World War II. David Eskenazi Collection.

17. (*Opposite bottom*) O'Doul shakes hands with fifteen-year-old Crown Prince Akihito, the future emperor of Japan, before the game played on October 17, 1949. David Eskenazi Collection.

Souvenir
BASEBALL *Program*
SEALS vs GIANTS

CHARLIE GRAHAM   PAUL I. FAGAN   FRANK "LEFTY" O'DOUL

HONOLULU STADIUM

MARCH 19-20-21-22-23, 1947

PRICE TEN CENTS

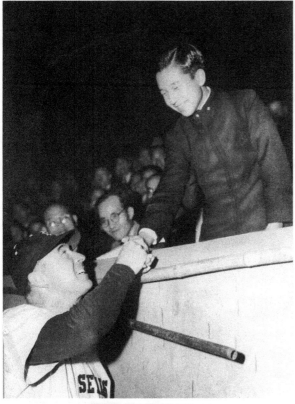

18. O'Doul fulfilled his promise to pinch-hit during the 1949 tour. San Francisco History Center, San Francisco Public Library.

19. Lefty O'Doul in the San Francisco Seals' dugout. David Eskenazi Collection.

20. During their 1950
visit, O'Doul and
Joe DiMaggio gave
instruction to Japanese
youth baseball players.
U.S. Army photo.

21. O'Doul with General
Douglas MacArthur and
Joe DiMaggio in Japan
in 1950. David Eskenazi
Collection.

22. Lefty invited four of the top Japanese professionals to spend spring training with the Seals in Modesto, California, in 1951. From left to right: O'Doul, Fumio Fujimura, Shigeru Sugishita, Makoto Kozuru, and Tetsuharu Kawakami. All five of the men in this photograph are members of the Japanese Baseball Hall of Fame. David Eskenazi Collection.

23. O'Doul as manager of the San Diego Padres in 1952. David Eskenazi Collection.

24. Lefty O'Doul, Marilyn Monroe, and Joe DiMaggio during a stop in Honolulu on the way to Japan in February 1954, less than a month after DiMaggio and Monroe married in San Francisco. Their faces reveal a lot about the trip. © Bettman/CORBIS.

25. O'Doul returned to the Bay Area in 1955 as manager of the Oakland Oaks. Photo by Kayo Harris, from the Doug McWilliams Collection.

26. Lefty with stepson James Gold shortly after the Oaks moved to Vancouver in 1956. While Lefty always loved kids, he never had any of his own, and his relationship with his stepson, while cordial, was not close. David Eskenazi Collection.

27. Rainiers slugger Joe Taylor is congratulated by O'Doul as he rounds the bases after a home run. Taylor was a Major League–caliber hitter when sober. Otherwise, Lefty had to "cross his fingers." David Eskenazi Collection.

28. Seattle was Lefty's last stop as manager. Photo by Dick Dobbins, from the Doug McWilliams Collection.

29. O'Doul in spring training in 1958 with San Francisco Giants veteran outfielder Hank Sauer. © S.F. Giants.

30. In March 1958 O'Doul was joined by San Francisco mayor George Christopher and business partner Al Pollack for a ceremony to open his iconic restaurant on Geary Street. San Francisco History Center, San Francisco Public Library.

31. Lefty O'Doul, circa 1960, as a special hitting instructor for the San Francisco Giants. © S.F. Giants.

32. Lefty traveled the world during the 1950s and 1960s. David Eskenazi Collection.

33. In September 1963 Lefty O'Doul was joined by Willie Mays, Joe DiMaggio, and sportswriter Prescott Sullivan signing autographs for kids at a B'nai B'rith event. San Francisco Examiner Collection, Bancroft Library, University of California, Berkeley.

34. The Oakland A's honored Casey Stengel in 1968 on the twentieth anniversary of his championship season as manager of the Oakland Oaks. Stengel and O'Doul play tug of war with the 1948 Governor's Cup as Charlie Finley and Joe Cronin look on. © Ron Riesterer Photography.

35. O'Doul's plaque in the Japanese Baseball Hall of Fame. He was inducted in 2002. Courtesy of Japanese Baseball Hall of Fame and Museum.

Manager for Life

After winning their first game in Japan, the Seals blasted an Armed Forces All-Star team the next day, 12–0, even turning a triple play.[1] That game provided one of the more emotional scenes of the 1949 tour, as fourteen thousand war orphans were invited to attend. Five of them were chosen to present artwork to O'Doul that they had created; Lefty in turn presented one dozen baseballs to each of them.[2] An editor from *Asahi Shimbun* was especially touched by the scene, writing about the harsh lives these children faced. It was noted that American GIs were asked to make room for the orphans, and that had it been up to the Japanese, the orphans—if invited at all—would have been placed in the far reaches of the ballpark, not in first-class seats. The editorial concluded, "The Japanese should not forget this humanism together with the art of ball playing."[3]

Crowds grew larger for every contest, each game becoming an event, really, as some of the parks swelled far beyond capacity— Japanese fans sometimes scrunching two or even three to a seat. The players were followed everywhere by fans seeking autographs. "A group of us went to a shrine in Nikko," Joe Sprinz recalled. "It was four miles . . . and naturally we had a bus. On the way back, just outside the shrine, we saw two Japanese boys with papers in their hands. They had run the four miles to get our autographs." The Seals gave the boys a ride back.[4]

The Seals played a night game on October 17 at Tokyo's Stateside Park (Meiji Shrine Stadium) where sixty thousand people, including Crown Prince Akihito and his younger brother, gathered to see the team battle the Tokyo All-Stars. It was the first professional game ever played under lights in Japan, and the first game the prince had ever attended; it was arranged for Akihito and O'Doul to shake hands for the benefit of photographers."[5] Two hundred students from St. Paul University weaved through the stands, hawking hot dogs, ice cream, chocolates, and popcorn—items not usually available to the Japanese—hoping to raise six million yen during the tour to rebuild Holy Trinity Church at Aoyama.[6]

Victor Starffin was the starting pitcher for Yomiuri. Despite his being the son of Russian refugees and therefore not a Japanese citizen, Starffin, who was in his early thirties, had become one of the country's greatest stars, leading Japanese baseball in wins in 1949 with twenty-seven.[7] Wearing his iconic number 17, Starffin pitched four shutout innings against San Francisco before leaving due to a sore elbow. Left-hander Hiroshi Nakao added two more scoreless frames before the Seals touched him for a pair of unearned runs in the seventh. Playing their first game under the lights—and substandard ones at that—the Japanese managed only two hits off Cliff Melton and Milo Candini, who combined to strike out fifteen batters in a 4–0 win.[8] Nevertheless, the Seals voiced praise for both Nakao and Starffin.[9]

Amazed as the Japanese fans were with the Seals, Seals players were equally amazed by the country of Japan and its fans during their 1949 tour. Times were tough, with extreme food shortages and whole neighborhoods in ruin. Con Dempsey, who had fought against the Japanese during the war, was concerned about resentment he might face. But, at least on the surface, he had nothing to worry about.

The players were treated as major celebrities. They wore special badges with their names printed in both English and Japanese so they would be recognized individually wherever they went. Reno Cheso remembered that every team member was assigned his own taxi driver, standing at the ready behind the wheel of an automobile bearing a number corresponding to the one emblazoned on that player's uniform. The drivers were available twenty-four hours a day to take the Americans wherever they wanted to go.[10]

For his part, O'Doul was surprised at how well he was remembered. Shortly after arriving, he had stopped by the Imperial Hotel, where he had lodged in 1934. He was immediately greeted by a clerk at the concierge desk who gleefully shouted, "Hello, Mr. O'Doul. Remember me? I took care of you when you were here before!"[11]

• • •

In 1937 Charlie Graham was the subject of a *Sporting News* profile on the occasion of his fortieth year in baseball. Asked his opinion of the players sold during his tenure with San Francisco, Graham selected Lefty Gomez as the best pitcher the Seals had ever graduated to the Major Leagues, and accurately predicted Joe DiMaggio would prove to be the best all-round player. Yet Graham singled out Lefty O'Doul as the most talented. "Frank had more ability than any man I have sent up," Graham insisted. "He was manhandled in the big leagues in many ways and yet he came through to be a leading hitter."[12]

Even past age forty, O'Doul remained an exceptional athlete. Tom Laird, sports editor of the *San Francisco News*, asserted, "Give Lefty O'Doul one week in which to practice and he will beat anybody at any sport."[13] O'Doul was a master skeet shooter. He was an excellent bowler with an average near two hundred, and outstanding at billiards. He was a near-scratch golfer. He was excellent at sleight-of-hand, especially card tricks. Butchertown old-timers insisted he could have been a great prize fighter. After admitting that he could never master skiing, O'Doul insisted, "Sports of all kinds are easy, if you have the proper coordination. And if you can do one, you should be able to do them all."[14] Following his being hired by the San Francisco Seals in early 1935, he discovered he could run a baseball team.

When O'Doul held his first meeting as manager of the San Francisco Seals, he greeted his charges with a brief, but sincere, promise. "I want to treat you," he vowed, "the way I wanted to be treated as a player."[15]

That succinct statement summed up O'Doul's managerial philosophy over the next quarter century. Of course, that is not to say he never chastised his men. Upon rejoining the Seals following an eight-year absence, O'Doul detected a coziness among the league's players. Living in what at that time remained a remote part of the country, many of them knew each other well—O'Doul thought *too* well. He began drilling into his players the importance of winning games over maintaining friendships, insisting that they always hustle, and always slide hard into second when attempting to break up double plays. Les Powers dutifully followed orders, hurtling into Los Angeles Angels second baseman Jimmie Reese, in the process nicking him in the ankle. After checking to make sure Reese was okay, Powers headed back to the bench.

Confronting the player as he reached the dugout, O'Doul scolded the Seals first baseman. "You are entitled to the baseline and I want you to slide hard," he snapped. "It is up to the baseman to protect himself. You are not playing ping-pong, you know."[16]

O'Doul did have a temper, and would display it every once in a while. He had little patience for lack of hustle, and hated losing more than anything; hearing abuse during or after a loss could set him off—on at least one occasion he chased a fan out of the stands.[17] He was not afraid to resort to fisticuffs if his authority was challenged, and he could be downright petulant if he felt wronged by umpires; early in his second season as manager, he reacted to an ejection by attempting to watch the remainder of the game in a box seat.[18]

It became clear almost from the start of his managerial career that, strategically, O'Doul was decidedly unorthodox, doing whatever he could to prevent his team from hitting into double plays, which he labeled the cancer of baseball.[19] He aggressively ordered hit and runs, steals, and bunts. From the third base coach's box he frequently signaled for his players to take chances on the base paths—many of which observers thought reckless. He managed by gut instinct, with the goal of pressuring opponents into mistakes. O'Doul's unpredictability made it difficult to manage against him.

He gained a reputation for "babying" his pitchers in the early part of the season, reasoning they would be fresher than their opponents down the stretch—as the year wore on, he would be criticized for leaving them in too long in a desire to give them experience in

working out of jams.[20] He was always teaching and always looking out for his men—he was what today would be called a "player's manager." And if he was a "player's manager," he was also a
"fan's manager." He waved, and cajoled, and incited the crowd.
He "fainted" in response to umpires' bad rulings. He was a show.

O'Doul was always trying to find ways to get the fans behind him
and his team—and rattle the opposition. During his first season,
the Seals were hosting the Angels, and O'Doul suddenly pulled a
handkerchief from his pocket and began waving it in the direction of Los Angeles pitcher Mike Meola as a distraction. Some fans
picked up on it and also began waving hankies. Unnerved, Meola
was soon knocked out of the box, and a Seals tradition was born.[21]

O'Doul developed variations on the theme, sometimes pulling
out a red bandanna, or one that was hilariously oversized. Fans
soon brought their own, making the stadium a sea of whirling
white semaphores, exhorting the Seals to rally. O'Doul once went
to home plate as a pinch hitter with a white handkerchief in one
hand and a red one in the other, anything to get the crowd behind
him—and gain a psychological advantage.[22]

Lefty also utilized a few, more traditional trade secrets he had
picked up along the way; his players quickly discovered that their
manager was a master of deciphering the opposition's signs. Though
he refused to disclose his methodology, he did tell of his easily intercepting Rogers Hornsby's signals when the great second baseman
was managing the Cubs.

"When he'd put his head back and shake it," recalled O'Doul, "that
was the knock down sign. We knew we were getting knocked down
before the catcher knew it. [One day Gabby] Hartnett is catching and
[Guy] Bush is pitching and I'm standing at the plate. Hornsby's in the
dugout giving the sign to Bush for a fastball—he'd give the sign to the
pitcher and then the catcher would flash all the signs, but the pitcher
would shake them off, except for the right one. So Hartnett gives the
curve ball sign to Bush and he shakes it off, and I turned to Hartnett
and says, 'Don't you know Hornsby wants the fastball, Gabby?'"[23]

When one of O'Doul's players pleaded with him to divulge his
secret, he refused. "I can't tell you," he explained, "because these

tricks are my stock in trade and it would be like taking tools away from me. . . . Besides, you might be traded to some other team next year."[24] In summary, O'Doul was smart, he was observant, and he knew people. Few could spot a "tell" like Lefty O'Doul.

In addition to coaching players on the ballfield, O'Doul also took a page from Rose Stolz and coached his players in becoming gentlemen—including lessons in dressing properly; more often than not he paid for their tailored suits at MacIntosh's out of his own pocket.[25] Players wore coats and ties on the road—he wanted them to understand what is was like to be a big leaguer. Bill Werle, who later played for the Pittsburgh Pirates, recalled a conversation with O'Doul early in his career: "Lefty said maybe he'd never make a ball player out of me, but when he was finished with me I'd at least look and act like a gentleman. He said the kids looked up to ballplayers and if we acted up, it reflected on baseball."[26]

O'Doul's life lessons included the responsibility for players to interact positively with the public and the press. Joe DiMaggio's San Francisco nickname "Deadpan" had followed him during his rookie season in New York. That winter, O'Doul took DiMaggio aside and worked with him on cultivating a better relationship with sportswriters. The next spring, reporters noticed that the outfielder was more relaxed and making an effort to connect with them. The young star openly credited O'Doul.[27]

Pitcher Con Dempsey still raved about O'Doul decades later: "To me, he was like a second father. He knew more about you than you did yourself. He tried to guide you, not only on the baseball field, but also in personal life."[28]

The Pacific Coast League of the mid-1930s consisted of eight teams—including two in Los Angeles (Hollywood and the Angels), two in San Francisco (the Seals and the Missions), and teams in San Diego, Oakland, Sacramento, Seattle, and Portland. (For those counting, that of course makes nine—during the decade, one Hollywood franchise moved to San Diego and was replaced two years later by the Missions, leaving one team—the Seals—in San Francisco at the end of the decade.)

Despite challenging economic conditions, the PCL remained largely independent, as it had since its founding in 1903—and to its fans, cut off from the Major Leagues by two thousand miles of mountains and comparatively empty prairie, it *was* their Major League. Philip Wrigley, owner of the Chicago Cubs, also owned the Los Angeles Angels, both of which he had inherited upon the death of his father in 1932. The Sacramento Senators were saved from bankruptcy thanks to their purchase by the St. Louis Cardinals in 1936 and were given the new nickname "Solons." But there were no other formal ties at that time, although some teams had arrangements with Major League counterparts somewhat akin to having the right of first refusal.

The PCL was a strong league, arguably the best outside of the Majors, and O'Doul originally envisioned himself as a player-manager; he opened the 1935 season in left field, alongside Joe Marty in center and Joe DiMaggio in right. O'Doul batted himself fourth, between the two young prospects. The lineup remained in that configuration for the first week of the season, at which point O'Doul was sidelined by a sore hip. He then inserted Ted Norbert into his outfield spot and moved DiMaggio to cleanup in the batting order.[29] From that point on O'Doul was primarily a bench manager, although he would remain on the active roster for the next five years, serving mostly as a pinch hitter or occasional mop-up relief pitcher. New York Yankees scout Joe Devine gave his rundown on the PCL for Yankees business manager Ed Barrow during the summer of 1935 and, upon reaching the space in his report reserved for the Seals manager, seemed as if he meant to skip him entirely before writing, "O'Doul all finished as a player."[30]

Despite Devine's assessment of his declining skills, O'Doul was productive as a part-timer, driving in twenty-five runs in only 134 at bats during the 1935 season. He poked a two-run pinch-hit home run over the right-field wall in Sacramento.[31] Later in the year he hit a game-winning pinch-hit home run against Hollywood.[32] When injuries depleted the Seals' lineup at the end of June, O'Doul manned left field in Seattle and, after being held hitless in two starts (his first in more than a month), finished out the series with five hits

in nine at bats and a pair of runs batted in. He followed that with a
pinch-hit single in the first game of the series against the Missions.

O'Doul's mini-streak seemed to spark his team. San Francisco
smashed fifty hits off Missions pitching in sweeping a doubleheader
on the Fourth of July. That was followed the next day by another
twenty-five hits in a 24–6 victory. Over the three games, the Seals
scored fifty-eight runs. During the eight-game series, the team
stole twenty-six bases and averaged more than ten runs per game.

Like John McGraw, O'Doul hated the sacrifice bunt, preferring
aggressive base running. O'Doul had the Seals seeking every opportunity to take advantage—and when opportunities failed to present themselves, he sought to create them.

The PCL employed a split-season format in 1935, with the Seals
capturing the second-half title. Prior to commencing the championship series against first-half winner Los Angeles—a series San
Francisco won in six games—Seals players presented O'Doul a silver cigarette case.[33] A month later, a pleased and satisfied O'Doul
reflected on his first year as a manager during a conversation with
Hugh Bradley of the New York Post.

"I like managing," he told Bradley. "My ambition is to graduate
to a major league managing job. You'll believe me, Hugh, when
I say I am applying the same methods of study to managing that
I applied to hitting. It is a new field and I am as ambitious as a
seventeen-year-old kid breaking into the West Texas League.

"I don't believe in bawling out a player in public when he pulls
a mechanical boot or a mental boner," he added. "It is crawfishing
on the part of the manager and it beats down the player. I believe
in telling the player in private what he did wrong and I think they
appreciate this common courtesy."[34]

It was clear from the start that O'Doul had a natural feel for the
job. He had a strong sense of each man on his team and, as someone who had chafed against authoritarian regimes, believed that
if a player wanted to play he would take care of himself—no one
could do it for him. In the 1940s he told Larry Jansen, "If you want
to play, you don't need any rules."[35]

He did not impose a curfew on his players, and in fact threatened to fine them if they saw him sitting in the hotel bar and failed to join him for a drink, or at least say hello—something almost unheard of at a time when players were expected to frequent watering holes away from the hotel, which the manager and coaches jealously guarded as their private sanctuary.

In his later years, O'Doul would point to lessons he learned while playing for great managers such as Miller Huggins, Frank Chance, and John McGraw, as well as lessons learned from managers he did not want to emulate, such as Rogers Hornsby.

"Never played for Hornsby, thank God," muttered O'Doul. "He didn't smoke, so he didn't want anybody else to smoke. He got up at six in the morning, so every one of his boys had to get up at six in the morning. He didn't read a newspaper in the clubhouse, so *you* weren't supposed to read a newspaper in the clubhouse. Now I don't think that's fair, do you? But he liked to sit around in the lobby and wink at girls!"[36]

Lefty O'Doul Day returned to San Francisco on September 1, 1935. Being the first in eight years, it was a spectacle of course, with Lefty making his entrance via stagecoach, escorted by the Butchertown Cowboys. As the driver screamed at his horses, brutally yanking the reins and grinding the coach to a skidding stop, O'Doul suddenly appeared atop the cab and waved to his cheering fans. Six thousand free bags of peanuts were distributed to kids in attendance, among the sixteen thousand fans on hand for the big day. Seals staffers joined O'Doul in grabbing as many bags as they could carry and showering the stands like so much confetti. At one point O'Doul disappeared; when he returned, he was laden with an armful of baseballs commandeered from the Seals offices and tossed those to excited youngsters as well. There were skits and baseball tricks, and a ballgame that the Seals won easily.[37]

Unlike the first O'Doul Day in 1927, when he pitched a two-hit shutout, Lefty did not play—he had not done so for nearly a month, save for a trio of pinch-hitting appearances—but the children of San Francisco were satisfied nonetheless.

It was a memorable day that morphed into an annual tradition. And it was a thrill not only for the kids but for the players as well. Asked by the *Syracuse Journal* to describe his greatest thrill in baseball, Ed Longacre, who played outfield for the Seals in 1937, described the O'Doul Day in which he participated. "That day," he remembered, "about ten thousand kids under twelve years of age were admitted to the ballpark free of charge, and all were handed miniature baseball bats as they came through the gate.

"The big thrill came after the game when several of the players, including myself, took places on stands spaced around the field and began the task of tossing out several hundred baseballs to the kids. They were a swarming, yelling mob of baseball-conscious kids, all of whom seemed to want a real, official baseball more than anything in the world. I'll never forget that scene.

"I have been in some exceptionally fine games, extra-inning affairs, sensational pitching battles, and I have made a catch now and then in a pinch, or come through with a timely hit that gave me satisfaction. But never have I had the thrill that came to me in that Pacific Coast holiday for the kids."[38]

O'Doul Day in 1938 was a typically festive occasion—the stadium was packed with nearly seventeen thousand screaming fans, at least half of them youngsters admitted free at the invitation of their hero. After the game, O'Doul signed autograph after autograph for kids waiting at the players' gate. Pointing to the crush that seemed ready at any moment to take him off his feet, he yelled to reporters, "See, they say baseball is dead. There are just as many kids hanging around the players' gate today as there was twenty years ago at Old Rec, when I broke into baseball."[39]

The next year's event was even grander. Although it was billed as Lefty O'Doul Day, it would have been more accurate to call it "Lefty's Day with the Kids." Twenty-two thousand were on hand for the doubleheader—at that time the largest crowd to see a game in Seals Stadium. Three actors from the popular "Dead End Kids" film series were on hand, as were members of the Winterland Ice Follies. Six thousand miniature bats signed by O'Doul were distributed to children as they streamed through the gates. Between games, Seals publicity director Walter Mails announced that everyone should remain in their seats while platforms were set up. Meanwhile, a truck bearing a giant, oversized baseball sat at home plate. Impatient children began screaming for Lefty—but he was nowhere to be seen. Suddenly, their hero popped out of the giant baseball and, to delighted screams and laughter, began throwing balls to the kids.[40]

It was, as all the others had been, a day to remember for young baseball fans of Lefty O'Doul and the San Francisco Seals.

During road trips, O'Doul typically loitered in hotel lobbies, wearing his trademark green suit and swapping stories with reporters. He simply loved talking baseball, especially reveling in visits to Los Angeles and Hollywood, basking in the glamour of those places.[41] He mingled just as easily with movie stars as with baseball men. And he enjoyed rainouts—it gave him an opportunity to walk the streets of a city he was visiting and take in the sights, the sounds, and the people.

When at his home base, he was a celebrity—the most popular attraction this side of the cable cars. The Mayor of Powell Street. And no one was allowed to buy him anything in San Francisco—it was Lefty O'Doul's town and if you were visiting, everything was on him.

O'Doul had always harbored ambitions to become a businessman. He had posed in ads for clothing and sports equipment while playing in New York, Philadelphia, and Brooklyn. In 1937 he landed a shoe endorsement with Brooks Sports of Philadelphia: "This shoe designed and used by Lefty O'Doul is made from the finest yellow-back kangaroo."[42] A year later he partnered in a roller rink with Charlie Graham's old manager, Mike Fisher—the man who in 1908 had been the first to take professional baseball players to Japan.[43]

Following the 1939 season, O'Doul opened his first bar, bearing his name and located at 209 Powell Street, just off San Francisco's landmark Union Square. O'Doul had always wanted his own gathering place where he could buy drinks for everyone, talk baseball, and celebrate life. An outsized baseball graced the entrance, to be signed by players when they visited the establishment. Cutouts of baseball greats were posted in the picture windows, and inside were a pair

of murals commissioned by O'Doul, one depicting women baseball teams in action—all of the players left-handed—and another
portraying a game played in the nineteenth century. Framed carica-
tures of the more prominent local sportswriters lined the wall behind
the forty-seven-foot-long bar—O'Doul never took for granted the
impact newsmen had on his career. Lefty had designed for himself
a home away from home. "It will be a place for people to meet and
chin a bit—and of course the drinks will be nothing but the best
and reasonable, too. One thing I know, I'll never get rich off it."[44]

After games, one of the great traditions was watching Lefty O'Doul
build a sandwich. Charlie Graham always laid out a spread in the
second-floor office where O'Doul would hold court for sportswriters, with the opposing manager usually joining them. Will Connolly
of the *San Francisco Chronicle* never got over the sight of O'Doul
telling stories as he built his Dagwood Bumstead work of art, commencing with four layers of different cheeses, swallowed by piles
of pumpernickel and every kind of lunch meat in existence, topped
off with hot English mustard or Mexican chili sauce, the final product stacked to such heights that it tottered "sixteen feet beyond the
center of gravity."[45] Then the day's events would be replayed, a practice that usually lasted well past midnight amid laughter and none
too serious bragging, to the amusement of reporters and combat-
ants alike.

    Having begun his career on the mound before transitioning to
the outfield, O'Doul was a unique manager able to relate to—and
coach—both pitchers and everyday players. He still toed the rubber
on occasion, throwing eight scoreless innings as a reliever in 1937
(plus another inning and a third in the playoffs). At a time when
specialized coaching was almost unheard of, with players expected
to work out problems on their own, O'Doul was always teaching,
even in the midst of a ballgame.

    And it did not matter to O'Doul whether a player was property
of the Seals or not; when pitcher Frank Dasso was on loan to San
Francisco from the Cincinnati Reds, O'Doul worked with him on
his mechanics as if he belonged to the Seals.

Dasso recalled O'Doul's patience. "I could throw as hard as any of them, but I had a tendency to get a little wild," he recalled. "O'Doul would come to the mound and say, 'Now Frank, you're releasing the ball too quick. On the very next pitch when I leave this mound, I want you to hit home plate.' So I'd hit home plate and he would yell, 'See, now you can throw low when you want to.' Lefty was a true manager. . . . As far as managing and teaching, there's only Del Baker and Lefty O'Doul, and I'd have to strain real hard to come up with somebody else."[46]

Elmer Singleton credited O'Doul with improving his control—after working with the Seals manager, the right-hander gradually cut his bases on balls per nine innings in half. Singleton called O'Doul "the greatest manager I ever played for besides Casey Stengel."[47]

O'Doul was certainly not infallible, and occasionally guilty of hyperbole when it came to prospects—but it was more out of a genuine desire to see someone succeed. He had oversold Joe Marty, and later convinced Connie Mack that Bill Lillard was baseball's next great shortstop—Lillard's Major League career lasted all of eighty games.

In 1939 O'Doul was very high on the potential of a hard-throwing young right-hander named Jack Bowen. Arguably the best all-round athlete in camp, Bowen had played freshman football and basketball at the University of Washington, and had once bested Fred Hutchinson in a thirteen-inning duel in American Legion ball.[48] During spring training, O'Doul labeled the nineteen-year-old the best-looking prospect he had seen since taking over as Seals manager. However, after a few weeks with the Seals, he was farmed to Tucson, where he lost sixteen of nineteen decisions and walked seven batters per nine innings. He was gone a year later.[49]

But quite often Lefty got it right. Taking a page from his old manager, Burt Shotton, O'Doul utilized psychology and his own passion for self-education as tools for helping players. At one point the Seals acquired a pitcher named Jack Brewer, a University of Southern California grad who had once ushered at Wrigley Field in Los Angeles. Brewer was an introvert who preferred rooming alone and hated to fly, which the Seals did in the 1940s, well before

Major League teams began doing so. Brewer was not the stereo-typical athlete—he was a much more intellectual sort than is usually found in the clubhouse.

O'Doul noticed Brewer studying the night sky and purchased a book on astronomy. He then ran into Brewer outside the hotel one evening and made observations about various constellations. This delighted the pitcher, who was thrilled that someone was taking an interest in his hobby. Brewer won thirty-one games over two seasons for O'Doul, despite arm problems that would end his career shortly after that.[50]

Following initial success under O'Doul's tenure, the Seals sagged a bit. With the Depression making a dent in the formerly lucrative market for the buying and selling of Minor League talent to the Major Leagues, and lacking a working agreement with a Major League team, Charlie Graham and the Seals struggled to keep the doors open, much less prosper. But O'Doul loved San Francisco, even as rumors continually swirled about his being offered this or that job as a Major League manager.

Observations had been made over the years that O'Doul should have been a politician, but he was not political at all. He was personable and popular but did not automatically cater to authority—sometimes defying it—and would not campaign for something he felt he deserved. Respect was his watchword, and he had little regard for those who did not show it, especially to others. To that end he was polite, thoughtful, and generous, but failed to overtly cultivate allies. He simply had them or he didn't. That had been true in the former case with Burt Shotton, Wilbert Robinson, and Charlie Graham. It had been equally true in the latter with Miller Huggins, Oscar Vitt, and Joe McCarthy. This attitude sometimes cost O'Doul, but not with Charlie Graham.

Following the 1937 season, when O'Doul's initial three-year contract as manager of the San Francisco Seals expired, Graham wanted O'Doul to continue as manager, and O'Doul felt the same. The two men settled on an arrangement that would make O'Doul manager of the Seals "for life." Graham told reporters that O'Doul "wanted to be sure of the future, and so did we. That's why the contract was made for 'from now on.'"[51]

But there was no document. The two men trusted each other and the agreement was consummated with a handshake. Graham allowed O'Doul one escape clause—if the New York Giants ever came calling, he would allow Lefty to go, no questions asked.

Over the next decade the two men would meet at the end of each season and agree to continue their relationship with a handshake. It was an arrangement that proved mutually satisfying to O'Doul and Graham. Despite its informality, O'Doul would eventually become one of the highest-paid managers, not only in the Minor Leagues, but in all of baseball.

Lefty O'Doul remained a capable hitter, even as his appearances dwindled. During the 1937 season he collected seventeen hits—including six doubles—in forty-four at bats for a .386 batting average. In late August his bases-loaded pinch-hit double against Oakland drove in three runs and ended an eighteen-inning scoreless string by the Seals. He then scored on Larry Woodall's single, making him responsible for all of San Francisco's runs in a 4–2 win.[52]

On September 1, O'Doul pitched at the end of a 10–5 loss to the Padres. Ted Williams had hit two home runs that day, giving him three in two games. Unfortunately, Lefty finished two batters shy of facing Williams, who would have been the next batter in the on-deck circle had O'Doul not retired George Myatt to end the eighth.[53]

During the 1938 season, the forty-one-year-old O'Doul managed a feat never before accomplished in the PCL. The San Francisco Seals were trailing, 7–3, in the ninth inning of the first game of a doubleheader on May 29 in Seattle. O'Doul, determined to shake his team's lethargy, grabbed a bat and pinch-hit; he promptly homered, as did the next man up, Dominic DiMaggio. Before the inning was over, the Seals had blasted four home runs and rallied to win the game.

The Seals were again trailing in the nightcap, this time by one run in the sixth inning, and O'Doul decided to see if he could replicate his pinch-hitting magic of the first game. Incredibly, he again hit a home run, tying the score, and the Seals went on to win that game, too. Lefty O'Doul had become the first player in PCL history to crack pinch-hit home runs in both games of a doubleheader.[54]

By 1939 O'Doul was feeling his age and rarely left the bench. Early in the season he pitched an inning in a blowout loss at home against Sacramento and pinch-hit twice, both times successfully, including a bases-loaded tenth-inning single down the right-field line that defeated San Diego.[55] But he had made no other in-game appearances.

However, in late June, the Seals outfield was decimated by injuries. Dominic DiMaggio was banged up, a sprained wrist and injured hand limiting his playing time. O'Doul put himself in the lineup in right field against Seattle; outside of his one inning pitched in the lopsided defeat to Sacramento, it marked the first time he had played in the field since taking over at first base for a few innings during the 1938 Governor's Cup playoffs.

After failing to collect a hit in four at bats and, according to game accounts, misplaying a single into a triple in right field, O'Doul sat the next day and put catcher Joe Sprinz into the outfield; the result was an unmitigated disaster. Sprinz committed three errors and sprained a finger as the Seals lost, 11–1.[56] O'Doul recognized he was out of options. The forty-two-year-old laced up his spikes and somehow the magic returned.

Seattle's ace pitcher, rubber-armed roly-poly curve ball specialist Dick Barrett, walked Ted Jennings to lead off the first inning. O'Doul then snapped his wrists inside-out on a Barrett curve and slapped a looping liner behind third base. Brooks Holder followed with a single to score Jennings while O'Doul sprinted all the way to third. O'Doul then scored on a grounder to shortstop.

It was one of those days. O'Doul felt good; his legs were under him and the old juices were flowing. In his second at bat he pulled Barrett's pitch over the first baseman's head and down the line for another single—a humpbacked liner similar to the first one, except into right field. After Holder walked, O'Doul called for a hit and run play, counting on an element of surprise. Ted Norbert struck out, but with Holder and O'Doul breaking on the pitch, they managed a successful double steal. Both men ultimately scored on an infield error.

O'Doul smacked a line drive single in the fifth, his third hit of the game. Then, to everyone's shock, he stole second. After moving to third on an infield out, he got carried away and was thrown out at home plate on a ground ball hit to third base; the play left him with a serious strawberry on his right hip.

Wisely calling it a day, O'Doul had the hobbled Dominic DiMaggio finish the game in his place. The Seals won, 4–1, but O'Doul grabbed the headlines with three hits, two runs scored, and two stolen bases.[57]

What's more, he played in the doubleheader the next day, collecting three more hits in seven at bats and driving in a run.[58] When the Seals returned home on June 27 to face Oakland, O'Doul started his fourth straight game.

He added another single in three at bats before pulling a hamstring running to first. Forced to use a cane the next day, he ruled himself out of the lineup and the Seals signed veteran Harlin Pool to take his place until DiMaggio could return.[59] In starting five out of six games, O'Doul had collected seven hits in eighteen at bats. It was a noteworthy achievement for a forty-two-year-old who had played neither a full game in the outfield in nearly three years, nor consecutive games defensively in four seasons. O'Doul made one more start—in the final game of the season, against Portland—singling in three at bats and scoring twice.

With that, the 1939 season was history, and after falling painfully short of doing so on a couple of occasions—once in the PCL and once in the Majors—O'Doul could finally lay claim to a .400 batting average for a season, thanks to his fourteen hits in thirty-five at bats.

O'Doul played less in 1940, collecting only two hits in thirteen at bats, and pitching in relief three times for a total of three and two-thirds innings. After the season, having played in four different decades, he announced his retirement as an active player.[60] It was a vow he stuck to—for the most part.

The year 1941 would not prove to be Lefty O'Doul's favorite; it began with one serious fight—in a bar that nearly cost him the sight in his left eye—and ended with another, on a global scale that caught up his old friends in the Far East.

During the early morning hours of April 30, O'Doul and a friend, former boxer Specs Ramies, stopped at the bar located in the Hollywood-Roosevelt Hotel in Los Angeles. The Seals had lost the opener of a series against the Angels that evening after coming back from a 6–0 deficit, only to commit five errors and drop a 12–9 decision. O'Doul had planned to meet another friend of his at the hotel bar, veteran character actor Eugene Pallette, a big frog-voiced man best known for roles in *Mr. Smith Goes to Washington*, *My Man Godfrey*, and *The Adventures of Robin Hood*.[61]

While they waited for Pallette to arrive, another party began razzing O'Doul about his team's ragged play. Although O'Doul would deny it, several witnesses described the group as denigrating the Seals because of a lost bet on the game. These witnesses claimed that O'Doul asked one man in particular to quiet down; when he refused, Lefty bought the party a round of drinks and threw cash onto the bar, barking, "If you lost two dollars on the game, here it is!"[62]

Everyone agreed that O'Doul approached the most belligerent of the group—Lefty claimed for the purpose of apologizing for reacting with profanity before realizing there were women in the party. In relating his version of events, O'Doul sighed, "I guess he thought I was going to hit him." (Everyone would agree no punches were thrown.) The heckler reacted by swinging a glass at O'Doul's head. O'Doul attempted to avoid the blow, but the glass, which was chipped on the rim, caught his left eye, lacerating his cornea.[63] As O'Doul fell to the floor, grabbing his face, the man took off, jumping into his car. Specs Ramies chased the assailant on foot for a short distance before returning to the scene. O'Doul was hustled into a taxicab and rushed to the hospital. Several stitches had to be taken in the injured eyeball, and it was feared he might lose sight out of it.[64]

"I never saw the man before in my life," insisted O'Doul. "I paid so little attention to him at first that I would have a hard time picking him out of a lineup."[65]

O'Doul phoned his mother to assure her he was all right, and also called Abbie, who jumped on a plane for Los Angeles. A shaken Charlie Graham swore that he had witnessed numerous instances of O'Doul being verbally abused and had never seen him fail to de-escalate the situation. "Lefty never gets into an ill-humored argument," insisted a pained Graham. "His greatest asset is his ability to make friends. . . . I cannot understand why anyone should do this awful thing to him"[66]

Attention turned to tracking down the man responsible for injuring O'Doul. No one at the hotel admitted to knowing the identity of the assailant. Eugene Pallette hired a private investigator in an effort to find the suspect, who was vaguely described as a "short, dark man." Seals players milled about their hotel lobby, some discussing the idea of forming a posse and finding the wanted man themselves.[67]

Meanwhile, doctors placed patches over both of O'Doul's eyes and assessed the damage. "He has stronger than a possibility of keeping the left eye," said one of the surgeons. "I would say it is a probability, and an encouraging one."[68] A photo of O'Doul, his eyes bandaged and a nurse leaning over to check on him, ran nationwide while newspapers up and down California churned out daily updates on O'Doul's condition and the status of the investigation.[69]

The next day a detective investigating the case, influenced by witness accounts that referenced betting, told reporters that in his opinion the act had been committed by a gambler who had lost money on the Seals. "The staff of the Hollywood-Roosevelt Hotel told our inspectors that the man is known to bet on ball games," he said. "They have seen him many times, but they claim they do not know his name."[70]

O'Doul became livid at any mention of gambling—but what he and the public did not know was that Los Angeles Angels pitcher Julio Bonetti was under active investigation for taking money from a known gambler named Albert Reshaw. The Angels had been plagued by such rumors since the latter part of the 1940 season. Because of that, it was quite natural for gambling to cross the minds of investigators. Within a week of O'Doul's injury, Bonetti was charged in the unrelated investigation, and two months later was indefinitely suspended by Organized Baseball.[71]

O'Doul stuck to his assertion that he was attacked when he left his table to confront a trash-talking wise guy, who was simply berating the play of the Seals rather than being angry at losing a bet. However, both Bob Ray of the *Los Angeles Times* and Bob Hunter of the *Los Angeles Examiner* concluded that the argument *was* over a lost bet; neither man was suggesting that O'Doul or his players had wagered on or thrown the game, only that a drunk hothead had reacted to seeing O'Doul, his anger fueled by lost money.[72]

With his attacker having disappeared, O'Doul sounded almost relieved and eager to let bygones be bygones. "I guess the man who hit me now feels more sorry about it than I do. I don't think he intended to do the damage he did."[73]

Three days later, the attacker was finally identified as Buddy Jackler, a thirty-one-year-old fur dealer. Far from apologetic, Jackler claimed he was with his wife and that O'Doul had instigated the fight. He insisted he had been in the right. "O'Doul was very drunk, very profane, and very mean," Jackler claimed. He added that he had thought O'Doul was about to hit him and had "tossed the glass in self-defense."[74] Jackler claimed that he had not left the scene until it became apparent to him that no one intended to ask him any questions. After investigating, police prepared a complaint for O'Doul to sign, but he declined. Will Connolly speculated that O'Doul was embarrassed about being involved in a bar fight, and was unenthusiastic about appearing to be a poor role model during what would have been a very public trial.[75] O'Doul seemed to verify that assumption when he later told Dick Williams of the *Seattle Times*, "Prosecute him? Why the people with him would have had me going after him with a knife in one hand and a gun in the other. I'd have to commute between San Francisco and the Los Angeles courthouse. At best it wouldn't do baseball any good."[76]

Insisting he bore no hard feelings about the incident, O'Doul said that he "didn't want to make trouble for anyone."[77] By this time it was determined he would not lose his sight.[78] After spending two weeks in the hospital, O'Doul was released on May 12 and was back at his Seals Stadium office, wearing sunglasses while posing for a photographer.[79] By the end of the month he was back on the bench. But for the first time in his life he would have to wear glasses.

Shortly after O'Doul recovered from his eye injury, rumors began circulating that the New York Giants were going to fire Bill Terry and hire Lefty as his successor. In July, Terry was forced to deny reports he was being booted to the front office to make room for O'Doul. Noting that he had a year remaining on his contract, Terry said that if something like that were being contemplated, "the board of directors certainly would consult me."[80]

It was not the first time O'Doul's name had been attached to rumors related to other managerial positions. In 1939 his name was mentioned in conjunction with the Chicago Cubs.[81] At about the same time the Hollywood Stars of the PCL, recently purchased by Brown Derby restaurant owner Bob Cobb, and looking for a big name to hire alongside the celebrities that had invested in the team, were rumored to want Lefty in their dugout.[82] Nothing came of either story—but this one involving the New York Giants had legs.

Tom Meany of New York PM insisted that Giants president Horace Stoneham "told at least two people around town that Lefty O'Doul would be the next manager."[83] There were rumors of O'Doul not only taking over the Giants but also bringing along his two best players, Ferris Fain and Nanny Fernandez.[84]

A couple of months later, O'Doul attended the World Series and stopped by the newsroom of the New York Daily News. Asked again about the possibility of his taking the helm of the Giants, O'Doul quipped, "Sports writers do a pretty good job of managing ball clubs in this town—they don't need me."[85]

Upon returning to San Francisco at the end of October, O'Doul declared he wasn't going anywhere and that his priority was rebuilding the Seals.[86] A month later, the Giants fired Terry and hired Mel Ott as his replacement. O'Doul once again shook hands with Charlie Graham and continued as Seals manager.[87]

As the San Francisco Seals slipped to the middle of the league standings during the early 1940s, O'Doul grew frustrated at his inability to compete on a level playing field. He bemoaned the fact that he was forced to challenge the likes of Los Angeles and Sacramento— and their Major League connections—while being handicapped by a roster developed on a shoestring. There were some good young players signed by the Seals, such as Larry Jansen, Ferris Fain, and Nanny Fernandez, but they had not arrived PCL ready, and increasingly O'Doul's role was to develop these talents at the expense of winning so that the Seals could package them to the big leagues.

O'Doul's competitive nature got the best of him and frustration bubbled to the surface. "Why kid ourselves?" he asked near the end of the 1942 season, as Sacramento and Los Angeles battled for the pennant during the final week.[88] That frustration led him to entertain the notion of managing the Philadelphia Phillies in 1943.

The Phillies were being sold to a syndicate headed by William Cox, owner of an American League Football franchise in New York. Cox was aggressive—he had made a big splash signing Heisman Trophy winner Tom Harmon before the gridiron league suspended play due to the war, and he wanted to create the same sense of excitement with the Phillies.[89] Never one to keep his own counsel when he could announce to the world what he was planning, Cox provided reporters the scoop that O'Doul was his first choice as manager. But Lefty opted to remain in San Francisco, and Bucky Harris was hired instead.[90] The decision was a wise one for O'Doul—an impatient and unrealistic Cox thought the Phillies, coming off their fifth straight one-hundred-loss season, a contender. Harris lasted only three months, as Philadelphia lost ninety games and finished seventh in the National League. After the season, Cox received a lifetime ban for betting on his own team.[91]

Even though he might not have had the most talented rosters to work with, O'Doul could always inspire his charges to play hard, and his aggressiveness and unpredictability paid off, if not over the long haul, at least in short series. For more than a decade, the PCL had held a postseason, second-chance playoff among the league's top four finishers. The Seals claimed the trophy, dubbed "The Governor's Cup," three years in a row, beginning in 1943, defeating teams of superior talent including a Los Angeles Angels team that had won the PCL pennant with 110 victories while only losing 45 games. That success merely added to O'Doul's conviction that with proper financial backing and the right players, he could win a regular season championship.

After the Seals captured their third straight Governor's Cup in 1945, O'Doul was named Minor League Manager of the Year by *The Sporting News*.[92] He was recognized for being a deft handler of men, and of taking inferior rosters and getting the most out of them. He took retreads and never-were ballplayers—such as pitcher Bob Joyce, who won thirty-one games for the Seals in 1945—and made something of them.

O'Doul was officially presented the *Sporting News* award by Charlie Graham at a banquet in San Francisco held at the Fairmont Hotel. Graham led the tribute, telling the audience, "Year in and year out, I've seen O'Doul finish in the first division when, by any player by player comparison, he should have finished seventh or eighth. He gets more out of men than they know is in themselves, and nobody deserves the honor of being selected as the minor league manager of the year more than he does."[93]

The award seemed a sign that a new era was on the horizon. Following years of scraping by, the fortunes of both the San Francisco Seals and Lefty O'Doul were about to change, thanks to the personal fortune of another man who had recently arrived on the scene. Initially, O'Doul would see Paul Fagan as the savior of the franchise—a man whose ambition was to make the San Francisco Seals a Major League team. In recognition of winning the award, Fagan would join with Graham in making O'Doul the highest-paid manager in Minor League Baseball.[94] However, within a few years, Paul Fagan's ardor for the Seals would cool, and he would kick both O'Doul and the franchise to the curb.

10

It Is Epidemic

On October 21, 1949, the San Francisco Seals played in front of fifty-five thousand fans at Nishinomiya Stadium, near Osaka, taking on the All-West Japanese All-Stars. Once again the Japanese put up a good fight as Bill Werle pitched a complete-game, 3–1 victory; Tadashi Wakabayashi pitched two innings in relief and allowed two hits and one run in a game the Americans never trailed. But Joe Sprinz was correct, the Japanese did catch on quickly.[1] O'Doul had noticed—not without some pride—that the gap between the Americans and Japanese was closing. His players would have to remain alert if they were to complete the 1949 tour with an unblemished record.

Never forgetting that his role included that of being a baseball diplomat, O'Doul visited Keio University in central Tokyo, where he presented a letter to the school's newspaper editor, sharing his thoughts on Japanese baseball and offering advice to students on improving their skills.[2]

The Japanese were continuing to notice differences in play—and attitude—of the Americans. Retired pitcher Kyoichi Nitta spoke at length with Joe Sprinz. "Among the many things I learned," revealed Nitta, "I was most impressed to find out that each of his players think of baseball as a serious business, play only with the team in mind, and constantly behave like sportsmen." He added that Sprinz told him, "There are people who come to see the games, after buying an expensive ticket from pocket books that are slim. Thus it's not right to play lazy baseball." Nitta also noted that Seals players listened to O'Doul, even during a game. "I can well understand," he told his readers, "that they are being polished each moment and improving with each play."[3]

There were those who wondered why Japanese fans would continue coming out to see their players lose. O'Doul explained that their attitude was opposite of Americans—they wanted to see how superior the American players were. "That's their psychology. If they [could defeat the Americans], nobody would go to another game. What's the use of seeing something inferior?" He then contrasted that to American attitudes, pointing out that if it were reversed and the Japanese were superior and defeating American teams in the United States, the reaction of American fans would be different. "If they beat us, nobody would come. They'd say [of the American players] well . . . those bums."[4]

Between eighty and ninety thousand people greeted the Seals at Koshien Stadium in Nishinomiya on October 23—and the games were getting tougher. The All-Japan team led the game in the third inning thanks to a double, a sacrifice, and a successful squeeze play. The Seals tied the score in the sixth, and the game remained tied, 1–1, into the ninth when the Seals loaded the bases with no one out. All-Japan brought in Hiroshi Nakao to stem the tide, but he promptly walked in the lead run. Nakao quickly regrouped, eliciting rousing cheers from his countrymen for striking out Jim Moran. Then, the All-Japan team executed a sparkling double play—Jim Westlake grounded back to Nakao, who threw to catcher Takeshi Doigaki at home for the first out, and Doigaki then fired to first to nip Westlake to end the inning. It was an outstanding play, but it went for naught. Cliff Melton struck out the side in the bottom of the ninth to clinch a 2–1 win.[5]

O'Doul praised the Japanese defense after the game, as well as the manager's moves with his pitching staff. "I have no criticism of such a fine game," he said. Joe Sprinz advised that the Japanese batters should have been more aggressive against Melton in the ninth, but he also praised the All-Japan team. "This is the best game since we came to Japan."[6]

• • •

A few months after Lefty O'Doul's first visit to Japan in 1931 with Lefty Grove, Lou Gehrig, and the other American Major Leaguers, the first player billed as being of Japanese ancestry to play professionally in the United States made his debut with the Sacramento Senators of the Pacific Coast League.[7]

Kenso Nushida was born on the big island of Hawaii shortly after it became a territory of the United States. A star pitcher in the islands, Nushida settled in California after traveling there with a barnstorming baseball team. He played several years during the 1920s in the fast semi-pro leagues in central California, eventually earning his tryout with Sacramento thanks to a scrapbook that documented his exploits in Hawaii.[8] Team owner Lew Moreing, sensing the opportunity to tap into the fan base of the large Japanese population that inhabited California's Central Valley, signed the pitcher to a contract in late summer.

The thirty-two-year-old right-hander was, at best, five-foot-one and weighed 110 pounds—some articles of the time claim he was less than five feet tall. No uniform could be found that fit, so one had to be tailored for him. He became popular with teammates, stereotypically profiled as joyfully strumming his ukulele while the team traveled between cities. Because of his size Nushida was, as one would almost certainly surmise, a "junk ball" pitcher. But he did possess some skill, including an impressive curve ball and decent control—teammate Laurie Vinci told Oakland reporters, "It is comical to watch him break a slow curve here, there and just about where he pleases."[9] When he was not pitching, Nushida toiled in a hardware store in Stockton, California.

While Lefty O'Doul was in Brooklyn, wrapping up his second National League batting title and preparing for his second trip to Japan, Nushida won two games and lost four for Sacramento; his best performance came against Seattle, when he no-hit the Indians for seven innings before surrendering three runs in the eighth and losing, 3–1, despite throwing a two-hitter.[10]

Near the end of the season, Oakland and Sacramento drew a larger than normal crowd of three thousand people to a Wednesday night game thanks to an unusual matchup. For the first time, two Asians faced each other in the PCL—Nushida for the Senators and recently signed Chinese pitcher Lee Gum Hong for the Oaks.

The twenty-one-year-old Hong had pitched for Oakland High School under his American name, Albert Bowen—his catcher there, Billy Raimondi, would later become an Oakland Oaks legend. More recently, Hong had been ace pitcher of the successful semi-pro Wa Sung Chinese Baseball club, also based in Oakland.[11] The Wa Sung club purchased a block of one hundred tickets to Hong's professional debut, in which the pitcher was reunited with Raimondi.[12]

The contest itself was somewhat anticlimactic. Hong's supporters set off firecrackers to show their support, and both pitchers received floral horseshoes for good luck from their former semi-pro teams. But Nushida was hit hard early, surrendering three runs in the first two innings, while Hong allowed only one hit through the first five. Nushida went to the showers after striking out Hong for the first out in the fifth, trailing 3–2.

Hong unraveled in the sixth, three singles loading the bases with no one out, followed by an error on a double play ball and a triple. Hong took the loss, 7–5, despite pitching well for the most part— four Oakland errors behind him hurting his cause.[13]

The two pitchers met in a rematch on the last day of the season, in the seven-inning nightcap of a doubleheader. Hong won the game by a score of 7–1, with the Oaks scoring all of their runs off Nushida in the fifth inning. It was all over in an hour and five minutes.[14] Neither Hong nor Nushida played again in Organized Baseball. Three years would pass before another player of Japanese ancestry appeared in the PCL—and he would arrive in a most roundabout way.

Nushida's signing a legitimate contract to play professional baseball, for a team in what was arguably the fastest Minor League in the country, was a greater accomplishment than it might at first seem. Asians living on the West Coast of the United States had long been subjected to distrust and unrelenting discrimination. A number of anti-Chinese and anti-Japanese laws had been adopted, and groups dedicated to Chinese and Japanese exclusion popped up in

California, Oregon, and other states in the West. Much of the tension had to do with the foreign language and culture of the Asians, which aroused suspicion and fear among the majority white population. The belief that Asians were taking employment opportunities away from American citizens was also a factor.

During the 1910s and 1920s, concern grew in official circles over the increasing property holdings of the Japanese in California, and the perception that they might move into areas in high concentration and could effectively "take over" sparsely populated portions of the state. Legislation was passed denying citizenship to the Japanese, coupled with laws prohibiting noncitizens from owning or leasing land.

As a result, Asians, as most minorities at the time, lived in segregated areas. That became true of baseball as well—Asians rarely played alongside Caucasians, even in high school. Japanese had played baseball regularly in San Francisco since shortly before the 1906 San Francisco earthquake, developing their own teams and leagues, the remnants of which continue more than a century later. The first team of note in San Francisco was the Fuji club, founded by a domestic servant, Chiuri Obata, who later became a famous artist. Teams in other California cities soon fielded strong teams, especially in San Jose, Stockton, Fresno, and Los Angeles.

Meanwhile, across the Pacific Ocean, baseball was rapidly becoming Japan's national sport. In 1920, fifty thousand people attended the collegiate baseball championships at Keio University, filling not only the stands but also the structures above them, the rooftops of surrounding homes, and any trees with a sight line of the baseball diamond.[15]

The next year, Adachi Kinnosuke, American correspondent for the *Tokyo Jiji Press*, was informing readers of the *New York Tribune* that his nation of fifty million people was shifting its attention away from wrestling in favor of a bat and ball—indeed, he revealed that a squad of sumo wrestlers had formed a baseball team; wearing the sport's traditional headdress, they were dubbed the Topknot Nine. Adachi told American readers that the game of baseball was "like a sizeable avalanche . . . so that today an American visitor after landing at Yokohama recalls the days of his youth every time he passes the athletic field of a Japanese school. The game is played by the boys of all the colleges of Japan. More than that, it is being played by the boys of all the higher schools of the empire. Still more than that, it is being played now by almost all the children of the common schools. It is epidemic."[16]

Less than fifteen years after Kinnosuke's article, Japanese baseball, with the help of Lefty O'Doul, was ready to show America how widely that epidemic had spread. On February 14, 1935—seven weeks after O'Doul had helped organize the franchise—eighteen members of Japan's first modern professional baseball team, the Tokyo Giants, along with their manager, Tadao Ichioka, and a coach, Daisuke Miyake, set sail for the United States aboard the *Chichibu Maru*.

Ichioka's players ranged in age from seventeen-year-old Tamotsu Uchibori to thirty-three-year-old captain Nobuaki Nidegawa. Ichioka, Miyake, and Nidegawa would eventually be enshrined in the Japanese Baseball Hall of Fame, as would Eiji Sawamura, Shigeru Mizuhara, Victor Starffin, Hisanori Karita, Takeo Tabe, and Sotaro Suzuki, who was serving as the team's business manager. Suzuki predicted that if the tour was successful, it would lead to other Japanese professional teams crossing the Pacific.[17]

One of the team's future Hall of Famers, Starffin, was a citizen of Russia instead of the Soviet Union, and since the United States did not recognize the exiled pre-communist regime, he could not be issued a passport. Starffin, who was not listed among the passengers on the *Chichibu Maru*, possibly because of his lacking documentation, was briefly detained several weeks into the tour and reached out to Lefty O'Doul, who vouched for him so he could remain with his teammates rather than being sent back to Japan.[18]

One of the Tokyo Giants, Fumito "Jimmy" Horio, carried an American passport. He was a Hawaiian-born outfielder who had traveled to Japan the previous October to play against Babe Ruth and the All-Stars.[19] Horio, who began his career with the powerful Southern California semi-pro team, the LA Nippons, had spent the 1934 season in the Class D Nebraska State League, gaining the indelicate nicknames of "The Yellow Peril" and "The Jaunty Jap" while playing for the Sioux Falls Canaries. Now, he had joined the new Japanese professional team for their tour of the United States, hoping to land another contract, hopefully with a Major League team.

Lefty O'Doul was on hand to meet the Giants as they disembarked. Jimmy Horio's wife, Yoshiko, who had accompanied her husband on the voyage across the Pacific Ocean, was photographed handing a ridiculously oversized bat to O'Doul as a gag gift from the Japanese.[20] O'Doul later posed alongside Giants second baseman Takeo Tabe, the bat standing on end to emphasize Tabe's lack of height.

The team began play on the second of March with a schedule that eventually stretched to more than one hundred games in the United States and Canada.[21] O'Doul asked his friend Webster K. Nolan, a former White House correspondent for the Hearst Corporation, to serve as publicity director for the tour, and also ensured that old friend Sotaro Suzuki had ready competition, arranging for PCL teams to play the Giants during March and early April.

O'Doul was considered vital to the success of the endeavor; several decades later, Giants shortstop Hisanori Karita wrote, "This was truly an arduous barnstorming tour for the newly born professional baseball team. Once again, O'Doul was very helpful to us. Although he was busy managing his new team, the San Francisco Seals, he made every effort to make our tour successful."[22]

It was the PCL teams that the Giants were most anxious to play; they provided the high level of competition against which the Giants could measure themselves—and the opportunity to prove to fans back home the viability of the professional game. The Giants began their tour in Marysville, California, north of Sacramento, splitting a pair of games against the PCL Missions; Eiji Sawamura won the second game, 12–5, and Jimmy Horio hit a home run.[23]

Two weeks later, the Giants were in Fresno to play against the Seals, with O'Doul barking orders from the bench through a megaphone. Joe DiMaggio, who had recently ended a holdout, was held hitless in three at bats as the Giants won, 8–1. O'Doul's only appearance resulted in a pinch-hit single after the game got out of hand.[24]

O'Doul put himself in the lineup the next day against Eiji

Sawamura; he was particularly anxious to hit against the teenage sensation, not being allowed the opportunity in Japan in 1934
because the National League had withdrawn its support of the tour,
limiting his role to that of coach and spectator.

Sawamura did not last long, knocked out of the box in the fifth
inning. In the seventh, O'Doul collected his second hit of the game,
a lead-off single, and then scored on DiMaggio's home run, a blast
that brought a grin to Lefty's face as he rounded the bases—the
Japanese were getting their first glimpse of a future legend. An
inning later, O'Doul got a little too enthusiastic and became overly
aggressive running the bases, resulting in his being trapped in a
rundown between third and home. Catcher Takeshi Nakayama
finally ended O'Doul's embarrassment, saying "Excuse it, please"
as he tagged the thirty-eight-year-old Seals player-manager. O'Doul
responded by shaking hands with each player involved in the successful rundown play.[25]

The Tokyo Giants' players, who according to O'Doul were being
paid $150 per month, year-round, proved a big hit with American
fans, who were especially impressed by their hustle—they ran full
out to first base on every play, be it a solid single to center or a
pop-up on the infield.[26] They also lined up before each game and
bowed to the grandstands, and between each inning they formed
a huddle around manager Ichioka, listening intently to his instructions. The Seals drew more fans in their two-game series at Seals
Stadium than for all of their exhibition games combined in 1934.[27]

Eiji Sawamura, whose curve ball was earning him the nickname
"Nippon's Schoolboy Rowe" in honor of the Detroit Tigers ace, was
an early star, pitching a shutout against Oakland after defeating
Mission.[28] In Sacramento, Sawamura hurled a 2–1 victory over the
Senators, striking out six while walking only one. Nearly five thousand were on hand, many of them Japanese.[29] Ironically, Sawamura's mound opponent, Jerry Angelich, would perish six years later
during the attack on Pearl Harbor.[30]

The reception for the Giants was especially enthusiastic in Fresno,
a stronghold of Japanese baseball in California. It was there that
they played against a powerful team headed by Kenichi Zenimura, a

Japanese-born player living in California. Even smaller than Kenso Nushida, Zenimura had traveled to the land of his birth many times to play against the Japanese, and is today considered the father of California's strong Japanese American baseball culture. Zenimura had helped organize the very successful 1927 tour of Japan by the Negro League All-Stars; that same year he played against Lou Gehrig and Babe Ruth in Fresno near the end of their famous postseason cross-country barnstorming trip.[31]

Most American observers were impressed with the talent and competitiveness of the Japanese. Henry Nelson wrote in *The Sporting News*, "The members of the Tokyo team have shown they know how to play ball, and inside baseball at that. It is true that they have met with a number of defeats, but most of those losses have been by close scores, and the Nipponese have won several games. They have employed keen speed, marked agility on the bases and in the field, and are displaying a knowledge of the game that surprised thousands of fans."[32]

The Giants played a three-game series in Los Angeles against Jimmy Horio's former team, the LA Nippons. It was an event billed by the English-language *Rafu Shimpo* newspaper as the "Japanese World Series," the paper's enthusiasm no doubt influenced by its decision to underwrite the games. The series was played at White Sox Park, a well-known semi-pro lot at Thirty-Eighth and Compton.[33] The teams split the first two games, with Starffin losing the second.[34] But Sawamura clinched the "title" by striking out fourteen in a lopsided win.[35] While the Giants were happy to claim victory, it was in reality not all that important to the Japanese professionals; they were more interested in playing fellow pros instead of semipros. In fact, they would have greatly preferred playing a Major League team, but would not receive that opportunity.

Nevertheless, Bob Ray of the *Los Angeles Times* was very impressed with the Giants, especially second baseman Takeo Tabe, who he insisted "can beat out a two-hop grounder to any infielder . . . and slides into a base either feet first or head first, a la Frankie Frisch."[36] The Japanese completed the California portion of their tour with twenty-two wins in forty-two games, plus one win in Mexicali, just across the Mexican border.[37] They won six and lost seventeen against PCL competition, and later split four other games against Minor League teams. During their other eighty-two games against semi-pro and amateur teams, they won sixty-six and had one tie.[38] They barnstormed as far east as Detroit—where they were honored with a parade through the city streets before defeating the Ford Motor Company corporate team, 6–0—and then on into Canada.[39]

At one point, before a game in Milwaukee, Sawamura was approached by a man wanting his autograph, and the pitcher complied. After Sawamura pitched six innings, allowing only six hits and one run in a 9–4 victory against the semi-pro Milwaukee Red Sox, the man waved the piece of paper in Sotaro Suzuki's face, revealing that Sawamura had unknowingly signed a contract. Suzuki reportedly paid the man a small sum to drop the matter.[40]

The trip was not without controversy among Japanese back home. The Giants played up their cultural differences as a way to drum up interest—critics viewed it as crass commercialization, tarnishing the purity of amateurism. That scorn toward what was viewed as mercenary behavior had long delayed the development of the professional game in Japan, a battle that was continuing. At the same time Matsutaro Shoriki was attempting to establish professional teams, the Japanese Board of Education was banning the playing of baseball by youth in favor of war calisthenics.[41]

The Giants' mainland tour ended in June 1935 at Seals Stadium against Ty Cobb's semi-pro team, after which the players sailed out of San Francisco for Honolulu on June 24, where they played the final five games of their tour before heading home. One player remained behind—Jimmy Horio caught the attention of the Sacramento Senators, who signed him on the condition that he join them only at the conclusion of the tour.[42] As with Kenso Nushida three years earlier, the Senators hoped Horio would prove a drawing card for local Japanese baseball fans.

Horio did become an instant favorite in the PCL, celebrated in Seattle, San Francisco, Los Angeles, and Sacramento during the summer of 1935. The ceremony in San Francisco was conjoined with a day honoring O'Doul, who was presented a silver cup from the Japanese Association of San Francisco in recognition of his contributions to Japanese baseball.[43] Unfortunately, Horio's season took a tragic turn. His wife, badly injured in an automobile accident a few weeks after being greeted by Lefty O'Doul, succumbed to internal injuries on August 3.[44]

In the end, Jimmy Horio played sparingly, batting only forty-four times. Overmatched as a hitter, he was dropped by Sacramento after the season.[45] He tried out with Seattle in spring training in 1936 but did not make the team.[46] Horio returned to Japan and played there until June 1941. Although he wanted to stay, Horio had remarried; his new wife, a Nisei born in Berkeley, California, but living in Hiroshima when they met, wanted no part of the war and convinced him to take her back to the United States.[47] They moved to Hawaii, and six months later Horio watched as Japanese war planes flew overhead and smoke billowed from the direction of Pearl Harbor. Less than four years after that, his brother perished when the atomic bomb was dropped on Hiroshima.

In addition to Jimmy Horio, a few other Americans went to Japan to play—most, like Horio, were born in Hawaii or were Japanese Americans. But not all.

African American pitcher James Bonner was a standout in the Berkeley International League, a fascinating integrated semi-pro circuit in which Lee Gum Hong's Wa Sung team was a cornerstone franchise. Bonner, who earned the nickname "Satchel," was added to an All-Star team that was to travel to Japan after he threw three complete-game victories in two days for a California Conservation Corps team. While in the Far East, he was signed to contract and agreed to remain behind; a decade before Jackie Robinson, Bonner was in a Dai Tokyo uniform for the inaugural season of Japanese professional baseball.[48] He would play only the fall season (baseball seasons were split between fall and spring), pitching four times for a total of less than ten innings, allowing an average of more than ten runs per game. While he also played a few games around the infield and managed to hit .458 in limited playing time, collecting eleven hits in twenty-four at bats, he was released in mid-November.[49]

Another American made a big mark on the Japanese professional landscape. Sotaro Suzuki had been impressed by Andrew Harris McGalliard, a Caucasian catcher for the LA Nippons playing under the nom de bat "Bucky Harris." A former PCL player, McGalliard had been considered the team's sparkplug when the team toured Japan. He jumped at the chance to play professionally across the ocean.

McGalliard, who continued playing under the name Harris in Japan, became popular in his new surroundings thanks to his hustling style of play.[50] He captured the Most Valuable Player Award in Japan in the fall 1937 season and led the Japanese League in home runs in the spring of 1938. However, McGalliard's stay ended when his wife, who had remained behind in the States, insisted he return home.[51]

Lefty O'Doul had originally hoped to take his San Francisco Seals to Japan in the fall of 1935, reciprocating the Giants' visit, but the plan was scuttled for reasons said to involve a lack of available playing venues.[52] The Tokyo Giants returned to the States in 1936, playing a seventy-five-game schedule against PCL, Japanese, and semi-pro teams in the western United States as well as Oklahoma and Texas. Sotaro Suzuki arrived stateside wearing a garish green suit, a tribute to his old friend O'Doul, and grandly claimed that it was every Japanese boy's dream to play on a team that could challenge the Major Leaguers. "That would be a real world's series," he declared. Suzuki then added, "We hope Lefty O'Doul will bring a team over next fall, for he is the most popular of all the players who ever visited Japan."[53]

On March 1 the Giants played against the San Francisco Seals reserves at Seals Stadium. Before the game, Suzuki presented O'Doul a silver baseball that opened up to reveal a compartment for cigarettes and a lighter. Eiji Sawamura then pitched a complete-game shutout, striking out ten and not walking a batter as the Giants won, 5–0.[54] But the Giants would once again return home without having the opportunity to play against Major League competition.

Despite his inability to travel to Japan, O'Doul continued making an impression on the people of that country. A year after the

Berlin Olympics, John Kieran of the *New York Times* spoke to Japanese sportswriter Y. Muraoka, who was covering a squad of Japanese track and field athletes competing in the United States. Standing beside pole vaulter Sueo Ohe, Muraoka told Kieran that the young men in Japan wanted to be like O'Doul.

"He is very popular in Japan," said Muraoka. "The boys, they all imitate him—his clothes—his walk—nice, big fellow—chest out." Ohe, who had won a bronze medal at Berlin a year earlier, and would set a meet record at the Millrose Games at Madison Square Garden, eagerly piped in, "He dresses up!"

"Yes," nodded Muraoka, "they try to wear suits like Lefty. He sets the fashion for them."[55]

However, continued unrest and the hostilities between Japan and China curtailed O'Doul's quest to expand his influence. In early 1937 he traveled alone and watched the construction of a new baseball venue in Tokyo, Korakuen Stadium.[56]

That summer, he promised Fumitaka Konoe, a student at Princeton and son of the Japanese prime minister, that he would bring a baseball team to Japan in the fall.[57] However, as O'Doul related to Lawrence Ritter in 1963, he later received a telegram that it would not be wise to do so "due to the confliction in China. Confliction— that's what they called it," he told Ritter.[58]

A 1938 visit was canceled due to increasing tensions between Japan and the United States that caused O'Doul to question his safety should he travel there.[59] Soon it became all too obvious that there would be no further journeys to Japan for the foreseeable future, and a saddened O'Doul turned his attention stateside.

Lefty O'Doul was heartbroken—and angered—by the Japanese attack on Pearl Harbor. Like Babe Ruth, he considered it a personal betrayal. And understanding the Japanese way of thinking, he recognized that the battle between Japan and the United States would be a long one.

"See, there's one thing I know about them; that they were going to be tough opponents . . . their God is the Emperor. And they have no fear of death, none whatsoever. You know that anytime a boy goes up in an airplane and drops [a bomb] down a smokestack of a ship, he certainly isn't showing fear. If the Emperor's their God, then they all become heroes. They figure on reincarnation. When you battle against that, it's bound to be rough."[60]

Distraught at the news of the December 7 attack on Hawaii, a number of high-profile Japanese rushed to proclaim their loyalty to the United States and condemn the actions of their former homeland.

The day after the bombing of Pearl Harbor, Katsuma Mukaeda, president of the Los Angeles–based Japanese Cultural Society, declared, "This is an unprecedented crisis for us but we will acquit ourselves proudly. America is our home, our permanent residence."[61] Togo Tanaka, editor of *Rafu Shimpo*, pointed out that the Japanese-American Citizens League had been working with the Federal Bureau of Investigation and intelligence services for years and added, "We think the Japanese government is stupid and has embarked on a campaign it has absolutely no chance of winning. We have not been in sympathy with Japan's expansion program. This may well be the end of Japan as a power."[62]

Nevertheless, the fear on the West Coast was palpable. In the wake of FBI sweeps of areas thought to be vulnerable to sabotage, especially ports and rail lines, Mukaeda and Tanaka were placed in internment camps, along with thousands of others including Kenichi Zenimura and the father and sister of Cappy Harada.

The fear was exacerbated by several Japanese attacks on West Coast targets in the weeks following Pearl Harbor. On December 20, Japanese submarines attacked two oil tankers off the Northern California coast, hitting one while the other escaped unscathed.[63]

Two months later, a Japanese submarine lobbed several shells at an oil refinery at Goleta, California, near Santa Barbara on the Southern California coast, causing minor damage.[64] This was soon followed by another engagement with an oil tanker, which was armed and managed to return fire off Half Moon Bay, south of San Francisco. Other minor attacks continued into the fall.[65]

O'Doul openly speculated that the Japanese had aimed poorly on purpose, calculating that it would cause American military leaders to underestimate them.[66] Meanwhile, filming for *Pride of the Yankees*,

for which O'Doul was serving as technical advisor to lead actor Gary
Cooper, began at Wrigley Field in Los Angeles and was limited to a
maximum of two weeks because the Cubs had to train there rather
than at Catalina Island because of the potential for Japanese attacks.[67]

These episodes brought the war home to those on the West
Coast. Japanese Americans especially felt the impact, dragged as
they were from their lives and into the segregation of internment
camps. A year after Pearl Harbor, a Gallup poll of those living in the
western states revealed that tensions remained. One-third of those
surveyed felt that no Japanese, regardless of where they were born,
should be allowed to return to the coast. Of those, two-thirds were
of the opinion that they should be sent to Japan. More than half of
the Gallup participants said they would not conduct business with
Japanese after the war. Ninety-seven percent thought relocation of
the Japanese was the right thing to do.[68]

During the war, Matsutaro Shoriki continued publishing *Yomiuri
Shimbun*. He was close to Prime Minister Hideki Tojo and was
promoted to a position of councilor to the Tojo cabinet, representing the Japanese press to that body. While he later insisted that he
had no great regard for the military or its aims, his newspaper, as
others, was a source of propaganda in support of the war effort. In
May 1944 Shoriki was selected to serve in the House of Peers, and
later that year received a silver cup from Emperor Hirohito in recognition of his outstanding service to his country.

After the war, several of Shoriki's employees charged that he had
colluded with Tojo, and questions were raised about the actions of
Yomiuri's editors in contacting Hawaii on the eve of Pearl Harbor,
inquiring about the military situation there. On December 1, 1945,
a warrant was issued for Shoriki's arrest, and twelve days later he
surrendered to Sugamo Prison, where accused war criminals were
being held over for trial.

Two weeks later, former prime minister Fumimaro Konoe, who
only weeks earlier had told Harry Brundidge that Lefty O'Doul should
have been a diplomat rather than a ballplayer, committed suicide
rather than surrender as an accused war criminal, ingesting potas-

sium cyanide the day he was due to turn himself in.[69] Konoe's son, Fumitaka, the former Princeton student O'Doul knew well, had been captured by the Soviets earlier that year; he eventually died in a Siberian prison camp in 1956 after reportedly refusing to spy for them.[70]

In June 1946 Matsutaro Shoriki wrote a defense of his actions and asked for an appeal of his charges, which consisted of crime against the peace, participating in the plan for preparation and waging an illegal war by promoting militaristic propaganda, and urging Japanese adherence to the Axis.

In the end, it was determined that Shoriki was not a war criminal and he was released without standing trial in September 1947, after spending twenty-one months in prison.[71]

During the summer of 1945, Lefty O'Doul had confidently predicted victory over the Japanese. "American boys always beat the Japanese in baseball," he defiantly announced. "American boys think faster, run harder, hit harder. In this war it will be the same old story of baseball. The American boy is better than the Japanese boy. We will win."[72] Two years earlier, he had converted his famous O'Doul Day event into a fundraiser to pay for athletic equipment to be shipped overseas to American soldiers. Roughly ten thousand fans attended the game and made donations.[73]

Still angry about the attack on Pearl Harbor, O'Doul said, "The only victory the Japanese understand is to kick the hell out of a guy. When Babe Ruth and us fellows barnstormed Japan . . . they wanted to get licked then. The government officials told us so. It would impress the Japanese boys and the people and make them work harder to become proficient in this American game that they dearly loved."[74]

O'Doul also harkened back to his arrest in 1932, when he and Joe Cohen were nabbed by police for taking photos of Tokyo Harbor. He told San Francisco Chronicle sportswriter Bob Stevens that he had gotten back at the Japanese for detaining him.

"I got the last laugh," he told Stevens. "I took pictures until my arms grew weary. Pictures of everything I could see. And those pictures have since been turned over to Army intelligence. I hope they make the road to Tokyo a little easier."[75]

But as angry as O'Doul was, he still had a soft spot for the Japanese people, as he would soon demonstrate.

In November 1945, with Japan vanquished, O'Doul's old friend and co-organizer of the 1934 tour, Sotaro Suzuki, now sports editor of *Yomiuri Shimbun*, predicted a comeback for baseball in Japan. Keio and Waseda universities had staged their first contest on November 18, a few weeks after the Big Six universities had staged a game marking baseball's return.[76] Suzuki, who was a director of the Tokyo Giants, told reporter Red Patton, "I have confidence that our league will be in full operation by next spring."[77]

He had been pleased to learn that O'Doul was doing well, and had sent a message through the press only days after Japan's surrender to let O'Doul know he was safe and sound, and that Matsutaro Shoriki—who had not yet been arrested—was interested in restarting professional baseball.[78]

Suzuki had kept the flame of baseball alive during the war, holding onto autographed photos, trophies, and other memorabilia from Americans despite threats from security police if he continued displaying them at his home in Yokohama. He even had a run of *The Sporting News* going back to 1920—receiving some of the contraband via South America during the conflict. Toward the end of the war, Suzuki took his prized possessions to a shelter cave, where he remained as a mass bombing raid destroyed the city. "One of the big bombs hit a corner of my home and it burned," Suzuki said. "But all of my souvenirs were saved."[79]

When asked about the state of baseball in his country, Suzuki bemoaned the decision to end youth baseball a decade earlier, and noted that the professionals had to stop playing in 1945. Even before that, Japanese versions of American terms used in baseball had been banned by a government anxious to stamp out any Western influence. "We admired baseball officials and the government in the United States for keeping the game alive during the war," Suzuki told Red Patton. "I wish we were as fortunate."[80]

Dozens of Japanese professional ballplayers died during the war, including Eiji Sawamura, who reportedly grew to dislike Americans during the 1935 tour; he perished when his ship was sunk in

1944 by an American submarine. Five others from that first Japanese professional team that O'Doul had helped bring to the United States in 1935 died during the war, fighting the Americans they had played against.[81] The ship that had carried O'Doul to Japan on his first visit in 1931, the *Tatsuta Maru*, also failed to survive; called into service as a troop ship during the war, it was sunk in February 1943 by the USS *Tarpon*, resulting in the deaths of more than one thousand Japanese soldiers.[82]

The war over, Lefty O'Doul traveled to Japan for the first time in nearly nine years. It was a sobering experience, and he betrayed a sense of nervousness about his return.

"Oh Jesus, so many of my friends in Japan got killed during the war. So many. Well, you know, in time of war we all get bitter. When I got there . . . I thought all they'd talk about was the bomb. But they didn't seem to be excited or vicious about it at all. At least those I talked to didn't."[83]

He reconnected with Sotaro Suzuki, and also discovered that he had not been forgotten. "Somebody told our interpreter that one Japanese had been able to trade a bat with my name on it for a bottle of whisky," laughed O'Doul. "I only hope it was good whisky."[84]

O'Doul was optimistic about the potential for reopening Japan and hoped to mount official tours. In May 1947 he announced his intention to take the San Francisco Seals as a "goodwill gesture" after the conclusion of the PCL season, but the American Occupation forces withheld approval.[85] In January 1948 O'Doul again announced he had applied for permission to bring the Seals to Tokyo and several other cities.[86] But a few weeks later, after returning from a vacation in Hawaii with Seals owner Paul Fagan, he revealed that permission had once again been denied.[87] O'Doul was disappointed, but undaunted. The 1934 tour had not forestalled an inevitable war between the two countries; everyone involved had been naive in thinking that it had. But O'Doul remained convinced that the game provided an opportunity to develop common ground and facilitate reconciliation between the nations. In 1949 his persistence paid off.

11

In Fact, We Are Major League!

The Seals finally lost on October 26 in Nagoya, but not to Japanese ballplayers. Rather they were bested, 4–2, in eleven innings by the Far East Air Force All-Stars they had humbled earlier in the tour.[1] San Francisco quickly rebounded against an All-Japanese team, winning, 13–4, in a game played despite torrential rain courtesy of Typhoon Patricia; mindful of it being the only opportunity these fans would have to see them play, O'Doul and his men soldiered on, even as the Seals manager coached third base while holding a Japanese paper umbrella and standing atop a pair of cinder blocks to keep from sinking into the mud.[2] "We had advertised that we'd play rain or shine," explained O'Doul. "So we figured if [the fans] could sit in the rain, we certainly could play in it."[3] He told a *Yomiuri Shimbun* reporter, "I have never seen in all my life such enthusiastic fans." He then joked, "However, I must say that it's natural for the Seals to win in water."[4]

Reno Cheso hit a grand slam through the downpour in what was scheduled to be the penultimate game of the 1949 trip.[5] He was treated as a hero after that blow; when he walked into a local camera shop the next afternoon, every employee recognized him and bowed in respect. Cheso's attempt to pay for a camera was refused—they insisted it was an honor to give it to him as a gift.[6]

Two days later, before an overflow crowd of seventy thousand in Tokyo, the Seals narrowly escaped defeat in what was possibly their toughest battle against the Japanese. The game remained scoreless into the ninth, with the Seals managing only two hits off Victor Starffin and submariner Shisho Takesue; San Francisco finally triumphed thanks to outfielder Dick Steinhauer, who hit a solo home run for a 1–0 win.[7] Steinhauer admitted afterward, "I was expecting a curve . . . but it came in higher than I expected. . . . It was pure accident that I hit the home run."[8]

By that time the Seals had played before nearly as many fans in Japan as during their entire 1949 home season in San Francisco, where they had drawn a very healthy 460,000 as a seventh-place team.

The Japanese could not get enough of the Americans, and in particular Lefty O'Doul. The only complaint was that the number of games was insufficient to satisfy demand. And with prices being what they were, many schoolchildren were essentially shut off from the experience.

O'Doul suggested a solution—a version of his San Francisco O'Doul Day. "The idea came to me when I was driving in from Haneda airdrome," O'Doul explained. "Thousands of kids lined the route, waving flags and shouting at the players as they went by. I realized that for most of these youngsters it would be their only opportunity to see the team, and yet they seemed happy and contented. I determined then and there to make it possible for those youngsters to see a game.

"These kids are the future diplomats, businessmen, politicians, industrial leaders, bankers and teachers of Japan. I wanted to stage a contest that would be their game."[9]

As had been the case for the O'Doul Day celebrations in San Francisco, the event Lefty staged in late October in Tokyo would become something to remember. For everyone.

• • •

A pair of developments in 1945 altered the baseball landscape in San Francisco and brought new life to Lefty O'Doul and the Seals. First, the team negotiated a working agreement with O'Doul's old team, the New York Giants.[10] The second was a new partner in Seals ownership—a multi-millionaire with big league ambitions.

Paul Fagan, who had long been involved with Crocker Bank in San Francisco before marrying into the Crocker family itself, purchased the share of the franchise once owned by George Putnam, who had died eight years earlier. Fagan's portfolio included significant holdings in Hawaii, including thousands of acres on Maui and Molokai. He owned a cattle ranch and resort properties there, and had built a palatial estate near Diamond Head.

Originally interested in relocating a team to Honolulu, Fagan came to terms with the impracticality of regular air travel to and from the mainland and heeded a friend's advice to look into acquiring a portion of the San Francisco Seals. Within weeks he had secured the one-third share held by the Putnam estate for a quarter million dollars. The infusion of cash meant that for the first time since the beginning of the Depression, the Seals were on solid financial footing.[11]

Although lacking anything more than a rudimentary knowledge of baseball, Fagan had a clear vision of what he wanted—Major League status. He was willing to invest in the stadium, the players, and the future. "Baseball is the same as any other business," he reasoned. "You have to meet your competition on equal footing. We are selling seats in a ballpark and we must give the fans a good show. That means a good club. And we must be in a position to meet any competition offered."[12]

Fagan spoke of covering the stands at Seals Stadium, installing theater seats for a more upscale experience, and adding steam heat to make patrons more comfortable during night games. The locker rooms were updated, with the players' lounge expanded and brightened. To generate additional revenue, he proposed constructing an ice rink at the stadium that could be opened to the public during the winter.[13]

Paul Fagan had instantly rejuvenated one of the Pacific Coast League's flagship franchises. Following several lean years, Lefty O'Doul eagerly accepted what Fagan was offering, having long argued that a quality setting was important for a good performance.

"A ball player should be presented in the same manner as a stage actor," O'Doul had declared. "In the theatre they write the script, shade the lights, tune the music, arrange the billing and employ every means in the producer's power to bring out the best in the performer. [A player is] made to feel welcome," Lefty gushed, "and he wants to play here and will hustle to hold his job."[14]

After more than a decade of scratching and clawing to survive, O'Doul was seduced by the promise made possible by Fagan's riches. Over time he began to think he was going back to the Majors after all, just not in a conventional manner. Which seemed appropriate— after all, little about Lefty O'Doul was conventional.

With money in the bank and wartime travel restrictions lifted, the Seals made plans to spend 1946 spring training in Honolulu as guests of Paul Fagan.[15] Among the thirty-seven players bound for Hawaii aboard the *Aleutian* were two young stars, returning after the war had forced one, first baseman Ferris Fain, into the service and the other, pitcher Larry Jansen, onto his family's farm to aid the war effort. O'Doul was thankful to be past the era of teenagers and forty-year-olds—the latter usually signed during the war years to trade off their names, briefly prolonging their careers before it became obvious that their eyes and/or legs had already betrayed them. It was true that the Seals players were not exactly young, but at least none were senior citizens in baseball terms, as had been the case during the war.

O'Doul felt on top of the world, even as rough seas made the voyage to the islands a bit of an ordeal. Confined to his cabin, he eagerly mapped out his plans for training camp. Once the ocean calmed a bit, he sought to alleviate the tedium by staging a sort of junior Olympics for the youngsters on board.[16]

The Seals were accorded a royal welcome when they reached Hawaii, each player greeted with a lei as he walked off the gang-plank. Charlie Graham was presented the key to the city of Hono-lulu, and the team was paraded through the streets, the mile-long convoy headed by O'Doul, perched in the front seat of a fire truck in a manner reminiscent of a proud peacock.[17] The players were delighted to discover that their hotel was located steps from Waikiki Beach, and that they would be working out at Honolulu's Munic-ipal Stadium, a twenty-year-old wooden structure that had hosted Irving Berlin the previous year, and where Babe Ruth had once

played. A new locker room was constructed expressly for the Seals'
visit—Paul Fagan had spared no expense.[18]

O'Doul was ecstatic about what was happening to the franchise.
He was said to be surprising himself by turning in every night at
nine-thirty, and then arising each morning to greet the sunrise and
swim in the surf at Waikiki.[19] Although there were a few injuries
not usually associated with spring training—Neill Sheridan cut
his hand on some coral while diving, and right-hander Frank Cvi-
tanich strained the muscles in his pitching arm pulling the oar of
an outrigger canoe—the trip was considered a rousing success.[20]

When O'Doul brought his team home to San Francisco, he
was ready to prove what he could accomplish with real backing.
The result would be one of the most successful seasons in franchise history.

Paul Fagan's quest for Major League status was far from folly—nor
was it a new one for the Pacific Coast League. From its inception,
the league's owners had been desirous of greater status than the
established Major Leagues were willing to allow. More than forty
years earlier, original Los Angeles Angels owner Jim Morley had
railed against the draft and openly advocated for Major League status. He successfully negotiated contracts with big leaguers such as
Dummy Hoy, Frank "Cap" Dillon, Doc Newton, and Frank Chance.[21]

The PCL adopted rules limiting the drafting of its players by
the Major Leagues during the 1920s. Teams held onto their stars
much longer—and reaped greater rewards when they did part with
them by selling them to the highest bidder. Lefty O'Doul had been
one of those laboring in the PCL during that period, even though
he was arguably performing at a big league level. During the postwar boom years, the clamor for big league status rose again, with
Paul Fagan one of its staunchest advocates. The league boasted
two major cities in San Francisco and Los Angeles, and another of
good size in Seattle. It had owners of means—Philip Wrigley and
Pacific Northwest beer barons Emil Sick and George Norgan. And
now Paul Fagan. The new Seals part-owner also had a sympathetic
ear for his ambitions in Charlie Graham—a man with connec-

tions and highly respected by the baseball establishment. Graham
believed in the primacy of his organization, arguing that com-
paring the International League and American Association to the
PCL was so much apples to oranges—the other "Triple A" leagues
were constricted by salary limits in the range of a half million dollars. According to Graham, the PCL's league-wide salaries would be
twice that by 1947—making the average team salary in the league
roughly equivalent to many of their Major League counterparts.[22]

The Seals' success in 1946 would only fan the flames of Fagan's
ambition. But to an extent it was a race against time. The Los Angeles Chamber of Commerce continued efforts to attract Major League
Baseball to California—the St. Louis Browns had proposed moving in 1942, but the window had slammed shut with the attack on
Pearl Harbor.[23] As fans began hearing more and more talk about
Major League Baseball, the question among more and more of them
became, "Why settle for the Minor Leagues if we can get the Majors?"

Lefty O'Doul found another motivation to stimulate his competitive
juices as he entered his twelfth season in charge of the Seals. The
Oakland Oaks had hired a colorful manager of their own, among
the most colorful in baseball history—Casey Stengel. O'Doul knew
Stengel well, and privately carped about the man with nine seasons of Major League experience as a manager, but most famous
for releasing a sparrow from beneath his cap during an argument
with an umpire. Sacramento sportswriter Bill Conlin offered his
opinion that O'Doul's disdain masked a streak of jealousy.[24] After
all, Stengel could give O'Doul a run for his money with Bay Area
reporters—heretofore his exclusive audience. Casey was a colorful
and quotable character, and a serious rival suddenly planted in his
backyard. O'Doul, who had become comfortable as the big fish in
the little pond, as it were, wanted to beat him.

When the 1946 season began, O'Doul struggled to formulate a
successful lineup as the team committed sixty-seven errors through
its first thirty-three games. Slowly the players jelled, the offense
coalescing around Ferris Fain and third baseman Ted Jennings—
another pet project of O'Doul's despite the fact that he could never

seem to comprehend even the simplest signs from the coach's box. But he could hit the ball hard.

The pitching staff was led by Larry Jansen and ex–New York Giants star Cliff Melton, who had won twenty games as a rookie for New York nine years earlier; Melton was sold to San Francisco after holding out the entire 1945 season while battling elbow problems dating back to a fateful request of Carl Hubbell to teach him the screwball.

Melton won his first six games while Jansen, having mastered a slider taught to him by Seals coach Larry Woodall, became a phenomenon.[25] By June, Jansen's record stood at 15-3 and his earned run average was 1.14. Jansen won his twentieth game with a week remaining in July, ending that encounter against Sacramento with a flourish by striking out the side in the ninth inning of a 7–3 victory.[26] He was soon sold to the New York Giants for delivery in 1947, where he would match Melton's feat of winning twenty games as a National League rookie.[27] The Seals were running away from the rest of the league—except for Oakland.

The rivalry between the Seals and the Oaks—and O'Doul and Stengel—was fueling fan interest and generating record attendance. Twice during a series in early August, the teams drew crowds of greater than twenty thousand. With more than five weeks remaining in the season, the Seals broke the all-time single-season Minor League attendance record, held by the 1939 Seattle Rainiers, who had drawn a little more than a half million.[28]

On September 19 Larry Jansen duplicated Bob Joyce's achievement of the previous year, defeating Portland, 2–1, to win his thirtieth game of the season.[29] The right-hander credited O'Doul for his development, calling him "the man who most influenced my thinking in baseball."[30]

San Francisco went on to capture its first regular-season title of any kind in eleven years, as the tightness of the pennant race and a pair of charismatic managers proved a boon for baseball in the Bay Area. The Seals and Oaks both drew more than 600,000 fans, with San Francisco attracting a Minor League record 670,563, a mark that would stand for more than three decades.[31] Never before had the PCL enjoyed the level of success at the turnstile as in 1946. More than 3.7 million fans bought tickets, led by the Seals' record. According to *The Sporting News*, every PCL team had turned a profit.[32]

The Seals' championship was celebrated with a parade to City Hall, where five hundred people crowded into the rotunda to listen to congratulatory speeches. For O'Doul it was a particularly proud moment, and he betrayed a bit of the chip he carried on his shoulder when it came to the popularity of Casey Stengel. As he concluded his remarks to raucous applause, O'Doul admitted, "Never in my life have I wanted anything as much as I wanted this flag. Not only for San Francisco, but for the boys who made a big league manager out of me, because I managed to finish ahead of that big league manager in Oakland."[33]

O'Doul's men followed the celebration with a defense of the Governor's Cup. Larry Jansen starred in the first round against Hollywood, shutting out the Stars in the opening game, and then pitching seven and two-thirds innings of relief and hitting a home run in the clincher that sent them to the championship series.[34] In the finals, San Francisco defeated Stengel's Oaks in six games, bringing another measure of satisfaction to O'Doul, and a fourth consecutive Governor's Cup to his team.

Lefty O'Doul was as popular as ever in San Francisco—as much a city landmark as the Coit Tower or the cable cars. And he was living the high life, courtesy of Paul Fagan; vacationing in Hawaii and spending his days on the beach, or reliving his Butchertown Cowboy days, riding the range on Fagan's cattle ranch.[35]

He loved it.

Shortly after the 1946 season ended, Lefty O'Doul's name once again surfaced in connection with managing the New York Giants. It had been Mel Ott, not O'Doul, chosen to succeed Bill Terry in 1942. The Giants had twice finished last in Ott's five seasons, including in 1946, and his hold on the job had become tenuous.

Frank Graham of the *New York Journal–American* attempted to force the issue, anointing O'Doul as "not only the best, but the most colorful manager in the minor leagues and, by any baseball standard you can set, belongs in the majors because at heart and in manner he is a big leaguer, on and off the field."[36]

When asked whether he would accept the job if it was offered, O'Doul replied, "I would never do anything to harm [Charlie] Graham and his associates. My first duty will always be to them. I guess what I am trying to say is that any decision I might make would only come after a full consultation with them."[37] While he did not say yes, O'Doul's love for the Giants made it extremely difficult for him to simply say no. At the same time, he recognized that in San Francisco he could do as he pleased as manager. He knew that would not be the case in New York.

O'Doul was a hot commodity. Larry MacPhail admitted he had O'Doul on his short list to manage the New York Yankees, succeeding Joe McCarthy (and Bill Dickey and Johnny Neun—all of whom had managed the team during the 1946 season). Dan Daniel of the *New York Telegram* reported that O'Doul had turned down an offer from MacPhail.[38]

In the end, O'Doul decided to stay in San Francisco, Mel Ott remained with the Giants, and Bucky Harris, as had been the case with the Phillies four years earlier, was hired in O'Doul's stead and took the reins of the Yankees.

The attention provided O'Doul a forum to expound on the managerial style he had developed over twelve seasons. "Today I gamble more," he explained. "I still figure percentages, but the older I get, the more radical I become." He still eschewed sacrifices, declaring, "I never play for a tie. I play to win."[39]

San Francisco Examiner sportswriter Abe Kemp informed his readers that an unidentified catcher on another team had confided to him that O'Doul drove opposing managers crazy. "There is only one way to get the best of O'Doul," the catcher told Kemp. "Figure the last thing in the world you would think of doing in a given situation and then figure on O'Doul and his boys to try and do it."[40]

It was noted that O'Doul no longer wore green suits—though he still owned one that he dragged out each St. Patrick's Day. His wardrobe now most commonly consisted of gray or beige whipcord and maroon neckties. "I confess I am superstitious," he admitted.

"I figured a green suit was the answer. Since becoming a manager, I've found out green or pink or blue or red doesn't help you in the least."[41]

Near the end of the year, Dan Daniel flew to San Francisco and spent a day with O'Doul, Charlie Graham, and Paul Fagan. As the four men sat in O'Doul's cocktail lounge on Powell Street, Daniel asked O'Doul why he turned down offers to manage in the Major Leagues.

O'Doul explained, "I have a fine job with the Seals. I have a thriving business. Out here I am somebody about town. I am my own boss. Sure, it would be an honor to run a club back East. I always have been very ambitious, always determined to be tops. But what's lacking in my position here? Charlie Graham is like a father to me. Paul Fagan and I see eye to eye on everything in baseball.

"This is my home. Here I was born. Here I intend to stay just as long as they will let me. I was born South of the Slot, in Butchertown. I like the folks of San Francisco . . . I'm already in the major leagues. This is major class. This is a major city. In fact, we are major league!"[42]

O'Doul's refusal to leave his home made him even more popular in San Francisco. In 1947 he was profiled by Collie Small in the *Saturday Evening Post*. It was said that Charlie Graham refused to walk down the street with his manager.

"He has tried it," wrote Small, "and finds he spends all his time lingering anonymously on the curb while the grinning O'Doul fends off innumerable 'old friends' and hysterical young admirers. One of O'Doul's 'old friends' is an ancient derelict to whom Lefty has been donating fifty cents a day for years. Several weeks ago, O'Doul emerged from Seals Stadium and, as usual, was confronted by his old pal, the tramp.

"'Gimme my half, Lefty,' he pleaded.

"O'Doul reached obediently into his pocket. Slowly he withdrew his hand. It was empty, except for his car keys.

"'Holy Smoke!' O'Doul exclaimed. 'I haven't got any money with me.'

"The tramp was shocked. O'Doul, of all people, had failed him. O'Doul was shocked too. He was also perplexed. Suddenly his face lit up.

"'Look,' he asked hopefully, like a small boy caught without his allowance, 'will you trust me until tomorrow?'"[43]

O'Doul remained popular with kids—though Lefty O'Doul Day had ended during the war, he remained focused on taking his time to chat with children, both boys and girls, when they crossed his path. He carried baseball equipment of all kinds in the trunk of his Cadillac—green, of course—and would stop to hand out bats, gloves, and baseballs when he came upon a group of kids playing ball. Future Oakland Raiders coach and sportscaster John Madden was playing ball in the street as a twelve-year-old with a friend when O'Doul pulled up and invited the boys to a Seals game that day. It made a lasting impression on Madden, who was a big fan of the Seals and of Lefty O'Doul. Madden reflected, "It taught me to be myself . . . but always think of others."[44] He later caddied for O'Doul on occasion and was often rewarded with tickets to the ball game. "Then, you had it made as a kid," he recalled.[45]

As O'Doul departed for spring training in 1947, he was at the top of his game, achieving the status of icon in his hometown, two pennants and four straight playoff championships in his portfolio, and two Major League teams representing New York City clamoring for his services. It was said that with bonuses tied to attendance, he could earn as much as $50,000 from the Seals in the coming season.[46] Bill Conlin claimed that O'Doul showed him his paycheck and the base pay was thirty-nine thousand.[47]

The Seals had lost their two biggest stars from the 1946 champions, Larry Jansen and Ferris Fain, to the Major Leagues, but O'Doul was confident the team would contend once again. They returned to Hawaii for spring training, this time flying so as not to repeat the viral bouts of seasickness that had swept through the players on the way over the previous spring. They trained in Hana, a wide spot in the road on the island of Maui and home to some five hundred people near Fagan's cattle ranch, on a plot of ground he had picked out the year before. The players were lodged in a brand-new hotel Fagan built for them that faced the beach.[48]

When rain damaged the practice field, Fagan picked out another spot four miles down the road and less vulnerable to daily rain showers. Within a day the new playing field was ready, along with a shuttle service established from the beach to the new facility. Players ate steak every day and were treated to hulas and Hawaiian music each evening.[49] O'Doul had slow motion film taken of each Seals pitcher and analyzed their mechanics with them on an individual basis.[50] It was no wonder he felt his surroundings were Major League.

O'Doul celebrated his fiftieth birthday on March 4 at Homoa Beach with the rest of the Seals and several sportswriters. Suddenly, Bob Stevens saw fellow scribe Bucky Walter struggling in the water, about seventy-five yards from shore. Pitcher Larry Powell saw him too and tried to reach him, but he tired before he could get there. O'Doul suddenly appeared and grabbed Walter who, in a panic, nearly pulled both of them under. Lefty managed to break Walter's grip and hauled him to the surface. O'Doul then pulled Walter to shore, saving his life.[51]

That night, Fagan threw a birthday party for O'Doul on his front lawn, complete with hula dancers, pig roasted underground Hawaiian style, shrimp, clams, and local delicacies. O'Doul even favored the group with a brief hula.[52] No man ever had a more memorable fiftieth birthday.

The New York Giants had tagged along to Hawaii, training in Honolulu and playing several games against the Seals. While there, Giants owner Horace Stoneham pulled Charlie Graham aside at Paul Fagan's home and asked, "If at mid-season Ott is no longer my manager, could I have Lefty as his replacement?" Graham said, "If O'Doul would want to go to you, you can have him."[53] Stoneham did just that, pulling Lefty into a side room, with Ott standing a floor below, and offering him the job. O'Doul turned him down.[54]

Paul Fagan continued dressing up Seals Stadium. He rebuilt the press box and added a Plexiglas backstop—the first in all of baseball.[55] He established a sporting goods shop at the stadium where fans could buy bats, gloves, and balls, as well as Seals caps. He allowed fans to reserve tickets by phone and held them until the last out of the game, trusting that most people were honest.[56] He also opened a ticket office downtown at Geary and Market Street.[57]

Fagan provided full medical coverage for his players and their families.[58] He hired five men to work year-round to keep the Seals' playing surface among the best in baseball. He employed female ushers, dressing them in smart outfits custom-ordered from premier clothier I. Magnin.[59] An aquarium was installed inside the stadium entrance, complete with a live seal.[60] The team instituted a new tradition, placing a star on the fence when a player hit a particularly long home run—Joe Brovia was the first to earn one with a blast off Seattle's Sig Jakucki.[61]

Pitching continued to be a Seals bedrock, even as Larry Jansen's replacement, Bob Chesnes, complained of a sore arm while pitching spectacularly. No one could find anything wrong while Chesnes missed several weeks, contacted a famed arm specialist, and then followed the advice of a local insurance salesman to eat garlic and put diced onions in his socks. Every day. Unorthodox as it was, Chesnes was soon back on the mound and finished the season with twenty-two wins.[62]

When the Seals lost veteran center fielder and lead-off hitter Frenchy Uhalt to a broken ankle, they seriously investigated the possibility of replacing him with Sam Jethroe, an outfielder with the Negro American League's Cleveland Buckeyes; Jethroe would have become the first African American in the PCL. It was almost unheard of for Charlie Graham to acquire players from other organizations once the season started, and when pressed about the need for the Seals to be the first to have an African American on their roster, Graham retorted, "Why should the Seals be last?"[63]

But the proposed transaction fell through, and when reporters asked Charles J. Graham, son of the legendary owner, whether O'Doul was aware of the deal—they had assumed the pursuit of Jethroe had been in response to a request by O'Doul—the answer shocked them. "I'm not sure that O'Doul knows of it," snapped the younger Graham. "But it doesn't matter. It's none of his business anyway."[64]

It was an ominous signal that, with the senior Graham beginning to phase himself out, O'Doul was only appreciated by the
front office as long as he knew his place. It was also a sign that
his continued pleas for quality reinforcements were unlikely to be
heeded, although Bill Leiser of the *San Francisco Chronicle* wrote
that another newspaper—not in favor of having black ballplayers
on the Seals—had reported O'Doul's saying he did not need help.[65]
Publicly, O'Doul remained silent.

There was speculation Charlie Graham had caved to hate mail protesting the signing of a black player, while some reporters attributed
the collapse of the deal to Graham's reticence in spending the money
it required. While always willing to pay his players a good salary,
Graham had never paid much to acquire them. His reputation was
that of someone fixated on getting the better of a deal—buying low
and selling high as it were—rather than investing money in players
to win pennants. Others claimed the deal failed because the Cleveland Indians had been promised first call on the outfielder.[66] But
the racial tenor of the protests unquestionably stunted Graham's
initial resolve; he expressed dismay at the abusiveness of the correspondence he received, and claimed he did not receive one call
or letter in favor of signing Jethroe.[67]

Despite injuries and an inability to replace their wounded, the Seals
hung in the pennant race after trailing at one point in August by
seven and a half games, making a mad rush during the final weeks
of the 1947 season to enter the final day in a flat-footed tie with the
Los Angeles Angels.

An opportunity arose when the Angels split their season-ending
doubleheader and the Seals won their first game that day against
San Diego—their twelfth win in thirteen contests. But San Francisco
would drop the nightcap in dramatic fashion when Dino Restelli
was called out on an attempted steal of home with the bases loaded,
a controversial call that culminated in O'Doul pretending to faint
and falling onto home plate.[68] The Seals went on to lose the game
in extra innings, forcing a one-game playoff against Los Angeles.[69]

The Angels hosted the winner-take-all contest at Wrigley Field, matching their twenty-three-game winner Cliff Chambers against San Francisco's Jack Brewer, winner of sixteen. The game was, as expected, a pitcher's duel; three times the Seals had potential rallies snuffed out by double plays, and neither team was able to score during the first seven innings.

But Brewer surrendered a grand slam to Clarence Maddern in the bottom of the eighth, dashing San Francisco's dreams of a second consecutive PCL pennant.[70] Chambers, pitching on one day's rest, would always call the shutout he pitched that day the highlight of his career—a notch above the no-hitter he tossed in the Major Leagues four years later.[71]

To add insult to injury, O'Doul would then see the Seals' streak of four straight Governor's Cup championships ended in the first round by Stengel and the Oaks.

The Seals drew 640,645 in 1947, slightly off their record pace a year earlier, but still impressive. Shortly after the 1948 season began, Paul Fagan, disappointed by the fact that the Seals would spend another season sans Major League status, vowed that his team would reclaim the PCL pennant. Insisting that the Seals would no longer sell players to the Major Leagues, except for those who were draft eligible, he maintained that the only way to raise the level of competition was to sign the best talent available, even if that meant San Francisco won the PCL pennant by twenty games every year. If the Seals destroyed the league's competitive balance, so be it, declared Fagan. "Eventually the weaker clubs will have to meet the higher level. Competition dictates that."

Fagan also forced Lefty O'Doul to curtail his business plans, which included opening a restaurant and a haberdashery, in order to focus on managing. Not only that, he ordered O'Doul to cease his active interest in his cocktail lounge—a disappointed O'Doul did as he was told, taking down the Lefty O'Doul's sign while remaining a silent partner in the enterprise, which was renamed "On the Hill."[72]

Despite this setback, O'Doul enthusiastically charged into the 1948 season, privately endorsing Fagan's assertions of the Seals' dominance, boasts that became public and caused no little amount

of embarrassment. O'Doul had no choice but to stick by his statement, while at the same time denying stories that had him proclaiming the Seals would outdistance the rest of the league by twenty-five
games. "I said we'd win the pennant," admitted O'Doul. "I meant
it. I'm stuck with it and my job now is to make good on it."[73]

And it appeared that he would. New outfielder Gene Woodling
took to O'Doul's batting lessons and was flirting with the .400 mark.
Outfielder Dino Restelli was developing as a hitter, and among league
leaders in all major offensive categories.[74] The team won eleven of its
first seventeen games and boasted three hitters with averages of .391
or better. Even light-hitting shortstop Roy Nicely was batting .359.
The pitching was solid as well—arguably the deepest staff O'Doul
ever had. Con Dempsey, a second-year side-arm pitcher acquired
from Salt Lake City, began the season in the bullpen by throwing
thirty-three consecutive innings without allowing an earned run.
Before long he became a starter, led the league in strikeouts, and
was one of four Seals pitchers with at least fifteen wins.

Fagan was also going out and acquiring players from other leagues
after the season started. As Memorial Day approached, San Francisco was seven games in front. Then they lost Gene Woodling for
the better part of two months after he tore ligaments in his ankle on
the base paths, a setback that O'Doul termed "the greatest blow to
me since I've managed the Seals."[75] But a greater blow was to come.

The San Francisco Seals—and the entire PCL—struggled with the
loss of one of the league's giant figures. On August 29, 1948, seventy-
year-old Charlie Graham died.

Although Graham's son had assumed the duties of general manager of the franchise, the elder Graham had remained an active advisor, and one of the league's champions in the fight to attain major
league status for the PCL. He was also serving as president of the
Association of Professional Baseball Players of America, which
assisted retired ballplayers in need.

Five days before his death, Graham was stricken with food poison-
ing. At first he seemed to recover, but then he developed pneumonia
and lapsed into a coma.[76] He died with his family at his bedside.[77]

The flags at Seals Stadium stood at half-staff while a crowd of slightly more than seven thousand stood for a moment of silence before the start of a Sunday doubleheader in the ballpark Charlie Graham had built. A fifty-year career in baseball was at an end, and the PCL had lost its most respected voice.

Like the 1947 season, 1948 would end in disappointment—in less dramatic but still heartbreaking fashion. The Seals weathered the loss of Gene Woodling and held on to first place for most of the season. They lost Joe Brovia to appendicitis and then a broken hand, and still remained in front. They even played well after Charlie Graham's death, winning twenty-two of their final thirty-three games. But somehow it was not enough to hold off Casey Stengel and his hard-charging Oakland Oaks. On August 25 the Seals led the Oaks by three and a half games. But Oakland would win thirty-one of forty down the stretch to take the pennant by two games.

After the season ended, Casey Stengel was hired by the New York Yankees to begin a managerial stint that would earn him a place in the Baseball Hall of Fame. Lefty O'Doul had fallen short for the second year in a row, and he was about to find out what life was like without Charlie Graham. He would not like it.

Ignoring Paul Fagan's displeasure with at least one of his outside pursuits, O'Doul continued playing golf, and playing it well. In January 1949 he teamed with professional Bill Nary to capture the Bing Crosby Pro-Am Golf Tournament in Monterey, California. The "nattily attired" O'Doul was said to have "helped his pro teammate many times during the three-day scramble." The team shot best-ball rounds of 61, 66, and 60 to win the Pro-Am portion of the tournament by two strokes; individually, Nary finished fourth among the professionals, five strokes behind winner Ben Hogan.[78]

Although Paul Fagan had insisted he would be a hands-off owner in the team's new management structure, with O'Doul having the final say in player matters, it did not take long for him to breach that pledge. Joe Brovia was a holdout that spring and Fagan, who was obsessed with appearance, disliked him because he refused to use a handkerchief while spitting or blowing his nose while in the

field. Fagan was also upset that Brovia pulled the legs of his baseball pants down so that very little of the sock was showing. When
Fagan ordered Brovia to pull his pant leg up—Brovia wore his that
way as a tribute to Ted Williams—the outfielder responded, "I'm
not bringing them up around the knee."[79]

One morning, Fagan pulled aside recently hired team announcer
and public relations man Don Klein and informed him that he
would be holding his first press conference the next day. He was
to tell reporters that Joe Brovia had been sold to Portland.

Klein was flabbergasted. He remembered, "O'Doul was upset
about it. Brovia was a hero to the fans. I had to tell the writers and
they didn't believe me. They thought I was kidding. And I said,
'No, it's true. He's been traded to Portland.'"[80]

The announcement ignited a firestorm in San Francisco. Dump-
ing Brovia after he had hit .322 in 1948 puzzled not only writers
but also die-hard followers of the team.[81] O'Doul was left to explain
the deal, and all he could come up with was that Brovia did not figure into the team's plans.[82]

San Francisco Examiner columnist Curley Grieve snorted, "Any
time a .322 hitter doesn't fit in your plans, it's time to change the
plans."[83]

Often, a public figure's popularity turns on such matters. Although
it had been Fagan's doing, fans held O'Doul responsible for Brovia's departure; and so did Brovia, certain that O'Doul could have
forestalled the sale had he been so inclined.[84] The resulting rift
between Brovia and O'Doul lasted several years. For the first time,
O'Doul would hear criticism from the fans of San Francisco; the
Seals were blasted by the press during spring training in 1949,
with O'Doul the target for much of the vitriol.[85]

When Brovia returned to Seals Stadium with the Portland Beavers on Opening Night, Seals fans lustily cheered their former
favorite, and unfurled banners deriding O'Doul as "Marble Head."
Brovia enjoyed one of the most satisfying days of his career, bang-
ing out three hits as the crowd jeered the home team, and especially
O'Doul.[86] It was the beginning of the end of the city's love affair
with the Seals. A disillusioned O'Doul began quietly rebelling—

often showing up to the ballpark just before game time. Infielder Dario Lodigiani loved playing for Lefty—he said it was like playing for a big brother. At the same time, he told PCL historian Dick Dobbins that if the Seals had a big lead in the late innings, O'Doul would hand the team over to his coaches and take off.[87]

There were not a lot of big leads in 1949. The team struggled, losing 103 games and finishing seventh. That winter, there were no rumors of O'Doul being hired as a Major League manager. Meanwhile, old foe Casey Stengel won the first of five straight World Series as manager of the New York Yankees.

In early 1950 Paul Fagan bought out Doc Strub, the last of the troika that had owned the franchise for three decades, and became majority owner of the San Francisco Seals. He announced there would be no changes in the structure of the franchise but noted, "Now that I've got all this money tied up in the club, I'm certainly going to take more active interest."[88] Lefty O'Doul was named a vice president, and stock that had been promised him upon Charlie Graham's death was activated.

Fagan then created an uproar when as his first action as majority owner, he took on the messiness of peanut shells at Seals Stadium. Upset by the cost of sweeping them up each night, which more than swallowed the profits generated by the snack item, Fagan announced they were banned from the ballpark.

Fans revolted and vendors made plans to set up shop outside the stadium entrance. The story threatened to make Fagan a laughingstock, and he had to give in.[89] To make amends, he gave every fan a free bag on Opening Day.[90]

Fagan turned his attention to the draft, joining with Oakland owner Brick Laws in calling for an end to the practice. Laws was particularly upset about losing pitcher Milo Candini, standing by helplessly as the Philadelphia Phillies drafted him for only $10,000.[91]

Fagan once again declared that the only cure involved the PCL operating as a third Major League. Noting the failure of Minor League football and hockey, Fagan feared the PCL was next and pointed to what he called weak ownership in Southern California, with Los Angeles operating as a de facto Cubs farm team and Hollywood beholden to the Brooklyn Dodgers for their survival.

"Let us buy, sell and draft players from the major leagues and we'll do all right," the Seals' owner argued.[92]

In addition to the draft, television was becoming an increasing problem. Attendance in Los Angeles and Hollywood declined precipitously as the two teams began televising all of their games. Joe Wilmot of the *San Francisco Chronicle* noted the resulting small size of the crowds and said, "Evidently the only people who came out to watch were the poor souls who didn't own a television set—and brother, that isn't many."[93]

Unfortunately for the PCL, neither the Major Leagues nor television was giving in or going away. The Seals finished fifth in 1950, winning exactly as many games as they lost. There were rumors during the season that O'Doul was unhappy and would resign. O'Doul scoffed at the gossip, saying he planned to manage another eight or nine years. "That's all a lot of nonsense," he insisted. "Mr. Fagan and I are personal friends and I respect him very much. I'm happy here, and why shouldn't I be?"[94]

But that was before Paul Fagan bought out Charles J. Graham and O'Doul at the end of the season to become sole owner of the franchise.[95]

Following his first postwar barnstorming foray to Japan in 1949, O'Doul made plans to return a year later; but instead of bringing along a team of professional players, he recruited one of baseball's biggest names, Joe DiMaggio. In late October 1950, O'Doul and DiMaggio readied for their departure and Lefty briefed reporters. "We plan to stay there for three weeks and, if the military agrees, we'll visit Korea and talk to the kids there. I know they'll love to be near and hear DiMaggio."[96]

DiMaggio and O'Doul landed in Tokyo on November 1 and lunched with General MacArthur, who posed for a photograph with the two baseball heroes.[97] They were accorded special receptions in Kobe, Osaka, Nagoya, and Hiroshima.

The two were mobbed everywhere they went—dozens of chil-

222

dren stood outside their hotel all night, pleading with the two stars to make an appearance. They kept DiMaggio awake; at four o'clock one morning he received a call from O'Doul, who shouted into the phone, "Do you have any kids over there?" "Yeah," answered DiMaggio. "Do you want some?"[98]

With O'Doul proclaiming, "I'm here this time as bat boy to the greatest player in the game today," DiMaggio participated in home run contests against various Japanese professionals, including Makoto Kozuru, who was coming off a season in which he had hit fifty-one home runs.[99] The five-foot-nine Kozuru defeated DiMaggio in the first competition, four home runs to two.[100] DiMaggio lost two more contests before locating a good, American bat. He then won the final seven. In between, he and O'Doul were sometimes on the go for twenty hours at a time, holding baseball clinics for Japanese kids and visiting eighteen military hospitals in seventeen days.

Cappy Harada accompanied Lefty O'Doul and Joe DiMaggio as they flew to Korea, traveling in an L-17; the runway was so small in one of the towns that the pilot had to use its streets for a landing strip. Sirens sounded to warn the townsfolk to stay off the roadway as the plane took off. The two baseball stars, close enough to the front they could hear mortar shells falling, were amazed as their convoy passed mile after mile of abandoned Russian trucks and equipment—South Koreans stripping the vehicles of anything of value.

At Seoul the two met a Private Eugene Jones, a survivor of the Sunchon Tunnel massacre.[101] As Private Jones grasped the Yankee Clipper's hand he exclaimed, "Gee, I never dreamed I'd get to meet Joe DiMaggio." Lefty quickly interjected, "And Joe never dreamed he'd get to shake hands with a guy who went through what the Jones kid did."[102]

Joe and Lefty met another soldier from Texas who had most of his jaw shot off. The soldier attempted to speak, but with what was left of his jaw wired shut he could not make himself understood. A shaken DiMaggio took a baseball from his back pocket and autographed it before giving it to the young soldier. The man asked a nurse to hang the baseball from a string so he could see it; he barely took his eyes off it for the next couple of days.[103]

O'Doul was definitely the more comfortable of the two men, cracking wise with the soldiers, while DiMaggio conversed more seriously about the game and life at home. It seemed that O'Doul knew someone in almost every town in America, so when a soldier answered where he was from, Lefty had a story to tell.

On November 22, 1950, O'Doul and DiMaggio returned to Japan and teamed up to deliver the opening pitch in the country's inaugural championship series, the Japanese having added a second league that year. DiMaggio swung and missed at O'Doul's offering, with General William Marquat catching. Then the two baseball stars watched the Mainichi Orions of the Pacific League defeat the Shochiku Robins, 3–2.[104]

O'Doul and DiMaggio toured Hiroshima, only five years after the city had been leveled by the atomic bomb, and then spent Thanksgiving at General Marquat's home, where the two were presented medals in honor of their visit and contributions to troop morale.[105] For O'Doul, the trip had been an eye-opener. Politicians back home, all too aware of the public wariness for further bloodshed, were reticent to label the Korean conflict for what O'Doul recognized that it was—war. He was so exhausted—and depressed—by the trip, and what he had witnessed, that he slept for more than twenty-four hours after his return.

"It's a brutal fight," O'Doul told the *San Francisco Chronicle*. "[The soldiers] want people here to know this isn't a police action but a bitter all-out war. They're doing a great job. But conditions are almost impossible. The enemy is tough and resourceful. He has Communist equipment that is really good. It's difficult to tell a North Korean from a South Korean. Ambushes are frequent. The psychological pressure of fighting a fanatical enemy that may strike from anywhere builds up almost to a breaking point. I saw things at those hospitals that made me heartsick."[106]

Depressing as the battlefield had been, O'Doul returned to the United States enthusiastic about the progress being made by Japanese baseball. Hoping to tap into the wealth of talent—and perhaps open the door to Japanese playing in the United States, maybe even for him—he invited four Japanese stars as guests during spring training in Modesto with the Seals in 1951: Makoto Kozuru, first baseman Tetsuharu Kawakami, third baseman Fumio Fujimura, and pitcher Shigeru Sugishita.[107]

Training camp proved a surprise to the Japanese, who had always been taught to train year-round and push themselves past their physical limits, breaking body and spirit, and then rebuilding— the willingness to sacrifice themselves and persevere being part of their code. Americans used spring training to get into shape, taking things slow so as to not overdo it.

Nevertheless, the Japanese players were excited by the opportunity to learn from someone they saw as a hero. Kawakami told reporters, "Lefty taught most of us all we know about baseball. O'Doul is one who takes an interest in an individual and he sincerely believes in good will between Japan and the United States."[108] All four visiting players would eventually earn places in the Japanese Baseball Hall of Fame.

O'Doul also made plans to take a team of Major League players to Japan for another tour in October 1951. Joe DiMaggio agreed to join the squad, hopefully after another World Series win. But 1951 was to prove a difficult year for both O'Doul and DiMaggio, bringing both men to a crossroads in their lives at the same time they were embarking on their second trip together to Japan.

The spring training visit by the Japanese—and the experimentation with a new invention, an "Iron Mike" pitching machine— arguably provided the only real highlights of the 1951 season for Lefty O'Doul; despite a working agreement with the New York Yankees, the Seals got off to a terrible start, losing their first thirteen games, a start from which they would not recover. Following the ninth loss, O'Doul was photographed with a "crying handkerchief," embossed with the image of a seal in tears—a play on the handkerchief O'Doul had for years famously waved from the coach's box as a way to rally fans.[109] The bright promise of Paul Fagan's entrance into the world of the San Francisco Seals only six years earlier had dimmed appreciably, and the Seals' owner proclaimed it was time to decide the issue of Major League status once and for all. On July

27 the directors took a vote on a motion made by Damon Miller, representing the Seals on behalf of Fagan, for the PCL to go outlaw.

Oakland, Portland, and Sacramento joined San Francisco in favor, but the three Southern California franchises and Seattle voted instead to push for individual contracts that gave players the option to exempt themselves from the draft. The proposal for Major League status effectively died on a tie vote.[110]

Paul Fagan reacted to the news by threatening to quit the league. "Everything is first class in San Francisco except for baseball," he complained. "You can't operate a minor league in a great town like that."[111] If a buyer could be found, Fagan said he would sell the team while retaining title to Seals Stadium. He said he would offer to rent the stadium to the buyer of the franchise for $60,000 per year.[112] If a buyer could not be found, he would fold the team.

The Seals foundered—finishing the 1951 season in last place, only the second time they had ever done so. There were some talented young players, pitcher Lew Burdette and first baseman Dale Long chief among them, but the relationship with the Yankees proved disappointing. And there were whispers that O'Doul was upsetting Fagan by not showing up on time for games, staying at hotels away from his players, and prioritizing golf over baseball.[113]

As the season ended, Fagan shocked the local sports world by informing O'Doul, general manager Joe Orengo, and team secretary Damon Miller that their jobs no longer existed. Only a groundskeeper would remain.[114]

There was a group interested in buying the franchise from Fagan, who seemed willing, in what could only be seen as spite, to let the team bottom out. If the group, which included members from coast to coast, could wrest control of the franchise, their intention was to retain O'Doul as manager.[115]

In the midst of this drama, O'Doul was honored at San Francisco's Fairmont Hotel. It was a difficult moment for a man who had proudly represented his city for seventeen seasons.

Sotaro Suzuki was among the five hundred people on hand; he was in town to finalize arrangements for O'Doul's trip to Japan the next month. California governor Earl Warren, who had recently returned from the Far East, turned to Lefty and proclaimed, "Every one . . . inquired about O'Doul's coming trip to Japan with his All-Stars, and I can think of nothing more to cement the friendship between Japan and the United States than Lefty's baseball trip."

District attorney Tom Lynch raised the spirits of the crowd when he declared, "I didn't come here this morning to say good-by to Lefty O'Doul. This is just a hello as he and his Seals will be with us for many years to come."

There were telegrams of support from Casey Stengel, Joe DiMaggio, Dan Topping, Frank Crosetti, Gene Woodling, Billy Martin, Pants Rowland, Bob Cobb, Fred Haney, and scores of others. There was no greeting from Paul Fagan. Nor was he mentioned.

Fighting back tears in response to the emotional outpouring, O'Doul began his remarks by talking about his parents, saying, "My mother and father were born in San Francisco. Even when I was in the big leagues I couldn't wait for the season to end so I could return to San Francisco." Then, pausing slightly as he choked up, he brought those in the room to their feet. "Baseball is my life, and I'm going to stay in it. I expect to stay in San Francisco, too, believe me."[116]

12

There Are No Trick Plays, No Short Cuts

Fifty thousand children, admitted free of charge, crammed into Korakuen Stadium on October 30, 1949, for Lefty O'Doul Day; the demand was such that those taking advantage of the offer had been chosen by lot. It was simply impossible to satisfy every child wanting to see Lefty O'Doul and his team.[1] But for those who did secure a ticket, it promised to be a grand event. When O'Doul, Del Young, and Dario Lodigiani appeared on the field at about ten-thirty that morning, the kids on hand went wild with excitement. Impatient, they charged toward the playing field to get a closer look and a protective screen gave way, sending several dozen children tumbling to the ground. None were seriously hurt; several, as they were brushed off and shooed back into the stands, anxiously asked, "Is Mr. O'Doul angry?"[2] They were assured that, of course, he was not.

Once everything settled down, O'Doul opened the festivities by proclaiming, "I am really glad to have such a large crowd of children. I am fifty-two years old but to show how glad I am, I will pitch at the beginning of the game," a declaration that elicited an explosion of wild cheering and applause. Then he told them, "In order to become a great man, you should study hard. In the same way if you want to become a good ball player you must study hard by obeying the instruction of your teachers."[3]

O'Doul then informed the crowd that every boy and girl would receive a free program. On cue, teachers passed out souvenir booklets to each student; then the children held them up in unison, yelling "thank you" and creating a beautiful sea of blue. The Seals, led by "Dear Uncle," the nickname bestowed on O'Doul by the *Asahi Shimbun* newspaper, then faced the stands and batted one thousand soft sponge baseballs into a seemingly inexhaustible sea of hands, grabbing for the prizes in frenzied bursts of motion.

As another treat, children could purchase a Coke for half-price— outside of the tour, the drink was only available to soldiers at their px, but special permission had been granted to sell it to the Japanese at games during the Seals tour.[4]

A group of children from four deaf schools presented O'Doul a flower basket. Then every member of the Seals was presented a hapi coat and a Japanese ceremonial towel. The players all put on their coats and tied the towels around their heads; O'Doul posed for a photo with one of the boys who had presented the ceremonial dress, his coat bearing his name spelled in Japanese. Then the Seals posed for a group photo with all of the presenters.[5]

As promised, O'Doul began the game on the mound, and he managed to shut out the Japanese Collegiate All-Stars for the first two innings. But he weakened in the third, allowing three hits and two runs before departing with the score tied, 2–2.[6] The Seals finally won, 4–2, in thirteen innings—the college players giving San Francisco all it could handle.[7] Afterward, O'Doul posed with sumo star Maedayama, and tirelessly signed autograph after autograph. As *Asahi Shimbun* put it, "This was the best day ever for young baseball fans."[8]

The festivities complete, O'Doul retreated to the clubhouse and addressed reporters: "The Japanese are playing good ball now. They learned a lot since I was here fifteen years ago and are coming along well." O'Doul singled out three players that he felt could play successfully in America—catcher Takeshi Doigaki, first baseman Tetsuharu Kawakami, and outfielder Kauro Betto.[9]

There was no question the day had been an unqualified success. The vice chairman of the Tokyo Metropolitan Board of Education penned a letter to O'Doul about the impact of the event, telling him, "This splendid program contributed much to implant sportsmanship and international comity in the minds of Japanese boys all over the country."[10]

• • •

During the first three games of the 1951 World Series, Joe DiMaggio had batted eleven times against the New York Giants and failed to register so much as a loud foul ball. Lounging in his robe while sipping coffee in his hotel suite, DiMaggio explained to reporters, "I'm not looking for sympathy. I don't want sympathy. I don't deserve sympathy. I've just been lousy."[11]

It had been a tough year for the Yankees' star—chronic foot problems had limited him to fewer than one hundred twenty games, in which he had hit only twelve home runs and batted a mere .263. Speculation was that "The Yankee Clipper" would retire after the Series—and he did not seem to be going out on a high note.

O'Doul was in New York, finalizing his roster for the upcoming All-Star trip to Japan and Korea, and DiMaggio approached Lefty for advice. After agreeing with his choice of bats, O'Doul told DiMaggio, "You're swinging too hard. You've been pressing—lunging at bad balls. Your body is ahead of your arms, so that you're pushing the ball." He finally suggested, "Joe, try to hit the ball just over the shortstop's head."[12]

DiMaggio told reporters, "I suspected that I have been doing all those things wrong. Now that O'Doul has spotted them I'll just have to try to cut down on my swing. Lefty should know. He was a great hitter."[13]

O'Doul was not around for the next game—he had to return home to complete tour arrangements—so another San Franciscan, former American League batting champ Lew Fonseca, offered a few suggestions and DiMaggio came away from his mini-clinic feeling he was swinging the bat better than he had for months.

In his first at bat in Game Four at the Polo Grounds against Sal Maglie, DiMaggio hit a line drive foul that barely missed being a home run. The next time up he collected his first hit of the Series, a solid single. In his third time at bat, DiMaggio hit a Maglie curve for a home run into the upper tier in left field. "It was a great feeling to see it going out to the seats. Lefty O'Doul told me last night that I was swinging high and taking my eye off the ball. I corrected that, but Lefty wasn't here to see it," said DiMaggio.[14] Then, as flashbulbs popped, he added, "When I get ten more hits I'll tell you fellows I owe all my success to O'Doul and Fonseca."[15]

DiMaggio did not get ten more hits, but he did go three for five with three runs batted in during Game Five, and one for two with two walks, both intentional, in Game Six, which the Yankees won to clinch their third straight World Series.

On the way to Japan in October 1951 with the All-Star team, O'Doul addressed the players, most of whom had never been to the country. He stressed that they should show respect and remember it was the Japanese military, not the Japanese people, that had brought war between their countries.[16]

General Marquat and Sotaro Suzuki met O'Doul and the All-Stars at the airport. General Matthew Ridgway, who had succeeded Douglas MacArthur, issued an official statement: "From the sandlots through the minor leagues . . . baseball has become an important part of the pattern of democratic life in both the United States and Japan. It is with this understanding of the significance of this occasion that I express my appreciation for the kind invitation which the Japanese have extended to the American group, and it is with great pleasure that I welcome the American All-Star Baseball Team."[17]

The first team consisting of Major Leaguers to visit since 1934 was of course mobbed on its arrival; it took the fifteen-car motorcade an hour to traverse the route from Shimbashi Station to the Owaricho crossing, a journey that usually took no more than five minutes.[18] O'Doul arranged for several of the All-Stars, including Billy Martin, Dom DiMaggio, Mel Parnell, Ferris Fain, George Strickland, and Jackie Price, to visit soldiers stationed in Korea. Upon their return, they joined the rest of the team for an appearance at Nippon Geiko, one of the most famous cinema houses in Tokyo. The event was sold out—the intensity of fan interest was such that one hundred policemen were brought in for crowd control.

O'Doul implored the audience, "Let's promote Japanese-American friendship by means of baseballs and gloves rather than cannons and machine guns. There is no sport like baseball to promote friendship between two countries."[19]

Boston Red Sox pitcher Mel Parnell, who had been amazed by the reception accorded O'Doul, related that as the two teams traveled by train, O'Doul would hold impromptu clinics with the Japanese players, "explaining the techniques of each position."[20] O'Doul's lessons aside, the Americans were, as expected, dominating during the tour, outscoring the Japanese during the first ten games by a combined score of 76–15, although they did drop one game, a 3–1 loss to the Pacific League All-Stars—the first defeat an American team of professionals had suffered at the hands of the Japanese since O'Doul's first visit to the country twenty years earlier.[21]

News during the tour centered on rumors of Joe DiMaggio's potential retirement—irritating "The Yankee Clipper" no end—and Lefty O'Doul's fate as manager of the Seals.[22] The brothers DiMaggio both homered in the second game, an 11–0 victory over the Mainichi Orions, but Joe missed several contests due to a sore back, and then left for California a week early to tend to personal business.[23] He did hit a home run in his final game before leaving, an eighth-inning shot into the left field bleachers at Stateside Park in Tokyo—it would be his last as an active Major Leaguer.[24]

The tour concluded with another Lefty O'Doul Day, against the Yomiuri Giants, champions of Japanese baseball. Actor-comedian Danny Kaye, on his way to visit troops in Korea, sat on the American bench during the game, while a happy O'Doul was hounded by children seeking his autograph throughout the contest. Thirty thousand screaming children enjoyed the game, which ended in a 5–5 tie when it was finally called due to darkness.[25] Afterward, O'Doul donated several thousand dollars to a school for mentally handicapped children.[26]

Before O'Doul left Japan, Paul Fagan phoned to formally dismiss him as Seals manager. Lefty knew of course that Fagan's announcement was inevitable, but experiencing the finality of the decision—a termination of something that had over the course of seventeen seasons become his identity— was not the same as knowing of its coming, and it was a blow. "I have no comment at present," he sputtered to reporters, "but I will have plenty to say when I get back to San Francisco."[27]

O'Doul predictably lashed out upon his return to California. "What does that guy expect of a man?" he ranted. "I've sent play-

ers up to the majors for big dough during every one of my seventeen years as manager of the Seals. I worked under restrictions,
protected Fagan, and took the rap. He'll regret it."[28]

Lefty was not unemployed for long. Bill Starr, president of the struggling San Diego Padres, saw O'Doul as a means to reinvigorate interest in his franchise—Starr was pressing hard for a new stadium to
replace rickety Lane Field, and he knew O'Doul's star power would
raise the team's profile. It was said that O'Doul's contract included
bonuses for attendance that could net him $25,000—a drop from
his peak years with the Seals, but still a considerable sum.

O'Doul was happy because he was well-liked in San Diego. Even
when Padres fans rode him, it was good-natured. He was taunted
by them during a game in 1949, thousands mocking his signature handkerchief wave during a game when the Seals fell behind.
Suddenly, and with great fanfare, he produced a sail-sized handkerchief from his back pocket and waved it, turning the jeers into
cheers and laughter.[29]

"I asked for the job managing the Padres because I wanted it,"
he declared. "Naturally, it's no fun getting released. But I'm not the
first manager to get fired. And I won't be the last."[30] Reaction in San
Diego was universally positive; Paul Fagan publicly extended his
best wishes to O'Doul and noted, with some foresight, "I'll bet he'll
sure be gaming to knock us into the creek when we play next year."[31]

A press conference officially announcing Lefty's appointment was
held at the El Cortez Hotel in downtown San Diego.[32] That event
was followed by O'Doul's official coming-out party at the annual
San Diego Hot Stove League banquet held at the Balboa Park Club,
where Joe DiMaggio joined George Jessel, William Frawley, Rogers
Hornsby, Phil Harris, Ray Boone, Luke Easter, and several other
stars of the diamond and the silver screen in honoring him.[33] Los
Angeles Angels first baseman and aspiring actor Chuck Connors
performed "Casey at the Bat."[34] O'Doul addressed the gathering of
nearly 1,400 people—two hundred beyond capacity—finishing his
short speech by unfurling an enormous red handkerchief from his
pocket, which brought a roar of approval from the crowd.[35]

O'Doul's popularity in a new setting was a tonic of sorts—over the previous few years he had been crowded from his perch as the biggest personality in the Pacific Coast League. During the late 1940s and early 1950s, the PCL had enjoyed a prosperity that enabled owners to hire big name managers—Rogers Hornsby, Casey Stengel, Bucky Harris, Del Baker, Charlie Dressen, Jimmy Dykes, Stan Hack, Mel Ott, and Joe Gordon among them. Even his enter- taining antics were overshadowed by the likes of Bobby Bragan in Hollywood, who could match O'Doul's fainting spells, order bat boys to the coach's box after being ejected, engineer eight consec- utive batting lineup changes, and send a coach to home plate with a lineup card, displaying an arm loaded down with wristwatches the day after a curfew disagreement.

Nevertheless, O'Doul's name still had marquee value, and it was quickly apparent that he and the San Diego baseball community were a good marriage. He hosted a television program on Saturday mornings, and local entrepreneurs began marketing the famous bandanna that he employed to rally fans. The team produced sou- venir cigarette lighters, complete with a replica of his distinctive sig- nature. He volunteered for the local American Heart Association fundraising campaign. He put on a baseball clinic; eighty local high school and college coaches were invited to participate in the two-day camp, which included other baseball notables, including Bob Elliott, Riggs Stephenson, and Hollis Thurston.[36] The hiring of O'Doul worked wonderfully; people were talking about the Padres again.

The San Francisco Seals' home opener in 1952 was an event. There was nothing else it could have been. Lefty O'Doul was making his return to the city, as manager of the opposition. As had been the case with Joe Brovia three years earlier, fans were almost beside themselves to see a former hero.

More than twelve thousand of them showed up in Seals Sta- dium following a parade through the streets in honor of the team's ex-manager.[37] O'Doul arrived at the ballpark at six o'clock sharp— unprecedented for him in recent years—and spent an hour going over the Seals' lineup with his team. He did everything he could to avoid Paul Fagan, and seemed uncharacteristically stoic during warm-ups.[38] He even resisted acknowledging the ovation when he took up his familiar post in the third base coach's box. But O'Doul warmed to his task as the game progressed, laughing and joking with fans between innings. His day ended with an ejection after coming to Guy Fletcher's defense when the pitcher began arguing balls and strikes; O'Doul continued managing the game from the clubhouse anyway, via messages transmitted to and through coach Jimmie Reese.[39] The Padres lost, 6–2, disappointing their manager, who desperately wanted to defeat the Seals every time he played them. But he would not lose to the Seals many more times in 1952, eventually winning twenty-one of twenty-eight games; Fagan would discover what Joe McCarthy and John McGraw had learned—O'Doul was very focused in response to slights.

There were unusual tributes from Seals fans that season. During the middle of a game at Seals Stadium, O'Doul was standing in the third base coach's box when five men bolted onto the field and handed him a watermelon. Why that—why then? Why him—why them? No answers were ever made public—it was simply one of those colorful things that always seemed to happen in the PCL.[40]

O'Doul's distaste for Paul Fagan failed to dissipate as the season wore on. He and the Padres visited Oakland in May, and O'Doul decided to play a round of golf at one of his favorite courses. That night, he was presented several gifts by the Oaks, including a television set that he immediately donated to an orphanage. The Padres defeated Oakland, and O'Doul shouted to reporters, "Why don't you tell Paul Fagan that I can still play golf and win games?"[41]

The Padres were not thought to be a contender in 1952—San Diego had finished sixth under Del Baker the year before, and the roster was filled with past-their-prime players. Lane Field seemed to be past its prime as well; termites claimed a section of the right-field bleachers—stands that were a holdover from the stadium's days as a motorcycle race track.[42]

But by mid-May the Padres were surprising everyone, holding onto first place with a 28-15 record and leading the league in attendance. O'Doul's competitive spirit was fueled by the renewed enthusiasm for baseball in San Diego. "I want to win this one more than any race I've been in," he confessed.[43] However, the team's fortunes turned shortly after forty-one-year-old reliever Al Benton was sold to the Boston Red Sox in June. Likely the team's most valuable player to that point, Benton was allowed to decide on his own if he was needed, in which case he would begin warming up; he always seemed to know when O'Doul should call on him.[44]

Age eventually caught up with the Padres, and O'Doul could not halt his team's slow but inevitable slide. They finished fifth, four games under break-even; the only satisfaction O'Doul felt was that the Seals finished seventh. He told Will Connolly, "Some fans expect miracles of managers, like they do of a football coach. There are no trick plays, no short cuts."[45]

On March 4, 1953, his fifty-sixth birthday, O'Doul granted an interview to Connolly. He mused about the loss of Benton and the Padres' resulting collapse, before acknowledging, "We surprised everybody, including me by going into July on top. Then the old geezers collapsed. You can nurse them only so long."[46]

The PCL continued clinging to its elusive dreams of Major League status, even as attendance began to erode like so much sand against the ocean tide. The last gasp was something called "Open Classification," which set supposedly attainable goals that would allow the PCL to earn equal status with the Major Leagues.[47] The designation allowed players the option to sign contracts exempting them from being drafted by Major League teams, and officially placed the league a step above all other Minors. O'Doul was an ardent supporter, pleading, "The fans have to go along with us. The whole league is building for the future. Three or four years from now you'll see much better ball. Be patient."[48]

During the winter following his first season in San Diego, O'Doul spent his energies on his burgeoning import-export business. He arranged for television programs to be broadcast in Japan—with commercial stations on the horizon, there was a need for programming. O'Doul engineered deals for American sports, travel, and technical films. He also marketed items made in Japan for the American market, including electrical appliances, dishware, and cigarette lighters.[49]

He formed a corporation—Frank J. O'Doul Enterprises—with Cappy Harada as a partner. In addition to the import-export business, the new corporation arranged for the Yomiuri Giants to spend spring training in the United States in 1953.[50]

San Francisco Examiner columnist Prescott Sullivan reported on O'Doul's effort to become a successful businessman. Lefty's financial advisor, former glove and hosiery entrepreneur Art Mesler, told Sullivan, "O'Doul has a good business head on him and it is my guess that he'll soon be making ten times in Japan what he could make here in baseball." But O'Doul would never become a great businessman. While he loved making and utilizing connections, and discussing business ideas, the tedious nature of day-to-day operations held no interest for him. He had successes here and there, but never put his business ventures ahead of his true passions. As he told Sullivan, "Baseball is one of two things I'll never give up. The other is golf."[51]

O'Doul was at the airport in San Francisco in February 1953 to greet the Yomiuri Giants as they arrived on American soil. Newspaper and newsreel cameramen were on hand to record the event, after which Harada, several of the players, and Giants manager Shigeru Mizuhara accompanied O'Doul to San Diego for a dinner in their honor.[52] Among the Giants players was outfielder Wally Yonamine, a former professional football player for the San Francisco 49ers and a Hawaiian native who went to Japan on Lefty O'Doul's recommendation. Yonamine would win three batting titles in Japan and earn a place in the Japanese Baseball Hall of Fame in 1994.[53]

But the tour was only a marginal success. Its cost was said to be in the range of $100,000, and overall attendance was poor for the exhibition games—the Giants were no longer a novelty in America, and they won only six of eighteen contests.[54]

Lefty O'Doul decided 1953 was the year to change his personal life. He and Abbie had no children, and they had been separated for at least three years. She had also spent considerable time in New York for several years before that while O'Doul managed the Seals.[55] During this period, O'Doul met Jean Gold, a model and divorcee living in San Francisco; as a result, Abbie filed for divorce in early 1953 after moving temporarily to Las Vegas to establish residency. The split was granted by the court in late March.[56]

Six weeks later, fifty-six-year-old Lefty married thirty-two-year-old Jean in Las Vegas. Emerging from the courthouse waving a marriage certificate in celebration, O'Doul announced the couple would not be taking a honeymoon until he went on his next trip to the Orient that winter.[57] O'Doul's family was far from supportive of the union; divorce in a Catholic family was bad enough, but the fact that Jean—who brought an eight-year-old son into the marriage—was Jewish didn't help.

Despite the upheaval, O'Doul remained close to his mother, even after the new marriage. She had been at his side in New York when the Giants won the World Series in 1933, and he often drove her to PCL games so she could watch him in action as manager. A widow, she too had gone through a second marriage, to James Fennell in the 1920s, and was now a widow once again.

Lefty's personal life proved a bigger story than did the Padres in 1953. The season began tragically, with the death of popular outfielder Herb Gorman, who suffered a heart attack and collapsed during a game a week into the season.[58] The team never got on track, failing to reach the first division, or even move above the .500 mark at any point beyond the first four games of the year. But O'Doul did develop two players into big payoffs for the franchise. He worked with Tom Alston and turned him into a marketable Major League prospect—accurately predicting he would become the league's next big hitting star after batting only .244 the previous year. Following the season, the Padres received in excess of $100,000 and two players from the St. Louis Cardinals in exchange for Alston, who became that team's first African American player.[59] And pitcher Memo Luna also went to St. Louis, for between $75,000 and $100,000.[60] Those transactions would lead to a much brighter outlook for San Diego in 1954.

When Paul Fagan announced his intention to finally sell the San Francisco Seals in 1953, rumors swirled that O'Doul would join forces with Joe DiMaggio to purchase the team. O'Doul quickly threw cold water on the suggestion, noting that new owners would be forced to assume an annual tax bill of $36,000, as well as $100,000 per year rent. He insisted, "That is too rich for my financial blood."[61]

Meanwhile, O'Doul's name was once again connected to a possible managerial slot, this time with the Brooklyn Dodgers. Jimmy Powers, veteran sports editor of the *New York Daily News*, endorsed the idea of having O'Doul succeed Charlie Dressen who, after winning two straight pennants, had insisted on a three-year deal rather than the customary one-year contracts offered by Walter O'Malley.

Powers provided several reasons for considering O'Doul, including his continued popularity in Brooklyn, dating back to his days as a player, the still flourishing youth leagues he had sponsored, and his public relations acumen. He also argued that O'Doul would be the ideal man to mentor Pee Wee Reese as his eventual successor.[62]

However, while O'Doul and his wife traveled to Hong Kong for an extended honeymoon in November 1953, the Dodgers hired the relatively unknown Walter Alston.[63]

On a January morning in 1954, Joe DiMaggio and Marilyn Monroe took a stroll in San Francisco's Funston Park, one of the many places the young DiMaggio had played baseball while growing up.[64] That afternoon, he and the actress invited six people, including Lefty and Jean O'Doul, to witness their wedding at City Hall. A crush of photographers waited expectantly outside. Reno Barsocchini, partner with DiMaggio in his restaurant, served as best man, and Barsocchini's wife served as matron of honor for the two-minute ceremony.[65]

The next day, Lefty headed for Monterey to play in the Bing Crosby Pro-Am Golf Tournament. He won for the second time, teaming with pro Walter Burkemo to tie three other teams for first; O'Doul clinched a share of the title for his team with a four-foot birdie putt on the eighteenth hole.[66]

After that Lefty, Jean, Joe, and Marilyn took off for a three-week trip to Japan, where the wives would made a side trip to Korea so Marilyn could entertain the troops, while the husbands provided hitting lessons to Japanese Central League players. During a stop-over in Honolulu, Lefty and the DiMaggios were photographed by the paparazzi, and the resulting image reveals much about the attitudes of those on the trip. Marilyn is front and center, eating up the attention. A clearly annoyed Joe DiMaggio is to one side in the photo, while O'Doul is on the other side of Marilyn, wearing a nervous, sheepish grin on his face.

Thousands of people greeted the couples at the airport in Tokyo; Marilyn was the biggest hit among the Japanese—men tried to smash the front door of the Imperial Hotel to get a look at her. An irritated DiMaggio complained, "Remember, she is not here on her own. She's here with me and we are on our honeymoon."[67]

Jean O'Doul accompanied Marilyn on her side trip to Korea, while Lefty and Joe remained behind in Japan, coaching as planned. Unfortunately, the famous photograph in Honolulu revealed more than intended. Before the trip was complete, the honeymoon was over between Joe DiMaggio and Marilyn Monroe. Literally. By the end of the year, they had divorced.

The San Diego Padres used the money and players acquired for Tom Alston and Memo Luna to make a run at the PCL pennant, which had belonged two years running to Bobby Bragan and the Hollywood Stars. They signed hometown hero and former National League MVP Bob Elliott to play third base. Outfielder Harry Elliott was loaned by the St. Louis Cardinals, and Dick Sisler, an outfielder for the 1950 Phillies "Whiz Kids," was acquired as part of the Alston deal. The latter two, along with holdover Earl Rapp, would com-prise three of the PCL's top four hitters in 1954.

Harry Elliott recalled that O'Doul had not lost his disdain for double plays—when Harry, who would win the PCL batting title with a .350 average, took it on himself to attempt a surprise bunt with a runner on first, only to harmlessly tap the ball back to the pitcher for an easy twin-killing, O'Doul met him at the top step of the dugout, screaming at him. Elliott screamed back, beginning an argument that went back and forth for several tense minutes. Elliott encountered Lefty in a bar that evening—the manager bought his outfielder a drink.[68]

As the weather warmed, so did the Padres, winning nineteen of twenty-eight games in June and carrying a ten-game winning streak through July 8 to vault into contention, running their record to 57-38. Thousands of pennant-hungry fans greeted their heroes on a return from a road trip. The mayor proclaimed July 12–18 "Padre Week," and at the end of the month, the front office had to secure 2,300 additional bleacher seats in order to accommodate the number of fans eager to see the team play a series against Hollywood.[69] The Padres then slumped slightly, falling four games off the pace. At that point, the Cleveland Indians sent Luke Easter back to San Diego, where five years earlier the former Negro League star had been one of the greatest drawing cards in PCL history.

During the nightcap of a doubleheader his first day back, Easter crushed a 490-foot home run that cleared the Pacific Coast Highway and caromed off the loading ramp at the Santa Fe depot on one bounce.[70]

From that point on it was a two-team race between the Padres and Hollywood. From the middle of August to the final day of the 1954 season, never more than two games separated them in the standings. Milt Smith had replaced Bob Elliott when the former National League star failed to hit. But Smith slumped late in the year, and O'Doul put Elliott, who had hit four home runs all season, back in the lineup during the final week of the season. Elliott responded with six home runs in eight days.

The season ended in dramatic fashion, Roger Bowman pitching a perfect game for Hollywood with Bobby Bragan at catcher and hitting two home runs—his first all year. Meanwhile O'Doul, having run out of pitchers, tapped outfielder and sometimes pitcher Al Lyons, who responded with a wonderful 7–2 win in his first start of the season. After 168 games, Hollywood and San Diego had identical 101-67 records. There would be a one-game playoff, to be held at Lane Field in San Diego; the last time a playoff was necessary, seven years earlier, O'Doul had lost to Los Angeles.

Bob Kerrigan pitched for the Padres against Hollywood's Red Munger, both men taking the mound on only one day's rest. The hero was Bob Elliott, who hit his seventh home run in nine days to put the Padres ahead, 2–1, with a blast in the second inning. After the Stars tied the game, Harry Elliott singled in the go-ahead run for San Diego, followed by Bob Elliott's second home run of the day, a three-run shot off Mel Queen. Kerrigan easily handled Hollywood the rest of the way, and the Padres captured their first PCL championship since winning the 1937 Shaughnessy Playoffs.

The crowd of more than eleven thousand rushed the field after the final out, lifting Kerrigan onto their shoulders. Bob Elliott, who had won a Most Valuable Player Award in the National League and hit two home runs in the 1948 World Series, shouted above the din in the clubhouse, "This game was the top thrill in my life!"[71]

The city of San Diego staged a parade down Broadway for the Padres, each player riding in his own convertible, followed by a rally before thousands of people at Horton Plaza. But not all was well; despite the team's success, Padres president Bill Starr was frustrated by the city's lack of progress toward a new stadium, and was said to be interested in selling the team and devoting his time to developing shopping centers.[72]

The season over, the question was, what was next for Lefty? Whatever that next step was, he wasn't saying, but what he did say sent shockwaves through the San Diego baseball community. Although Bill Starr had said O'Doul was welcome to return in 1955—"the job is his if he wants it"–Lefty was resigning as manager of the Padres.[73] Starr insisted that he and O'Doul were parting on the best of terms, despite their occasional disagreements about Lefty's dedication to his outside interests at the expense of managing.

Sid Ziff of the *Los Angeles Mirror* reported that O'Doul had left because of interference on the part of Starr, who was overheard before the playoff game ordering Lefty to play Luke Easter at first base and Dick Sisler in the outfield.[74] There were also rumblings that Starr was unhappy with the amount of time O'Doul spent on the golf course, and that he was often the last person to arrive in the clubhouse and the first to leave. Cliff Chambers, who pitched for the Padres in 1954, said of O'Doul, "He'd come out to the ballpark and put his uniform on, rub his elbows a couple of times while we finished hitting, and then he'd coach the game. He never broke a sweat."[75] Bob Stevens said he always felt O'Doul never got over being fired by Paul Fagan.[76]

There were rumors that O'Doul was interested in forming a group to purchase the Padres.[77] Walter Winchell reported that Lefty would soon be managing a Major League team; Fred Hutchinson had recently resigned as manager of the Detroit Tigers, and there were false rumors that O'Doul had been offered the job and accepted it.[78] The Oakland Oaks publicly courted O'Doul. So did the Sacramento Solons. Portland was interested in him as general manager. The hottest rumor involved the Philadelphia Athletics, who were for sale. If a local group could secure the franchise, new ownership wanted Eddie Mulligan as general manager and O'Doul as manager.[79]

"I have several irons in the fire," revealed Lefty, "and they all have to do with baseball." When asked about the Oaks rumor, he replied, "Sure, I'd like to manage Oakland if Brick Laws wants me. Yes, it's one of the irons I mentioned. Let's just say the Oaks are in the running."[80]

13

I'd Rather Be a Bad Winner

Japan's first ever O'Doul Day complete, Lefty quickly changed out of his uniform and hopped into a limousine with Paul Fagan and Charles J. Graham. The three were driven to the National Athletic Meet, where arrangements had been made for them to meet Emperor Hirohito. The emperor shook their hands and told them, "I am heartily pleased that you are trying to promote goodwill and friendship between the United States and Japan through baseball games."[1]

According to the American press, the emperor turned and addressed Lefty. "It is a great honor to meet the greatest manager in baseball," he said. "I am very happy to meet you and I certainly am appreciative and proud of the good work the Seals have done on the tour and very happy it has been successful. It is by means of sports that our countries can be brought closer together. I am glad I can thank you personally for it."

"I've waited a long time for this day," replied O'Doul.[2] Later noting that he had lost one hundred games for the first time in his managerial career during the 1949 season, O'Doul quipped to reporters, "It's a good thing he didn't know I finished in seventh place last season."[3]

Douglas MacArthur was gratified by the outcome of the tour, and congratulated O'Doul and his players: "Eighty million people heard about you, five million saw you and five hundred thousand watched you play." The general added, "This trip is the greatest piece of diplomacy ever. All the diplomats put together would not have been able to do this."[4] Decades later, MacArthur's successor,

General Matthew Ridgway, likewise singled out O'Doul's efforts, saying, "Words cannot describe Lefty's wonderful contributions, through baseball, to the postwar rebuilding effort."[5] By the end of the tour when Lefty O'Doul yelled "Banzai," the Japanese answered back in kind. Communists, who had been visible on street corners in the cities, had vanished.

Masao Date recognized the impact the 1949 tour had on the Japanese people. "When [the war] was over," wrote Date some forty years later, "we were [destitute]. We had hard times in daily life, even in getting food. So we spent day after day without hopes or dreams. In this hardship situation Lefty O'Doul [returned]. What he did was, through baseball, encourage Japanese people to work for recovery. Especially, he cheered up our children . . . who were to carry this country in the future."[6]

The trip netted a profit of nearly $100,000, nearly all of it designated for the building of a youth baseball field and donations to various health organizations and orphanages.[7]

The Japanese showed their gratitude by inundating the players with gifts: silver cigarette cases and lighters, suede jackets, coats, Noritake china, and other items. Every man received five professionally produced scrapbooks, personalized for each player, documenting his trip. It was an incredible outpouring of appreciation.

• • •

It turned out Lefty O'Doul's 1955 destination was home, or more accurately, across the bay from it, as manager of the Oakland Oaks, a team whose fans for nearly two decades had regularly hung him in effigy when he was leader of their hated rivals, the San Francisco Seals.[8]

Constant rumors had circulated that the Oaks were pursuing O'Doul at the same time both parties awaited a final decision from the Philadelphia Athletics.[9] Interest was intense. Brick Laws was attending a football game at Kezar Stadium between the San Francisco 49ers and the Chicago Bears when he was paged to the press box by the public address announcer during the fourth quarter. The

reason? To learn whether the Oaks' owner had made a final decision about signing Lefty.[10]

The path to Oakland was cleared when the Philadelphia Athletics
were sold to a group that moved the team to Kansas City and chose
Lou Boudreau as their manager. The announcement of O'Doul's
hiring by Oakland was met with great enthusiasm—thought by
many to forestall the franchise being moved, as had been rumored,
to Vancouver. Even Oscar Vitt, who had attempted to run O'Doul
out of Salt Lake City thirty years earlier, was supportive of the Oaks'
choice, pointing out how diligently O'Doul had labored to convert
from pitcher to outfielder. "I never knew a player who was more
determined to make good than O'Doul," said Vitt.[11]

Laws insisted that, unlike Paul Fagan and Bill Starr, he had no
problem with O'Doul playing golf before night games, telling James
McGee of the *San Francisco Call-Bulletin,* "As long as he does his
job, and I know he will, what difference does it make what he does
on his free time?"[12]

A clearly delighted O'Doul held court with the New York press,
on hand to cover spring training of the Major League teams. "I am
one who says the game is better today," he volunteered. "Defense
is vastly superior than it used to be. I make one exception—for Ty
Cobb. I think he was the greatest hitter."[13]

He began to reconcile with the San Francisco Seals, which had
been purchased from Paul Fagan by a group of the team's employees, who were dubbed "The Little Corporation." O'Doul's first such
gesture had involved his participation in an Old-Timers' Game at
Seals Stadium, along with Joe DiMaggio, the previous summer.[14] In
May 1955 he was elected to the newly created San Francisco Baseball
Hall of Fame along with Charlie Graham, Joe DiMaggio, Paul Waner,
and Harry Heilmann; Lefty appeared in person to accept his bronze
plaque, which was then affixed to the entrance at Seals Stadium.[15]

Lefty displayed some enthusiasm upon donning an Oaks uniform, clowning with both the fans and the players. He devised a
special signal when he wanted to bring pitcher Al Gettel into the
game: Gettel dreamed of becoming a movie-star cowboy, so O'Doul

would pantomime holding the reins of a galloping horse to summon the right-hander.

O'Doul was also reunited in Oakland with Joe Brovia, who performed so well in spring training that Lefty predicted forty home runs for the thirty-three-year-old slugger. Brovia would fall short of that mark, but that summer O'Doul was able to give Joe the news that, fifteen years after signing his first contract, he would finally get a shot at the Major Leagues with the Cincinnati Reds.[16]

O'Doul remained in demand as a hitting instructor. In mid-April, old friend Joe Cronin, now general manager of the Boston Red Sox, sent prize bonus baby infielder Billy Consolo to Oakland, specifically so he could work under O'Doul. The former Los Angeles high school baseball star had received a $60,000 bonus and, under rules in force at the time, had spent the required two years with the Red Sox before he could be farmed out. The twenty-year-old Consolo enjoyed a successful year with the Oaks, batting .276 in what would be his best season in professional baseball.

O'Doul clearly enjoyed teaching more than managing—it had almost always been so, and especially since Charlie Graham's death. Tommy Munoz, a young first baseman who spent spring training with the Oaks in 1955, remembered O'Doul standing behind the cage during batting practice and continually nagging him to "hit *down* through the ball" in order to drive it farther. The more he attempted to do so, the more O'Doul emphasized the point. Recognizing that O'Doul was asking the impossible, Munoz became angry but kept at it, until suddenly realizing he was lacing out line drives instead of lazy fly balls—the instruction was meant to force him to change his approach. Every time O'Doul saw Munoz after that, he would always remind him to swing down through the ball. It was advice the player never forgot.[17]

But it was not a successful season in Oakland for O'Doul; despite boasting two of the league's three top hitters and an excellent season from Consolo, the Oaks spent all but a few days of the season in the second division with a losing record, and they finished seventh. O'Doul sometimes let his frustration show. After being ejected from one game, he sent wooden planks, groundkeeper's tools, and even part of the dugout water fountain flying onto the field.[18]

The Pacific Coast League as a whole was also struggling. The San Diego Padres could not escape their termite-ridden stadium and were for sale. The San Francisco Seals were broke and in danger of folding. League attendance had dropped by more than two-thirds what it had been immediately after the war, as television fed the desire for Major League Baseball, a desire that ate away at the PCL and rendered "Open Classification" little more than an empty gesture from Major League owners who had no intention of opening their exclusive club to what they viewed as interlopers.

In the end, hiring O'Doul only bought Oaks fans one year. After the last pitch of the 1955 season, Lefty, Brick Laws, and the franchise headed to Canada.

There was some question about O'Doul's interest in following Brick Laws to Vancouver. He had re-formed his failed Lefty O'Doul Corporation, joining forces with California-based importer/exporter Michael Shigeru Yasutake, who had worked with orphanages in Japan during his time in the U.S. military.[19] O'Doul, who remained popular in San Diego, had invested in a par-three golf course at Colina Park, a couple of miles from San Diego State University.[20] New ownership in San Diego was pursuing him as general manager of the Padres, and there were rumors he was planning to build a home in Del Mar, twenty miles north of the city.

The struggling San Francisco Seals were purchased by the Boston Red Sox, who paid $150,000 for a franchise that had cost Paul Fagan $250,000 for a one-third share only a decade earlier. O'Doul was immediately mentioned as a possible manager of the team, as was Dominic DiMaggio, but Eddie Joost was hired instead.[21]

That winter, O'Doul was profiled in *Sport Magazine*, an article in which he declared, point-blank, his interest in managing in the Major Leagues.[22] Dick Young of the *New York Daily News* later wrote that when the Giants parted ways with Leo Durocher after the 1955 season, O'Doul had hoped they would hire him, but Horace Stoneham opted for Bill Rigney.[23] O'Doul had simply waited too long. There were no offers.

So, O'Doul moved with the Oaks to Vancouver, where they were rechristened the Mounties.[24] There, in a city he had praised during his first visit with the Major League All-Stars en route to Japan in 1934, Lefty once again plunged into youth baseball, sponsoring a team that he would underwrite for the rest of his life, called O'Doul's Angels.[25] After signing his contract, O'Doul visited the Mounties' home field, Capilano Stadium, and sounded an optimistic note— the *Vancouver Sun* credited O'Doul with admirable restraint as he surveyed an infield half-submerged by several inches of water. "That means it will be easy on the players' legs next summer," he quipped. "That's one of the big problems with some fields. They get so hard and sunbaked along about August, it's very hard on the legs." O'Doul also vowed a stronger commitment to managing, declaring, "I'm losing my golf sticks in the ash can. I've got to get around and meet my Vancouver fans."[26]

No one took him seriously about ditching golf, but Lefty O'Doul remained every bit the baseball diplomat.

The Vancouver Mounties were the PCL affiliate of the Baltimore Orioles, and during spring training, Orioles manager Paul Richards handed O'Doul a Baltimore uniform and asked him to work with some of the big league team's young hitters. Richards explained that he and O'Doul shared the same hitting philosophy, and he thought Lefty could be of help. It would also provide O'Doul the opportunity to look over some of the young players he would employ during the coming season. Lefty quickly declared that the three he most wanted were eighteen-year-old third baseman Brooks Robinson, twenty-two-year-old first baseman Tito Francona, and speedy outfielder Angelo Dagres.[27] Unfortunately, O'Doul would receive only Dagres.

The fifty-nine-year-old O'Doul was noticeably trimmer—he was nearly at his playing weight, having shed some forty pounds. And he seemed energized—perhaps due to his being in a new city full of yet to be discovered people, sights, and sounds. One day, he was providing instruction to several players when he decided to get in the cage. Within minutes he was imitating various hitters he had seen over the years—Babe Ruth, Ty Cobb, Joe DiMaggio, Mel Ott, and Paul Waner—all while lining shots into right field.

The Mounties opened the 1956 season with a sixteen-game road trip, beginning at Seals Stadium. In the team's second game, Vancouver pitcher Bob Harrison was having control problems, walking eight batters in the first four innings. O'Doul finally spotted the problem. "Bob was pitching to the glove. His pitches were going low. I told [catcher Len] Neal to stand up a bit and hold the glove up."[28] Harrison did not walk a batter the rest of the way and the Mounties had their first win.

But it became obvious that the Mounties were not very good. They returned for their April 27 home debut in last place. Fans, excited to be rooting for a new team, braved forty-four-degree weather and watched the Mounties play well before losing their opener in late innings. With his team's record standing at 5-11, O'Doul was in a sour mood afterward; when asked what Vancouver's historic Opening Day had meant, he snapped, "To me it means that there were 8,146 disappointed fans, eighteen disappointed ballplayers, and one disappointed manager."[29]

The situation did not improve—the Mounties were soon mired in the basement. Brick Laws spent most of the summer alternately feuding with the press, lobbying the city to allow Sunday baseball, or trying to sell the team. O'Doul groused, "Managing this club, you've got to be a good loser. But I'd rather be a bad winner."[30]

O'Doul did have a success story in Vancouver—one that again demonstrated that his teaching skills encompassed more than hitting. The Orioles had given up on twenty-seven-year-old pitcher Ryne Duren, whose eight seasons as a professional included exactly two Major League innings. The coke-bottle-glasses-wearing right-hander threw harder than just about any pitcher alive, but he was off to a terrible start in 1956, dropping five of his first six decisions largely due to an inability to throw the ball over the plate on a consistent basis. O'Doul was asked if he was going to cut the pitcher. He assured the press he had no such plans.[31]

A few days later, O'Doul approached Duren as he threw between starts. He told Duren to fire a ball high and inside, which he did. Using the same seemingly nonsensical approach he had used with Tommy Munoz, O'Doul kept telling Duren to throw the ball higher and further inside, persisting until an angry Duren threw one to the screen. O'Doul told Duren, "Now you've got it. Now throw a ball low and outside." Again, O'Doul kept making him throw lower and wider until he skidded one off the dirt. He made Duren repeat what seemed to be nonsense until the pitcher practically threw a ball out of the stadium in annoyance. "That's it!" cried O'Doul. Then he told Duren to look at his footprints. "Look at where your feet were when you threw those pitches," he said, showing how footwork factored into where pitches were going.

"It wasn't until I pitched for Lefty O'Doul," said Duren, "that anyone took the trouble to teach me how to throw the ball. His approach was entirely different from anything I'd ever seen before."

Duren explained, "The first thing [Lefty] told me was to forget all about putting the ball over the plate. 'Instead,' he said, 'visualize a rectangle that represents the batter's strike zone. Now move that all around, and always aim for an imaginary spot in that rectangle—a high ball inside, a low ball outside. Then, as you gain experience, you'll come to know what pitches certain batters like, what they don't like; concentrate on that, and that speed of yours will finally pay off.'"[32]

The results were almost instantaneous. On June 27 Duren struck out seventeen and walked only one in a win against the Los Angeles Angels, one of the strongest offensive teams the PCL had seen in thirty years.[33]

A month later the right-hander once more dominated Los Angeles, striking out thirteen batters and again walking only one in a shutout victory; this performance occurred during a stretch of four straight wins by Duren, in which he allowed only twelve hits and no earned runs in thirty-seven innings.[34]

Duren ended the year with a record of 11-11, balancing his wins and losses thanks to an eleven-strikeout one-hitter on the next to last day of the season. He reduced his bases on balls from between

six and seven per nine innings to less than four, pitched in the PCL
All-Star Game, and was sold after the season to the Kansas City Athletics, who in turn traded him in the middle of the 1957 season to
the New York Yankees in the famous Billy Martin deal.[35] Assigned
by New York to Denver of the American Association, Duren won
thirteen of fifteen decisions, striking out 116 batters in 114 innings
while walking only 33, an average of 2.6 per 9 innings.

The next year, the Yankees brought Duren to the Majors and
he made the All-Star team, and then did so twice more. He never
became a control pitcher by any means—his wildness was part of
his effectiveness—but he knew where the ball was going. His well-
documented struggles with alcohol addiction likely played a role in
that wildness, both on and off the mound, but he achieved success.
To the end of his life, Ryne Duren gave credit to Lefty O'Doul.[36]

A week before the end of the 1956 season, O'Doul's Mounties
defeated San Francisco, 4–3, at Seals Stadium in the first game of
a Sunday doubleheader.[37] No one noted it at the time, but it was
the two thousandth victory of O'Doul's career as a Minor League
manager, to go along with three PCL pennants and four Governor's
Cup championships. It is a milestone few have reached—he was
the seventh to have done so at that time, and through the 2016 season he remains among the ten men to have accomplished the feat;
he and Jack Dunn are the only ones to accomplish it entirely at the
top rung of the Minor Leagues.

O'Doul would have one last fling with the bat, on the final day
of the 1956 season, against Sacramento. Not counting the 1949
trip to Japan, his previous at bat had occurred eleven years earlier, when in a similar situation he grounded out as a pinch hitter against Hollywood.[38] With nothing at stake, O'Doul grabbed
a bat and stood in against Solons veteran Gene Bearden. Sacramento manager Tommy Heath obliged by bringing his outfielders in close, and the fifty-nine-year-old O'Doul promptly lined a
pitch over the center fielder's head and raced—at least for someone a few months shy of turning sixty—all the way to third for a
triple before the ball was retrieved.[39] He would later claim that he

had finally discovered the secret of hitting—"make sure the other guy is laughing so hard that you can race around the bases before he can recover."[40]

The Mounties wanted O'Doul back, but immediately after the 1956 season ended, Lefty announced that his old friend, Seattle general manager Dewey Soriano, had invited him "to go for a little ride."[41] The next day it was announced O'Doul had signed a contract for roughly $18,000 to manage the Rainiers. He insisted he had long wanted to manage in Seattle, declaring, "The only goal I have in mind right now is to get on top and win a pennant."[42] At his reception dinner, he mentioned the Yomiuri Giants, proudly noting, "I see that my team beat the Brooklyn Dodgers today."[43]

O'Doul spent spring training praising young players, perhaps overly so—he dubbed outfielder Jerry DiMartini, who did not end up making the team, as another Joe DiMaggio.[44] He did have two younger players of note—pitcher Charlie Rabe and young shortstop Maury Wills, the latter serving as the team's lead-off hitter.

But the 1957 Seattle Rainiers were ultimately a mix of old and new, with the old mixing in more and more as the year went on. Larry Jansen, who was down from the New York Giants, hit a home run in the first series at San Francisco. O'Doul pretended to faint in the third base coach's box and used a stage whisper as Jansen went by so the pitcher would stop and "revive" him.[45] Another veteran, thirty-one-year-old former Negro Leaguer Joe Taylor, was an impressive slugger who in the early going battled Los Angeles Angels legend Steve Bilko for the league lead in home runs, including three in an early season doubleheader against San Francisco. But Taylor had a "casual approach to training," another way of saying he had great difficulty remaining sober. O'Doul said, "When Taylor is 'right' he is definitely a major league hitter." For those times when Taylor was not "right," O'Doul could only cross his fingers.[46]

The majority of the roster consisted of veteran Minor Leaguers, such as charismatic Filipino outfielder Bobby Balcena, pitcher Red Munger, and infielder Eddie Basinski, or big leaguers on the way down, including outfielder Jim Dyck and pitchers Joe Black, Larry Jansen, Duane Pillette, and Lou Kretlow. "Open Classification" had become a boon for veterans no longer able to make it in the Majors. The league that had produced Williams, DiMaggio, and Waner was no longer signing and developing its own young talent.

When it became apparent 1957 was to be only marginally better for him than 1956, or 1955, O'Doul lost interest. Years later, Maury Wills claimed that O'Doul generally showed up a half-hour before game time and asked coach Edo Vanni for the lineup. According to Wills, O'Doul would say, "Yeah—that looks good." Then, said Wills, O'Doul would disappear until about the fourth inning, at which point he would surface to find out the score. "If we were winning," Wills explained, "he would say, 'Okay, I'll handle it from here.' If we were losing, he'd say, 'You take it, Edo. I'll see you tomorrow.'"[47]

Lefty's final games as a manager came in a doubleheader on September 15—a twelve-inning, 8–5 win over Vancouver, followed by a 2–2 tie in the nightcap. The Rainiers finished with a winning record at 87-80 but ended the season in fifth place, O'Doul's third-straight second-division finish, and his eighth in the last nine years.

With that, the Brooklyn Dodgers and New York Giants moved to California, and an era was over. The PCL would continue, but it would not be the same. And it would not be the same for Lefty O'Doul.

Lacking big league offers to manage or coach, and certain that a diminished PCL would likewise result in diminished salaries, Lefty O'Doul decided it was time to call it quits. On November 30, 1957, he announced he was retiring to become a full-time bar owner and restaurateur in San Francisco—or as full-time as his golf game would allow.[48]

While, of course, playing golf, he told legendary *Seattle Post-Intelligencer* sports columnist Royal Brougham, "A fellow has to settle down sometime. If it wasn't that baseball was my whole life I would have quit years ago. I guess a real baseball man like an old soldier never wants to retire."[49] He announced his intention to root for his former team, now transplanted to San Francisco. "While I have retired from baseball to open a restaurant," he declared, "I plan to remain close to the game by occupying a box seat at all home games of the Giants."[50]

Harkening back to his first experience as a bar owner, O'Doul was enthusiastic about returning to his hometown and christening another one; with Major League Baseball coming to San Francisco, he envisioned his new establishment as a West Coast version of New York's legendary Toots Shor's. He secured a prime location just off Union Square, across the street from the landmark St. Francis Hotel.

While unveiling his plans to reporters, O'Doul reminisced about growing up in Butchertown, about Rose Stolz—he confirmed that they remained in touch—the sore arm that ended his pitching days, and his managerial career. He confirmed that he had accepted an offer from the Giants to visit Phoenix that spring to work with some of their hitters during training camp—Horace Stoneham remained a big fan of O'Doul and considered him a logical bridge between the Giants of New York and San Francisco. "When Horace Stoneham asked me to return to the Giants, it was like coming home," allowed an obviously pleased O'Doul.[51]

On Friday, March 21, 1958, Lefty O'Doul opened his restaurant at 333 Geary Street in San Francisco, in a building originally constructed four decades earlier as a movie theater.[52] Although his old bar around the corner was using his name—when O'Doul sold the business on Powell Street upon leaving the Seals for San Diego in 1952, its name was changed from "On the Hill" to "Lefty's"—he had no association with it and was irritated that the public was being misled to think otherwise. The best remedy for that was to make sure everyone knew about his new digs.

In the wake of a publicity blitz, American Airlines sent representatives, as did Pan American in what was some kind of mix-up. Actor Eddie Nugent escorted two stewardesses to the entrance while a trumpet played a fanfare. Nugent carried with him a box of sod from the center field of the Polo Grounds.

Pan American sent a ribbon of flowers for a ceremony, and the press was out in force. Mayor George Christopher handled the honors of the ribbon cutting while O'Doul and his restauranteur partner Al Pollack looked on. There was some clowning—Christopher pretended to cut Lefty's throat with the scissors, and Lefty then commandeered the shears and pretended to cut the grass in the box of sod.[53] He posed under a life-size mural depicting him swinging a bat and wearing his New York Giants uniform under the caption, "When Lefty O'Doul Was a Giant."

When the festivities concluded, everyone entered and had a few drinks and lunch on Lefty. A landmark was open for business.

O'Doul's bar almost immediately became a watering hole for fans and players alike. He frequently held court, usually drinking "a brew" (always a local product called Acme Beer) while bartenders mixed his family's special Bloody Mary recipe. The atmosphere was that of a Hofbrau house, with a menu featuring a wide range of drinks at the bar and food served cafeteria style, dominated by corned beef sandwiches, roast beef, and turkey and gravy with mashed potatoes. Mementoes from O'Doul's long career lined the walls—there were photos of Lefty with Douglas MacArthur, with Babe Ruth, with Gary Cooper, Ty Cobb, Joe DiMaggio. It was a second home, and a celebration of his accomplishments.

He continued his entrepreneurial ventures in Japan and lent his name to a group in California doing business as "Lefty O'Doul's Batting Range."[54] But his heart and soul would remain in his establishment on Geary. And in teaching hitting. And in playing golf.

14

The *San Francisco* Giants

Many of the Seals left Japan immediately after O'Doul Day, accompanied by Charles J. Graham, on a clipper ship bound for Hawaii. Lefty O'Doul and Paul Fagan remained behind for a week, continuing their public relations effort along with several players, including second baseman Dario Lodigiani, who had become especially popular with Japanese fans.

O'Doul acknowledged the overwhelming reception the team had received, telling reporters, "When we first arrived at the Haneda Airport I felt that all the Japanese were our good friends. And the longer we associate with them, the wider they open their heart's door to us."[1] The Japanese were anxious to hear O'Doul's opinion of their play, prepared for an honest critique from someone they considered a master or a father-figure. He noted their improvement since the 1931 and 1934 tours, and offered the opinion that their fielding was near Major League caliber, although, as he pointed out, there was always room for growth. O'Doul told the Japanese that their pitchers threw too much, risking the weakening of shoulders, and he advised them to learn to save their strength. He also told them not to worry about their physiques, pointing to the example of Paul Waner, who became a star despite his small stature.

O'Doul also discouraged the Japanese tendency to showboat for the crowd—he declared that it demonstrated a lack of team play and unity, as well as a lack of seriousness.

He stressed the importance of sportsmanship, noting that Japanese catchers tended to shout "strike" on pitches in an attempt to sway the umpire, and that infielders made fake tags without the ball, causing baserunners to slide unnecessarily, risking injury. He lectured them that it was not the honorable way to play baseball.

O'Doul also leveled with them about their play, explaining that if the Yomiuri Giants, the best team in Japan, were to join the Pacific Coast League, they would finish in the cellar. He explained that Japanese baseball did not yet have a long enough tradition, pointing to the PCL's nearly fifty years in existence. He encouraged the Japanese to create a farm system so players could gain experience and polish their technique, explaining that by the time a player reaches the American Major Leagues, he has already refined his skills, unlike in Japan.

"Baseball should be given greater latitude and good players be given a chance to train," said O'Doul. "I feel therein lies the difference between the professional baseball of Japan and that of the United States."[2] Far from being insulted, the Japanese regarded O'Doul's honesty as a sign of respect.

Kyoichi Nitta viewed the 1949 tour as a landmark in Japanese baseball history, and he was certain the visit would prove a catalyst in the development of quality baseball in his country. To illustrate the importance of the Seals' visit, he invoked the Japanese adage "Frogs in a well do not know of the wide ocean." Counseling against being fooled by games that had been closely decided, Nitta reminded fans and players alike that the Seals were an inferior team in a league a step below the American Major Leagues. Nitta wrote, "We should learn from the admirable and the superior technique based on fundamentals of the Seals and start all over again." He added, "Japanese baseball clubs should realize that they are little frogs in a well that have been allowed to catch a glimpse of the wide ocean."[3]

On November 6, 1949, O'Doul prepared to leave Japan. General William Marquat was on hand to say goodbye to Lefty and the remainder of the team. At the airport, the players were "besieged with flowers" while a band played "Auld Lang Sine."[4]

One by one the players boarded the aircraft, until only O'Doul remained outside. He turned and addressed those who had gathered. "I'm very happy that our tour was a great success," he said. "I shall never forget the rest of my life the kind welcome shown to us during our stay. I would like to come again next year.

"To the children of Japan, I'd like to say, 'Take good care of yourselves,' and to the professional ballplayers of Japan, I'd like to leave the message, 'Practice alone will perfect your techniques.'

"Once again then, Sayonara."[5]

• • •

A few weeks before opening his new saloon in March 1958, Lefty O'Doul celebrated his sixty-first birthday the best way possible, sitting on a stool in a clubhouse in Phoenix, Arizona, and pulling on a Major League uniform—this one bearing the number 63 on the back. He had been asked to serve as a special hitting instructor for the San Francisco Giants during spring training, and it felt good to him, as did the fact he could wear a baseball cap bearing the letters "SF" for the first time since being forced to say goodbye to Bay Area baseball fans in 1951. O'Doul's interactions with Giants players that spring reflected his being sensitive to the temporary—and to a degree honorary—nature of his role. He recognized that it was, in part, a public relations move. There were rumors that Giants manager Bill Rigney, a former PCL player, was merely tolerating O'Doul because of his status as a San Francisco icon. Always mindful of showing respect, O'Doul was careful to act as more of a guest than an employee.

Publicly, all was harmonious. Rigney told reporters, "The kids know of him, know his name, and will listen to him. It has always been my opinion that Frank is in a class by himself as a hitting instructor."[6]

Rigney then added, "Lefty has sort of a roving mission. He has my carte blanche to operate as he sees fit on the batting stances of any player in camp."[7] O'Doul was asked to work specifically with outfielder Felipe Alou and shortstops Daryl Spencer and Andre Rodgers, the latter a Bahamian cricket star who had recently become the first Major Leaguer from his country. O'Doul stayed after hours, eager to assist those three, and any other young players interested

in learning. When Spencer hit two home runs in an early exhibition game, it was noted that O'Doul had been working with him.[8]

When asked about Willie Mays, O'Doul cracked, "What is there
to tell Willie about hitting? He has a style all his own. I'd be fool-
ish to tinker with it. I think he has a chance to become the greatest right-handed hitter of modern times."[9]

Reporters pressed him to elaborate on his legendary ability to
teach, but O'Doul deflected the request, instead downplaying the
role of batting instructors. "Nine times out of ten when a hitter is in
a slump, it's mental," he argued. "Often, if you change the position
of his hands, or remind him of some fundamental he has ignored,
it will work wonders. First thing he knows, he has hit one out of the
park. His confidence is restored, and he goes on a hitting streak.
What happened? I hadn't told him a thing he didn't already know.
I had merely given him a pep talk."[10]

It fit the credo O'Doul had always followed as a manager—to
empathize when a player is down on himself. The key, as always,
was to restore confidence. There was a time to teach, and a time to
encourage—they were of equal importance. The stint in Phoenix
was good for O'Doul's ego, demonstrating he had not been forgotten by the Giants, and it excited him as reality set in that San Francisco was now officially a Major League Baseball city.

On April 15, 1958, Lefty O'Doul was at Seals Stadium, the Giants'
temporary home while they awaited a new stadium that would
open in 1960. As promised, he occupied a box seat for the first
game played by the *San Francisco* Giants. There had been a parade
to the ballpark, with actress Shirley Temple Black acting as parade
queen. Toots Shor was on hand, flying in from New York City to
say a melancholy goodbye to his beloved team, and to pass the
torch to a new group of fans. Ty Cobb was there too, along with
Mrs. John McGraw. O'Doul cheered as his protégé, Daryl Spencer,
hit the first-ever Major League home run on the West Coast.[11] But
it was undeniably strange for O'Doul, now a spectator in the stadium he had called home for seventeen seasons, and visited as an
enemy manager for another six.

The Giants won, 8–0, and O'Doul departed Seals Stadium slapping backs and telling everyone what a great day it had been for the city. Returning to his bar, he overheard a news crier erroneously proclaim, "New York Giants Win Opener!" O'Doul popped his head through the door and called out in mock anger, "What team was *that*, Charlie?"[12]

He was at the ballpark the next evening when Dodgers pitcher Johnny Podres got into a jam and fans began waving handkerchiefs— the tradition initiated by O'Doul more than two decades earlier.[13]

Although glad to see Major League Baseball in San Francisco, O'Doul could not fathom the plan to replace Seals Stadium. After asking why more thought was not given to adding a second deck to the diamond he had called home for so long, O'Doul cried, "What a crime to tear down the most beautiful ballpark in the country."[14]

In August, he was saddened by the death of Rose Stolz at age eighty-four. Never married and with no family other than her sister Minnie, she had served at Bay View School beginning as a substitute teacher and ending her career as principal upon her retirement in 1936. She had remained an informal counselor and guide to neighborhood children—and their parents—throughout her life. Among those had been Lefty O'Doul.[15]

A few months earlier, O'Doul had spoken fondly of Rose Stolz. "She's growing older," said Lefty, "but she's still a great fan. I know it is an old cliché, but Miss Stolz is my severest critic. Every time I pulled a boner, all through the years, I heard from her. We exchange notes, and talk on the telephone about my past, present and future."[16]

During the summer of 1958, Bill Rigney invited O'Doul to resume tutoring Giants hitters and help out as long as he wanted to—Felipe Alou, for one, reported every day to Seals Stadium to work out with him, and O'Doul predicted an All-Star future for the outfielder from the Dominican Republic.[17] But while O'Doul received praise for his work with Giants hitters, it seemed as if he had crossed the line from being a figure of the present to one of the past. Most of these young men did not really know who he was. Although a former big league star, he wasn't viewed as such by many Giants players because his reputation over the past two decades had been forged in the PCL, not the Majors. Articles about him increasingly focused on his past career, and he unwittingly played into the perception that time had passed him by through the repeated telling of twenty-five-year-old stories involving Joe DiMaggio and Ted Williams.

Willie Mays did not seek him out for advice as Williams and DiMaggio had. O'Doul began taking slight digs at the Giants star, remarking that if he had Mays's talent he would hit .400. There was no question he admired Mays and recognized his greatness. It was likely frustration at not being consulted by the new generation of baseball stars; the game was entering a new era.

O'Doul returned to help out Giants hitters again in 1959, and it was said publicly that Bill Rigney was again giving him "carte blanche." Lefty expressed delight at continuing his duties. "It enables me to run my string of years in organized ball to forty-three," he noted. "Baseball is still my life, although I wouldn't say it is my livelihood any longer."[18]

He ran into a bit of a roadblock his first day at training camp when he discovered the batting cage had been locked, since Rigney wanted conditioning drills completed before hitting began. But O'Doul sneaked the cage out the next day. Horace Stoneham laughed when he saw what had happened. "Sure, that's okay. Spring training is no fun without hitting," he said.[19] O'Doul pulled out the old rope trick he'd famously used on Ferris Fain to help Minor League catcher Al Stieglitz.[20] He praised young third baseman Jim Davenport, calling him every bit the equal of Pie Traynor and Willie Kamm.

"I saw them both. Most old guys are too prone to look backwards and accept the past as unmatchable," said O'Doul. "But this Davenport boy . . . well, he makes the same plays Pie and Willie did, and equally effortlessly." He added, "The past has no monopoly on excellence."[21]

O'Doul also spent time working with a young slugger, still limping on a knee injured the year before. The big left-hander, named Willie McCovey, had a swing that reminded Lefty of Ted Williams. He also displayed impressive power to all fields. McCovey would credit O'Doul with his mental and physical development that spring.

"Mr. O'Doul," said McCovey, "saw I was favoring my knee and not going through with my swing and reminded me of it. He kept picking at me until I lost the small fear that the knee would cave in on me."[22] Although the Giants sent McCovey to the Minor Leagues to begin the 1959 season, he would not stay there for long.

Later that spring, O'Doul joined Ty Cobb, Dizzy Dean, and former Giants pitcher Artie Nehf in signing three hundred baseballs after an automobile parade down the streets of Scottsdale, Arizona. The four retired stars wore green carnations in honor of St. Patrick's Day—O'Doul added his own touch with a shiny tie of shamrock green.[23] While signing, O'Doul was asked about the practice of handing out big money to young ballplayers. "I wouldn't pay any of them a bonus," he declared while shaking his head. "Most of these kids should be glad to get off the farm. I was happy to leave a sausage factory for $100 a month."[24]

When the season began, he was back at his restaurant.

The San Francisco Giants played their final game at Seals Stadium on September 20, 1959. A crowd of nearly twenty-three thousand was on hand to see the Dodgers smack San Francisco, 8–2. Los Angeles's Duke Snider hit the last home run in the ballpark, and Giants shortstop Eddie Bressoud hit into a double play to end the game.[25] The Giants drew 1,422,130, nearly 150,000 more than in their first season in San Francisco, and the greatest number the franchise had seen click through the turnstiles since 1948. It was quite a turnaround for a team that—despite playing in the nation's largest city—had finished dead last in National League attendance during its final two seasons in New York prior to moving to California.

On April 12, 1960, the Giants opened a new season in their new home, Candlestick Park. The first stadium constructed entirely of reinforced concrete, it was built not far from the Butchertown neighborhood in which Lefty O'Doul was raised. Vice President Richard Nixon, a California native running for president, praised the stadium as "the finest ball park in America."[26]

From his box seat, O'Doul could look up and see Bay View Hill—rising some four hundred feet above the lip of the stadium on the third base side—and shook his head at the thought of the days he spent on its slopes when it was known as Morvey Hill, picking daisies for Rose Stolz. The hill was relied on as a windbreak, of sorts, against the stiff, prevailing breezes that blew off the ocean in frigid gusts across the small point jutting out into the bay and into the open end of the stadium; enclosing the ballpark was more than a decade away. O'Doul still could not believe that Seals Stadium had been abandoned, and he blasted the new location as the most ridiculous site for a ballpark he'd ever seen. Lefty scoffed, "When I was a child, the wind would blow the sheep I was herding off [that] hill."[27]

The Giants won that first day, 3–1, defeating the St. Louis Cardinals. And it was cold.

O'Doul was asked to assist Giants hitters again in 1960—since he'd had success with Willie McCovey the year before, it was natural to give Lefty the assignment to turn the twenty-two-year-old left-handed slugger into a pull hitter, so he could take advantage of the wind blowing out to right field in the new ballpark.[28]

But being converted into a pure pull hitter in the wake of a successful Major League season was a change that McCovey would not remember with fondness. He struggled—after winning the Rookie of the Year Award while hitting .354, with a .656 slugging average in less than a half season in 1959, McCovey would slump to .238, even returning to the Minors for a brief stint to regain his batting eye.

Orlando Cepeda was another pupil who professed having mixed feelings about working with O'Doul. In his autobiography, *Baby Bull*, Cepeda grumbled that O'Doul constantly wanted him to pull the ball, even though he, like McCovey, enjoyed success hitting to all fields. The son of a legendary baseball player in Puerto Rico, Cepeda was resistant to O'Doul's entreaties.[29] O'Doul praised the young slugger anyway, declaring, "I don't see any reason why Cepeda shouldn't be one of the great stars of all time. He's got all the utensils. A good arm. Good eye. He's not afraid of the plate. And he's strong."[30]

In 2004, for an official Giants publication, Cepeda changed his tune about O'Doul. "In spring training that year he was great," said Cepeda. "He knew so much about hitting. He taught fundamentals and discipline and not to over-swing. I learned a lot from him. We all learned."[31]

The Giants abruptly fired Bill Rigney in June 1960, with the team in second place. He was replaced on an interim basis by Tom Sheehan; Lefty was not mentioned as a possible successor. In fact, Horace Stoneham publicly removed him from consideration, along with Leo Durocher and Hank Sauer.[32] According to Charles Einstein, O'Doul was not seen as a solution—his career had been about working with players he had been given. He had never had to build a team.[33]

For his part, O'Doul publicly expressed an indifference for the post. However, in an article published in *Sports Illustrated* once it became clear the Giants would not win the pennant, O'Doul, who was close to both Stoneham and Sheehan, expressed mystification at Sheehan's hiring, and for whom the Giants had posted a losing record and dropped to fifth in the eight-team National League.

"Horace can be a very stubborn man," said O'Doul. "If somebody tells him he should hire so-and-so to manage the club, you can bet right there that Horace is going to hire somebody else. He doesn't like people telling him how to run his ball club.

"No, I don't know how it happened—but it might have happened like this. Tom sat there for so long telling Horace how Rigney should have done this and that until Horace finally decided, 'Well, now, old Tom's pretty smart, we'll let him run the ball club.' Now I don't say that's what happened. But it might have."[34]

The San Francisco Giants had another new manager in 1961, thirty-nine-year-old Alvin Dark, who had been traded to the Giants from the Milwaukee Braves for Andre Rodgers.[35] If O'Doul was disappointed, he kept it to himself. "Alvin Dark is a fine choice," he insisted. "He has always been a hustler and knows the game. San Francisco fans will welcome him with open arms." Asked his opinion on ways the Giants could improve on their second-division finish, O'Doul replied, "I don't know what's going on with this club and don't care to butt in. I'm keeping my mouth shut."[36]

But O'Doul's attempts at magnanimity went nowhere; Dark had

no interest in tolerating O'Doul's presence as Rigney had—he had no ties to either O'Doul or the old Pacific Coast League. Lefty reported to spring training, same as he had since the Giants had arrived, but Dark ignored him. Lacking a role, O'Doul decided against appearing in uniform, instead stationing himself behind the batting cage in civilian clothes. Dark never acknowledged his existence.[37]

Charles Einstein, in his book *A Flag for San Francisco*, related Dark's old-school views of hitting, the Giants manager telling reporters, "I don't want anyone tampering with my hitters. A hitter doesn't get to the big leagues unless he knows how to hit. Changing him can do more harm than good."

Einstein asked Dark whether that meant O'Doul was not welcome. "You said that," muttered Dark. "I didn't."[38]

At one point, according to Einstein, O'Doul was watching newly acquired outfielder Harvey Kuenn, a season removed from an American League batting title, and remarked that he lunged too much when he swung. Willie McCovey supposedly overheard the remark and retorted, "What I need is some lunging lessons."[39]

Rejected by Alvin Dark and the Giants, Lefty spent the summer of 1961 in Japan, attempting to convince the country to embrace pizza. He also served as an announcer, along with Buddy Blattner, for the Japanese All-Star Game in Nagoya, which was taped for later broadcast back to the United States for a new program on the American Broadcasting Network called *Wide World of Sports*. O'Doul predicted the game would be a hit among Americans, saying, "Everywhere I go in the States, people ask me how good those Japanese guys are and how much they get paid. Now they can see for themselves."[40] A year later, ABC producer Roone Arledge visited Japan to secure rights to a second All-Star broadcast, and he claimed to have conceived the idea for slow-motion instant replay while watching samurai movies there—more than forty years after O'Doul had been featured in the first sports-themed motion picture utilizing slow motion.[41]

Horace Stoneham kept O'Doul on the Giants' payroll part-time for the next couple of years, having him instruct Minor League players during spring training, away from the big league complex and Alvin Dark. With each year, O'Doul's relationship with the Giants became more tenuous as San Francisco fans found new local baseball heroes—Mays, McCovey, Cepeda, and Marichal. Dark and the team began having success; the Giants claimed the National League pennant in 1962 and played in Northern California's first World Series, against the mighty New York Yankees—a Series that ended on a line shot hit by Willie McCovey that was famously (or infamously, according to Giants fans) speared by Bobby Richardson to send the Giants to defeat in the seventh game. O'Doul could only root for his beloved Giants as a fan.

Though nothing was said publicly, after Stoneham had O'Doul work with the 180 or so Minor Leaguers the Giants had under contract in the spring of 1963, Lefty's official duties with the Giants came to an end.[42] According to Bob Stevens, the final indignity came when O'Doul spotted a promising young hitter he wanted to work with. When the rookie was told this, he responded, "O'Doul, who's he?" Stevens said O'Doul overheard the exchange and walked away.[43] After forty-seven consecutive years connected to professional baseball, Lefty's time in baseball had run out.

In August 1963 O'Doul sat down with author Lawrence Ritter, who was conducting interviews for an oral history of baseball as it had been played in the early part of the twentieth century. The project would become the best-selling book *The Glory of Their Times.* O'Doul was one of twenty-two men Ritter profiled in the book, including Hall of Famers Sam Crawford, Paul Waner, and Edd Roush. (Goose Goslin, Stan Coveleski, Harry Hooper, and Rube Marquard would become members of baseball's shrine following the book's publication in 1966.) O'Doul later gave Ritter two tickets to a Giants game at Candlestick Park, along with a note saying, "This is the most absurd place for a ballpark I've ever seen."[44]

During the interview, O'Doul at times fell back into the time-worn tradition of arguing that players weren't as tough as in his day—how they were overpaid, whined too much about bean balls, and how they were more focused on commercial endorsements than on the game. He complained, "They think the old-timer is living in the past. They don't care to discuss baseball."

He remarked that Willie Mays was a great fielder and a good base runner, but that he was not in the class of Ty Cobb, Joe Jackson, or Babe Ruth. One of his famous banquet lines circa 1960 was that Cobb would only hit around .320 if playing today. When questioned, O'Doul would remind the audience, "Well, you have to remember he's seventy years old."

O'Doul often spoke with pride about his role in the development of professional baseball in Japan, and he lamented the fact that the Japanese were more coachable than Americans. "They want to learn," O'Doul said of the Japanese ballplayers. "They don't think they know everything."[45] More and more, Lefty would turn his attention toward Japan.

15

A Big, Big, Big, Big Thing

Lefty O'Doul returned to Japan more than a dozen times after his 1949 visit, most significantly in 1950 with Joe DiMaggio, and with a Major League All-Star team in 1951. During a 1953 trip he had arranged on behalf of the New York Giants, O'Doul stopped off in the midst of his delayed honeymoon and sat in the Yomiuri Giants' dugout, calling pitches against Leo Durocher's team. To Lefty's delight, the Japanese won, 2–1.[1]

O'Doul traveled during the 1950s to other venues as well, including both Alaska and Nicaragua with the Seattle Rainiers, with mixed results. While the Alaska venture was somewhat successful, the six-game trip to Nicaragua was rained out after only one contest.[2]

The most ambitious of O'Doul's other junkets was to Australia in November 1954, when the Japanese attempted to utilize O'Doul, Cappy Harada, and baseball to mend the war-driven rift between the countries. O'Doul did not organize the trip, but he did lend his name and presence to the endeavor, joining Harada and the Yomiuri Giants in "The Land Down Under." Expressing high hopes for the diplomatic potential of the trip, O'Doul declared, "The way things are going in this world now, it is important that better understanding between countries should prevail. This will be the first time since the war that Japanese athletes have been granted admission to Australia and I am confident that once competition is restored between these two countries, it will lead to a closer and better understanding."[3]

In his sendoff speech to the team, Matsutaro Shoriki admitted, "In her relations with Australia, Japan made mistakes in the

past. Now we are deeply repenting." Shoriki added that he wanted
to convey "fond wishes of Japan for a brighter tomorrow between
the two countries."[4]

But the goal of lessening the deep animus the Australians felt
for Japan was derailed by the early misstep of scheduling a game
on Memorial Day. The resulting cacophony of protest from war veterans reverberated nationwide. The offending exhibition was canceled, even as the Japanese made a futile attempt to make amends
by wearing posies to honor the war dead.[5]

Mindful of the controversy already plaguing the trip, O'Doul
repeatedly emphasized that Cappy Harada had fought with American troops, and that several of the Giants ballplayers were American citizens born in Hawaii.[6] But Australian bitterness toward the
Japanese continued unabated.

It did not help that the games were anything but exciting—most
of the locals were cricketers and lacked experience playing serious baseball. It was said that no more than five hundred people
attended any of the games—exorbitant ticket prices, in some cases
eight times what local baseball teams charged, was said to have contributed to poor attendance.[7] The effort was mercifully abandoned
after eight of the scheduled fifteen exhibitions had been played.

O'Doul blamed the failure of the trip squarely on the Aussies'
residual feelings about the war. "The Australians were not ready
to accept the Japanese as friendly foes," he complained. "We were
boycotted before we arrived . . . [and] the war veterans just refused
to forgive and forget."[8]

Lefty continued his efforts in Japan, but there was an interesting "what if" involving O'Doul and the Soviet Union. San Francisco mayor George Christopher hit it off with Soviet leader Nikita
Khrushchev during the latter's famous tour of the United States
in 1959, leading Christopher to undertake a reciprocal visit to the
Soviet Union the next year. The mayor spoke of cultural exchange
possibilities with Khrushchev, hoping to close the deal by proposing
that the Soviets invite O'Doul, who would bring sports equipment
and teach baseball to the Russians. Christopher further suggested
the possibility of future athletic contests between teams represent-

ing San Francisco and Moscow.[9] But the Russians, unlike the Japanese, had absolutely no interest in importing an American game. In the end, only a proposal for the exchange of animals between the Moscow and San Francisco zoos moved forward.

. . .

A few days before Christmas 1960, Lefty O'Doul decided to visit some of his old haunts in the Tenderloin, wandering into a bar on Ellis Street. While he waited for his drink to be served, he noticed a man in his mid-forties staring at him. Suddenly the man pointed his finger and said, "You're Lefty O'Doul and you hit .398 in 1929 and your lifetime batting average was .349." The man introduced himself as Budd Schulberg, the famous novelist and screenwriter of *On the Waterfront*, *A Face in the Crowd*, and *The Harder They Fall*. Schulberg was visiting San Francisco "incognito," as columnist Herb Caen put it.[10]

O'Doul was of course flattered by the recognition. But as Budd Schulberg had unintentionally pointed out, that recognition was for what Lefty had done in the past, not the present. It is difficult for someone when he recognizes time passing him by. It is doubly difficult when that person has tasted celebrity and its attention, and knows he still has much to offer. Such was the lot of Lefty O'Doul in the 1960s.

Once it became clear that managing a Major League team, or even a coaching role, was not in the cards, O'Doul visited Japan more than ever. During a trip to spring training in Tokyo in 1959, he spied a left-handed-hitting, nineteen-year-old rookie whose swing was triggered by an exaggerated leg kick that had to have reminded him of his old teammate Mel Ott. O'Doul told reporter Leslie Nakashima of the *Mainichi Daily News*, "The Giants have a great potential hitter in a player named Oh. He has an excellent swing and I predict he will become the best hitter in Japan."[11]

Lefty had not lost his eye for talent; although Sadaharu Oh hit only .161 in his rookie season, he ultimately hit 868 career home runs, including 40 or more per season thirteen times, during seasons that typically ran only 130 games. Oh was named his league's

Most Valuable Player nine times and played for eleven Japanese baseball champions.

That winter, O'Doul met with Matsutaro Shoriki for the purpose of arranging a visit by the San Francisco Giants following the 1960 season; it was hoped that the Giants would emerge as World Series champions, leading to the tantalizing possibility of a match between American and Japanese pennant winners—an unofficial "World Series," so to speak.[12]

O'Doul then caused a stir when he mentioned he would love to sign ace right-handed pitcher Tadashi Sugiura of the Nankai Hawks, a submariner who had recently pitched and won all four games of a Japan Series sweep of the Yomiuri Giants; the remark was interpreted by the Japanese as a plan to poach their talent for American teams.[13] Although Horace Stoneham *was* secretly hoping that O'Doul would prove a conduit for a new pipeline of talent to his team, and during his Pacific Coast League days O'Doul had openly courted Japanese professionals, Lefty backtracked from his statement about Sugiura, assuring local fans, "I definitely think Japanese players should stick to professional ball in their own country."[14]

Despite the dustup, O'Doul's popularity remained intact. A few months later, Cappy Harada was lunching with Commissioner Ford Frick as the two men discussed the long-range future of Japanese baseball. Questioned about O'Doul's influence in Japan, Harada replied, "Lefty O'Doul has meant so much to Japan that he could live like a king. . . . We call Lefty the Father of Professional Baseball in Japan. As General MacArthur once said, 'He's the best ambassador the United States ever had over here.'"[15]

On October 15, 1960, sixty-two people gathered at San Francisco International Airport at one-thirty in the morning to board a Pan American flight to Honolulu, the first stop on a postseason tour that would include sixteen games played by the San Francisco Giants in Japan. Lefty O'Doul was on hand to act as tour guide, the sixty-three-year-old on crutches thanks to forgetting his age and rupturing an Achilles tendon while playing softball two months earlier at a charity event at Lake Tahoe. "I was showing them how I used to dig for first," he lamented. "The left leg went 'pop.'"[16]

O'Doul was nonetheless upbeat, predicting that Willie Mays would prove a sensation. At the same time, he warned, "The Giants aren't heading for any soft touch. If the Giants loaf, the Japanese will beat them."[17]

Ten convertibles awaited the players upon their arrival in Tokyo; a pair of schoolgirls managed to poke their head into Willie Mays's car and shout, "Say Hi, Say Hi," which was their version of his famous nickname "Say Hey."[18]

The welcome parade wound through downtown, the crowd ignoring the rain along the ten-mile route and dousing the Americans with ticker tape and confetti. The weather caused more than one player to remark, "Gee, this is just like Candlestick Park," evidence the new stadium was already gaining a dubious reputation.

Mays was unquestionably the biggest attraction, and he addressed a horde of reporters "who nearly trampled him in their eagerness." As order was restored, Mays said, "I'll try my best on the field. I heard so much about Japan and am thrilled to see it for myself." He had to deny a report that had him predicting he would hit twelve home runs on the trip; he simply shook his head and grinned. "You know ballplayers don't commit themselves like that."[19]

The visiting big leaguers got off to a slow start, seemingly unable to shake their jet lag. They lost two of their first three games—including the first contest by a 1–0 score when Mays dropped a long fly ball that was generously scored a triple. The winning run then crossed the plate on a suicide squeeze.[20] Asked afterward about his bobble of the fly ball, Mays shrugged, "It was just one of those things. I thought I had it." He then added, "These Japanese play a fine brand of baseball. I was very impressed."[21]

Mays started slowly but warmed up as the trip went along, while manager Tom Sheehan admitted that he had indeed underestimated the Japanese. San Francisco won six of the next seven, with Willie McCovey belting four home runs, including two in one game at Sendai against the Japan All-Stars.[22]

As the trip neared its end, O'Doul was ecstatic. He could see that the Japanese had continued to progress; they were bigger and faster than a generation before. He vowed to approach Commissioner Frick with the idea of an annual Japan-U.S. championship series, beginning in 1964 when Tokyo was to host the Summer Olympics. "It would be a dream come true," he said. "I wouldn't say the Japanese could win, but by 1964 they should be able to make it competitive."[23]

While O'Doul did not come out and say it, he clearly would be rooting for the Japanese in such a series—in the same way he had felt slighted by Joe McCarthy and John McGraw and Paul Fagan, to a certain extent he felt slighted by baseball in his home country. A couple of years later he would confess his frustration to Lawrence Ritter. "See, I like people who you're not wasting your time trying to help. Teaching Americans and teaching Japanese is just like the difference between night and day. The American kid, he knows more than the coach. But not the Japanese kid.[24]

At one point he admitted, "I have more friends [in Japan] than in the U.S."[25]

There was no U.S.-Japan championship series in 1964, although O'Doul did host more than two dozen friends at the Olympic Games—finally held in Tokyo twenty-four years after their cancellation on the eve of the Second World War.

There was another major development that year as the San Francisco Giants made history, signing Japanese pitcher Masanori Murakami and two other players in a deal brokered by Cappy Harada. It was the first time Japanese nationals had signed with an American Major League team, and it would prove one of the highlights of O'Doul's life.

The nineteen-year-old Murakami had been sent to the United States by the Nankai Hawks on a temporary basis—at least that was their intention. The Hawks were enthusiastic about the youngster's prospects but thought the left-hander would benefit from tougher competition. Although he no longer worked for the Giants, O'Doul was on hand for the news conference introducing the players at Candlestick Park, and when asked about the significance of the occasion, he indirectly referenced the title of the recent hit comedy film *It's a Mad, Mad, Mad, Mad World* by declaring, with considerable pride, "This is a big thing in Japan. A big, big, big, big thing."[26] O'Doul went on to predict, "Someday, Japan will have many of its sons playing major league baseball in America."[27] Later, he posed with the three in a comic photograph, wearing a ridiculously oversized fielder's mitt.[28]

Following a whirlwind spring training that included a trip to Disneyland, Murakami was assigned to Fresno, the Giants' Class A affiliate in the California League, where his manager, Bill Werle, understood a little Japanese, and also understood Japanese culture thanks to his travels with O'Doul. Murakami had studied English but possessed only a rudimentary understanding of it, and he did not speak it well at that point. Werle told Murakami's teammates what to say—and what not to say—around him, and then set about converting the teenager from a starter to a relief pitcher.[29]

Even though he had at first seen it as a demotion, Murakami thrived in his new role out of the bullpen. By the end of August he had won eleven games for Fresno and posted an earned run average of 1.78, while striking out an incredible 159 batters in 106 innings and walking only 34.

San Francisco recalled Murakami on September 1; Giants president Chub Feeney insisted, "We brought him up here to pitch." Through an interpreter, Murakami told reporters that he relied on his fastball and breaking pitches and avoided throwing change-ups. "Change-up not good," he insisted. "Relief man come in, men on bases. Throw change-up. Boom. Long ball. No good."[30]

Three thousand miles away, Lefty O'Doul threw open the door to his bar on Geary Street, arriving around five o'clock. The sunlight cast a red glow that reflected through the windows, as the always-smiling ex-ballplayer maneuvered his way behind the counter. He was where he wanted to be. O'Doul spread his arms wide and shouted his welcome to the crowd, which shouted back its traditional greeting, "How are you, Lefty?"

The Japanese press, on hand to record O'Doul's reaction to Murakami's debut against the New York Mets, described him as balding and gray, but also muscular, and noted that "his suntanned face looked healthy as if he might be playing golf." O'Doul joked with customers while keeping one eye on the black-and-white television above the bar, the set flickering with fuzzy images from Shea Stadium, the brand-new home of the nearly brand-new Mets, who were managed by the far from brand-new Casey Stengel.

In the eighth inning, Alvin Dark sent Murakami to the mound; O'Doul and his customers immediately crowded closer to the television, watching as the left-hander walked in from the bullpen to the applause of forty thousand people and the stadium organist pounding out the popular hit song "Sukiyaki."

Lefty O'Doul had always predicted that the Japanese would eventually produce players to compete in the American Major Leagues, and now his prophecy had come true. As Murakami threw his first pitch to Charlie Smith, O'Doul raised his glass in a toast and shouted, "Tonight drinks will be my treat!"[31] The Geary Street crowd roared when Murakami struck out Smith to lead off the inning. After allowing a single to Chris Cannizzaro, Murakami then struck out Ed Kranepool and retired Roy McMillan to complete his first inning in the Major Leagues.[32]

An emotional O'Doul cheered with everyone else as Murakami walked off the mound. Turning to address his patrons—whom he truly viewed as friends—his eyes welled with tears as he explained, "I've been patiently waiting for this day for thirty years."[33]

Japan opened its own Baseball Hall of Fame in the summer of 1959; its first inductee was Matsutaro Shoriki, who had owned the Yomiuri Giants since their inception twenty-five years earlier. Shoriki was the only living inductee among the eight men selected.

In addition to early mementoes of Japanese baseball dating back to the 1870s, the Hall included an American Room, featuring artifacts from the various tours of Japan. One of O'Doul's uniforms was prominently displayed, along with Babe Ruth's bat and warm-up jacket from the 1934 junket. Douglas MacArthur II, nephew of the famous general and serving as America's ambassador to Japan, remarked that the museum "stands today as a monument to all

Japanese who love baseball and who wish to honor the heroes of that great game."³⁴

Lefty O'Doul was famously unable to pronounce the word "statistics," but he was extremely proud of his nonetheless, and had always been hopeful his .349 lifetime batting average would result in his election to Cooperstown—he had received votes every year between 1948 and 1953, and also from the Veterans Committee in 1956 and 1958. O'Doul reached his voting peak in 1960 when he received forty-five votes and finished thirteenth—of the top sixteen that year, he is the only one not in the Hall of Fame today.

But the rules for induction ignored O'Doul's contributions to youth baseball, and as a hitting instructor, and his two thousand wins as a Minor League manager, and his role in the development of the game in Japan. Voting was based only on his Major League playing career, which, although spectacular once he became an outfielder, was shortened because he was trapped in the Pacific Coast League during several of his peak years.

O'Doul's vote tally dropped to thirteen in 1962, while Bob Feller and Jackie Robinson made it—Feller in a near landslide, Robinson just squeaking in. Lefty collected one less vote than Goose Goslin and Johnny Mize, and one more than Lou Boudreau.³⁵ That represented O'Doul's last chance on the regular ballot, as the rules were changed to allow voting only for athletes who had played in the past twenty years, rather than thirty.

Attempting to disguise his disappointment, he refused to speculate about the reasons for being passed over for Cooperstown, deflecting such questions by insisting, "The game has been good to me, so I'm just going to talk about that." At the same time he worried about the game's future, noting, "When I was a kid everybody, kids from eight to twenty-five, played baseball. Take a walk around town now and you'll be lucky if you see even one sandlot game. That, I believe, is baseball's great weakness today."³⁶

Several years later O'Doul was honored at a banquet in Japan. The speaker lauded Lefty's contributions to baseball and concluded his remarks by suggesting that he be inducted into the Japanese Baseball Hall of Fame. The room exploded in cheers while dozens of people spontaneously paraded around the room shouting "Banzai!" to Lefty O'Doul.

Once decorum was restored, O'Doul cleared his throat and addressed the audience. "I am deeply touched," he said. "If there's room for me in Japan's Hall of Fame I'd sure like to be in it."[37] That elicited another energetic burst of celebration.

Afterward, O'Doul granted an interview to Kent Nixon of *Pacific Stars and Stripes*. Sitting in a downtown Tokyo hotel, the old ballplayer claimed it would mean more to him to be voted into the Japanese Baseball Hall of Fame than the one in Cooperstown.

"The only way you can get into Cooperstown is in a coffin, or on crutches," he told Nixon. "Besides, it would be a tremendous thing for me to be honored in Japan because I'd be the only foreigner so honored."

When told how grateful Joe Medwick had been for his recent election to the Hall of Fame, O'Doul shrugged and, betraying both bitterness and a touch of envy, insisted, "If getting enough votes means that much to Joe, okay. Maybe he needs it. I got a saloon. Business is great. Why should I complain?" After the interview was published, Shigeru Mizuhara and Sotaro Suzuki agreed to join with other baseball figures in Japan and begin pushing for O'Doul's election to the Hall there.[38]

In early 1966, writer Gay Talese arrived in San Francisco to pen a profile of Joe DiMaggio for *Esquire*. DiMaggio had previously agreed to talk to Talese, but the writer was given the cold shoulder until he contacted O'Doul, who invited Talese to tag along on the golf course while he and DiMaggio played a round.

What followed was a highlight of sports journalism—a poignant look at the afterlife of a hero, in this case DiMaggio, with O'Doul serving as comic relief of sorts. At one point in the article, Talese related the interactions of O'Doul and DiMaggio, portraying them as men who got a kick out of life, while sometimes engaging in behavior more akin to that of overgrown kids. There was an extremely energetic sixty-nine-year-old O'Doul chiding DiMaggio on the golf course, the two driving to parties together and ogling women half their age—or less.[39] Talese's story ran in the July issue, and was as entertaining as it was enlightening. It was, and is, considered a landmark, stripping away the mystique of celebrity to reveal the person behind the public mask.

Shortly after Talese returned to New York to file his story, O'Doul learned, to his delight, that he was to be honored by the San Francisco Giants. It had been Horace Stoneham's idea. As the day of the event drew near, he confided to *San Francisco Examiner* columnist Jack McDonald, "It's the thrill of my life—me a guy born and raised in Butchertown and having great players come from miles away to honor me. I've hardly slept for a week, lying in bed thinking about it."[40]

On May 21, 1966, the Giants held Lefty O'Doul Day at Candlestick Park. Joe DiMaggio, Casey Stengel, Carl Hubbell, Joe Cronin, and Frankie Frisch were among those on hand to salute their friend.[41] A ceremony was held at home plate, and O'Doul was moved to tears as he listened to tribute after tribute. Former Seals teammate Sammy Bohne implored the crowd to begin a campaign to get Lefty elected to the Hall of Fame—singer Bing Crosby, a longtime part-owner of the Pittsburgh Pirates, remarked, "That's interesting. I always thought he was in."[42] Bohne then handed O'Doul a $1,500 check from the Merced Golf Club. Lefty immediately turned it over to the Police Athletic League.

Baseball commissioner William Eckert was on hand and made a few remarks. Horace Stoneham presented O'Doul $5,000 in savings bonds. Lefty also received lifetime passes from the NBA's San Francisco Warriors and the San Francisco 49ers. Casey Stengel reminded those in attendance, "At one time O'Doul was the biggest man in the state of California. Bigger than a Supreme Court Justice or the Governor." Joe DiMaggio said simply that O'Doul was, as he put it, "a great teacher."[43]

Lefty was overwhelmed. "They've given guys just retiring from the game a day, but I'm an old codger who's been out of it for a long time. It's wonderful. It's the thrill of my life. And the unbelievable part of it is that Candlestick is in the very shadows of where I was born and raised, right here in Butchertown. Who could visualize

then that the New York Giants would become a San Francisco club
and that they would honor me in my old neighborhood?"[44]

There could not have been a more meaningful tribute to O'Doul
than being recognized in San Francisco. He was not recognized in
Cooperstown. He no longer wore a baseball uniform. But he had
been honored by his hometown. And he *was* honored.

16

He Was Here at a Good Time

During the 1970s, there were intermittent efforts to have Lefty O'Doul inducted into the Japanese Baseball Hall of Fame. In 1976 Sotaro Suzuki published his book *History of Japanese Professional Baseball*, in which he detailed O'Doul's contributions to the 1934 tour and his convincing Matsutaro Shoriki to start professional baseball in that country. That summer, Leslie Nakashima, of the *Mainichi Daily News*, pointed out that Japan's *Baseball Weekly* had recently celebrated its one thousandth issue by noting the fifty-two men who at that point had been inducted into the Japanese Baseball Hall of Fame. Then he noted, "But there's one important name sadly lacking. It is that of Frank 'Lefty' O'Doul."[1]

That oversight was finally rectified in 2002, when O'Doul was selected by a committee recognizing special contributors to the game in Japan.[2]

Unfortunately, Lefty was no longer around to enjoy the honor, but many who had known and loved him were. On a typically fog-shrouded summer Sunday morning in San Francisco, a group of baseball fans gathered in Lefty's restaurant just off Union Square, toasting to his memory—the boy from Butchertown who was now a member of the Japanese Baseball Hall of Fame. O'Doul's second cousin Tom was there, as was Con Dempsey, who called O'Doul his "second father," saying of his former manager that he was like a "second emperor" in Japan. Former Seals outfielder Dino Restelli also noted O'Doul's accomplishments as a baseball ambassador.

Cappy Harada said of his old friend, "He always lived up to

whatever he said."[3] Baseball historian Kerry Yo Nakagawa noted that O'Doul had "opened up a positive bridge across the Pacific between Japan and the United States."[4]

Highlights of Lefty's career were screened, eliciting gales of laughter and sustained applause from those in attendance. The Japanese consul was well represented, as a barrel of sake was broken open in a traditional Kagamiwari ceremony, utilizing wooden mallets designed specifically for the purpose. A saxophonist played "Take Me Out to the Ballgame" as those present toasted O'Doul's memory, and his Hall of Fame selection, using square wooden cups called *masu*.[5]

A month later, O'Doul was formally inducted in a ceremony held during the Japanese All-Star Game at the Tokyo Dome. That August, Tetsuharu Kawakami and Shigeru Sugishita, Hall of Famers who had been invited by O'Doul to spring training with the San Francisco Seals in 1951, called on the United States' ambassador to Japan, former U.S. Senator Howard Baker, and showed him the bronze plaque bearing O'Doul's image that was to be displayed at the Hall of Fame. Several months later, a duplicate was presented to Giants managing partner Peter Magowan and Tom O'Doul during a ceremony at AT&T Park (then called Pacific Bell Park).

The plaque's inscription notes O'Doul's visit to Japan in 1931, his assistance in establishing professional baseball and naming the Tokyo Giants, the 1949 tour, the invitation of the four Japanese stars to training camp in America in 1951, bringing the San Francisco Giants to Japan in 1960, and his helping develop and improve baseball in Japan.[6]

The San Francisco Giants have embraced their history in recent years, coinciding with their occupying a new stadium, just across the estuary from the Lefty O'Doul Bridge. The nearest entrance, by the Willie McCovey statue and McCovey Cove, is at Lefty O'Doul Plaza and is named the Lefty O'Doul Gate. The second Japanese Hall of Fame plaque is located at the stadium on the Club Level, with a replica posted just inside the entrance of the O'Doul Gate.

• • •

As his assignments with the San Francisco Giants tapered off into irrelevance during the 1960s, Lefty O'Doul's daily existence evolved into a series of banquets, fund-raising events, celebrity golf tournaments, and old-timers' games—Mets, Giants, A's, Yankees, it made no difference. If he was called, he was there. He signed autographs at every invitation—one memorable event sponsored by B'nai B'rith involved him signing baseballs for kids along with Willie Mays and Joe DiMaggio.

O'Doul continued his ritual of traveling to training camp every year to swap stories, feel the sun, and enjoy the sights and sounds of baseball in spring. Willie Mays taped segments for a fifteen-minute pregame television show during training camp in the late 1960s, and he was once asked about the experience of switching places and interviewing others. After lamenting the challenges he had endured with several guests who turned out to be less than talkative, Mays volunteered that his easiest interview was Lefty O'Doul. "I just said four words," he recalled, laughing, "and he didn't stop talking. Man, that's an easy job."[7]

O'Doul began serving as a celebrity host of sorts at his restaurant, chatting up friends and customers. He arranged for buses to Giants games at Candlestick—an effort to shore up the significant drop in his business since the team had moved from downtown. He also organized weekend tours to Los Angeles for Giants-Dodgers series, during which he gladly played tour guide.

At one point he converted the back of his restaurant into what he called "Lefty O'Doul's Hideaway Room," inviting celebrity friends to headline in an attempt to secure a foothold in the highly competitive nightclub circuit of San Francisco. But the concept failed.[8] Most of the time O'Doul was content having Don Figone, who began working at the restaurant in 1961, handle day-to-day operations, although Lefty insisted on closing the restaurant two days each year—Thanksgiving and Christmas—to provide free meals to the downtrodden, or the "less lucky" as he put it, from the nearby Tenderloin. In 1966 Lefty bought out his partners to take over 100 percent of the business—with the financial assistance, rumor had it, of Horace Stoneham.[9]

Lefty remained incredibly popular—both locals and tourists sought him out at his bar and found him always willing to talk, not only about baseball but also about people he had met and places he had been. Lefty *was* San Francisco, and if you visited San Francisco, you wanted to visit Lefty. He would explain to outsiders that it was okay to call the city "Frisco," explaining that only folks who had transplanted from elsewhere were offended by the phrase.

Golf increasingly took up Lefty's time and interest; his back bothered him, as did his arthritic shoulder, but he was not about to give up the game, admitting to columnist Art Rosenbaum, "I love golf more than I love myself."[10] There is plenty of evidence to support that—he played in the Crosby Clambake every year, and in virtually every amateur tournament staged anywhere on the West Coast. He was perpetually accompanied by Joe DiMaggio, and often with Ernie Nevers and Reno Barsocchini as well; O'Doul and DiMaggio even traveled to Lake Tahoe to film a segment for a popular television golf show.[11] Most often, Lefty played in celebrity fund-raising tournaments, usually in the Bay Area or Idaho or Nevada—at one tournament in Reno he missed a hole-in-one by inches that would have won him a car and his weight in silver.[12] He also took an interest in boosting the women's professional tour, befriending young future Hall of Famers Donna Caponi and Kathy Whitworth.

As a result, much of the press coverage O'Doul received in the 1960s related to golf, not baseball. When a reporter or columnist did ask Lefty about the national pastime, it was generally to compare present-day players with those who, like him, were part of the past.

Baseball returned to Oakland in 1968 when the Athletics were transferred from Kansas City by Charlie Finley, who gave several nods to the area's ties with the old PCL. He hired Joe DiMaggio as a coach and vice president, and on August 18 staged a Casey Stengel Day, coinciding with the twentieth anniversary of Stengel's Pacific Coast League championship, which had launched his Hall of Fame stint with the New York Yankees. Stengel and O'Doul posed the day before, hamming it up while playing tug of war with the 1948 PCL Governor's Cup, while Finley and Joe Cronin looked on.[13]

More than forty-one thousand people showed up for an exhibition between former Oakland Oaks and San Francisco Seals staged prior to the regular game. Comedians Tom Smothers and Pat Paulsen were introduced as umpires, while O'Doul posed in a sports coat along with the three DiMaggio brothers, who wore A's uniforms. Lefty was demonstrating something or other with a baseball bat for the benefit of photographers—it's not entirely clear what instruction would have been relevant to the DiMaggios at that point in their lives, but they were having fun.

So it came to pass that O'Doul and Stengel managed against each other one last time, with Stengel's Oaks taking the two-inning contest, 3–1.[14] The seventy-seven-year-old Stengel was so enthused he even praised the quality of play in his inimitable style, exclaiming, "There was some hitting and there was some fielding which is pretty remarkable when you consider they had a party last night."[15]

Lefty would attend one more Old-Timers' Day, as a guest of the Giants at Candlestick Park in 1969. He mugged for a publicity photograph, pretending to choke "umpire" Babe Pinelli while Stengel looked on, as if to study O'Doul's technique. Don Larsen took the mound, as he had for Pinelli's last assignment as a home plate umpire—calling balls and strikes for Larsen's perfect game in the 1956 World Series. Larsen, of course, pitched a perfect inning.[16]

It was a wonderful day of memories and tall tales plus, of course, the inevitable bending of the elbow at Lefty's saloon.

During the summer of 1969, Lefty O'Doul made what would be his final trip to Japan. He labeled it "a sentimental journey," one that involved looking up old friends and renewing long-lost acquaintances. While there he made plans to visit the Osaka Exposition the next summer.[17] But Lefty was not well.

He had been suffering numbness in his left arm for a couple of months, which he chalked up to his arthritis. He was mistaken. On November 12 O'Doul suffered a stroke that crippled his left leg and arm. Admitted to French Hospital, located in San Francisco's Richmond district, he was to remain there for several weeks in order to gain strength for surgery to clear a blood clot—publicly his condition was reported as not serious. "They want to get more blood to my brain," O'Doul quipped from his hospital bed. "These French and Italians can't get an Irishman down."[18] Jean O'Doul told reporters, "He's not feeling good. But he's kidding all the nurses just the same. He's a tough old bird and he'll come out of this."[19]

As O'Doul lay in bed, he naturally grew restless. A week into his hospitalization, he told the *San Francisco Chronicle*, "I'm feeling about as good as a guy can under the circumstances. Only trouble is I can't move my left arm. If I could, I'd get out of here and have a belt and that would loosen me up."[20]

A few days later, O'Doul received a phone call that meant the world to him, from Joe DiMaggio. Lefty and Joe had fallen out a few months before—over what, no one was quite sure. Joe was just that way sometimes.

A mutual friend, unidentified but quite possibly Reno Barsocchini, told DiMaggio that O'Doul was in the hospital and that a call would mean a lot to him. Joe immediately dialed up O'Doul's hospital room and, according to *Oakland Tribune* columnist Ed Levitt, the two men talked for an hour.

"I'm glad it happened," Levitt reported the unidentified friend as saying. "That was one thing in Lefty's life that disturbed him the most. He had to feel better knowing Joe was still his pal."[21]

O'Doul's surgery was finally scheduled for December 8. A day earlier, as animated as ever, he traded stories with friends and talked of plans for another trip to Japan, "as soon as I get out of here, probably in the spring."

Looking around a hospital room overflowing with cards and letters from all over the world, Jean remarked, "Few of us ever have such expressions of love come to us while we're still alive."[22] One of the get-well letters was from President Richard Nixon; O'Doul cried when he read it.

At noon he telephoned Prescott Sullivan and told him that he was regaining use of his left leg, and that the operation would take care of the paralysis of his left arm.

Sullivan told O'Doul, "You sound good. You must be feeling better."

"A lot better," he replied. "I'm gonna beat this thing. I'm bat-tling it all the way."[23]

O'Doul laughed about a sign he had tacked onto his hospital room door, a sheet of paper with large red block letters spelling out "HELP!"

Lefty phoned several other friends that afternoon, sounding buoy-antly optimistic. He was still joking and laughing at about four-thirty when, without warning, he suddenly slumped, unconscious. Efforts to revive him were unsuccessful. He was officially declared to have died at ten minutes to five o'clock. The attending physician said of the seventy-two-year-old, "It was very quick. He never knew what hit him."[24] Ironically, the man who had so loved Japan succumbed on the anniversary of the bombing of Pearl Harbor.

Lefty's passing was front-page news in San Francisco and was car-ried in newspapers nationwide. Prescott Sullivan wrote movingly of his old friend. "It isn't easy to write about, it is something we know to be true, but still can't believe it. In our mind, Lefty O'Doul was the one person who would never get old and would never die."[25]

Casey Stengel said, "Baseball has lost a great man . . . one of the greatest hitters and one of the greatest hitting instructors of all time."[26] Red Smith paid tribute in his nationally syndicated column.[27]

Columnist Art Rosenbaum remembered Lefty as one who "loved the action, day or night." He added, "That man could talk, and he always drew a circle of listeners. His baseball tales were endless and he never gave himself the worst of it. But with his wonderful ego, there was always a sense of believing. He could pitch or hit better, putt better, play cards better, stay up longer, make friends faster than—well, there was only one O'Doul."[28]

In Tokyo, longtime Central League president Ryuji Suzuki called O'Doul his personal friend and, recalling the 1949 tour, declared, "He was the man who built the bridge of goodwill between Japan and the United States."[29]

Cyril "Pinkie" Green, a local baseball fan who had spent fifteen years attempting to get O'Doul into Cooperstown, recalled Mark Twain's famous quote, "I want to live so that when it comes time

to die, even the undertaker will feel sorry." Green told Art Rosenbaum that the sentiment fit O'Doul.[30]

O'Doul's funeral was held on December 11, a gloomy, gray day
punctuated by intermittent showers; it was if the city itself was sad
to see him go. He was eulogized as the "Mayor of Powell Street"
and "The Father of Baseball in Japan." Among the pallbearers
were Prescott Sullivan, Sammy Bohne, and former San Francisco
49ers placekicker Joe Vetrano. Charlie Graham's daughter Claire
represented her family. Horace Stoneham, Carl Hubbell, Willie
Kamm, Joe Sprinz, Buddy Baer, Ernie Nevers, and Del Webb were
listed as attendees.[31]

An organist softly played "Take Me Out to the Ballgame" as
O'Doul's casket was carried out of St. Edward the Confessor Church
to the hearse that would take him on his final motorcade to Cypress
Lawn in Colma, where he was laid to rest.

Today, O'Doul's four-foot-high grave marker lists the statistics of
which he was always most proud. It bears his lifetime batting average of .349, stenciled onto a baseball attached to the monument.
The marker also notes his National League record for base hits in a
season and his two batting championships. Underneath his name
and the dates of his birth and death is written his nickname, "The
Man In The Green Suit," and his epitaph: "He Was Here At A Good
Time And Had A Good Time While He Was Here." A baseball bat
crosses the marker diagonally across the bottom. He is buried near
the roadway, his distinctive gravestone hard to miss—after all, as
he had once told Lawrence Ritter, what's the use of doing something where nobody's looking?

Lefty O'Doul's will was straightforward. He was far from destitute,
but as would be expected of someone who habitually gave away
what he had, O'Doul's list of assets was modest. His estate was val-
ued at slightly less than $160,000, all but $20,000 of that amount
representing the value of his restaurant on Geary Street. He also
owned shares in a British Columbia copper mine, some clothing
and jewelry, a couple of television sets, a few gold coins, and the

two hundred shares of the Dai Nippon Baseball Club given him at the creation of the franchise in December 1934.

O'Doul's mother had died in 1961, so he directed that first wife Abbie be given a stipend of $250 per month, and the same amount to Jean's mother. Jean got the rest.[32] Jean married Don Figone nine months before her death in November 1977, a little more than a year after Abbie O'Doul passed away. At that point, Don Figone took over the business.[33]

Lefty O'Doul's continued on, run by Figone until 1997, when he announced it would be closing. At that point, Nick Bovis agreed to run the business for his father—who had been a good friend of O'Doul's—and they purchased it.[34] The restaurant has thrived over the past two decades, enjoying a revival as a historic watering hole for players and fans alike, and has gained additional fame through an extremely successful toy drive held each Christmas. Lefty O'Doul's name also lives on through a foundation chaired by Lefty's second cousin Tom O'Doul that provides sports equipment and tickets to ballgames for needy children—echoing Lefty's contributions to the community during his lifetime.

There were a number of efforts to memorialize O'Doul following his death. One of the first was an effort to rename Candlestick Park in his honor.[35] That ran into a snag when the San Francisco 49ers reached an agreement to share the stadium with the Giants. The matter was put up for a vote in November 1970 but failed by a nearly three-to-one margin, as many pointed out that O'Doul had never been involved with the stadium, had publicly voiced his displeasure with the ballpark, and likely would not have wanted his name associated with it.[36]

O'Doul did have a street named in his honor, in the area known as South of Market, or SOMA; it had been an Irish enclave for decades and seemed an appropriate place for an "O'Doul Lane." But by the end of the 1970s the street's name, along with a half-dozen others, was changed to reflect a shift in the neighborhood's demographics, which had become predominantly Filipino. In August 1979

the San Francisco Board of Supervisors voted to change the name
from O'Doul Lane to "Tandang Sora."[37]

As an accommodation, O'Doul was honored through the renam-
ing of a bridge on Third Street, a major thoroughfare that had tra-
versed old Butchertown. The 143-foot span, constructed in 1933,
was designed by Joseph Baerman Strauss, who also designed the
Golden Gate Bridge. A steel truss bascule type bridge—the only
one remaining in the vicinity of San Francisco—it crosses a ship-
ping channel emptying into the bay.[38] It has also served as a location in several television shows and motion pictures, including the
1985 James Bond film *A View to a Kill*. Sixty-seven years after it
was built, and thirty-one years after O'Doul's death, the San Francisco Giants built a new ballpark on the other side of that bridge—a
more than fitting coincidence.

In 1981, around the same time the bridge was renamed, O'Doul
was elected to the Bay Area Sports Hall of Fame—there had been
an uproar when he was not one of the original inductees the year
before, supposedly because of rules allowing only one of the five
inductees to be inducted posthumously. His selection in the second year was essentially a forgone conclusion. (It was not his first
Hall of Fame induction—in the 1940s he had been honored by the
Helms Athletic Foundation, whose inductees were later rolled into
the current Pacific Coast League Hall of Fame.) Fellow inductees
included Lefty Gomez, Bob Matthias, and Helen Wills Roark. Dominic DiMaggio flew in at his own expense from Boston to accept the
award on Lefty's behalf. He told the audience, "I congratulate the
Bay Area Sports Hall of Fame for having the wisdom to do what
Cooperstown didn't."[39]

A decade later there was a serious effort to gain Lefty's enshrine-
ment in Cooperstown, taking up the torch first carried by Pinkie
Green in the mid-1950s. At the suggestion of San Francisco supervi-
sor Quentin Kopp, Daniel Woodhead, who had headed up a Downtown Ballpark Boosters Club for the San Francisco Giants, initiated
a "Lefty O'Doul for Cooperstown" letter-writing campaign. Aided by
Japanese baseball historian Yoichi Nagata, the campaign garnered

the support of dozens of veteran ballplayers from both America and Japan, as well as sportswriters and other notables. General Matthew Ridgway, in his nineties, emphasized O'Doul's importance to U.S.-Japan relations, while Warren Buffett, who had been a fan of Lefty's since childhood, also wrote in support.[40] *Sports Illustrated* took notice and published an article about the effort.[41]

Hisanori Karita, a member of the 1935 Tokyo Giants and the Japanese Baseball Hall of Fame, detailed O'Doul's contributions to baseball in his country and concluded, "I hope that Frank O'Doul will be honored in Cooperstown due to his great achievements in American baseball and also in the international scene of baseball."[42]

Toru Shoriki, eldest son of Matsutaro Shoriki, and his successor as owner and president of the Yomiuri Giants, wrote, "He devoted himself as a bridge between the two baseball countries. I would like to call him an American Ambassador of Baseball to Japan. I can hardly wait to see Frank J. 'Lefty' O'Doul in the Hall of Fame. I am confident it will be a great honor to the Japanese baseball society as well as the same in the States."[43]

The drive ultimately fell shy of its goal—Veterans Committee member Buzzie Bavasi remained in contact with Daniel Woodhead, and confided that many on the committee felt O'Doul's peak as a player was too short.[44] There was another brief push in the late 1990s, and a book about O'Doul was written by Richard Leutzinger; it was also published in Japan.

Ten years later, San Francisco attorney John Ring joined with Woodhead for another attempt. Ring helped organize a tribute to O'Doul in San Francisco to kick off the effort.[45] The old Hall of Fame Veterans Committee had been reconstituted into a voting body consisting of all living Hall of Fame members, plus those writers honored at Cooperstown. They would vote every other year. A subcommittee of ten sportswriters had in 2003 generated a list of two hundred players meriting consideration but ineligible for the annual Baseball Writers Association of America voting—O'Doul was among them, although he did not receive any votes in either 2003 or 2005.

Ring and Woodhead sensed an opportunity to make the case

before a different set of judges. The effort caught the attention of
USA Today, which ran a story that summer about campaigns for
induction into baseball's shrine on behalf of forgotten players. Ring
and Woodhead were photographed at Lefty O'Doul's pub, posed
underneath the photo of O'Doul receiving his field day award for
fastest runner to first base in 1931, a group shot that included Babe
Ruth. It was noted that written materials and DVDs had been sent
to more than 260 potential supporters.[46]

O'Doul also had the public support of several Hall of Famers,
including Bob Feller; when asked who should be in the Hall of
Fame but wasn't, he told *San Francisco Chronicle* reporter John Shea,
"Lefty O'Doul is number one in my book." He compared O'Doul's
length of career to that of Dizzy Dean and then added, "He should
be the next player elected by the Veterans Committee."[47]

In 2007 twenty-five finalists were chosen from the list of two
hundred, and this time O'Doul made the cut. In the balloting, he
tied Roger Maris and Luis Tiant for ninth place with fifteen votes
out of eighty-two cast—a respectable showing after being shut out
twice.[48] But the rules were changed again after that year, and since
that time O'Doul has not appeared on a final ballot.

Thirty-one years after Lefty O'Doul sat in on a press conference
at Candlestick Park announcing the signing of the first Japanese
native by a Major League team, another press conference was held
at the same stadium as the second Japanese Major Leaguer, Hideo
Nomo, prepared to make his Major League debut for the Los Angeles Dodgers against the San Francisco Giants, in the shadow of what
had once been the Morvey Hill O'Doul knew so well.

A group of fans in Section 12 unfurled a Japanese flag and celebrated, rising in unison as Nomo walked to the mound for the
first time; many were Japanese nationals visiting or working in
San Francisco. Mitsuko Iwama called it a special day for Japan—
she had taken her son out of school to see the historic moment.
"I wanted my son to see this because young people see him as a
symbol of excellence."[49]

Nomo would surrender only one hit in his five-inning debut,

allowing no runs while striking out seven and walking four. Retired Japanese All-Star outfielder Isao Shibata called it "a very, very big start. How he performs shows how far Japanese baseball has come. By him being successful, it will open the door to Japanese people."[50]

Nomo would go on to capture the Rookie of the Year Award, win 123 Major League games and throw two no-hitters, and lead both leagues in strikeouts. In 2014 he became the youngest man elected to the Japanese Baseball Hall of Fame, in large part because of his Major League career. And he did open the door to others from Japan. Through the 2016 season, more than fifty native Japanese had played in the American Major Leagues. One of them, Ichiro Suzuki, set a new Major League record with 262 hits in a season, and in August 2016 he became the first former Japanese professional to accumulate 3,000 hits in Major League Baseball. He is certain to earn a plaque in Cooperstown after his playing days; undoubtedly, there will be many more great Japanese players to come.

No one would be more proud of this than Lefty O'Doul.

The tranquil morning at the farmhouse in Gorham, Maine, was suddenly interrupted by a knock on the door. The visitor responsible for the intrusion on this fine spring day in 2001 was from Japan—specifically, *Asahi Shimbun*. The man was polite and apologetic. Although he did not speak English very well, it soon became clear that he hoped to discover more about Horace Wilson, the English professor credited with introducing baseball to Japan in 1872. This stranger, standing on a porch more than six thousand miles from his home, was delighted to learn that the farm was owned by a great-grand-daughter of Wilson's youngest brother. A researcher named Phil Block had discovered Wilson's original home and contacted the Japanese Hall of Fame, hence the visit.[51] The family knew little about Wilson, and nothing about his role as Japan's Alexander Cartwright, so to speak. So they were learning about him as well.

Born and raised in Maine, Wilson had served in the Union Army and moved to San Francisco in the late 1860s. While there, he received an invitation from the Japanese government to travel to the country and teach. Wilson remained in Japan for five years and, according to his obituary, received the country's prestigious Order of the Rising Sun.[52] In 1877 he and his young family returned to San Francisco, where he was initially employed as a librarian at the iconic Mechanic's Institute. He also served as secretary to the Japan Society of San Francisco.

Wilson became a prominent citizen of San Francisco, active in the Grand Army of the Republic and local Republican politics. He was appointed in 1900 to the San Francisco Board of Supervisors by Mayor W. A. Phelan and was elected the next year for a term in his own right. While in that role, he served on the commission that drafted the city's charter. Wilson was later appointed by two California governors to the board of managers of Agnew State Hospital and was a member of the famous Bohemian Club.[53] In his later years Wilson was one of the city's most prominent insurance men.[54] Thanks to a visit to a Maine farmhouse, in 2003—three-quarters of a century after his death—Horace Wilson became the fourth American to be inducted into the Japanese Baseball Hall of Fame. And there were a number of strange coincidences involving Wilson and his fellow American inductee Lefty O'Doul.

Wilson died at his home at 711 Post Street in San Francisco at age eighty-four on March 4, 1927—Lefty O'Doul's thirtieth birthday. Not only that, at the time O'Doul lived at 890 Bush Street, only three blocks from Wilson's residence.[55]

Did Horace Wilson ever see Lefty O'Doul play? Or perhaps sell him insurance? No one knows. It is not clear whether Wilson was in fact a big baseball fan. But in 1935, eight years after Wilson's death, O'Doul, who had never visited Japan prior to Wilson's passing, was presented an award at Seals Stadium by the Japan Society of San Francisco—the same organization Wilson had for many years served as secretary.

Horace Wilson was buried in Cypress Lawn Cemetery in Colma, south of San Francisco. His grave marker, set in place decades before his being credited with planting the Japanese branch of the baseball tree, is simple, listing his birth and death dates, as well as those of his wife and children. It is certain that Wilson had no inkling of

his eventual place in Japanese baseball history; his marker reads
only "Civil War Veteran."

Four decades later, Lefty O'Doul was laid to rest in the same cemetery.

Today, people in San Francisco, and beyond, know the name Lefty
O'Doul. But nearly a half century after his death, a surprising number who visit his restaurant are under the impression he is a fic-
tional character. Many more are unaware of his full legacy, which
is far from simple to measure. It includes his batting skills—two
batting titles and coming within one hit of a .400 batting average,
the highest batting mark of any National League outfielder during
the 1900s. He was a champion for kids and baseball worldwide,
through his famous O'Doul Days and sponsorships of youth baseball leagues, as well as gifts to orphanages and foster homes. He was
batting guru to Ted Williams, Joe DiMaggio, and other stars—in
both Japan and the United States—and one of baseball's all-time
greatest hitting instructors. He was, and is, a San Francisco icon
who created one of San Francisco's enduring landmarks with his
Geary Street restaurant.

In 2013 the Baseball Reliquary, which describes itself as an organization dedicated to fostering an appreciation of American art
and culture through the context of baseball history, inducted Lefty
O'Doul into its "Shrine of the Eternals," a sort of "people's" Hall
of Fame. He was recognized as one of the greatest sports legends
in San Francisco history, a legendary Minor League manager, and
a great hitter.[56]

But the Baseball Reliquary also recognized O'Doul for his most
important contribution—his role in the growth and development
of Japanese baseball. Although—as with Horace Wilson—it is not
on his tombstone, O'Doul's efforts inspired generations of Japanese
players, ultimately leading to the contributions of Ichiro Suzuki,
Hideki Matsui, Hideo Nomo, Yu Darvish, and Masahiro Tanaka to
the American baseball landscape.

Probably the best measure of O'Doul's impact on Japan is reflected
in a statement made by Toru Shoriki during a meeting he had with
then baseball commissioner William Eckert a year before Lefty's

death. After reminiscing for several minutes, Shoriki, whose father, Matsutoro, knew O'Doul so well, told Eckert, "Babe Ruth was very popular—I remember I saw him when I was quite young. But Lefty O'Doul—the Japanese loved him."[57]

EPILOGUE
LEFTY'S STORY CONTINUES

No one ever truly finishes a nonfiction project. One only reaches an intractable deadline. There is always more to be discovered, and relevant events sometimes accrue long after the demise of the biographical subject. Lefty O'Doul is no exception.

The following developments came too late for inclusion in the initial release of this book, even as they became front-page news in San Francisco.

In October 2016 the building on Geary Street in which Lefty O'Doul's long-running bar and restaurant operated turned one hundred years old. It had originally opened as a movie theater—the first in the western United States ever designed specifically for that purpose—called the Theater St. Francis, and remnants of its former identity were still visible upstairs.

But what should have been cause for celebration went unnoticed due to a battle brewing between restaurant owner Nick Bovis and Jon Handlery, whose family owned the building and much of the city block on which it sat. The building was in need of repair, and the lease was up soon with the rent to be increased substantially. By January 2017 the situation came to a head, and Bovis announced the landmark was going to close, saying of the February 3 date, "That is it. That is our last day here."[1]

Bovis announced plans to reopen at a new location as near to downtown as possible, declaring, "My only purpose is to keep the

Lefty O'Doul's restaurant and bar open as close to this location as possible and to keep . . . traditions alive."[2]

When Bovis attempted to remove furnishings and souvenirs from the restaurant, the Handlerys obtained an injunction barring him from doing so.[3] This was despite the fact that most of the "souvenirs" were copies, much of the original memorabilia having been sold off by Lefty's widow and stepson; the O'Doul Day trophy, the belt buckle from the 1934 tour, and the cigarette lighter from the Japanese in 1935 are among the items now in private hands. The remainder of the original photos and other items were last known to be in the possession of Don Figone's widow, transferred from the restaurant when he sold it to the Bovis family in 1997.[4] Figone had remarried after Lefty's widow passed away in 1977.

The farewell to Lefty O'Doul's was actually held two days early, on February 1. London Breed, then president of the San Francisco Board of Supervisors, announced, "Free drinks for everybody," and fans and family spent the evening swapping stories about the landmark watering hole.[5]

The marquee was then covered and the restaurant shuttered as the legal battles over the restaurant as well as the Lefty O'Doul trademark, which also included a well-established Bloody Mary mix based on Lefty's recipe, wound on for months.

Nick Bovis finally opened a new Lefty's in November 2018 at Fisherman's Wharf in a remodeled space that had previously housed a Rainforest Café. London Breed, now mayor of San Francisco, led the festivities, which included a large crowd and police on horseback, a tradition carried from the original Lefty's. A San Francisco Giants Dugout Store was housed on the bottom floor with the restaurant situated upstairs. Photos from the original restaurant were placed in the new space.

Despite the great fanfare, the new location lasted only a year, closing suddenly just before Thanksgiving in 2019.

The shuttering of the restaurant was blamed on broken water pipes, but it soon became clear there were other issues as well. On January 15, 2020, a seventy-nine-page federal complaint was filed against San Francisco public works director Mohammed Nuru, who was accused of accepting bribes and kickbacks in exchange for assisting, "or to promise to assist, in public business opportunities with the City."[6] Nick Bovis was among those accused of being involved in the scheme, and he eventually pled guilty to federal wire fraud charges and agreed to cooperate in the investigation of Nuru.[7] In October 2020 Bovis filed for bankruptcy. Lefty O'Doul's has never reopened. Sadly the Lefty O'Doul Foundation for Kids was caught up in various financial transfers related to the legal issues and also shuttered.[8]

Meanwhile there have been further efforts to honor Lefty O'Doul since this book's original publication. In both 2017 and 2020 there were campaigns for Lefty to receive the Buck O'Neil Award, which honors "an individual whose extraordinary efforts enhanced baseball's positive impact on society, broadened the game's appeal, and whose character, integrity and dignity are comparable to the qualities exhibited by O'Neil."[9] O'Doul fell short both times, to Rachel Robinson in 2017 and to former Philadelphia Phillies owner David Montgomery in 2020. He is eligible once again in 2023.

Then came a surprise. On November 5, 2021, the National Baseball Hall of Fame announced its ten finalists for the Early Baseball Era Committee, among them Lefty O'Doul, marking his first appearance on a Hall of Fame ballot in nearly two decades.[10]

The results were announced a month later on ESPN, with Bob Costas cohosting a program that reviewed the nominees. When it came to O'Doul, Costas remarked that many people probably thought he was already in, echoing Bing Crosby's comment during Lefty O'Doul Day at Candlestick Park more than fifty years earlier. Twelve votes from the sixteen committee members were needed for induction, and O'Doul did well, garnering five, but was obviously short of the number needed. Baseball pioneer Bud Fowler and Buck O'Neil were the only players to poll the necessary support.[11]

The Hall of Fame's Early Era Committee has now been folded into a new panel, christened the Classic Baseball Era Committee, which will now consider those eligible whose contributions came prior to 1980. Its next meeting to vet potential inductees and create a ballot of finalists, including Lefty O'Doul, will take place in 2024 for inclusion in the Hall of Fame class of 2025.[12]

Undoubtedly there will be more to follow for Lefty O'Doul in the coming years. Some stories never truly end.

NOTES

1. Butchertown

1. Einstein, *Flag for San Francisco*.

2. *The Sporting News*, March 12, 1958, 13–14.

3. Augustus O'Doul was also employed as a saloon keeper at one point, according to the 1880 census.

4. *Crocker-Langley San Francisco City Directory, for the Year Commencing 1897*. The partnership ended with the sixty-six-year-old Peguillan's death in 1899 (*San Francisco Call*, August 15, 1899).

5. *Seattle Times*, February 16, 1900; *San Francisco Chronicle*, February 17, 1900. August, who admitted to serving short stints in Folsom and San Quentin prisons, was arrested in mid-February in Seattle while using two aliases and allegedly participating in a home robbery. The man assaulted in San Francisco had been struck on the head by a rock following an argument, but the injury had not seemed serious. A month later the alleged victim developed symptoms of lockjaw and died; the tenuous connection to the New Year's Day incident certainly contributed to the charges being dropped. August's obviously troubled life ended in May 1915, when he died at age thirty-nine (California Death Index, 1905–40). *San Francisco Chronicle*, May 11, 1915.

6. *San Francisco Chronicle*, November 2, 1901.

7. *San Francisco Call*, June 8, 1904.

8. *Seattle Times*, April 28, 1940.

9. The information comes from the Crocker-Langley San Francisco city directories of the time period.

10. *San Francisco Chronicle*, April 21, 1952. This is a story/interview with Rose Stolz.

11. U.S. Census, 1910; *The Sporting News*, December 26, 1929, 5, and April 12, 1934, 4. Eugene is first listed as a salesman in the 1908 Crocker-Langley San Francisco city directory. Even as an adult, O'Doul said that some friends from his old neighborhood still called him "Young Froggy."

12. *San Francisco Chronicle*, June 12, 1912. Almost every account states that O'Doul led his team to the city championship, but Bay View in fact lost to John Hancock for the title by a score of 11–3. The tournament was divided into teams consisting of smaller players, weighing ninety-five pounds or less, and an unlimited classification. Bay View fielded its team in the unlimited class. There were four divisions in each classification, and Bay View went undefeated in District Four, which put it into the finals (*San Francisco Chronicle*, May 7, 26, and June 14, 1912; *San Francisco Call*, June 14, 1912).

13. *The Sporting News*, March 12, 1958, 13–14.

14. *San Francisco Chronicle*, November 6, 1939.

15. *San Francisco Chronicle*, April 21, 1952. Many accounts state Rose Stolz's last name as Stoltz or Stultz, but contemporary census records, news articles, and city directories confirm her surname was Stolz.

16. *The Sporting News*, October 23, 1946, 13.

17. Although there would be later references to his having green eyes, O'Doul's 1918 draft registration card lists his eyes as blue.

18. *The Sporting News*, October 23, 1946, 13. O'Doul mentioned in an interview that he had played "around 1914" for a team in Visitacion Valley—an area of southeast San Francisco that borders Daly City. He said his manager was "Puddin' Head" Toner and that Toner had taught him control as a pitcher. It is unknown whether this is the same Toner who had pitched for the San Francisco Seals.

19. *Brooklyn Daily Eagle*, August 14, 1932.

20. *American Legion Magazine*, April 1935, 66.

21. *Brooklyn Daily Eagle*, August 14, 1932.

22. *San Francisco Chronicle*, August 8 and 15, 1916.

23. *San Francisco Chronicle*, October 3, 1916.

24. Interview of O'Doul by Lawrence Ritter, August 29, 1963.

25. *San Francisco Chronicle*, November 9, 10, and 12, 1916. Stanford's roster included former Los Angeles Angels catcher Hughie Smith and former Minor Leaguer Bart Burke. O'Doul said that Smith introduced him to Harry Wolverton, facilitating his being signed by the Seals (*The Sporting News*, March 9, 1955, 18).

26. *San Francisco Examiner*, November 13, 1916.

27. *San Francisco Chronicle*, November 13, 1916.

28. *San Francisco Chronicle*, November 22, 1916. Kennedy had not played in the league prior to October 2, which under league rules rendered him ineligible.

29. *San Francisco Chronicle*, December 1, 1916; *San Francisco Examiner*, December 1, 1916; *San Francisco Call*, December 1, 1916.

30. *San Francisco Chronicle*, December 19, 1916.

31. *San Francisco Examiner*, December 1, 1916.

32. *San Francisco Chronicle*, January 4, 1915; *Detroit Free Press*, January 28, 1915.

33. *San Francisco Chronicle*, February 28, 1917.

34. Interview of O'Doul by Lawrence Ritter, August 29, 1963.

35. *The Sporting News*, March 9, 1955, 18.

36. *San Francisco Chronicle*, March 10, 1917.

37. *San Francisco Chronicle*, April 19, 30, and May 4, 1917. O'Doul allowed seven runs in eight total innings, while walking six batters and striking out four. He made one start, leaving with a lead against Portland after four innings—some records credit him with a victory in that game.

38. *San Francisco Chronicle*, May 8 and 10, 1917.

39. Interview of O'Doul by Lawrence Ritter, August 29, 1963.

40. Coffey eventually coached at Fordham for a total of forty-seven years.

41. *Des Moines News*, May 20, 1917.

42. *Des Moines News*, May 23 and 24, 1917. Kallio was also property of the Seals.

43. *Des Moines News*, May 29, 1917.

44. *Des Moines News*, June 2, 1917.

45. *Des Moines News*, June 5, 6, and 11, 1917.

46. *Des Moines News*, June 19, 1917.

47. *Des Moines News*, July 6 and 17, 1917.

48. Email from Tom O'Doul to the author, June 29 and 30, 2014. Many accounts of the incident state that O'Doul lost the tip of his finger, but Tom O'Doul confirmed that was not the case.

49. *Des Moines News*, August 31, 1917.

50. *Des Moines News*, September 10, 1917.

51. *Des Moines News*, September 4, 5, and 10, 1917.

52. *San Francisco Chronicle*, September 15 and 24, 1917. The Seals had suffered injuries to their pitching staff, and O'Doul and Rudy Kallio were brought back to provide additional depth.

2. As Great a Ballplayer as He Cares

1. *Portland (ME) Press Herald*, May 20, 2007. Wilson, who is often erroneously identified as a missionary, may or may not have been the first to introduce the game—there were other Americans who taught baseball to their students around the same time. However, the Japanese have settled on Wilson as the instigator of the game in their country.

2. *Nippon Times*, October 6, 1949. Hiraoka was also credited as being the first to use baseball uniforms and the first to throw a curve ball in Japan.

3. *San Francisco Call*, June 28, 1908.

4. *Philadelphia Inquirer*, July 18, 1948. The girls were stranded for several weeks when the tour ended suddenly (*New York Times*, December 1, 1925).

5. *San Francisco Chronicle*, October 10 and December 13, 1928.

6. Guthrie-Shimizu, *Transpacific Field of Dreams*, 149.

7. *The Sporting News*, January 1, 1931, 1.

8. *San Francisco Chronicle*, March 22, 1918. San Francisco's Olympic Club was, and is, a prestigious private athletic club. The oldest of its kind in the United States, having been founded in 1860, it has fostered the careers of Olympians and professional athletes in numerous sports, and its three golf

courses, among the finest in the country, have five times hosted the U.S. Open golf tournament.

9. *San Francisco Chronicle*, March 8, 1918.

10. *San Francisco Chronicle*, April 4, 1918.

11. *San Francisco Chronicle*, April 13 and 21, 1918.

12. *San Francisco Chronicle*, April 27, 1918.

13. *San Francisco Chronicle*, May 4, 1918.

14. *San Francisco Chronicle*, May 6, 1918.

15. *San Francisco Chronicle*, January 24, 1943.

16. *San Francisco Chronicle*, November 18, 1918.

17. Interview of O'Doul by Lawrence Ritter, August 29, 1963.

18. State of California Department of Public Health Standard Certificate of Death for Eugene Joseph O'Doul.

19. *New York Tribune*, March 18, 1919.

20. *New York Evening World*, March 25, 1919.

21. *Moving Picture World*, December 21, 1918, and January 18, 1919; *Reel and Slide*, May 1919; *Transactions of the Society of Motion Picture Engineers*, October 31–November 3, 1921.

22. *New York Tribune*, January 5 and March 18, 1919; *New York Evening World*, March 25, 1919; *New York Times*, December 12, 1920. *Analysis of Motion* was actually the title of a series of films; other subjects in the series included scenes of athletes jumping hurdles and cowboys riding horses and roping. Little information exists about these films, and there are no prints known to exist today. John McGraw was so impressed, he had Novagraph film each of his players during the summer of 1919, hoping to use the images for training purposes (*Motion Picture News*, June 21, 1919; *Variety*, May 13, 1921).

23. *New York Sun*, March 30, 1919.

24. *New York Tribune*, March 27, 1919. At the time the official world record for the 100-yard dash was 9.6 seconds.

25. *New York Sun*, April 1 and 3, 1919.

26. *Los Angeles Times*, January 2, 1919. The war had depleted the ranks of college football, so the 1919 Rose Bowl—which at that time was called the Tournament East-West Football Game—was staged with teams representing Mare Island Naval Station and the Great Lakes Naval Station.

27. *New York Sun*, April 1, 1919. Exactly when O'Doul hurt his arm has never been pinpointed; some stories have him injuring the arm during his 1918–19 stint in the navy. However, the *New York Evening World* stated that he had injured the arm early in spring training in 1919, and there are numerous references during that training camp about him cutting loose too early and being warned against throwing too hard from the outfield (*New York Evening World*, March 29, 1920).

28. *New York Times*, March 26, 1919.

29. *New York Tribune*, April 3, 1919.

30. *New York Sun*, April 7, 1919.

31. *New York Sun*, April 12, 1919.

32. *New York Times*, April 30, 1919.

33. *New York Times*, May 13, 1919; *New York Tribune*, May 13, 1919.

34. *New York Times*, June 2, 1919; *Washington Post*, June 2, 1919.

35. *New York Sun*, November 27, 1919.

36. *Washington Post*, July 6, 1919; *New York Times*, July 6 and 12, 1919.

37. *New York Tribune*, March 5, 1920.

38. *New York Sun*, November 27, 1919. O'Doul also played center field in one in-season exhibition game, on September 28 versus Brooklyn. He batted sixth and collected one hit in four at bats (*New York Sun*, September 29, 1919).

39. Halas was released to St. Paul by the Yankees in July and hit .274 in thirty-nine games, after collecting only two hits in twenty-two at bats for New York. He left baseball for the Decatur Staleys football team in 1920 and was given control of the club the next year. He promptly moved the franchise to Chicago, where it became the Chicago Bears.

40. *New York Times*, December 27, 1919.

41. *New York Times*, January 6 and 7, 1920.

42. *Boston Globe*, March 18, 1918; *New York Times*, September 25, 1919.

43. *New York Tribune*, January 7, 1920.

44. *New York Times*, January 13, 1920.

45. *San Francisco Chronicle*, November 9, 1919; *New York Times*, January 23, 1920.

46. *New York Tribune*, March 5, 1920.

47. *New York Tribune*, March 13, 1920.

48. *Bismarck Tribune*, January 12, 1921.

49. *Washington Times*, March 27, 1920.

50. *New York Post*, April 19, 1928. This quote was printed in a column written by Fred Lieb, eight years after Sparrow's death.

51. *New York Tribune*, April 10, 1920.

52. *New York Tribune*, April 17, 1920.

53. *New York Times*, August 12, 1932.

54. *Philadelphia Inquirer*, March 23, 1930. Over the years, Fred Lieb and a few others would often insist that it was Huggins who wanted O'Doul to remain a pitcher, stubbornly refusing to take advantage of his hitting skills because he had fallen in love with the fastball O'Doul had when he first signed, before hurting his arm. But this contradicts the opinion of other sportswriters, O'Doul's teammates, and often O'Doul that he wanted to be a pitcher.

55. *San Francisco Examiner*, February 17, 1935.

56. *Brooklyn Daily Eagle*, December 27, 1932. This would be one of O'Doul's most often told and popular stories over the years.

57. *New York Evening Telegram*, June 13, 1920.

58. *New York Times*, July 27, 1920.

59. *New York Times*, August 1, 1920.

60. *New York Times*, August 18, 1920.

61. *New York Times*, August 17, 1920; *New York Tribune*, August 17, 1920.

62. *Philadelphia Inquirer*, April 18, 1920. The incident occurred on April 15 at Shibe Park.

63. *New York Times*, May 8, 1920.

64. *The Sporting News*, February 17, 1921, 4.

65. *New York Tribune*, January 28, 1921. O'Doul was sent to San Francisco via the PCL Vernon Tigers, who were owed players by the Yankees from an earlier trade (*New York Times*, January 28, 1921; *San Francisco Chronicle*, January 29, 1921).

66. In May of 1920 and with his team in first place, Graham suddenly announced the release of two of his best pitchers, Tom Seaton and Casey Smith, with little explanation—but a clear implication that it involved issues around gambling and throwing of games. The Seals fell to fourth place while Graham was hailed as a man of integrity (*San Francisco Chronicle*, May 8 and 9, 1920; *San Francisco Examiner*, May 8 and 9, 1920).

67. *Oregonian*, April 9, 1921.

68. *San Francisco Chronicle*, April 22, 1921; *The Sporting News*, December 26, 1929, 14. Carroll was highly regarded in the Pacific Coast League and became a legend among trainers after joining the Detroit Tigers in the early 1930s, credited with reviving, or saving, the careers of Schoolboy Rowe, Dick Bartell, and Charlie Gehringer.

69. *San Francisco Chronicle*, May 2, 1921.

70. *San Francisco Chronicle*, May 28, 1921.

71. O'Doul collected five hits in eighteen official at bats as a pinch hitter for the Seals in 1921.

72. *San Francisco Chronicle*, June 12, 1921. The Brummell allusion refers to George Bryan Brummel, who became the last word on men's fashion during the early 1800s in Great Britain.

73. *Oregonian*, September 23, 1921; *San Francisco Chronicle*, September 23, 1921.

74. *San Francisco Chronicle*, December 6, 1921.

75. *New York Evening World*, March 25, 1922.

76. *New York Tribune*, February 17, 1922. Charles Comiskey had reportedly blocked an attempt by the Seals to acquire O'Doul from New York during the 1919 season by refusing to let him pass through waivers (*San Francisco Chronicle*, February 17, 1922).

77. *New York Times*, December 6, 1921.

78. *New York Evening World*, February 17, 1922.

79. *New York Tribune*, March 4, 1922.

80. *New York Tribune*, March 19, 1922.

81. *New York Evening World*, May 24, 1922.

82. Lefty O'Doul paycheck from the New York Yankees dated August 31, 1922.

83. *The Sporting News*, September 3, 1931, 4.

84. *New York Times*, August 11, 1922.

85. *Buffalo Evening News*, September 26, 1922. Ruth also pitched an inning in the game, as he often did during in-season exhibition games. O'Doul pitched in one other in-season exhibition game, on April 16 against Ruth's old Minor League team, the Baltimore Orioles. He entered the game in the sixth inning with the Yankees leading, 9–0, and surrendered one run in four innings (*New York Telegraph*, April 17, 1922).

86. *The Sporting News*, November 27, 1965, 5.

87. *New York Evening World*, October 13, 1922.

88. *New York Times*, August 12, 1932.

89. *San Francisco Chronicle*, February 1, 1923, and April 21, 1952.

90. *San Francisco Chronicle*, February 1, 1923.

91. *San Francisco Call*, November 30, 1922; *San Francisco Examiner*, November 30, 1922; *San Francisco Chronicle*, December 1, 1922. There was a macabre aspect to these events. The fifty-yard dash for inmates over sixty was won by a seventy-three-year-old "lifer." Apparently, San Quentin's chief surgeon, Leo Stanley, was performing experiments on some of the prisoners, including the winner of the dash, surgically implanting testicles of animals into their abdomens in order to demonstrate that they became quicker and more agile after the procedure. It was also thought that "rejuvenation," as it was called, would change their criminal behavior. While it may seem like mad science today, the procedures were popular for a time; in 1935 *The Sporting News* reported that O'Doul was treated by Dr. Stanley, who administered the procedure as treatment for his sore arm after he returned to the San Francisco Seals as player-manager. At that point, instead of surgically inserting glands, the surgery involved the injections of a "slurry" (*The Sporting News*, August 29, 1935, 4).

92. *Boston Globe*, March 7, 1923.

93. *Boston Globe*, February 18, 1923.

94. *Boston Globe*, March 10, 1923.

95. *Boston Globe*, April 5, 1923.

96. *Boston Globe*, April 11, 1923.

97. *Boston Globe*, April 20, 1923; *New York Times*, April 20, 1923.

98. *Boston Globe*, April 22, 1923.

99. *New York Times*, April 27, 1923.

100. *Boston Globe*, July 8, 1923. Chance did the same thing to his best pitcher, twenty-game winner Howard Ehmke, near the end of the season against the Yankees. After giving up six runs in five innings, Chance left Ehmke on the mound in the sixth as he allowed eleven runs and tied O'Doul's record by facing sixteen batters before retiring the side. The Yankees won, 24–4 (*New York Times*, September 29, 1923).

101. *San Francisco Examiner*, April 27, 1966. A look at the Red Sox's schedule in 1923 reveals that the Yankees left town a week and a half before the game with Cleveland, but all of Boston's intervening games were competitive until

July 7, a contest that provided Chance with his first opportunity to do exactly as O'Doul claimed. O'Doul had not pitched since June 19, eighteen days earlier.

102. *Boston Globe*, February 3, 1924.

3. A Sure Frank Merriwell

1. *The Sporting News*, March 30, 1949, 28.

2. Fitts, *Remembering Japanese Baseball*, 3.

3. *Salt Lake Telegram*, February 20, 1924.

4. *Salt Lake Telegram*, February 1, 1924.

5. *Salt Lake Telegram*, February 12, 1924.

6. *Salt Lake Telegram*, February 12, 1924.

7. State of Oregon Certification of Vital Record. The wedding took place on April 28. Lacey was always coy about her age—the marriage certificate states she was three months older than her husband. The 1930 census lists her being two years younger. Ten years later, the census has her four years older. Social Security records list her birthdate as January 27, 1887, which would have made her ten years older than Lefty. This latter birthdate matches a listing for a female of her name with a Lacey family in the 1900 census.

8. *Salt Lake Telegram*, March 30, 1924.

9. *Salt Lake Telegram*, April 10, 1924.

10. *The Sporting News*, March 12, 1958, 14.

11. *Salt Lake Telegram*, August 7, 1924.

12. *Salt Lake Telegram*, August 18, 1924; *San Francisco Chronicle*, August 18, 1924.

13. *Salt Lake Telegram*, August 25, 1924; *Los Angeles Examiner*, August 25, 1924.

14. *Salt Lake Telegram*, September 21, 1924; *The Sporting News*, March 12, 1958, 14. Portland second baseman Emmett McCann set a league record that game with seven hits in seven at bats—all singles. O'Doul would embellish the story over the years, and his version would be added onto by others. Some versions had him walking off the field after Poole's home run and declaring he was now an outfielder. Duffy Lewis supposedly would tell O'Doul, "But you don't know how to play the outfield." O'Doul would reply, "I'll learn." Clearly the story is false. By this point O'Doul was already a full-time outfielder.

15. *The Sporting News*, September 4, 1924, 3. Lewis took over as manager at Portland and had battles with players there as well. In early July 1925, news broke that Beavers pitcher Pat Martin had taken a swing at Lewis. Martin missed, Lewis did not. Martin was suspended and fined $100 (*San Francisco Chronicle*, July 8, 1925).

16. *Seattle Post-Intelligencer*, October 9, 1924.

17. *Salt Lake Telegram*, December 18, 22, and 24, 1914.

18. *The Sporting News*, June 5, 1924, 7.

19. *The (NY) Saratogian*, July 6, 1934. In this article, for example, O'Doul said, "In baseball you hit a rapidly moving ball with elbows bent. In golf, you

hit a stationary target on the ground and, at the time of contact, the left elbow should be straight as a ramrod. Those who excel at both games just happen to be able to play both well."

20. *Los Angeles Times*, July 17 and 19, 1925.

21. *Los Angeles Times*, July 21, 1925.

22. *Salt Lake Telegram*, July 17 and 19, 1925; *The Sporting News*, July 30, 1925, 3.

23. *Salt Lake Telegram*, July 14, 1925; *Nevada State Journal*, September 8, 1925.

24. *Seattle Times*, August 29, 1925; *Salt Lake Telegram*, August 29, 1925.

25. *Chicago Tribune*, September 12, 1925; *Salt Lake Telegram*, September 12, 1925; *The Sporting News*, October 15, 1925, 4.

26. *Chicago Tribune*, September 20, 1930.

27. *The Sporting News*, February 25, 1926, 2.

28. *Chicago Tribune*, February 17, 1926.

29. *Chicago Tribune*, February 20, 1926.

30. *The Sporting News*, March 4, 1926, 5.

31. *Chicago Tribune*, February 18, 1926.

32. *Chicago Tribune*, February 24, 1926.

33. *The Sporting News*, March 11, 1926, 2.

34. *Chicago Tribune*, March 12, 1926.

35. *Los Angeles Times*, March 6, 1926.

36. *Los Angeles Times*, March 12, 1926; *Chicago Tribune*, September 12 and October 13, 1929.

37. *Los Angeles Times*, March 14, 1926; *Chicago Tribune*, March 14, 1926; *The Sporting News*, March 18, 1926, 3, and March 25, 1926, 1.

38. *Los Angeles Times*, March 22, 1926.

39. *Los Angeles Times*, May 16, 1926.

40. *Los Angeles Times*, May 23, 1926.

41. *Los Angeles Times*, September 5, 1926.

42. *Los Angeles Times*, February 3 and 4, 1927.

43. *San Francisco Chronicle*, February 4, 1927.

44. *San Francisco Examiner*, February 4, 1927.

45. *San Francisco Chronicle*, February 4, 1927.

46. *San Francisco Chronicle*, October 13, 1927.

47. *San Francisco Chronicle*, September 8, 1927.

48. *San Francisco Chronicle*, October 2, 1933.

49. Email from Paula Lichtenberg to the author, April 12, 2016. Lichtenberg was contacted by a woman whose aunt had been a student at the school in 1927 and had related this story to her.

50. *San Francisco Chronicle*, August 31, 1927.

51. *San Francisco Chronicle*, September 10, 11, and 12, 1927.

52. *San Francisco Chronicle*, September 13, 1927.

53. *San Francisco Chronicle*, September 12, 1927; *San Francisco Examiner*, September 12, 1927.

54. *San Francisco Chronicle*, September 13, 1927. The loving cup Lefty received was inscribed, "Presented to Frank 'Lefty' O'Doul, O'Doul Day, Recreation Park Sept 11 1927, By Judge Mathew Brady, District Attorney." It has repeatedly been misidentified in photographs as being given for his Most Valuable Player Award.

55. *Oakland Tribune*, October 12, 1927; *San Francisco Chronicle*, October 13, 1927; *Los Angeles Times*, October 13, 1927.

56. *San Francisco Chronicle*, October 22, 1927.

57. *San Francisco Chronicle*, October 23, 1927.

58. *Oakland Post-Enquirer*, October 24, 1927.

59. *Oakland Tribune*, October 24, 1927.

60. *San Jose Mercury News*, October 27, 1927.

61. *Los Angeles Times*, October 29 and 30, 1927. If the ire was real, Ruth certainly got his revenge against Root in the 1932 World Series.

62. *Los Angeles Times*, October 31, 1927.

63. *San Francisco Chronicle*, October 5 and 8, 1927.

64. *San Francisco Chronicle*, October 8, 1927; *Binghamton (NY) Press*, April 20, 1928.

4. He Always Could Play Ball

1. *The Sporting News*, January 26, 1949, 26.

2. Guthrie-Shimizu, *Transpacific Field of Dreams*, 249.

3. Leutzinger, "Lefty O'Doul," 30–34.

4. *New York Sun*, December 6, 1927.

5. *Binghamton (NY) Press*, April 20, 1928.

6. *Rome (NY) Daily Sentinel*, March 1, 1928.

7. *New York Post*, March 6, 1928.

8. *New York Sun*, April 4, 1928. Emil "Irish" Meusel was the left fielder for the Giants' four straight pennant winners (1921–24) and drove in one hundred or more runs each year between 1922 and 1925. Bob Meusel was his brother.

9. *New York Post*, March 5, 1928.

10. *New York Sun*, April 16, 1928.

11. *New York Times*, March 9, 1928.

12. Letter from Colonel Russell "Red" Reeder to Ken Smith, director of the National Baseball Hall of Fame and Museum, November 8, 1971. Reeder was an army officer and author who commanded an infantry regiment that fought at Utah Beach on D-Day; he suffered wounds that led to the amputation of his left leg. After the war, he became assistant director of athletics at West Point and held that position until 1967. He then had a long career as a nonfiction writer of military history. In 1928 Reeder, who had been an excellent athlete at West Point, received a tryout with the New York Giants. It was there that he encountered Cobb, who worked not only with O'Doul and Reeder but also with Mel Ott, Les Mann, Buck Lai, and Andy Reese. Reeder wrote, "Cobb was a smart, crafty, dynamic and intense batting instructor. When he talked batting, if you

were absorbing the instruction, his eyes glittered." At the end of training camp, Reeder turned down a contract to play for the Giants in order to remain in the military. A baseball award named in Reeder's honor is presented annually at the U.S. Military Academy to the Most Valuable Player in the graduating class.

13. *New York Sun*, April 7, 1928.

14. *New York Post*, April 11, 1928.

15. *New York Post*, March 28, 1928.

16. *New York Times*, April 12, 1928.

17. *New York Post*, April 11, 1928; *New York Times*, April 12, 1928.

18. *New York Times*, April 12, 1928. The Giants also had a Jewish pitcher, Jacob Levy, who made the roster out of spring training. However, he was optioned to Hartford a week into the season without appearing in a game. The *New York Times* said, "Jake Levy, who came to the Giants as a pitcher, turned out to be a very good violin player. Unfortunately, that's all." Levy never made it back to the Majors (*New York Post*, April 11, 1928; *New York Times*, April 12 and 19, 1928).

19. *New York Sun*, April 12, 1928.

20. *New York Sun*, April 16, 1928.

21. *Philadelphia Inquirer*, April 16, 1928; *New York Times*, April 16, 1928.

22. *New York Times*, April 19, 1928.

23. *Philadelphia Inquirer*, April 19, 1928.

24. *New York Times*, April 22, May 9, and May 20, 1928.

25. *Brooklyn Daily Eagle*, June 16, 1928.

26. *New York Times*, July 13, 1928.

27. *Brooklyn Standard Union*, September 25, 1928.

28. *Chicago Tribune*, September 28, 1928; *New York Times*, September 28, 1928.

29. Alexander, *John McGraw*, 288.

30. *Philadelphia Inquirer*, October 29, 1928; *New York Times*, October 30, 1928.

31. *Geneva (NY) Daily Times*, March 25, 1929.

32. *San Francisco Chronicle*, March 20, 1979.

33. *Philadelphia Inquirer*, October 29, 1928.

34. *The Sporting News*, November 8, 1928, 1. The Phillies needed the cash from the Giants to replenish their coffers after having purchased shortstop Tommy Thevenow from the St. Louis Cardinals.

35. Philadelphia's record in 1928 was 43-109.

36. *Brooklyn Daily Eagle*, September 4, 1929; *San Francisco Examiner*, February 17, 1935.

5. I Am Going to Have a Great Year

1. *Pacific Stars and Stripes*, May 27, 1949.

2. *The Sporting News*, July 20, 1949, 26.

3. *The Sporting News*, August 3, 1949, 15.

4. Among those joining the team were Pittsburgh Pirates pitcher Bill Werle, Oakland Oaks pitcher Milo Candini, and New Orleans pitcher Bill MacDonald,

who lived in the Bay Area and, like Werle, was property of the Pirates (*The Sporting News*, October 19, 1949, 23, and November 16, 1949, 10).

5. *San Francisco Chronicle*, June 19, 1949.

6. Guthrie-Shimizu, *Transpacific Field of Dreams*, 250.

7. *Pacific Stars and Stripes*, July 2, 1949.

8. *The Sporting News*, October 19, 1949, 23.

9. *New York Post*, October 2, 1929.

10. *Philadelphia Inquirer*, April 19, 1929.

11. *Brooklyn Daily Eagle*, April 25, 1929.

12. *Brooklyn Daily Eagle*, May 20, 1930.

13. *New York Times*, April 26, 1929. Statistically, Leach had almost the exact same season in 1929 as O'Doul in 1928. Leach hit eight home runs, drove in forty-seven, and batted .290. A year earlier, O'Doul's line was eight home runs, forty-six runs batted in, and a .319 batting average.

14. *The Sporting News*, March 31, 1932, 4; *Providence Visitor*, June 2, 1933.

15. *Philadelphia Inquirer*, May 17 and 18, 1929.

16. *Philadelphia Inquirer*, June 20, 1929. The Phillies lost both games, 15–14 and 12–6.

17. *Brooklyn Daily Eagle*, July 1, 1929.

18. *New York Sun*, March 20, 1931.

19. *Brooklyn Daily Eagle*, September 24, 1929.

20. *Brooklyn Daily Eagle*, December 26, 1929.

21. *New York Post*, September 24, 1929.

22. *Brooklyn Daily Eagle*, May 20, 1930.

23. *The Sporting News*, December 26, 1951, 12.

24. *Brooklyn Daily Eagle*, March 17, 1931. According to the website Baseball-Reference.com, O'Doul struck out only six times in 280 plate appearances at Wrigley Field during his career, or roughly once every forty-seven at bats. At Redland Field he struck out four times in 229 plate appearances, or once every fifty-seven trips to the plate. That compares to once every thirty plate appearances over his entire career.

25. *Philadelphia Inquirer*, March 26, 1930.

26. *Baseball Magazine*, January 1930, 341–42.

27. *Baseball Magazine*, January 1930, 341–42.

28. *Amsterdam (NY) Evening Recorder*, December 6, 1933.

29. *Philadelphia Inquirer*, September 2, 1929.

30. *New York Times*, September 30, 1929.

31. *New York Times*, October 6, 1929. That was not the only National League record Rogers Hornsby lost that day—Chuck Klein hit his forty-third home run in the first game of the doubleheader to pass Hornsby's previous mark. New York Giants outfielder Mel Ott went into the day tied with Klein; despite losing the game, 12–3, Phillies pitchers walked Ott five times in six at bats in the nightcap in a successful effort to protect Klein's lead.

32. *The Sporting News*, September 14, 1944, 11.

33. *New York Times*, December 8, 1929. Eight sportswriters, one representing each National League city, ranked the top ten players in order. Hornsby collected sixty out of a maximum possible eighty points, including three first-place votes. O'Doul collected fifty-four points, including two first-place votes. He also received two third-place votes and single votes for fourth, sixth, and seventh.

34. In 1941 Joe DiMaggio hit thirty home runs for the New York Yankees and struck out thirteen times.

35. Leach would play two more years for the Giants before John McGraw sold him to the Boston Braves, batting .327 in 1930 and .309 in 1931. His runs batted in totals for 1929 and 1930 *combined* were fewer than Lefty O'Doul had in 1929 alone.

36. *The Sporting News*, September 26, 1929, 8.

37. *Brooklyn Daily Eagle*, April 18, 1930.

38. *San Francisco Chronicle*, February 9, 1930. O'Doul's financial situation was such that he borrowed $7,900 from Gus Oliva on January 2, 1930. This came to light in 1932, when a woman named Sheila Webster, who claimed to have acquired the rights to the promissory note from Oliva, sued O'Doul in December 1932 for the $7,900, plus interest. Webster's claim was ultimately dismissed (*Berkeley Daily Gazette*, December 22, 1932; *San Francisco Chronicle*, December 22, 1932; letter from Suzanne Leacy, Superior Court of California, County of San Francisco, to the author, October 20, 2015).

39. *Philadelphia Inquirer*, February 23 and March 5, 1930.

40. *Philadelphia Inquirer*, March 16, 1930.

41. *Philadelphia Inquirer*, March 26, 1930.

42. *Brooklyn Daily Eagle*, March 22, 1930.

43. *Philadelphia Inquirer*, December 12, 1929. The Phillies traded reserve outfielder Homer Peel and veteran pitcher Bob McGraw to St. Louis for Alexander and catcher Harry McCurdy.

44. *Philadelphia Inquirer*, March 29, 1930.

45. *Philadelphia Inquirer*, April 21, 1930.

46. *Brooklyn Daily Eagle*, May 20, 1930; *Philadelphia Inquirer*, March 23, 1930.

47. *Charleston (wv) Daily Mail*, December 9, 1969.

48. Interview of O'Doul by Lawrence Ritter, August 29, 1963.

49. *Philadelphia Inquirer*, September 10, 1930.

50. *Chicago Tribune*, May 29 and 30, 1930.

51. *Philadelphia Inquirer*, September 14, 1930.

52. *Chicago Tribune*, September 14, 1930; *Philadelphia Inquirer*, September 14, 1930. The *Inquirer* reported the count as being one ball and one strike when O'Doul homered, but the *Tribune* reported the count was two and one.

53. *Chicago Tribune*, September 14, 1930.

54. *Chicago Tribune*, September 15, 1930.

55. *Philadelphia Inquirer*, September 16, 1930.

56. *Philadelphia Inquirer*, September 16, 1930.

57. *Chicago Tribune*, September 16, 1930.

58. *New York Sun*, September 25, 1930.

59. *Philadelphia Inquirer*, September 16, 1930.

60. *Brooklyn Daily Eagle*, July 22, 1931.

61. *Chicago Tribune*, September 20, 1930.

62. *The Sporting News*, October 10, 1929, 2.

63. *The Sporting News*, October 2, 1930, 1. McCarthy was informed before the final series of the season that he was being replaced by Hornsby. There were rumors that Wrigley had been unhappy with McCarthy over the lack of player discipline after winning the 1929 pennant but losing the World Series. The lack of disappointment among the players in their World Series defeat led to disappointment in them by Wrigley.

64. *Philadelphia Inquirer*, September 24, 1930.

65. *The Sporting News*, October 23, 1930, 1.

6. Plenty on the Personality Ball

1. *Pacific Stars and Stripes*, July 8, 1949.

2. *Pacific Stars and Stripes*, October 13, 1949; *Nippon Times*, October 14, 1949.

3. *Nihon Keizai*, October 12, 1949; *Yomiuri Shimbun*, October 13, 1949; *Pacific Stars and Stripes*, October 13, 1949; *The Sporting News*, October 26, 1949, 19.

4. *Pacific Stars and Stripes*, October 13, 1949.

5. *Asahi Shimbun*, October 13, 1949.

6. *The Sporting News*, October 19, 1949, 1, 4.

7. *Pacific Stars and Stripes*, February 20, 1968. Roughly translated, "banzai" means "long live." It can also mean "ten thousand years."

8. Fitts, *Remembering Japanese Baseball*, 4.

9. *The Sporting News*, November 16, 1949, 10.

10. *Yomiuri Shimbun*, October 14, 1949; *Pacific Stars and Stripes*, October 14, 1949.

11. *The Sporting News*, October 26, 1949, 19.

12. *Pacific Stars and Stripes*, October 14, 1949.

13. *Yomiuri Shimbun*, October 14, 1949; *Mainichi Shimbun*, October 14, 1949.

14. *New York Times*, October 15, 1930. The team will be referred to in this chapter as the Dodgers for consistency's sake.

15. *Philadelphia Inquirer*, October 16, 1930.

16. *The Sporting News*, October 23, 1930, 1.

17. *Brooklyn Daily Eagle*, April 19, 1931.

18. Interview with Glenn Wright, conducted by Walter Langford and published in the 1990 edition of the *Baseball Research Journal*, 71–76.

19. *Brooklyn Daily Eagle*, October 14, 1930.

20. *Brooklyn Daily Eagle*, March 17, 1931.

21. *Brooklyn Daily Eagle*, March 4, 1931.

22. *Brooklyn Daily Eagle*, March 17, 1931.

23. *The Sporting News*, April 2, 1931, 6.

24. Interview with Glenn Wright, conducted by Eugene Murdock and published in the 1979 edition of the *Baseball Research Journal*.

25. *Brooklyn Standard Union*, June 13, 1931.

26. Offense in the National League exploded in 1929, and by 1930 the number of runs scored had increased by more than 20 percent of 1928. Home runs had increased by nearly 50 percent, from just over six hundred to nearly nine hundred.

27. *Brooklyn Daily Eagle*, May 11, 1931.

28. *New York Sun*, May 8, 1931.

29. *Brooklyn Daily Eagle*, June 28, 1931.

30. *Brooklyn Daily Eagle*, June 30, 1931.

31. *New York Sun*, July 16, 1931.

32. *Chicago Tribune*, July 22, 1931.

33. *Pittsburgh Post-Gazette*, July 25, 1931.

34. *Brooklyn Standard Union*, July 25, 1931.

35. *Brooklyn Standard Union*, July 25, 1931.

36. *Brooklyn Daily Eagle*, September 25, 1931. He circled the bases in 14.7 seconds.

37. Lieb, *Baseball as I Have Known It*, 200.

38. *The Sporting News*, December 3, 1931, 7.

39. Sendai was struck by a 2011 earthquake and tsunami that destroyed the Fukushima Daiichi nuclear plant.

40. *The Sporting News*, December 17, 1931, 4.

41. *New York Times*, December 23, 1931.

42. Lieb, *Baseball as I Have Known It*, 204.

43. *New York Times*, January 8, 1932.

44. *New York Times*, May 16, 1932. Film star Charlie Chaplin, a guest of Inukai, was fortunately away from the residence at the time of the attack. He was at a sumo match.

45. *New York Post*, November 26, 1932.

46. Lieb, *Baseball as I Have Known It*, 205. To that point, Gehrig had played in 1,042 consecutive games for the New York Yankees. O'Doul only played in seven of seventeen games; Gehrig was limited to five.

47. *New York Times*, December 23, 1931.

48. *The Sporting News*, January 14, 1932, 7; *Pacific Stars and Stripes*, April 25, 1948. O'Doul had sixteen hits in twenty-six at bats, including five doubles and two triples. The Americans hit .346 as a team, with Al Simmons leading the All-Stars in home runs with five.

49. Suzuki to O'Doul, February 5, 1932.

50. *New York Times*, April 12, 1932. The All-Stars had dropped a pair of games to the San Francisco Seals immediately prior to leaving for Japan. O'Doul bat-

ted second for the All-Stars in the games, with Lou Gehrig or Frankie Frisch hitting third behind him. The Seals pounded Lefty Grove, winner of thirty-one games for the Philadelphia Athletics that season, for six runs in the first inning of the second contest (*San Francisco Chronicle*, October 12, 13, and 14, 1931).

51. *Pacific Stars and Stripes*, April 25, 1949.

52. *Brooklyn Daily Eagle*, January 21, 1932.

53. *Brooklyn Daily Eagle*, October 6, 1932.

54. *Brooklyn Daily Eagle*, October 24, 1931. Robinson had won two National League pennants and 1,375 regular-season games for Brooklyn.

55. *Brooklyn Daily Eagle*, January 23, 1932. The Dodgers won out over the second choice, the "Kings."

56. *The Sporting News*, November 5, 1931, 1.

57. *Brooklyn Daily Eagle*, March 14 and 15, 1932.

58. *Brooklyn Daily Eagle*, January 24, 1932.

59. *Brooklyn Daily Eagle*, March 11, 1932; *New York Post*, March 11, 1932.

60. *Brooklyn Daily Eagle*, March 30, 1932.

61. *Brooklyn Daily Eagle*, April 22, 1932.

62. *New York Times*, May 5, 1932; Morris, *Game of Inches*, 341. Max Carey was reciting a litany of Dodgers injuries and said, "O'Doul's wearing that glove to protect his injured finger when he's batting. It's one of those golfer's gloves."

63. *Brooklyn Daily Eagle*, September 24, 1932.

64. *Brooklyn Daily Eagle*, July 28, 1932.

65. *Brooklyn Daily Eagle*, August 21, 1932.

66. *Brooklyn Daily Eagle*, December 27, 1932.

67. *Brooklyn Daily Eagle*, May 4, 1933.

68. *Brooklyn Daily Eagle*, August 14, 1932.

69. O'Doul demonstrated his batting and golf swings for a newspaper in 1928, showing that while the grip of a bat differed from that on a golf club, the finishes of the swings were similar (*San Francisco Examiner*, March 16, 1928).

70. *Brooklyn Daily Eagle*, August 14, 1932.

71. *Brooklyn Daily Eagle*, August 5, 1932.

72. *Brooklyn Daily Eagle*, August 5, 1932; *Pittsburgh Post-Gazette*, August 5, 1932.

73. *Brooklyn Daily Eagle*, August 11, 1932.

74. *Brooklyn Daily Eagle*, September 24, 1932.

75. *Brooklyn Daily Eagle*, September 24, 1932.

76. *New York Times*, October 19, 1932.

77. *Brooklyn Daily Eagle*, October 6, 1932.

78. *Brooklyn Daily Eagle*, October 6, 1932.

79. *San Francisco Chronicle*, January 4 and September 30, 1932. The truck was provided by Walter Schulken, who had teamed with O'Doul to sponsor a semi-pro baseball team consisting of young players deemed to be future prospects for the San Francisco Seals. The team was called the Schulken-O'Doul All-Stars.

80. *The Sporting News*, October 13, 1932, 5. In a 1968 interview, O'Doul said

he worked with every Big Six school except for the University of Tokyo (*Pacific Stars and Stripes*, February 20, 1968).

81. *Utica (NY) Daily Press*, January 28, 1942

82. *San Francisco Chronicle*, December 22, 1932.

83. *The Sporting News*, November 3, 1932, 8; *San Francisco Chronicle*, March 26, 1944. Cohen is often referred to as a reporter, but he was not.

84. *The Sporting News*, March 16, 1933, 5.

85. *Collier's Weekly*, July 11, 1936, 24, 26.

86. Letter written by Masao Date, Lefty O'Doul Clip File, National Baseball Hall of Fame.

87. *The Sporting News*, January 5, 1933, 2; *San Francisco Chronicle*, December 23, 1932. O'Doul and Cohen discovered the twenty-five-year-old stowaway, William Kelly, on the first day after the *Chichibu Maru* left Honolulu on the final leg of the return trip to San Francisco. After Kelly was placed in the brig, O'Doul and Cohen slipped chicken, ice cream, and cocktails to him through the porthole. Seeing Kelly as someone down on his luck, they repeated this every day and then finally persuaded the captain to have him sit as a guest at the captain's dinner on the final day of the voyage.

88. *San Francisco Chronicle*, February 20, 1933.

89. *San Francisco Chronicle*, March 1, 1933.

90. *The Sporting News*, January 26, 1933, 3.

91. Johnson, *Who's Who in Major League Baseball*, 303.

7. Banzai O'Doul

1. *Yomiuri Shimbun*, October 15, 1949.

2. *Yomiuri Shimbun*, October 15, 1949; *Pacific Stars and Stripes*, October 15, 1949. Masao Date, who had pitched against the Americans during their earlier tours, was given the honor of pitching batting practice to the Seals that day.

3. *Yomiuri Shimbun*, October 16, 1949.

4. Guthrie-Shimizu, *Transpacific Field of Dreams*, 251.

5. *Nippon Times*, October 16, 1949.

6. Fitts, *Remembering Japanese Baseball*, 4; John Holway, "Lefty and the Geisha," http://baseballguru.com/jholway/analysisjholway32.html. Retrieved October 22, 2015.

7. *Pacific Stars and Stripes*, February 20, 1968.

8. *The Sporting News*, October 26, 1949, 19.

9. *New York Post*, May 1, 1933.

10. *Brooklyn Daily Eagle*, May 1, 1933

11. *Brooklyn Daily Eagle*, April 30, 1933; *New York Post*, May 2, 1933.

12. *New York Sun*, May 12, 1933.

13. *Brooklyn Daily Eagle*, May 22, 1933; *Chicago Tribune*, May 22, 1933.

14. *Brooklyn Daily Eagle*, May 23, 1933. O'Doul was also criticized by the *New York Post*'s Gerald Sylvester, who wrote, "The only thing wrong with Brooklyn

at the present time is Lefty O'Doul, the smiling Irishman who has been letting in runs all season in left field" (*New York Post*, May 26, 1933).

15. *Brooklyn Daily Eagle*, June 12, 1933.

16. *The Sporting News*, June 15, 1933, 4.

17. *Brooklyn Daily Eagle*, June 15, 1933.

18. *New York Sun*, June 15, 1933.

19. *Brooklyn Daily Eagle*, April 18, 1930.

20. *New York Sun*, September 23, 1933.

21. *Amsterdam (NY) Evening Recorder*, December 6, 1933.

22. *The Sporting News*, June 6, 1940, 8.

23. *New York Post*, June 17, 1933.

24. *Brooklyn Daily Eagle*, June 27, 1933.

25. *The Sporting News*, June 29, 1933, 8. Chuck Klein received the most votes among National League outfielders, with 342,283. Paul Waner was second with 269,291 and O'Doul third with 230,058. Wally Berger finished fourth, nearly 100,000 votes behind O'Doul.

26. *Chicago Tribune*, July 4, 1933.

27. *Chicago Tribune*, July 7, 1933.

28. *New York Post*, August 29, 1933.

29. *The Sporting News*, October 5, 1933, 3.

30. *Philadelphia Inquirer*, October 5, 1933.

31. *Philadelphia Inquirer*, October 5, 1933.

32. *New York Sun*, October 5, 1933.

33. *The Sporting News*, September 14, 1944, 11.

34. *New York Sun*, October 5, 1933.

35. *San Francisco Chronicle*, May 7, 1950. The story was reprinted in *Baseball Digest* that July.

36. *The Sporting News*, October 12, 1933, 3.

37. *Philadelphia Inquirer*, October 5, 1933.

38. *New York Post*, October 5, 1933.

39. *New York Times*, October 5, 1933.

40. *New York Times*, September 2 and October 5, 1933.

41. *New York Times*, October 9, 1933.

42. *San Francisco Chronicle*, October 15, 1933; *The Sporting News*, October 19, 1933, 8.

43. *San Francisco Chronicle*, October 11, 1933.

44. *San Francisco Chronicle*, October 16, 1933.

45. *Berkeley (CA) Daily Gazette*, November 9, 1933; *San Francisco Chronicle*, November 10, 1933.

46. O'Doul to Suzuki, January 19, 1932.

47. Suzuki to O'Doul, February 8, 1932. O'Doul was close to company founder J. A. Hillerich and invited him and his wife to come along on the tour in 1934 (*San Francisco Chronicle*, June 15, 1944).

48. O'Doul to Suzuki, thought to be written in January 1933.

49. O'Doul to Suzuki, April 24, 1933.

50. Suzuki to O'Doul, June 5 and July 4, 1933.

51. Dossier for Matsutaro Shoriki, Tokyo War Crimes Trial Collection, Case File 181, University of Virginia.

52. Suzuki to O'Doul, July 4, 1933.

53. O'Doul to Suzuki, July 12, 1933.

54. Suzuki to O'Doul, June 5, 1933.

55. Suzuki to O'Doul, August 31, 1933.

56. O'Doul to Suzuki, August 8, 1933.

57. Earle Mack to Shoriki, October 12, 1933, Norman Macht Collection.

58. Shoriki to Earle Mack, November 8, 1933, Norman Macht Collection.

59. Suzuki to O'Doul, September 1, 1933.

60. Suzuki to O'Doul, September 12 and 14, 1933.

61. Earle Mack to Kenesaw Mountain Landis, December 28, 1933, Norman Macht Collection.

62. *The Sporting News*, January 25, 1934, 2.

63. *Japan Times and Mail*, December 1933.

64. *San Francisco Chronicle*, January 18, 1934.

65. *The Sporting News*, November 30, 1933, 2.

66. *New York Times*, May 3, 1934; *Brooklyn Daily Eagle*, May 3, 1934.

67. *Pittsburgh Post-Gazette*, May 28 and June 18, 1934; *New York Times*, May 28 and June 18, 1934.

68. *New York Times*, August 5 and 6, 1934.

69. *New York Times*, July 2, 1934.

70. *The Sporting News*, June 21, 1934, 4.

71. *The Sporting News*, December 20, 1969, 40.

72. *New York Tribune*, January 24, 1934.

73. *New York Times*, September 30, 1934.

74. *New York Times*, October 1, 1934.

75. *The Sporting News*, October 4, 1934, 6.

76. Ott drove in his 135 runs in 582 official at bats to lead the National League. If O'Doul had maintained his pace for the same number of at bats as Ott, he would have driven in 151 runs.

77. *Baseball Research Journal* 19 (1990): 21–22.

78. *The Sporting News*, November 22, 1934, 6.

79. *New York Times*, July 6, 1934.

80. *Brooklyn Daily Eagle*, July 5, 1934.

81. *The Sporting News*, October 18, 1934, 1. Robert Creamer, in his biography of Ruth, reported an additional portion of the conversation that had Ruppert asking Ruth if he was satisfied with McCarthy. Ruth replied that he was not and could do a better job of managing. That part of the conversation was not carried by *The Sporting News*.

82. William Benswanger to Earle Mack, October 19, 1933, Norman Macht Collection.

83. *New York Times*, October 21, 1934. Connie Mack filled out the roster with several players from his Philadelphia Athletics.

84. Fitts, *Banzai Babe Ruth*, 38.

85. *The Sporting News*, April 25, 1956, 2.

86. *The Sporting News*, April 25, 1956, 2.

87. *The (NY) Saratogian*, November 7, 1934.

88. *The Sporting News*, October 18, 1934, 3.

89. November 2, 1934, diary entry by unknown author, Norman Macht Collection.

90. Ijimino, *Father of Pro Baseball*, n.p.

91. *San Francisco Chronicle*, January 17, 1935.

92. November 2, 1934, diary entry by unknown author, Norman Macht Collection.

93. *New York Times*, November 3, 1934.

94. *New York Times*, November 5, 1934.

95. *The Sporting News*, November 22, 1934, 3.

96. *The Sporting News*, November 8, 1934, 1.

97. *New York Times*, November 10, 1934.

98. *New York Times*, November 10, 1934.

99. *The Sporting News*, November 15, 1934, 3.

100. Diary entry dated November 6, 1934, in *Ten Years in Japan* (New York: Simon & Schuster, 1944), n.p.

101. *The Sporting News*, November 22, 1934, 4.

102. Ijimino, *Father of Pro Baseball*, n.p.

103. *New York Times*, November 21, 1934. The *Times* and many other news outlets incorrectly credited Ruth with hitting the home run off Sawamura.

104. *New York Times*, December 2, 1934.

105. Fitts, *Banzai Babe Ruth*, 182–83. The truth about the attempted coup was the result of research by Fitts.

106. Ijimino, *Father of Pro Baseball*, n.p. It was said Shoriki and *Yomiuri Shimbun* lost 45,000 yen, more than twice what was lost in 1931. As a measure of the Americans' dominance, they hit forty-seven home runs. The Japanese hit three.

107. *The Sporting News*, December 6, 1934, 5. Berg's trip to the roof of the hospital building was mysterious, with him feigning illness and missing a game in order to do so. Since it is clear he was not a spy at the time (he did not show these films to the government until the 1940s), one must wonder whether he was attempting to avoid the difficulties that O'Doul had encountered two years earlier in his efforts to film the Tokyo waterfront. For a detailed account of Berg's life and activities, see Dawidoff, *Catcher Was a Spy.*

108. *New York Times*, February 22, 1935, and October 9, 1969; Fitts, *Banzai Babe Ruth*, 235–39.

109. *The Sporting News*, September 6, 1934, 9.

110. *New York Times*, January 22, 1935.

111. *San Francisco Chronicle*, January 17, 1935.

112. *New York Times*, January 22, 1935.

113. *New York Times*, January 22, 1935.

114. *The Sporting News*, March 14, 1935.

115. *San Francisco Examiner*, February 17, 1935.

116. *San Francisco Call*, February 16, 1935.

8. Greatest Hitting Instructor

1. *Yomiuri Shimbun*, October 16, 1949.

2. *Yomiuri Shimbun*, October 16, 1949.

3. *Yomiuri Shimbun*, October 30, 1949.

4. *The Sporting News*, November 16, 1949, 4.

5. *The Sporting News*, March 26, 1936, 3.

6. *San Francisco Chronicle*, November 22, 1934; *New York Times*, November 22, 1934.

7. *San Francisco Chronicle*, May 15, 1935.

8. *Sacramento Union*, August 6, 1935. Waner would win his third National League batting title in 1936, eventually collect more than three thousand Major League hits, and be inducted into the Hall of Fame in 1952.

9. *Brooklyn Daily Eagle*, June 28, 1941.

10. *New York Post*, November 7, 1935. DiMaggio collected the first of his three Most Valuable Player Awards in his fourth season, in 1939.

11. *The Sporting News*, November 14, 1994, 44.

12. *The Sporting News*, March 23, 1939, 4. This interaction would become one of the legends surrounding Ted Williams. In more romanticized versions, O'Doul is reported telling Williams, "Kid, don't let 'em change a thing."

13. Email from Troy Kinunen to the author, April 20, 2016. Kinunen is the president and CEO of MEARS Auctions. According to Hillerich & Bradsby records Kinunen has reviewed, Williams used an O'Doul model bat from 1940 through 1943, with Williams's signature on the barrel.

14. *The Sporting News*, December 16, 1937, 5.

15. *San Diego Union*, December 1, 1937.

16. *Albany (NY) Knickerbocker News*, January 25, 1940.

17. *Sporting Life*, December 14, 1912, 3, 8.

18. *Baseball Magazine* 19, no. 6 (October 1917): 542.

19. *1948 Famous Slugger Year Book*, 3–10.

20. Interview of Marcucci by the author, June 5, 1995.

21. Interview of Conlin by the author, May 28, 1995. Conlin (not to be confused with the Philadelphia sportswriter of the same name) was a legend in Sacramento and the longtime sports editor of the *Sacramento Union*, and he knew both Marty and Moreing well.

22. *The Sporting News*, January 7, 1937, 3.

23. *The Sporting News*, July 23, 1936, 7.

24. *The Sporting News*, May 14, 1936, 5.

25. *San Francisco Chronicle*, May 5, 1936.

26. *The Sporting News*, July 23, 1936, 7.

27. *The Sporting News*, January 7, 1937, 3.

28. Interview of Doerr by the author, August 20, 1991.

29. *The Sporting News*, April 9, 1942, 2.

30. *Philadelphia Inquirer*, May 8, 1942.

31. *Philadelphia Inquirer*, May 9, 1942.

32. *Philadelphia Inquirer*, June 20, 1942, and February 22, 1946.

33. *The Sporting News*, June 17, 1959, 13.

34. Interview of D. DiMaggio by the author, January 10, 1992.

35. *Los Angeles Times*, March 2, 1937. Joe DiMaggio was on hand for his brother's signing ceremony because he was holding out from the Yankees for the second year in a row. During his time in San Francisco, the New York outfielder consented to having his batting stroke filmed as part of a series of motion pictures O'Doul planned to use to demonstrate proper hitting, base running, throwing, and fielding techniques. O'Doul also planned to film players during training camp so they could review their performance. O'Doul and DiMaggio found time to visit Doc Strub's new creation, the Santa Anita racetrack, where they took in the $100,000 race and witnessed Seabiscuit lose to Rosemont (*Los Angeles Times*, March 1 and 6, 1937).

36. *Los Angeles Times*, March 2, 1937. After the tryout camp was over, the Seals had first choice of players and the Reds second. DiMaggio wanted to play for the Seals. He said that if the Reds had chosen him, he would not have signed.

37. *The Sporting News*, April 29, 1937, 9.

38. *The Sporting News*, May 11, 1939, 10.

39. *The Sporting News*, June 15, 1939, 6.

40. *The Sporting News*, August 3, 1939, 13.

41. *San Francisco Chronicle*, November 23, 1939.

42. *The Sporting News*, July 25, 1940, 5.

43. *New York Sun*, March 12, 1940.

44. Interview of D. DiMaggio by the author, January 10, 1992.

45. *San Francisco Chronicle*, November 20, 1939.

46. *The Sporting News*, January 11, 1940, 8.

47. *The Sporting News*, February 29, 1940, 7; *San Francisco Chronicle*, February 27, 1940.

48. Babe Dahlgren to Daniel Woodhead, January 10, 1992, Lefty O'Doul Clip File, National Baseball Hall of Fame.

49. *New York Sun*, March 6, 1940.

50. *New York Times*, February 27, 1940.

51. Dahlgren, *Rumor in Town*, 103.

52. *New York Times*, February 27, 1940.

53. *New York Times*, March 8, 1940.

54. *New York Times*, March 8, 1940.

55. Dahlgren, *Rumor in Town*, 193–94.

56. Dahlgren to Woodhead, January 10, 1992.

57. *New York Sun*, June 13, 1941. Two days later, Dahlgren was sold by the Boston Braves to the Chicago Cubs.

58. *The Sporting News*, April 2, 1942, 6. After the film was completed, it was said O'Doul was paid $12,000 (*The Sporting News*, July 23, 1942, 1).

59. *Santa Cruz (CA) Sentinel*, February 13, 1942.

60. *New York Post*, March 13, 1942.

61. In 2013 Shieber deconstructed many of the film's scenes and discovered that with the exception of some early shots, when Gary Cooper was in close-ups swinging a bat or catching a baseball left-handed, it was not a film trick. Shieber also explains a 1956 quote by Cooper in which he seems to admit he threw and batted right-handed (http://baseballresearcher.blogspot.com/2013/02/the -pride-of-yankees-seeknay.html).

62. *The Sporting News*, July 23, 1942, 1, 9.

63. *The Sporting News*, May 31, 1945, 12.

64. *Rockford (IL) Morning Star*, July 28, 1946.

65. *The Sporting News*, May 4, 1949, 30.

66. Kelley, *San Francisco Seals*, 21.

67. *The Sporting News*, May 7, 1942, 16.

68. Kelley, *San Francisco Seals*, 20.

69. *Philadelphia Inquirer*, November 2, 1946.

70. *The Sporting News*, May 21, 1947, 12.

71. Kelley, *San Francisco Seals*, 20.

72. *San Francisco Chronicle*, March 16, 1948.

73. Interview of Jansen by the author, December 29, 1991.

74. Interview of Brovia by the author, March 1990.

75. *Rome (NY) Daily Sentinel*, May 4, 1944. Metkovich had been in the Boston Braves' farm system, but they gave up on him, selling him to the Seals. By the middle of his year with O'Doul, five Major League teams were interested. He was purchased by the Boston Red Sox, resuming a ten-year Major League career. He later captured the Pacific Coast League's Most Valuable Player Award in 1950.

76. *The Sporting News*, April 23, 1942, 3.

77. *The Sporting News*, May 19, 1948, 19.

78. *The Sporting News*, July 6, 1949, 4.

79. *San Francisco Chronicle*, December 8, 1969.

80. *The Sporting News*, April 6, 1949, 3.

81. *The Sporting News*, April 6, 1949, 3.

82. Gene Woodling to the members of the Baseball Hall of Fame Veterans Committee, January 5, 1992, Lefty O'Doul Clip File, National Baseball Hall of Fame.

83. *San Francisco Chronicle*, December 8, 1969.

9. Manager for Life

1. *Pacific Stars and Stripes*, October 17, 1949.

2. *Asahi Shimbun*, October 17, 1949

3. *Asahi Shimbun*, October 18, 1949.

4. *The Sporting News*, November 16, 1949, 10.

5. *Yomiuri Shimbun*, October 18, 1949; *Nippon Times*, October 19, 1949.

6. *Yomiuri Shimbun*, October 18, 1949.

7. Starffin was the first Japanese pitcher to win 300 games, and he still holds a number of Japanese pitching records, including wins in a season (42), most consecutive 30-win seasons (3)—both records shared with Kazuhisa Iano—and most career shutouts (83).

8. *San Francisco Chronicle*, October 18, 1949.

9. *Pacific Stars and Stripes*, October 18, 1949.

10. Interview of Cheso by the author, November 11, 2010.

11. *Pacific Stars and Stripes*, October 14, 1949.

12. *The Sporting News*, May 27, 1937, 5.

13. *San Mateo (CA) Times*, January 26, 1949.

14. *San Mateo (CA) Times*, January 26, 1949. One of O'Doul's favorite tricks was taught to him by former teammate Carl Zamloch, who became a professional magician after his playing days. The trick involved having someone choose a card from a deck. The card was then replaced and a rubber band placed around the deck, which was then thrown against the ceiling. All of the cards would fall to the floor, except for the card that had been chosen, which would remain stuck to the ceiling.

15. Interview of O'Doul by Lawrence Ritter, August 29, 1963.

16. *The Sporting News*, May 2, 1935, 1.

17. *The Sporting News*, June 13, 1940, 1.

18. *The Sporting News*, April 16, 1936, 8.

19. Interview of O'Doul by Lawrence Ritter, August 29, 1963.

20. *The Sporting News*, October 23, 1946, 13.

21. *San Francisco Chronicle*, October 9, 1936.

22. *San Francisco Chronicle*, April 11, 1938

23. Interview of O'Doul by Lawrence Ritter, August 29, 1963.

24. *Nation's Business Monthly*, August 1953, 32-33.

25. Interview of Ed Cereghino by the author, October 16, 2015.

26. Undated United Press International article by Steve Snider, Lefty O'Doul Clip File, National Baseball Hall of Fame.

27. *The Sporting News*, April 8, 1937, 6.

28. *San Francisco Chronicle*, June 4, 2002.

29. *The Sporting News*, May 9, 1935, 9.

30. Joe Devine report to Ed Barrow, August 10, 1935, Dick Dobbins Collection.

31. *Sacramento Union*, May 27, 1935.

32. *San Francisco Chronicle*, September 5, 1935.

33. *The Sporting News*, October 3, 1935, 8.

34. *New York Post*, November 7, 1935.

35. Interview of Jansen by the author, December 29, 1991.

36. Interview of O'Doul by Lawrence Ritter, August 29, 1963. O'Doul also said of Hornsby, "Off the field, you know, he was a pretty good guy."

37. *San Francisco Chronicle*, September 2, 1935.

38. *Syracuse Herald-Journal*, April 19, 1940.

39. *San Francisco Chronicle*, September 12, 1938.

40. *The Sporting News*, June 15, 1939, 12.

41. Interview of Marcucci by the author, June 5, 1995.

42. *The Sporting News*, March 4, 1937, 8.

43. *The Sporting News*, October 5, 1939, 16.

44. *San Francisco Chronicle*, October 16, 18, and 21, 1939.

45. *San Francisco Chronicle*, April 15, 1952.

46. Interview of Dasso by the author, August 19, 1991.

47. Interview of Singleton by the author, May 19, 1995.

48. *The Sporting News*, March 9, 1939, 6.

49. *Seattle Times*, March 8, 1939; *The Sporting News*, March 9, 1939, 6; *San Francisco Chronicle*, March 12, 1942.

50. *New York Mirror*, March 30, 1964.

51. *San Francisco Examiner*, November 21, 1937.

52. *San Francisco Examiner*, August 22, 1937; *Oakland Tribune*, August 22, 1937.

53. *San Francisco Examiner*, September 2, 1937; *San Diego Union*, September 2, 1939.

54. *San Francisco Chronicle*, May 30, 1938; *Seattle Times*, May 30, 1938. Joe Gordon would match O'Doul's feat while playing for Sacramento in 1952. It has been accomplished twice in the Major Leagues—by Joe Cronin for the Boston Red Sox in 1943 and Hal Breeden of the Montreal Expos in 1973.

55. *San Diego Union*, April 26, 1939.

56. *Seattle Times*, June 24, 1939.

57. *Seattle Times*, June 25, 1939; *San Francisco Chronicle*, June 25, 1939.

58. *Seattle Times*, June 26, 1939.

59. *The Sporting News*, July 6, 1939, 2.

60. *The Sporting News*, January 9, 1941, 3.

61. *San Francisco Chronicle*, May 2, 1941.

62. *San Francisco Chronicle*, May 3, 1941.

63. *San Francisco Chronicle*, May 1 and 6, 1941; *Seattle Times*, June 29, 1941.

64. *Los Angeles Times*, May 1, 1941; *San Francisco Chronicle*, May 1, 1941.

65. *San Francisco Chronicle*, May 1, 1941.

66. *San Francisco Chronicle*, May 1, 1941.

67. *San Francisco Chronicle*, May 2, 1941; *Los Angeles Times*, May 2, 1941.

68. *San Francisco Chronicle*, May 1, 1941.

69. *The Sporting News*, May 8, 1941, 12, 14.

70. *San Francisco Chronicle*, May 2, 1941.

71. *Los Angeles Times*, May 8, July 3, 4, 5, 8, 9, and 10, 1941; *The Sporting News*, September 11, 1941, 1. Bonetti, an extremely popular pitcher, was ultimately reinstated in 1949, but he never played professional baseball again.

72. *San Francisco Chronicle*, May 2, 1941.

73. *San Francisco Chronicle*, May 2, 1941.

74. *Los Angeles Times*, May 4, 1941.

75. *San Francisco Chronicle*, May 8, 1941.

76. *Seattle Times*, June 29, 1941.

77. *Los Angeles Times*, May 4, 1941; *San Francisco Chronicle*, May 8, 1941.

78. *Los Angeles Times*, May 2, 3, 4, and 6, 1941.

79. *Los Angeles Times*, May 12 and 13, 1941; *San Francisco Chronicle*, May 28, 1941. Larry Woodall ran the team in O'Doul's absence.

80. *New York Post*, July 26, 1941,

81. *The Sporting News*, September 21, 1939, 1.

82. *San Francisco Chronicle*, August 12, 1939.

83. *New York PM*, November 23, 1941.

84. *Troy (NY) Times Record*, August 18, 1941.

85. *New York Daily Mirror*, October 15, 1941.

86. *The Sporting News*, November 6, 1941, 10.

87. There was another rumor that O'Doul was headed to Cleveland to manage the Indians, but they hired twenty-four-year-old shortstop Lou Boudreau as player-manager to replace Roger Peckinpaugh (*The Sporting News*, December 4, 1941, 6).

88. *The Sporting News*, September 24, 1942, 16.

89. *New York Times*, October 14, 1941.

90. *Philadelphia Inquirer*, February 20, 21, and 25, 1943.

91. *Philadelphia Inquirer*, November 24, 1943; *The Sporting News*, December 2, 1943, 4. Cox pointed the finger of blame for his banishment at Harris for revealing his betting habits (*New York Post*, November 24, 1943).

92. *The Sporting News*, December 27, 1945, 1.

93. *The Sporting News*, February 7, 1946, 11.

94. *The Sporting News*, November 22, 1945, 7.

10. It Is Epidemic

1. *San Francisco Chronicle*, October 22, 1949.

2. *Pacific Stars and Stripes*, October 20, 1949.

3. *Yomiuri Shimbun*, October 19, 1949.

4. Interview of O'Doul by Lawrence Ritter, August 29, 1963.

5. *Pacific Stars and Stripes*, October 24, 1949; *Yomiuri Shimbun*, October 24, 1949.

6. *Yomiuri Shimbun*, October 24, 1949.

7. Nushida was the first who was *billed* as Japanese. Andy Yamashiro, also born in Hawaii, played under the name Andy Yim in the Minors from 1917 through 1919 after touring the United States with a popular Chinese team from the islands.

8. *Honolulu Record*, August 30, 1956.

9. *Oakland Tribune*, September 27, 1932.

10. *Seattle Times*, August 25, 1932.

11. *Berkeley (CA) Daily Gazette*, September 27, 1932; interview of Raimondi by the author, March 21, 2009. Nushida was born on November 28, 1899, in the town of Honomu, not far from Hilo on the island of Hawaii.

12. *Berkeley (CA) Daily Gazette*, September 28, 1932.

13. *Oakland Tribune*, September 29, 1932.

14. *San Francisco Chronicle*, October 3, 1932. Hong managed to hit a run-scoring single in three at bats; the only blemish on his pitching line was a solo home run.

15. *New York Tribune*, April 17, 1921.

16. *New York Tribune*, April 17, 1921.

17. *San Francisco Chronicle*, February 28, 1935; List or Manifest of Alien Passengers for the United States, List 11, M.S. *Chichibu Maru*, Passengers Sailing from Yokohama, Japan, February 14, 1935. As mentioned, Victor Starffin was not listed on the ship's manifest but was on board the ship. Sotaro Suzuki was not on the *Chichibu Maru*, having arrived a couple of weeks before the team to finalize arrangements.

18. *Rafu Shimpo*, April 16, 1935; email from Yoichi Nagata to the author, September 9, 2015. Starffin's father was an exiled "White Russian" and therefore not recognized as a citizen by the Soviets. Since the United States officially recognized the Soviet Union and not the exiled White Russians, the Japanese could not issue him a passport. Instead, they provided a document verifying that Starffin was a resident of Japan.

19. Horio was born March 15, 1907, in Pa'ia, Hawaii, on the island of Maui.

20. *San Francisco Chronicle*, February 28, 1935.

21. The Giants also played against Seattle, Hollywood, and Los Angeles. Sawamura struck out fourteen in a twelve-inning 6–5 victory over Hollywood (*Los Angeles Times*, February 28, March 12, 16, 30, 31, and April 1, 1935).

22. Hisanori Karita letter, dated December 24, 1991, Lefty O'Doul Clip File, National Baseball Hall of Fame.

23. *San Francisco Chronicle*, March 4, 1935.

24. *San Francisco Chronicle*, March 26, 1935.

25. *San Francisco Chronicle*, March 28, 1935.

26. *The Sporting News*, March 28, 1935, 1.

27. *San Francisco Chronicle*, March 26 and 27, 1935.

28. *The Sporting News*, March 28, 1935, 1.

29. *Sacramento Union*, March 18, 1935; *Ogden (UT) Standard Examiner*, May 23, 1935.

30. *Los Angeles Times*, March 30, 1942. Angelich, who was killed at Hickam Field during the Japanese raid, made the Senators out of spring training in 1935 but was released before appearing in a regular-season game (*The Sporting News*, May 2, 1935, 9).

31. In 2014 the Nisei Baseball Research Project announced the discovery of silent film footage of Ruth, Gehrig, and Zenimura when the two Major League stars stopped in Fresno. The fifty-second clip shows Ruth taking some practice swings and Gehrig walking from home plate. The film ends with Ruth, Gehrig, and three Japanese players, including Zenimura, gathering to pose for what became an iconic photo of the Ruth-Gehrig barnstorming tour.

32. *The Sporting News*, March 28, 1935, 1.

33. *Rafu Shimpo*, March 28 and April 12, 1935.

34. *Rafu Shimpo*, April 13 and 21, 1935.

35. *Rafu Shimpo*, April 22, 1935.

36. *Los Angeles Times*, April 1, 1935. Interestingly, Ray confused Victor Starffin with Eiji Sawamura, crediting Starffin with pitching the 1–0 game against the Americans during the 1934 American All-Stars tour.

37. *Rafu Shimpo*, April 12, 1935; Nagata, *Tokyo Giants North American Tour*.

38. Nagata, *Tokyo Giants North American Tour*.

39. *The Sporting News*, May 9, 1935, 2.

40. *Milwaukee Journal*, June 12, 1935; Dennis Pajot, "Almost an International Incident in Milwaukee," March 5, 2009, www.seamheads.com; email from Yoichi Nagata to the author, September 9, 2015. The article in the Milwaukee newspaper does not mention the contract incident, nor would it be expected to.

41. *The Sporting News*, November 22, 1945, 9.

42. *San Francisco Chronicle*, June 24, 1935. The team would become known as the Solons in 1936, the name by which they are best known. Horio seemed to have promise—having hit five home runs and batting .264 in 110 games for Sioux Falls—but age was an issue. He claimed to be twenty-one years old but in reality was twenty-seven, an advanced age for someone playing at the bottom rung of the Minor League ladder (*Lincoln [NE] Star*, July 10, 1934; *Ogden [UT] Standard Examiner*, May 23, 1935).

43. *San Francisco Chronicle*, August 26, 1935. The cup is inscribed, "Presented To Frank O'Doul From Japanese Ass'n of San Francisco 1935" (email from David Eskenazi to the author, October 4, 2015).

44. California Death Index, 1905–1939, entry for Yoshiko Horio. Original image retrieved from www.familysearch.com, September 11, 2015.

45. Horio collected eleven hits in forty-four at bats for Sacramento in 1935.

46. *Los Angeles Times*, August 24 and September 1, 1935; *Seattle Times*, March

19, 1936. Before being cut by Seattle in the spring of 1936. Horio played in an exhibition game for the Indians against the team he had played for in 1935, the Tokyo Giants. He sparked a rally with a two-run single (*Oakland Tribune*, March 20, 1936).

47. Email from Yoichi Nagata to the author, February 19, 2016. Nagata spoke with Horio's second wife, Eileen, in Hawaii around 1995. Horio batted .236 over six seasons with the Hankyu team and the Osaka/Hanshin Tigers.

48. *Berkeley (CA) Daily Gazette*, July 5 and October 1, 1936.

49. Email from Yoichi Nagata to the author, February 19, 2016.

50. *Rafu Shimpo*, April 18, 1935.

51. Email from Yoichi Nagata to the author, February 19, 2016. It is usually stated that McGalliard changed his name to Bucky Harris in Japan because the fans there could not pronounce his name, but he played under that name both in the Minors and for the LA Nippons. McGalliard, a native of Los Angeles who had attended the University of Southern California, played three games for the Sacramento Senators in 1928 and in forty-six games in 1929 before joining Wichita of the Western League in 1930. One other white American played in Japan in 1936, a pitcher named Herbert North, who won two games and lost five for Nagoya.

52. *The Sporting News*, August 15, 1935, 8.

53. *San Francisco Chronicle*, February 18, 1936.

54. *San Francisco Chronicle*, March 2, 1936.

55. *New York Times*, February 4, 1937. Ohe would die less than three weeks after Pearl Harbor of wounds suffered during the Battle of Wake Island.

56. *Chicago Tribune*, January 30, 1937. The article says that O'Doul was supervising construction of the stadium, but there is no record that is the case.

57. *The Sporting News*, July 15, 1937, 13.

58. Interview of O'Doul by Lawrence Ritter, August 29, 1963. O'Doul had also been working with Sotaro Suzuki to take a PCL all-star team to Japan following the 1937 season (*The Sporting News*, April 25, 1956, 2).

59. *The Sporting News*, May 14, 1947, 22.

60. Interview of O'Doul by Lawrence Ritter, August 29, 1963.

61. *New York Times*, December 9, 1941.

62. *New York Times*, December 9, 1941. After the war, Mukaeda again became a leader in the Japanese community in Los Angeles, and in 1952 he gained American citizenship when the naturalization ban was lifted. In 1992, at age 101, Mukaeda was honored at the opening of the Japanese-American Museum in Los Angeles. He died in November 1995, only two weeks shy of his 105th birthday.

63. *Santa Cruz (CA) Sentinel*, December 21, 1941; *Los Angeles Times*, December 22, 1941; *Time*, December 29, 1941. The tanker *Emidio*, owned by the Socony-Vacuum Oil Company, was shelled by a submarine twenty miles off the California coast southwest of Eureka, resulting in the loss of five lives.

64. *Santa Barbara (CA) News Press*, February 24 and 25, 1942. The Japanese

submarine lobbed two dozen shells at the coastline, one of which hit an oil rig and some pumping equipment, causing approximately $500 in damage. Other shells hit nearby farms, leaving large holes in the ground.

65. *San Francisco Chronicle*, March 3, 1942.

66. *San Francisco Chronicle*, July 22, 1945.

67. *Chicago Tribune*, February 16, 1942.

68. *Los Angeles Times*, December 30, 1942.

69. *New York Times*, December 16, 1945.

70. *Japan Times*, July 25, 2000.

71. Dossier for Matsutaro Shoriki, Tokyo War Crimes Trial Collection, Case File 181, University of Virginia.

72. *San Francisco Chronicle*, July 22, 1945.

73. *San Francisco Chronicle*, June 6 and July 12, 1943.

74. *San Francisco Chronicle*, July 22, 1945.

75. *San Francisco Chronicle*, March 26, 1944.

76. Email from Yoichi Nagata to the author, February 19, 2016.

77. *The Sporting News*, November 22, 1945, 9.

78. *Charleston (wv) Gazette*, September 23, 1945.

79. *The Sporting News*, April 25, 1956, 1-2. This is from an interview of Suzuki by Carl Lundquist of United Press International.

80. *The Sporting News*, November 22, 1945, 9.

81. Among those perishing were Kenichi Aoshiba, a pitcher who died of disease in a military hospital in Korea at war's end; Nobuo Kura, a catcher who died during the Battle of Okinawa; Usaburo Shintomi, an outfielder who died after stepping on a landmine in Burma; Takeo Tabe, the fleet infielder who had so impressed Bob Ray, during combat on Okinawa; and Kumeyasu Yajima, an outfielder killed in Burma in late April 1945. In addition, as noted earlier, Shigeru Mizuhara served time in a Russian prisoner of war camp. Victor Starffin, as a noncitizen, was detained by the Japanese during the late stages of the war.

82. The *Tatsuta Maru*, renamed *Tatuta Maru*, was used by the Japanese to repatriate citizens living in the United States in the days leading up to Pearl Harbor.

83. Interview of O'Doul by Lawrence Ritter, August 29, 1963.

84. *Pacific Stars and Stripes*, February 20, 1968.

85. *The Sporting News*, May 14, 1947, 22.

86. *The Sporting News*, January 21, 1948, 25.

87. *The Sporting News*, February 4, 1948, 22.

11. We Are Major League!

1. *Pacific Stars and Stripes*, October 27, 1949.

2. *Yomiuri Shimbun*, October 28, 1949.

3. *Pacific Stars and Stripes*, October 28, 1949; *The Sporting News*, November 30, 1949, 16. The Seals actually trailed, 4–1, after five innings—another reason it would have been unwise to halt the game.

4. *Yomiuri Shimbun*, October 28, 1949.

5. *Pacific Stars and Stripes*, October 28, 1949; *The Sporting News*, November 2, 1949, 17.

6. Interview of Cheso by the author, November 11, 2010.

7. *Pacific Stars and Stripes*, October 29, 1949; *Mainichi Shimbun*, October 30, 1949; *Yomiuri Shimbun*, October 30, 1949.

8. *Yomiuri Shimbun*, October 30, 1949.

9. *Pacific Stars and Stripes*, October 21, 1949; *Yomiuri Shimbun*, October 21, 1949.

10. *New York Times*, January 24, 1945; *The Sporting News*, February 1, 1945, 6.

11. *The Sporting News*, April 12, 1945, 17.

12. *The Sporting News*, April 12, 1945, 17.

13. *San Francisco Chronicle*, May 26, 1945.

14. *New York Mirror*, March 30, 1964.

15. *The Sporting News*, February 14, 1946, 11, and February 21, 1946, 12.

16. *San Francisco Chronicle*, February 18, 1946.

17. *The Sporting News*, February 28, 1946, 9.

18. *The Sporting News*, February 28, 1946, 9.

19. *The Sporting News*, March 14, 1946, 4.

20. *The Sporting News*, March 21, 1946, 9.

21. *Los Angeles Times*, January 4, 1903, February 10, 26, and March 23, 1904. Chance took advantage of the long PCL schedule to earn some extra money after the Cubs' season ended.

22. *The Sporting News*, August 13, 1947, 24.

23. *The Sporting News*, December 18, 1941, 12.

24. Interview of Conlin by the author, May 28, 1995.

25. Interview of Jansen by the author, December 29, 1991.

26. *San Francisco Chronicle*, July 26, 1946.

27. *New York Times*, August 12, 1946.

28. *The Sporting News*, August 21, 1946, 24.

29. *San Francisco Chronicle*, September 20, 1946.

30. Interview of Jansen by the author, December 29, 1991.

31. The Louisville Redbirds of the American Association finally broke the Seals' record by drawing more than eight hundred thousand in 1983.

32. *The Sporting News*, October 2, 1946, 1–2.

33. *San Francisco Chronicle*, September 24, 1946.

34. *Los Angeles Times*, September 26 and 30, 1946.

35. *The Sporting News*, October 2, 1946, 1.

36. *The Sporting News*, October 2, 1946, 2.

37. *The Sporting News*, October 9, 1946, 29.

38. *The Sporting News*, October 16, 1946, 2, and October 30, 1946, 4.

39. *The Sporting News*, October 2, 1946, 2.

40. *The Sporting News*, December 4, 1946, 8; interview of Ed Cereghino by the author, October 16, 2015.

41. *The Sporting News*, October 23, 1946, 13.

42. *The Sporting News*, January 1, 1947, 3.

43. Small, "Too Good for the Majors," 26. Frank Graham told a story that happened about the same time that involved O'Doul, "busy straightening out a fellow who had gotten himself into a jam." Graham noted, "The fellow had been in jams before and was not the kind of fellow you would go out of your way to help if you were not Lefty O'Doul. 'Why do you bother about a guy like that?' somebody asked. 'Why,' [O'Doul] said, 'the guy is in trouble'" (*Baseball Digest*, November 1946, 45).

44. *San Francisco Chronicle*, July 9, 1991.

45. *San Francisco Examiner*, March 6, 1983.

46. *The Sporting News*, June 4, 1947, 23. An audit in 1951 showed what O'Doul had been paid during the years Paul Fagan owned the franchise. In 1945 he was paid $15,000. In 1946 that rose to $21,000. In 1947 O'Doul earned $37,000, and $41,000 in 1948, 1949, and 1950. In his final year with the Seals, O'Doul's pay was $30,000 (*The Sporting News*, September 26, 1951, 2).

47. Interview of Conlin by the author, May 28, 1995.

48. *The Sporting News*, February 26, 1947, 21.

49. *The Sporting News*, March 12, 1947, 13.

50. *San Francisco Chronicle*, March 30, 1947.

51. *San Francisco Chronicle*, March 5, 1947.

52. *The Sporting News*, March 19, 1947, 20.

53. *The Sporting News*, July 28, 1948, 8.

54. Stevens to Dobbins, March 4, 1992, Lefty O'Doul Clip File, National Baseball Hall of Fame.

55. *The Sporting News*, February 12, 1947, 11; *San Francisco Chronicle*, February 1, 1947. To demonstrate the backstop's shatterproof qualities, Fagan had Bob Chesnes hurl baseballs against it. The version used by Fagan was developed by Libbey-Owens-Ford, called "Tuf-flex."

56. *The Sporting News*, January 12, 1949, 17, and March 1, 1950, 5.

57. *San Francisco Chronicle*, January 8, 1947.

58. *The Sporting News*, January 1, 1947, 3.

59. *San Francisco Chronicle*, March 24, 1948.

60. *San Francisco Chronicle*, March 17, 1950; email from Bill Soto-Castellanos to the author, August 31, 2015. The "seal" was actually a year-old sea lion named "Major." When not frolicking on the field for the benefit of photographers, it swam in a tank located on the first-base side of the stadium, at the end of a ramp to the west of the main entrance.

61. *The Sporting News*, April 23, 1947, 29; *San Francisco Chronicle*, April 4, 1947.

62. *The Sporting News*, September 24, 1947, 23.

63. *San Francisco Chronicle*, August 29, 1947.

64. *The Sporting News*, August 20, 1947, 23.

65. *San Francisco Chronicle*, August 10 and 29, 1947.

66. *San Francisco Chronicle*, August 1, 1947.

67. *San Francisco Chronicle*, August 3 and 10, 1947. Jethroe eventually reached the Major Leagues in 1950 with the Boston Braves, winning the National League Rookie of the Year Award.

68. *San Francisco Chronicle*, September 29, 1947. O'Doul was certain that even if Restelli had been tagged, the pitch should have been called ball four, which would have meant he would have scored automatically.

69. *San Francisco Chronicle*, September 29, 1947; *San Francisco Examiner*, September 29, 1947; *San Diego Union*, September 29, 1947.

70. *San Francisco Chronicle*, September 30, 1947; *Los Angeles Times*, September 28 and 30, 1947.

71. Interview of Chambers by the author, January 7, 2010.

72. *The Sporting News*, December 3, 1947, 19; *Polk's Crocker-Langley San Francisco City Directory*, 1948–49.

73. *The Sporting News*, April 28, 1948, 23.

74. *The Sporting News*, May 19, 1948, 19.

75. *San Francisco Chronicle*, May 24 and 25, 1948.

76. *The Sporting News*, September 8, 1948, 18.

77. *San Francisco Examiner*, August 30, 1948.

78. *New York Times*, January 17, 1949.

79. Interviews of Brovia by the author, November 1989 and April 1990.

80. *San Francisco Chronicle*, March 2 and 3, 1949; interview of Klein by the author, February 3, 2009.

81. *The Sporting News*, March 16, 1949, 29.

82. *The Sporting News*, February 22, 1950, 19.

83. *The Sporting News*, February 22, 1950, 19.

84. Interview of Klein by the author, February 3, 2009.

85. *The Sporting News*, March 16, 1949, 29.

86. *San Francisco Chronicle*, March 31, 1949; *Los Angeles Times*, April 2, 1949; *The Sporting News*, April 13, 1949, 27.

87. Dobbins, *Grand Minor League*, 141.

88. *San Francisco Chronicle*, January 31, 1950; *The Sporting News*, February 8, 1950, 15.

89. *Los Angeles Herald-Express*, February 16, 1950; *Los Angeles Times*, February 17, 1950.

90. *The Sporting News*, April 12, 1950, 23.

91. *Oakland Tribune*, February 3, 1950.

92. *Oakland Tribune*, April 11, 1950.

93. *San Francisco Chronicle*, May 17, 1950.

94. *The Sporting News*, December 27, 1950, 14.

95. *San Francisco Chronicle*, September 28, 1950.

96. *San Francisco Chronicle*, October 25, 1950.

97. *Baseball News*, November 1, 1950.

98. *Salt Lake Tribune*, June 22, 1952.

99. *Nippon Times*, November 5, 1950.

100. *The Sporting News*, November 22, 1950, 9.

101. The Sunchon Tunnel massacre involved nearly 180 American and Koreans held prisoner by the North Koreans. After marching several hundred miles, the prisoners were loaded onto a train and traveled for several days. Stopping at a tunnel, the prisoners were unloaded in groups of twenty, supposedly to eat. Instead, North Korean soldiers shot and bayoneted them.

102. *The Sporting News*, November 22, 1950, 9.

103. *The Sporting News*, December 6, 1950, 22.

104. *New York Times*, November 23, 1950.

105. *New York Times*, November 25, 1950.

106. *San Francisco Chronicle*, November 28, 1950.

107. *San Francisco Chronicle*, January 23, 1951; *Los Angeles Times*, January 23, 1951. The fact that training camp was in Modesto was appropriate in a way because the Minor League team in that city, the Modesto Reds, had two years earlier fielded the first all-Japanese battery in American professional baseball history—catcher Henry Matsubu and pitcher Jiro Nakamura (*Modesto Bee*, March 6 and 27, 1951).

108. *The Sporting News*, March 7, 1951, 20.

109. Acme Telephoto, April 18, 1951 (author's copy).

110. *San Francisco Chronicle*, July 27, 1951; *Washington Post*, July 28, 1951.

111. *San Francisco Chronicle*, August 26, 1951.

112. *San Francisco Chronicle*, August 26, 1951. In addition, the renter would have to pay taxes of approximately $40,000 per year, so the total cost of operation would be about $100,000 annually.

113. *The Sporting News*, April 18, 1951, 20. The rumors were made public by *Los Angeles Times* sportswriter Al Wolf.

114. *San Francisco Chronicle*, September 6, 1951; interview of Klein by the author, February 3, 2009.

115. *San Francisco Chronicle*, September 6, 1951.

116. *San Francisco Chronicle*, September 10, 1951.

12. There Are No Trick Plays

1. *The Sporting News*, November 16, 1949, 10.

2. *Yomiuri Shimbun*, October 31, 1949.

3. *Yomiuri Shimbun*, October 31, 1949.

4. *Nippon Times*, October 31, 1949; Guthrie-Shimizu, *Transpacific Field of Dreams*, 253–54.

5. *Asahi Shimbun*, October 31, 1949.

6. *Nippon Times*, October 31, 1949; *Pacific Stars and Stripes*, October 31, 1949; *The Sporting News*, November 9, 1949, 14.

7. *Pacific Stars and Stripes*, October 31, 1949.

8. *Asahi Shimbun*, October 31, 1949.

9. *Pacific Stars and Stripes*, October 31, 1949.

10. *San Francisco Chronicle*, February 6, 1950.

11. *New York Times*, October 8, 1951.

12. *The Sporting News*, October 17, 1951, 14.

13. *New York Times*, October 8, 1951.

14. *New York Times*, October 9, 1951. There have been numerous stories told about O'Doul recommending a lighter bat, including from DiMaggio himself, but articles of the time indicate that was not the case.

15. *Buffalo Courier Express*, October 9, 1951.

16. Interview of Ed Cereghino by the author, October 16, 2015.

17. Statement by General Matthew Ridgway, October 15, 1951, Archives, U.S. Military History Institute, Daniel Woodhead Collection.

18. *Nippon Times*, October 18, 1951.

19. *Billboard*, December 8, 1951, 3.

20. Undated letter from Mel Parnell to Daniel Woodhead, Lefty O'Doul Clip File, National Baseball Hall of Fame.

21. *Pacific Stars and Stripes*, November 14, 1951. The losing pitcher was seventeen-year-old Yankees farmhand Ed Cereghino, who had spent the season with Lefty in San Francisco.

22. *The Sporting News*, November 7, 1951, 17, and November 21, 1951, 17.

23. *Nippon Times*, October 22, 1951.

24. *Pacific Stars and Stripes*, November 11, 1951.

25. *Pacific Stars and Stripes*, November 20, 1951.

26. *The Sporting News*, November 28, 1951, 18. The donation was made to the Asahide Gakuen.

27. *San Francisco Chronicle*, November 19, 1951.

28. *San Francisco Chronicle*, April 15, 1952.

29. *The Sporting News*, May 18, 1949, 28.

30. *San Diego Union*, November 28, 1951.

31. *San Francisco Chronicle*, November 28, 1951.

32. *San Diego Union*, February 12, 1952.

33. *San Diego Union*, February 10 and 13, 1952.

34. *San Diego Union*, February 10, 1952.

35. *San Francisco Chronicle*, February 18, 1952; *The Sporting News*, February 20, 1952, 23.

36. *San Diego Union*, February 20, 1952.

37. *The Sporting News*, April 30, 1952, 23.

38. *San Francisco Chronicle*, April 16, 1952.

39. *San Francisco Chronicle*, April 16, 1952.

40. *San Francisco Chronicle*, August 9, 1952.

41. *The Sporting News*, June 4, 1952, 32.

42. *San Diego Union*, April 30, 1952.

43. *The Sporting News*, June 11, 1952, 23.

44. *The Sporting News*, May 28, 1952, 23.

45. *San Francisco Chronicle*, November 30, 1952.

46. *San Francisco Chronicle*, March 5, 1953.

47. In order to move from "Open Classification" to Major League status, the Pacific Coast League cities were required to have an aggregate population of at least fifteen million, and the league had to average attendance of a minimum 3.5 million over three years, had to bring stadiums to a minimum capacity of twenty-five thousand, and had to create a pension fund. In return, the Major Leagues could not move a franchise into a PCL city without the league's permission, and PCL players with fewer than five years of experience were exempt from the draft.

48. *San Francisco Chronicle*, November 30, 1952.

49. *San Francisco Chronicle*, November 30, 1952. He also investigated the idea of signing Japanese star Kauro Betto to a Padres contract for 1953 but was unsuccessful in doing so (*The Sporting News*, July 30, 1952, 23).

50. *The Sporting News*, October 29, 1952, 24, and February 11, 1953, 30.

51. *The Sporting News*, March 11, 1953, 16.

52. *San Francisco Chronicle*, February 17, 1953; *The Sporting News*, February 25, 1953, 29.

53. *Pacific Stars and Stripes*, March 19, 1953; *New York Times*, March 4, 2011.

54. *The Sporting News*, March 25, 1953, 25 and April 1, 1953, 29.

55. *The Sporting News*, April 8, 1953, 30.

56. *San Francisco Chronicle*, March 25, 1953.

57. *San Francisco Chronicle*, May 12, 1953.

58. *San Diego Union*, April 6, 1953; *Los Angeles Times*, April 5, 1953; *The Sporting News*, April 15, 1953, 34. Gorman's death made O'Doul the only man present for the only on-field fatalities in both the PCL and the Major Leagues (Ray Chapman).

59. *The Sporting News*, April 22, 1953, 32.

60. *The Sporting News*, October 14, 1953, 17.

61. *The Sporting News*, May 27, 1953, 13.

62. *New York Daily News*, November 18, 1953.

63. *Pacific Stars and Stripes*, November 11, 1953.

64. Funston Park is now the Moscone Recreation Center.

65. *San Francisco Chronicle*, January 15, 1954. Joe DiMaggio's brother Tom and his wife were the other invitees.

66. *San Francisco Chronicle*, January 18, 1954.

67. *Buffalo Courier Express*, February 1, 1954.

68. Interview of H. Elliott by the author, July 2, 2010.

69. *The Sporting News*, July 21, 1954, 28, and August 11, 1954, 25.

70. *San Diego Union*, July 19, 1954.

71. *Los Angeles Times*, September 14, 1954.

72. *The Sporting News*, August 11, 1954, 25.

73. *The Sporting News*, October 6, 1954, 30; *San Francisco Chronicle*, November 1, 1954.

74. *The Sporting News*, November 17, 1954, 16.

75. Interview of Chambers by the author, January 7, 2010.

76. *San Francisco Chronicle*, December 8, 1969.

77. *San Diego Union*, October 22, 1954.

78. *Chicago Tribune*, October 1, 1954.

79. *New York Times*, October 17, 1954; *Oakland Tribune*, October 18, 1954; *San Mateo (CA) Times*, October 19, 1954; *Philadelphia Inquirer*, November 1, 1954.

80. *San Francisco Chronicle*, November 1, 1954.

13. I'd Rather Be a Bad Winner

1. *Yomiuri Shimbun*, October 31, 1949. The meeting was reported by some wire services as having taken place at the Imperial Palace, but *Yomiuri Shimbun* reported that the meeting was prearranged to occur at the athletic meet.

2. *Chicago Tribune*, October 31, 1949.

3. *The Sporting News*, November 9, 1949, 14.

4. *The Sporting News*, November 17, 1954, 21; *Pacific Stars and Stripes*, October 18, 1960.

5. Undated letter, Matthew B. Ridgway to the members of the Baseball Hall of Fame Veterans Committee, Lefty O'Doul Clip File, National Baseball Hall of Fame.

6. Masao Date letter, December 11, 1991, Lefty O'Doul Clip File, National Baseball Hall of Fame.

7. *The Sporting News*, March 8, 1950, 28.

8. *Oakland Tribune*, November 4, 1954.

9. *San Francisco Chronicle*, November 5, 1954.

10. *Oakland Tribune*, November 2, 1954.

11. *Oakland Tribune*, November 4, 1954.

12. *The Sporting News*, February 16, 1955, 14.

13. *The Sporting News*, April 6, 1955, 12.

14. *San Francisco Chronicle*, July 11, 1954.

15. *San Francisco Chronicle*, May 24, June 11 and 12, 1955.

16. Brovia's stay in Cincinnati would be brief and unhappy: eighteen official at bats—all as a pinch hitter—with only two singles to show for it. Teammate Don Ferrarese claimed that Brovia had been playing with a broken hand, which he did not want to reveal (interview of Ferrarese by the author, November 23, 2010).

17. Interview of Munoz by the author, November 17, 2015.

18. *Oakland Tribune*, May 23, 1955; *The Sporting News*, June 1, 1955, 27.

19. Articles of Incorporation of Lefty O'Doul Enterprises, Inc., filed with the Secretary of State of California, October 17, 1955.

20. *San Diego Union*, September 13, 1955.

21. *San Francisco Chronicle*, November 29, 1955.

22. *Sport Magazine*, November 1955, 20–21, 64–65.

23. *The Sporting News*, January 3, 1970.

24. *Vancouver Sun*, December 6, 1956.

25. *New York Times*, February 20, 1970.

26. *Vancouver Sun*, December 7, 1955.

27. *Vancouver Sun*, March 6, 1956.

28. *Vancouver Sun*, April 13, 1956.

29. *Vancouver Sun*, April 28, 1956.

30. *Vancouver Sun*, May 29, 1956.

31. *Vancouver Sun*, May 19, 1956.

32. *New York Times*, February 24, 1958.

33. *Vancouver Sun*, June 28, 1956; *Los Angeles Times*, June 28, 1956.

34. *Vancouver Sun*, August 2, 1956.

35. *New York Times*, June 16, 1957.

36. Interview of Duren by the author, November 27, 2010.

37. *San Francisco Chronicle*, August 23, 1956.

38. *Los Angeles Times*, September 13, 1945.

39. *Sacramento Bee*, September 16, 1956. O'Doul became the only man to play in five different decades in the PCL.

40. Interview of O'Doul by Lawrence Ritter, August 29, 1963.

41. *Seattle Times*, September 22, 1956.

42. *Seattle Times*, September 23, 1956.

43. *Seattle Times*, October 21, 1956. The Dodgers were on a goodwill barnstorming trip to Japan.

44. *Seattle Times*, March 5, 1957.

45. Interview of Jansen by the author, December 29, 1991.

46. *The Sporting News*, June 19, 1957, 29.

47. *Seattle Times*, April 12, 1981.

48. *San Francisco Chronicle*, December 1, 1957.

49. *Seattle Post-Intelligencer*, December 1, 1957.

50. *The Sporting News*, February 12, 1958, 20.

51. *The Sporting News*, March 12, 1958, 10.

52. The building was constructed on a lot that had remained vacant since the 1906 earthquake, and was the first theater in the West designed specifically for the screening of motion pictures. Named Theatre St. Francis, it opened on October 2, 1916, and seated 1,100 patrons. It closed in early 1919. The art nouveau style and distinctive façade remains intact. After briefly serving as a restaurant called the Virginia Hill Inn, the space was taken over by Wilson's Candy Shop. During the 1930s, a beauty shop occupied what was then the second floor. The

building was purchased in late 1935 and remodeled into a Gene Compton's Cafeteria, which was the building's final incarnation until becoming Lefty O'Doul's (*Moving Picture World*, December 2, 1916; *San Francisco Chronicle*, October 1 and 3, December 5 and 30, 1916; December 7, 1935; and May 27, 1937).

53. *San Francisco Chronicle*, March 22, 1958.

54. Articles of Incorporation of Lefty O'Doul's Batting Range, Inc., filed with the Secretary of State of the State of California, December 24, 1959.

14. The *San Francisco* Giants

1. *Mainichi Shimbun*, November 1, 1949.
2. *Asahi Shimbun*, October 30, 1949.
3. *Yomiuri Shimbun*, October 31, 1949.
4. *Yomiuri Shimbun*, November 7, 1949.
5. *Asahi Shimbun*, November 6, 1949.
6. *San Francisco Chronicle*, March 1, 1958.
7. *The Sporting News*, March 12, 1958, 10.
8. *The Sporting News*, March 26, 1958, 22. Years later Rigney would insist he had no problem with O'Doul, while at the same time revealing why he might have. "I didn't see much of a conflict there," he told author Steve Bitker, "but I think the San Francisco writers all thought Lefty O'Doul should have been manager, because he was a great pal of theirs" (*Original San Francisco Giants*, 52).
9. *The Sporting News*, March 19, 1958, 8.
10. *The Sporting News*, March 19, 1958, 8.
11. *San Francisco Chronicle*, April 16, 1958.
12. *The Sporting News*, April 23, 1958, 9.
13. *The Sporting News*, April 23, 1958, 22.
14. *San Francisco Chronicle*, May 22, 1958.
15. *San Francisco Chronicle*, August 16, 1958.
16. *The Sporting News*, March 12, 1958, 10.
17. *The Sporting News*, July 16, 1958, 14.
18. *The Sporting News*, November 26, 1958, 31.
19. *The Sporting News*, March 4, 1959, 16.
20. *The Sporting News*, March 25, 1959, 11, 16.
21. *The Sporting News*, April 15, 1959, 9.
22. *San Francisco Chronicle*, November 18, 1959.
23. *The Sporting News*, March 25, 1959, 11, 16.
24. *Chicago Tribune*, March 17, 1959.
25. *San Francisco Chronicle*, September 21, 1959.
26. *The Sporting News*, April 20, 1960, 3–4, 14.
27. www.foundSf.org, retrieved June 24, 2014.
28. *San Francisco Examiner*, December 22, 2013. According to *Examiner* sportswriter Glenn Dickey, Willie Mays claimed that McCovey lost a lot of home runs that blew foul down the right field line.

29. Cepeda, *Baby Bull*, 56. Pedro "Perucha" Cepeda was a legend in Puerto Rico and the Caribbean, playing alongside many of the greatest names in Negro League history.

30. *Boy's Life*, September 1960, 24.

31. *Giants Today*, advertising feature in the *San Francisco Chronicle*, July 31, 2004.

32. *The Sporting News*, June 29, 1960, 13.

33. Einstein, *Willie Mays*, 154.

34. Terrell, "Old Pals," 80–82.

35. *San Francisco Chronicle*, November 1, 1960. Dark had not retired as an active player and at first was not sure whether he might be a player-manager.

36. *Pacific Stars and Stripes*, November 2, 1960.

37. *San Francisco Examiner*, March 5, 1961.

38. Einstein, *Flag for San Francisco*, 37.

39. Einstein, *Flag for San Francisco*, 37. Interestingly enough, Kuenn, whose lifetime average through eight seasons to that point was .313, batted higher than .300 only one more time, and only .278 during the remainder of his career after being acquired by the Giants.

40. *Pacific Stars and Stripes*, May 10 and July 17, 1961.

41. Arledge, *Roone*, 38–39.

42. *The Sporting News*, February 23, 1963, 16.

43. *San Francisco Chronicle*, December 8, 1969.

44. Postcard, Lawrence Ritter to Daniel Woodhead, February 11, 1992, Lefty O'Doul Clip File, National Baseball Hall of Fame.

45. Interview of O'Doul by Lawrence Ritter, August 29, 1963.

15. A Big, Big, Big, Big Thing

1. *New York Times*, November 1, 1953.

2. *Seattle Times*, July 2 and 3, September 4, 10, and 23, 1957.

3. *The Sporting News*, November 17, 1954, 21.

4. *Newcastle (Australia) Sun*, November 8, 1954.

5. *San Francisco Chronicle*, November 11, 1954.

6. *Grafton (Australia) Examiner*, November 6, 1954; *Canberra Times*, November 18, 1954.

7. *Perth West Australian*, November 20, 1954.

8. *The Sporting News*, December 29, 1954, 29.

9. *New York Times*, March 9, 1960; *Sports Illustrated*, March 21, 1960, 33.

10. *San Francisco Chronicle*, December 23, 1960.

11. *Mainichi Daily News*, August 22, 1976.

12. *The Sporting News*, November 18, 1959, 9, November 25, 1959, 8, and December 2, 1959, 26.

13. *Seattle Times*, November 19, 1959.

14. *The Sporting News*, December 2, 1959, 26.

15. Associated Press News Features, July 30, 1960.

16. *San Francisco Chronicle*, August 14, 1960; *The Sporting News*, September 28, 1960, 12.

17. *Pacific Stars and Stripes*, October 18, 1960.

18. *Pacific Stars and Stripes*, October 21, 1960.

19. *Pacific Stars and Stripes*, October 21, 1960; *The Sporting News*, November 2, 1960, 15, 20.

20. *San Francisco Chronicle*, October 22, 1960.

21. *Pacific Stars and Stripes*, October 23, 1960.

22. *Pacific Stars and Stripes*, October 29, 1960.

23. *Pacific Stars and Stripes*, October 29, 1960. Back in the States, Frick, never one with the thickest of skins when it came to perceived challenges of his authority, immediately fired back, "No one is authorized to enter into any such discussions or negotiations" (*Pacific Stars and Stripes*, November 10, 1960).

24. Interview of O'Doul by Lawrence Ritter, August 29, 1963.

25. *Pacific Stars and Stripes*, November 2, 1960.

26. *San Francisco Chronicle*, March 11, 1964.

27. *The Sporting News*, March 7, 1964, 11. Murakami returned to the Giants in 1965 and was successful, but his stint was not without controversy. According to Robert Fitts in his biography of Murakami, *Mashi*, the Nankai Hawks claimed they were unaware that the deal they had signed with the Giants gave San Francisco the right to purchase Murakami for $10,000—the agreement had never been translated into Japanese. The $10,000 was given to Cappy Harada, who reportedly kept it, thinking it a bonus for bringing Murakami to the Giants. The Hawks, who wanted Murakami to pitch for them, pinned much of the blame on Harada. After a tug of war during the winter of 1964, Murakami was allowed to come back to the United States for the 1965 season, but under pressure he returned to Japan in 1966. Over the years Murakami would occasionally contact the Giants about the possibility of returning, but the rules of Japanese baseball prevented it from happening. He pitched into the 1980s and then attempted a comeback during spring training 1983 with San Francisco that fell short (Fitts, *Mashi*, 49–50, 119, 123, 133–37, 190–91; *The Sporting News*, February 28, 1983, 10, 42, and March 28, 1983, 38; *San Francisco Chronicle*, December 14 and 20, 1969, February 11, 1983, and March 29, 1983).

28. *San Mateo (CA) Times*, March 11, 1964.

29. *The Sporting News*, March 28, 1964, 13.

30. *The Sporting News*, September 12, 1964, 19.

31. *Shukan Baseball*, September 21, 1964. Translation by Keiko Nishi.

32. *New York Times*, September 2, 1964.

33. *Shukan Baseball*, September 21, 1964. Translation by Keiko Nishi. At a luncheon a few days later, O'Doul was still exulting over Murakami's debut and told a reporter for the *San Rafael Daily Independent* that more Japanese players would be coming. "Someday there will be many," he said (*San Rafael [CA] Daily Independent*, September 5, 1964).

34. *The Sporting News*, June 24, 1959, 23, 26.

35. *The Sporting News*, January 31, 1962, 6.

36. *Chicago Tribune*, August 20, 1967.

37. *San Francisco Chronicle*, March 3, 1968.

38. *Pacific Stars and Stripes*, February 20, 1968.

39. Talese, *Silent Season*, 238–42.

40. *San Francisco Examiner*, May 17, 1966.

41. *San Francisco Examiner*, March 10, 1966.

42. *San Francisco Chronicle*, May 23, 1966.

43. *San Francisco Chronicle*, May 22, 1966.

44. *The Sporting News*, June 4, 1966, 24.

16. He Was Here at a Good Time

1. *Mainichi Daily News*, August 22, 1976.

2. Also inducted was former Los Angeles Dodgers executive Akihiro "Ike" Ikuhara, who joined the Dodgers as they began to build on contacts made in the 1950s during the team's first visit to Japan.

3. *San Francisco Chronicle*, June 24, 2002.

4. *San Francisco Chronicle*, June 4, 2002.

5. These details were provided by Kerry Yo Nakagawa, who was present for the ceremony (email from Nakagawa to the author, August 4, 2016). A Kagami-wari ceremony is a celebratory occasion.

6. Translation by Mrs. Shizuko "Susie" Strom.

7. *Pacific Stars and Stripes*, April 6, 1969.

8. *San Francisco Chronicle*, April 13 and 20, 1963.

9. *San Francisco Chronicle*, September 26, 1966.

10. *San Francisco Chronicle*, January 22, 1961.

11. *San Francisco Chronicle*, July 16, 1964.

12. *San Francisco Chronicle*, July 1, 1965. He would have won $3,621, based on $17 per pound.

13. *Oakland Tribune*, August 18, 1968.

14. *San Francisco Chronicle*, August 19, 1968; *The Sporting News*, August 31, 1968, 31.

15. *Oakland Tribune*, August 19, 1968.

16. *San Francisco Chronicle*, August 31, 1969.

17. *San Francisco Chronicle*, August 7, 1969.

18. *San Francisco Examiner*, November 14, 1969.

19. *San Francisco Chronicle*, November 14, 1969.

20. *San Francisco Chronicle*, November 20, 1969.

21. *Oakland Tribune*, December 9, 1969.

22. *San Francisco Chronicle*, November 19, 1969.

23. *San Francisco Examiner*, December 8, 1969.

24. *San Francisco Chronicle*, December 8, 1969.

25. *San Francisco Examiner*, December 8, 1969.

26. *San Francisco Examiner*, December 8, 1969.

27. *Binghamton (NY) Press*, December 9, 1969.

28. *San Francisco Chronicle*, December 9, 1969.

29. *Pacific Stars and Stripes*, December 10, 1969.

30. *San Francisco Chronicle*, May 26, 1980.

31. *San Francisco Chronicle*, December 12, 1969; *San Francisco Examiner*, December 12, 1969. Some news accounts listed Joe DiMaggio as attending the funeral, while other accounts, including that in Richard Ben Cramer's biography of the Yankee Clipper, do not. Tom O'Doul remembers shaking DiMaggio's hand, but believes it was likely at the rosary the night before the funeral (email from Tom O'Doul to the author, April 21, 2016).

32. Last Will and Testament of Frank J. O'Doul, August 22, 1968.

33. *San Francisco Chronicle*, February 1 and November 3, 1977; *San Francisco Examiner*, September 5, 1976. Lefty's on Powell Street was a nightclub for several years before becoming a topless bar in the late 1960s, which brought O'Doul no small measure of aggravation. It finally closed in January 1972. There was also a restaurant in Vancouver named in honor of O'Doul shortly after his death. It was housed in the Listel Hotel on Robson Street and became a popular music venue, best known for hosting the Vancouver International Jazz Festival. The restaurant remained open for forty-one years before closing in June 2012, when it was replaced by an eatery called "Forage" (*San Francisco Chronicle*, January 18, 1972).

34. *San Francisco Chronicle*, July 18, 1997. Both Nick Bovis and Tom O'Doul told the author that Lefty was going to will the restaurant to Bovis's father on the day he died. Bovis had the papers ready for Lefty's signature and was to bring them to the hospital the night of December 7 (interview of Tom O'Doul by the author, June 29, 2014; interview of Nick Bovis by the author, September 30, 2015).

35. *The Sporting News*, January 24, 1970, 42.

36. *San Francisco Chronicle*, May 18, October 23, and November 4, 1970.

37. San Francisco Board of Supervisors Resolution No. 814-79, August 31, 1979.

38. San Francisco Planning Commission Resolution No. 11629, April 6, 1989. A bascule bridge has one end weighted to balance the structure when the bridge swings open to allow ships to pass.

39. *San Francisco Chronicle*, March 10, 1981.

40. Email from Daniel Woodhead to the author, February 20, 2016.

41. Fimrite, "Hall Monitor," 46.

42. Karita to Woodhead, December 24, 1991, Lefty O'Doul Clip File, National Baseball Hall of Fame.

43. Shoriki to Woodhead, December 5, 1991, Lefty O'Doul Clip File, National Baseball Hall of Fame.

44. Bavasi to Woodhead, various correspondence during 1995.

45. *San Francisco Chronicle*, June 15, 2006.

46. *USA Today,* July 27, 2006.

47. *San Francisco Chronicle,* August 2, 2009.

48. Ron Santo received the most votes, fifty-seven, which was short of the sixty-one required. It was the third consecutive time no one was elected.

49. *Los Angeles Times,* May 3, 1995.

50. *Los Angeles Times,* May 3, 1995.

51. Email from Yoichi Nagata to the author, February 22, 2016.

52. U.S. Census, 1880, 1900; *San Francisco Chronicle,* March 6, 1927. The Order of the Rising Sun is the third-highest honor bestowed by the Japanese government and the highest honor given to civilians.

53. *San Francisco Chronicle,* March 6, 1927.

54. U.S. Census, 1910 and 1920.

55. *San Francisco Chronicle,* March 6, 1927; *Crocker-Langley San Francisco City Directory,* 1927. Wilson's former home address lies only four blocks from the present-day location of Lefty O'Doul's on Geary Street. Tadashi Wakabayashi and Wally Yonamine, both born in Hawaii, are the other Americans enshrined in the Japanese Baseball Hall of Fame.

56. Baseball Reliquary, press release, May 4, 2013 (author's copy).

57. *Pacific Stars and Stripes,* July 28, 1968.

Epilogue

1. *San Francisco Chronicle,* January 13, 2017, A1.

2. *San Francisco Chronicle,* January 13, 2017, A9.

3. *San Francisco Chronicle,* January 21, 2017, C1.

4. Telephone interview with John Ring, December 5, 2015.

5. *San Francisco Chronicle,* February 2, 2017, A4.

6. Press Release, Department of Justice, U.S. Attorney's Office, Northern District of California, December 17, 2021.

7. Jaxon Van Derbeken and Michael Bott, "SF Restaurateur Nick Bovis Admits Corruption Charges," NBC *Bay Area,* May 21, 2020, https://www.nbcbayarea.com /investigations/sf-restaurateur-nick-bovis-admits-corruption-charges/2294795/.

8. Joe Fitzgerald Rodriguez, "Lefty O'Doul's charity used city contractor donations to pay for Public Works party," *San Francisco Examiner,* February 5, 2020, https://www.sfexaminer.com/the_fs/forum/lefty-o-doul-s-charity-used-city -contractor-donations-to-pay-for-public-works-party/article_da4bc82f-2ccd-5a7f -a8b3-7548ce91ea4f.html. Email correspondence with Tom O'Doul, June 11, 2022.

9. "Buck O'Neil Award," National Baseball Hall of Fame, accessed June 12, 2022, https://baseballhall.org/discover-more/awards/890.

10. "Early Baseball, Golden Days Era Committee Ballots Announced," National Baseball Hall of Fame, November 5, 2021, https://baseballhall.org/news /era-committee-ballots-announced-for-class-of-2022-consideration. The Early Era Committee was one of several committees formed from what was originally the Veteran's Committee.

11. "Fowler, Hodges, Kaat, Miñoso, Oliva, O'Neil Elected to Hall of Fame," National Baseball Hall of Fame, December 5, 2021, https://baseballhall.org /news/six-candidates-elected-to-hall-of-fame-as-part-of-class-of-2022. The Golden Days Era Committee votes were also released the same day, with Gil Hodges, Jim Kaat, Minnie Miñoso, and Tony Oliva elected to the Hall of Fame.

12. "Era Committees," National Baseball Hall of Fame, accessed June 12, 2022, https://baseballhall.org/hall-of-famers/rules/eras-committees.

BIBLIOGRAPHY

Archival Sources

Alan O'Connor Collection
    Translations of Japanese newspaper articles of the 1949 Tour of Japan
        for Paul I. Fagan (3 vols.)
Bancroft Library, University of California, Berkeley
California State Library, Sacramento
Crocker-Langley San Francisco city directories
Daniel Woodhead Collection
David Eskenazi Collection
Dick Dobbins Collection, California Historical Society
Doug McWilliams Collection
National Archives, Washington DC
National Baseball Hall of Fame and Museum, Cooperstown NY
    Lefty O'Doul Clip File
    Moe Berg Papers
Norman Macht Baseball Research Collection, DeGolyer Library, Southern Methodist University
Peter Shields Library, University of California, Davis
Ray Saraceni Collection
Richard Leutzinger Collection
San Francisco Public Library, History Center
Sotaro Suzuki Papers
Stanislaus County Library
Tokyo War Crimes Trial Collection, University of Virginia

Published Sources

Alexander, Charles C. *John McGraw*. New York: Viking Press, 1988.
Arledge, Roone. *Roone: A Memoir*. New York: Harper Collins, 2003.
Beverage, Richard E. *The Hollywood Stars: Baseball in Movieland, 1926–1957*. Placentia CA: Deacon Press, 1984.

Bitker, Steve. *The Original San Francisco Giants: The Giants of '58*. New York: Sports Publishing, 2001.

Cepeda, Orlando, with Herb Fagen. *Baby Bull: From Hardball to Hard Time and Back*. Dallas: Taylor, 1998.

Cobb, Ty. "Place Hitting." *Baseball Magazine*, October 1917.

Cunningham, Bill. "Three O'Clock Scholar." *Collier's Weekly*, July 11, 1936, 24–26.

Dahlgren, Matt. *Rumor in Town*. California: Woodlyn Lane, 2007.

Dawidoff, Nicholas. *The Catcher Was a Spy: The Mysterious Life of Moe Berg*. New York: Random House, 1994.

Diendorfer, Bob. "Baseball's Counterspies." *Nation's Business Monthly*, August 1953.

Dobbins, Dick. *The Grand Minor League*. Emeryville CA: Woodford Press, 1999.

Einstein, Charles. *A Flag for San Francisco*. New York: Simon & Schuster, 1962.

———. *Willie Mays: Coast to Coast Giant*. New York: G. P. Putnam & Sons, 1963.

Fimrite, Ron. "Hall Monitor." *Sports Illustrated*, December 11, 2006, 46.

Fitts, Robert K. *Banzai Babe Ruth: Baseball, Espionage, and Assassination during the 1934 Tour of Japan*. Lincoln: University of Nebraska Press, 2012.

———. *Mashi: The Unfulfilled Dreams of Masanori Murakami, the First Japanese Major Leaguer*. Lincoln: University of Nebraska Press, 2015.

———. *Remembering Japanese Baseball: An Oral History of the Game*. Carbondale: Southern Illinois University Press, 2005.

Franks, Joel. *Asian Pacific Americans and Baseball: A History*. Jefferson NC: McFarland, 2008.

Gershman, Michael. *Diamonds: The Evolution of the Ballpark*. New York: Houghton Mifflin, 1993.

Graham, Frank. "O'Doul—Frisco's Pride and Pal." *Baseball Digest*, November 1946.

Guthrie-Shimizu, Sayuri. *Transpacific Field of Dreams*. Chapel Hill: University of North Carolina Press, 2012.

Ijimino, Seiichi. *The Father of Pro Baseball, Shoriki Matsutaro*. Translated by Takamitsu Tanaka. Tokyo, 1966.

Johnson, Harold, ed. *Who's Who in Major League Baseball*. Chicago: Buxton, 1933.

Kelley, Brent. *San Francisco Seals, 1946–1957*. Jefferson NC: McFarland, 2002.

Leutzinger, Richard. "Lefty O'Doul and the Development of Japanese Baseball." *National Pastime* 12 (1992): 30–34.

———. *Lefty O'Doul: The Legend Baseball Nearly Forgot*. Carmel CA: Carmel Bay Publishing, 1997.

Lewis, Jerry D. "The Master of the Giants." *Baseball Magazine*, October 1933.

Lieb, Frederick. *Baseball as I Have Known It*. New York: Coward, McCann & Geoghegan, 1977.

Mackey, R. Scott. *Barbary Baseball: The Pacific Coast League of the 1920s*. Jefferson NC: McFarland, 1995.

Morris, Peter. *A Game of Inches: The Stories behind the Innovations That Shaped Baseball*. Chicago: Ivan R. Dee, 2006.

Nagata, Yoichi. *The Tokyo Giants North American Tour of 1935* [in Japanese]. Osaka: Toho Shuppan, 2007.

Nakagawa, Kerry Yo. *Japanese American Baseball in California: A History*. Charleston SC: History Press, 2014.

1948 Famous Slugger Yearbook. Louisville: Hillerich & Bradsby, 1948.

O'Brien, Tricia. *Images of America: San Francisco's Bayview Hunters Point*. Charleston SC: Arcadia Publishing, 2005.

O'Doul, Frank "Lefty," and John Wesley Noble. "I'd Like a Shot at the Big Leagues." *Sport Magazine*, November 1955, 20–21, 64–65.

Raley, Dan. *Pitchers of Beer: The Story of the Seattle Rainiers*. Lincoln: University of Nebraska Press, 2011.

Ritter, Lawrence. *The Glory of Their Times*. New York: Macmillan, 1966.

Small, Collie, "Too Good for the Majors." *Saturday Evening Post*, August 23, 1947, 26–27, 109–10.

Snelling, Dennis. *The Greatest Minor League: A History of the Pacific Coast League, 1903–1957*. Jefferson NC: McFarland, 2012.

Soto-Castellanos, Bill. *16th & Bryant: My Life & Education with the San Francisco Seals*. Pinole CA: Clubhouse Publishing, 2007.

Steinberg, Steve, and Lyle Spatz. *The Colonel and Hug: The Partnership That Transformed the New York Yankees*. Lincoln: University of Nebraska Press, 2015.

Stevens, Bob, "'Twas Fudger O'Doul in '33." *Baseball Digest*, July 1950, 17–18.

Talese, Gay. *The Silent Season of a Hero*. New York: Walker, 2010.

Terrell, Roy. "Old Pals in a Cold Wind." *Sports Illustrated*, September 26, 1960, 80–82.

Uhlan, Edward, and Dana L. Thomas. *Shoriki: Miracle Man of Japan*. New York: Exposition Press, 1957.

Wind, Herbert Warren. "The Bouncing Ball." *Sports Illustrated*, February 24, 1958.

INDEX

CPSIA information can be obtained
at www.ICGtesting.com
Printed in the USA
LVHW030726060223
738662LV00002B/2